Sense and Sensitivity

Explorations in Semantics
Series Editor: Susan Rothstein

This exciting series features important new research by leading scholars in the field of semantics. Each volume focuses on a topic or topics central to the field, including dynamic semantics, aspect, focus, anaphora, and type-shifting, and offers a pedagogical component designed to introduce the topics addressed and situate the new research in the context of the field and previous research. The presentational style emphasizes student accessibility without compromising the sophistication of the research involved.

Explorations in Semantics is an excellent series for students and researchers in the field, as well as scholars in adjacent areas such as syntax, philosophy of language, and computational linguistics.

1   *Compositionality in Formal Semantics: Selected Papers of Barbara H. Partee*
   Barbara H. Partee

2   *Structuring Events: A Study in the Semantics of Lexical Aspect*
   Susan Rothstein

3   *Indefinites and the Type of Sets*
   Fred Landman

4   *The Proper Treatment of Events*
   Michiel van Lambalgen and Fritz Hamm

5   *Sense and Sensitivity: How Focus Determines Meaning*
   David I. Beaver and Brady L. Clark

Sense and Sensitivity
How Focus Determines Meaning

David I. Beaver
and
Brady Z. Clark

A John Wiley & Sons, Ltd., Publication

This edition first published 2008
© 2008 David I. Beaver and Brady Z. Clark

Blackwell Publishing was acquired by John Wiley & Sons in February 2007. Blackwell's publishing program has been merged with Wiley's global Scientific, Technical, and Medical business to form Wiley-Blackwell.

Registered Office
John Wiley & Sons Ltd, The Atrium, Southern Gate, Chichester, West Sussex, PO19 8SQ, United Kingdom

Editorial Offices
350 Main Street, Malden, MA 02148-5020, USA
9600 Garsington Road, Oxford, OX4 2DQ, UK
The Atrium, Southern Gate, Chichester, West Sussex, PO19 8SQ, UK

For details of our global editorial offices, for customer services, and for information about how to apply for permission to reuse the copyright material in this book please see our website at www.wiley.com/wiley-blackwell.

The right of David I. Beaver and Brady Z. Clark to be identified as the authors of this work has been asserted in accordance with the Copyright, Designs and Patents Act 1988.

Library of Congress Cataloging-in-Publication Data

Beaver, David I., 1966–
Sense and sensitivity : how focus determines meaning / David Beaver and Brady Clark.
    p. cm. – (Explorations in semantics)
  Includes bibliographical references and index.
    ISBN 978-1-4051-1263-5 (hardcover : alk. paper) – ISBN 978-1-4051-1264-2 (pbk. : alk. paper)
1. Semantics. 2. Focus (Linguistics) 3. Pragmatics. 4. Discourse analysis. I. Clark, Brady. II. Title.
  P325.5.F63B43 2008
  401_.43–dc22

                                       2008002636

A catalogue record for this book is available from the British Library.

Set in 10/12.5 Palatino by SPi Publisher Services, Pondicherry, India
Printed in Singapore by Markono Print Media Pte Ltd

1   2008

But stress clearly does in fact on many occasions make a difference to the speaker's meaning [. . .]

In accordance with the spirit of Modified Occam's Razor, we might attribute conventional meaning to stress only if it is unavoidable. Thus we might first introduce a slight extension to the maxim enjoining relevance, making it apply not only to what is said but also to features of the means used for saying what is said.

Herbert Paul Grice, 1989, *Further Notes on Logic and Conversation*, p. 51.

Association with Focus is a Relevance implicature [. . .]

Craige Roberts, 2007, *Information Structure in Discourse*, handout,
LSA Summer Institute, Stanford, p. 10.

AWF [*association with focus*] in English as well as in Hungarian is an island sensitive syntactic process.

Hans Bernhard Drubig, 2000, *Towards a a Typology of Focus and Focus Constructions*, p. 36.

My general opinion about this doctrine is that it is a typically scholastic view, attributable, first, to an obsession with a few particular words, the uses of which are over-simplified, not really understood or carefully studied or correctly described; and second to an obsession with a few (and nearly always the same) half-studied *facts*. [. . .] It is essential, here as elsewhere, to abandon old habits of *Gleichschaltung*, the deeply ingrained worship of tidy-looking dichotomies.

John Langshaw Austin, 1962, *Sense and Sensibilia*, p. 3.

Contents

List of Figures		*x*
Preface		*xi*
1	Introduction	1
2	Intonation and Meaning	7
	2.1 Introduction	7
	2.2 Focus	7
	2.3 Intonational Phonology	10
	2.4 Focus Projection	12
	2.5 Questions and Focus	25
	2.6 The Interpretation of Focus	28
	2.7 Structuring Discourse with Questions	33
	2.8 The Quasi/Free/Conventional (QFC) Model	40
	2.9 Summary	43
3	Three Degrees of Association: Quasi, Free, and Conventional	44
	3.1 Introduction	44
	3.2 The First Degree: Quasi-Association	44
	3.3 The Second Degree: Free Association	52
	3.4 The Third Degree: Conventional Association	68
	3.5 Summary	78
4	Compositional Analysis of Focus	80
	4.1 Introduction	80
	4.2 Compositional Alternative Semantics	81
	4.3 Structured Meanings	84
	4.4 Focus with Events	87
	4.5 Relating the Frameworks	91

4.6   The President, the Boy Scouts, and a Trip to Tanglewood   95
4.7   Summary   115

5   Pragmatic Explanations of Focus   117

5.1   Introduction   117
5.2   Accentless Focus   119
5.3   Association with Presupposition   121
5.4   Roberts' Account of Focus Sensitivity   123
5.5   A Presuppositional Account of Focus Sensitivity   130
5.6   Summary   140

6   Soft Focus: Association with Reduced Material   142

6.1   Introduction   142
6.2   Second Occurrence Focus: Background   143
6.3   Second Occurrence Focus: Experiments   145
6.4   Leaners: a Contrast   149
6.5   Leaners: an Events-based Analysis   154
6.6   Summary   158

7   Lacking Focus: Extraction and Ellipsis   160

7.1   Introduction   160
7.2   Extraction   161
7.3   Cross-linguistic Evidence on Extraction   166
7.4   Analyzing the Extraction Data   169
7.5   An Extraction Puzzle   174
7.6   Ellipsis   176
7.7   Analyzing the Ellipsis Data   178
7.8   An Ellipsis Puzzle   180
7.9   Summary   181

8   Monotonicity and Presupposition   182

8.1   Introduction   182
8.2   Background on Monotonicity, NPIs, and PPIs   182
8.3   Polarity Item Licensing by *only*   184
8.4   Polarity Item Licensing by *always*   190
8.5   Monotonicity Inferences   192
8.6   A Formal Account of PI Licensing   197
8.7   Restrictions on PI Licensing by *only*   200
8.8   Association with Presupposition   204
8.9   What Does *always* Associate With?   208
8.10 Summary   211

9   Exclusives: Facts and History   212

     9.1   Introduction   212
     9.2   Positive and Negative Parts of Exclusive Meanings   214
     9.3   The Prejacent Presupposition Theory   215
     9.4   The Existential Presupposition Theory   218
     9.5   The Implicational Presupposition Theory   223
     9.6   Implicatures for Unembedded Exclusives   225
     9.7   Denial Isn't Just a River in Egypt   233
     9.8   The Arroyo Tequila Test   238
     9.9   Is the Prejacent Entailed?   244
     9.10   Summary   246

10   Exclusives: a Discourse Account   248

     10.1   Introduction   248
     10.2   The Discourse Function of Exclusives   249
     10.3   Examples of Scales   254
     10.4   Formal Analysis   260
     10.5   Unembedded Exclusives   264
     10.6   Negated Exclusives and Other Embeddings   267
     10.7   Association with Focus   272
     10.8   NPI Licensing   276
     10.9   Non-association with Presupposition   277
     10.10   Summary   278

11   Conclusion   280

     11.1   The Story so Far   280
     11.2   What Isn't (Conventionally) Focus Sensitive?   282
     11.3   Generalizations from the QFC Model   283
     11.4   Closing Remarks   285

Bibliography   287

Index   301

Figures

1.1	Generic depiction of core grammar architecture	3
2.1	Pitch accents	11
3.1	Focus sensitivity of *must*	62
5.1	Initial DRS for (5.17)	131
5.2	Global accommodation (Gloss: Butch is awake, and if he is barking Mary realizes he is awake.)	132
5.3	Intermediate accommodation (Gloss: If Butch is awake and barking, Mary realizes he is awake.)	133
5.4	Local accommodation (Gloss: If Butch is barking, he is awake and Mary realizes he is awake.)	133
5.5	Initial DRS for (5.18)	134
5.6	Intermediate accommodation (Gloss: Any event of Mary helping some x is an event of Mary helping Jim.)	134
5.7	Initial DRS for (5.19)	135
5.8	Global accommodation (Same truth conditions as *Mary helped Jim.*)	136
5.9	Intermediate accommodation	136
5.10	Initial DRS (for 5.19) with BPR induced presupposition	137
5.11	Intermediate accommodation	137
5.12	Global accommodation of quantificational presupposition	138
5.13	Geurts and van der Sandt representation for (5.22)	139
5.14	Initial DRS for (5.22)	139
5.15	Accommodation of BPR induced presupposition	139
5.16	Existential presupposition of *too* resolved	140
9.1	Purity wager results	220
9.2	*Only* vs. presupposition triggers	241

Preface

This book concerns the semantic and pragmatic effects of focus in natural language discourse. The term *focus* at a pragmatic level relates to a certain type of information status: something that is focused is pragmatically important, perhaps the answer to an explicit question. In the languages we will be chiefly considering in this book, Romance and Germanic languages, and English in particular, focus is commonly marked by prosody, with changes in pitch used to mark focused expressions.

Now, some words, like English *only, just, merely, also, too, even, specifically*, and emphatic *totally*, have meanings that are particularly affected by the position of focus. The book is about the meanings of *focus sensitive* expressions like these. We argue that for many such expressions (including all of those in the list above), their focus sensitivity is conventionalized, an intrinsic part of lexical meaning. But we also argue that many other terms, though they appear sensitive to focus, are not conventionally focus sensitive. The range of expressions which we argue manifest non-conventionalized focus sensitivity is very diverse, and includes, e.g. negation, comparative constructions, counterfactual conditionals, and many different quantificational expressions.

The centerpiece of the book is a new theory of focus sensitivity, the QFC theory, which involves a three-way distinction between different effects of focus:

- Quasi association, a special type of pragmatic inference;
- Free association, the resolution of a free variable; and
- Conventional association, a grammatical dependency on the current question under discussion.

Prior to our development of the QFC theory, it was generally assumed that focus is a uniform phenomenon. Yet there were no studies carefully comparing the behavior of different focus sensitive expressions to support the standard view. Our account shows that the standard view is incorrect, and backs this up with detailed study of how focus sensitive expressions vary, based on a series of new diagnostic tests and a variety of data from across a range of Germanic and Romance languages.

We argue that the reason some expressions have a conventionalized dependency on focus relates directly to the discourse function of those expressions. These expressions have what might be termed *lexically pragmatic meanings*. Specifically, a focus is the answer to a question, and conventionally focus sensitive items all mark the status of that answer. For example, the exclusive *only* marks an answer as maximal but below expectation, while the additive *too* indicates that an answer extends a previously salient answer to the same question.

Lexically pragmatic meanings: this might seem to some a contradiction in terms. For there is a long tradition of studying word meaning in terms of truth conditional significance, the mapping, if you will, between word and world. That is, *lexical meaning* was at least implicitly equated with *lexical semantics*. But the 1970s and 1980s brought a fresh look at the study of meaning – the *dynamic turn* as it has been called. Linguists and philosophers of language moved on from a static word-to-world model of meaning to a more nuanced view emphasizing in one way or another the dynamic nature of communication. The study of meaning now involved consideration not only of what is said about the world, but also about the process of information exchange.

Following the dynamic turn, many scholars take linguistic meaning to directly encode information about the state of the conversation, and even instructions about how a speaker intends the conversation to develop. Here are some examples. For Heim (1982) and Kamp (1981), an indefinite noun phrase signals that a new discourse marker must be added to a hearer's mental model of the state of the conversation, and a pronoun or definite signals that an existing discourse marker must be re-used.

Or consider presupposition theory: it is now standard (though not uncontroversial) to consider a vast slew of linguistic expression types to carry with them as part of their meaning a conventional signal about the prior state of discourse. See Beaver (2001) both for a model of this type, and for many references to other work based on such intuitions.

As a final, prominent example of a theory in which linguistic meaning directly encodes information about the state of the conversation, consider Herb Clark's multi-track model of discourse, e.g. Clark (1996: ch. 8). Like researchers in the Conversation Analysis and Discourse Analysis communities, Clark analyzes large amounts of discourse as conveying meta-commentary separate from the primary topic of conversation. In his terms, information about the main issues under discussion is exchanged via the first track, while commentary pertaining to regulation of that information exchange is conveyed on the second track, or even on further meta-meta-conversational tracks. Clark takes many expressions as having a conventionalized meaning which is primarily concerned with such meta-commentary, including back-channeling signals, markers of disfluencies, acknowledgments like *I see*, and discourse markers like *anyway*. Thus, our model is one in which the primary function of conventionally focus sensitive expressions is to convey information on Clark's second track. But this is a track that semanticists and philosophers of language are only just learning to follow.

In setting out a theory of the pragmatic meanings of focus sensitive expressions, alongside empirical argumentation based largely on discourse, we situate our work as an example of contemporary, dynamic, formal pragmatics. And it should be noted here that the switch to a dynamic view of language is paralleled by an empirical shift, from the study of sentence-level phenomena to the study of discourse-level phenomena. Thus, where Frege (1884) said *"nur im Zusammenhange eines Satzes bedeuten die Wörter etwas"* ("Only in the context of a sentence do the words mean anything"), we might paraphrase: only in the context of a discourse do the sentences mean anything useful. Indeed, we take it that the essence of formal pragmatics is to carry the reductive and analytic program set out in Frege's philosophy of language from the sentence level to the discourse level.

Who should read this book? And, less obviously, how should they read it? The book is a research monograph aimed at those who have taken at least one graduate level class in linguistic semantics, and who want more. We hope the book will be of interest not only to students of semantics and pragmatics, but also to philosophers of language, syntacticians, and maybe even phonologists who have a semantic bent. And if you already have interests in the interpretation of focus, discourse structure, or more specifically in the semantics and pragmatics of exclusives or other focus sensitive expressions, then we certainly hope this book will give you food for thought.

As regards technical apparatus, the reader is expected to have a general appreciation for how compositional semantic theories work, and of predicate logic and set theory. We included a generous slice of background material, especially in Chapters 2, 4, and 5, on basics of intonational phonology, discourse structure, question semantics, focus, and theories of focus interpretation. The reader is not assumed to have any specific background in these areas, and we hope that the book will make for a good introduction to them.

For most of the book, a basic background in semantics and some gumption will be adequate, but there are a couple of more technically demanding sections. Specifically, §4.2–§4.6, and §10.4 assume a high degree of comfort with intensional logic and lambda calculus. These sections can safely be skipped without grossly impairing the overall message of the book. Similarly, there is one section, §5.5, which assumes basic knowledge of Discourse Representation Theory (DRT). Again, this section can be skipped without impairing the overall integrity of the book, although for those who have previously taken a semantics class, Geurts and Beaver's (2007) short, online[1] introduction to DRT would provide all the background needed.

We embarked on this project nearly a decade ago, in mid-June 1999. In his comments on Brady's final paper for a Spring quarter graduate semantics course, David wrote "By the way, I thought of a neat argument for why

---

[1] Geurts and Beaver (2007) is on the Stanford Encyclopedia of Philosophy website at <http://plato.stanford.edu/entries/discourse-representation-theory/>.

'only' and 'even' do have structural focus sensitivity, but 'usually' and 'always' don't." And we were off! In the meantime we produced a number of other publications in which many of the ideas and arguments in this monograph first appeared. Chapter 6 (§6.2 and §6.3) leans heavily on joint work with Edward Flemming, Florian Jaeger, and Maria Wolters, reported in Beaver et al. (2007). The basic ideas for Chapters 6–8 were developed in Beaver and Clark (2002a, 2002b, 2003), while some discussion in Chapter 9 relates to Beaver (2004). As will become clear to the reader, the rest of the book borrows from a wide range of sources, but the theory we develop is especially influenced by work of Craige Roberts, Mats Rooth, and Henk Zeevat, if not Larry Horn.

We have many people to thank for their help on the project that culminated in this book. Maria Aloni was a key influence at an early stage. We learned a great deal from audiences at Cornell University, the Massachussetts Institute of Technology, Northwestern University, the University of California at Berkeley, the University of California at Santa Cruz, the University of California at San Diego, the University of Texas at Austin, the Ohio State University, the LSA 2000, 2003 and 2004 annual meetings, SALT XII in San Diego, WCCFL XXI in Santa Cruz, the Twelfth Amsterdam Colloquium, and the 2002 *One Day Only* workshop in Amsterdam. Comments from participants in courses at Stanford University, Northwestern University, and the University of Texas at Austin and the 2005 LSA Summer Institute at MIT helped a great deal as well.

For their direct help on this book, we would like to thank Kai von Fintel, Robert van Rooij, Henk Zeevat, two anonymous reviewers for Blackwell who provided extensive comments on earlier versions of the manuscript, and the series editor Susan Rothstein. Christine Ranft, Laura Whitton, Emile Destruel, Frederick Hoyt, and Eric Campbell did a fantastic job of proofreading, copy-editing, and indexing. Devyani Sharma took considerable risks to photograph the sign in Chapter 3. Many thanks Devyani! At Blackwell, Sarah Coleman, Danielle Descoteaux, and Kelly Basner have been great to work with – helpful and supportive in the extreme.

We received financial support from the Stanford Office of Technology Licensing, the Department of Navy (research grant N000140010660), the Stanford Humanities Center, the Andrew W. Mellon Foundation, the Scottish Development Office through the Edinburgh–Stanford Link project, and the University of Texas Department of Linguistics and College of Liberal Arts.

Our wives, Moni and Gina, and our children, Anna and Noah, Malachi and Riley, put up with a lot. Thank you!

Chapter 1

Introduction

Intonation is important, especially when it is cold.

Eugene Ormandy

This book is about the effect of intonation on meaning. Consider the many ways in which to say *This book is even sold at Wal-Mart*. Different pronunciations of the sentence convey different emotions, e.g. excitement, disappointment, anger. The imaginative reader can perhaps imagine vocalizations suggesting sarcasm, or even horror. Furthermore, the pronunciation of *This book is even sold at Wal-Mart* not only affects emotional attitudes, but also affects what the speaker asserts, and what the speaker presupposes.[1] Two possible renditions are presented in (1.1). We represent the word carrying the greatest prosodic prominence of a sentence with capital letters.

(1.1) a. This book is even sold at WAL-Mart.

  b. This book is even SOLD at Wal-Mart.

Among other things, the speaker of (1.1a) could convey that this book is sold at another outlet besides Wal-Mart and that Wal-Mart is a relatively unexpected place for the book to be sold. In contrast, the speaker of (1.1b) could be indicating that while it is clear that this book will be stocked at Wal-Mart, it is surprising that it would be sold there. The main source of the interpretational difference between (1.1a) and (1.1b) is *even*, a FOCUS SENSITIVE expression.

Different ways of pronouncing *This book is even sold at Wal-Mart* also affect the range of contexts in which the sentence can be used felicitously, as illustrated in (1.2). The disparaging rejoinder in (1.2c) cannot contrast with the statement in (1.2a), whereas (1.2b) can. We use the "#" symbol to indicate infelicity.

---

[1] That pronunciation affects meaning was observed by Paul (1888: 312ff.). In the particular case at hand, it could be argued that the assertion is unchanged for the two variant productions, although the presupposition changes. In many other examples we will consider, e.g. (1.3) and (1.4), both presupposed and asserted content are affected.

(1.2) a. This book is sold on Amazon.

      b. So what? This book is even sold at WAL-Mart.

      c. #So what? This book is even SOLD at Wal-Mart.

Prosody clearly affects the sense of an utterance in many different and amazing ways. How can we get a grip on such a varied phenomenon?

    In this book we are primarily concerned with just one key topic in the study of the interaction of prosody and meaning, FOCUS SENSITIVITY, as effected by *even* in (1.1).[2] We will devote considerable attention to two important sub-classes of focus sensitive expressions: exclusives (e.g., *only*) and adverbs of quantification (e.g., *always*).

    Consider the examples in (1.3). In a situation where Kim serves Pat and Sandy Johnnie Walker whiskey, but serves nobody anything else, (1.3a) is true while (1.3b) is false.

(1.3) a. Kim only serves Sandy JOHNnie WALker.
        'Kim serves Sandy nothing but Johnnie Walker.'

      b. Kim only serves SANDY Johnnie Walker.
        'Kim serves nobody but Sandy Johnnie Walker.'

The culprit in (1.3a) and (1.3b) is the exclusive *only*. We see a similar sort of interaction with adverbs of quantification such as *always*. Examples (1.4a) and (1.4b) have different truth conditions, just like (1.3a) and (1.3b).

(1.4) a. Kim always serves Sandy JOHNnie WALker.
        'Whenever Kim serves Sandy something it's Johnnie Walker.'

      b. Kim always serves SANDY Johnnie Walker.
        'Whenever Kim serves Johnnie Walker to someone, it's Sandy.'

As will become clear as we give more background on existing literature, most analysts tacitly assume that the class of focus sensitive expressions is monolithic, and they refer to a single mechanism, so-called ASSOCIATION WITH FOCUS, to explain the meaning difference between (1.3a) and (1.3b), and between (1.4a) and (1.4b).

    We think it a mistake to assume that a single mechanism is at work. In this book we will show that the class of focus sensitive expressions, or at least the class of expressions which have been termed focus sensitive in the past, is not at all uniform. Further, we will show how the type of focus sensitivity manifested by a particular expression is related to its meaning.

---

2 Fischer (1968) and Kuroda (1965) are important early references on focus sensitivity. Fischer's paper (a term paper for one of Chomsky's courses and cited by Jackendoff 1972 and Chomsky 1972) is, as far as we know, the first paper in the generative tradition to observe that the interpretation of *only* and *even* is linked to focus (what Fischer calls 'contrastive stress').

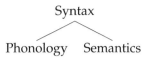

Figure 1.1 Generic depiction of core grammar architecture

The phenomenon of focus sensitivity has repercussions not only for semantics and pragmatics, but also for how and where SUPRASEGMENTAL information is encoded in the grammar, and in particular the intonational tunes which mark focus.[3] Many standard contemporary approaches to grammar separate phonology and semantics into components that cannot exchange information directly, as in Figure 1.1, so that any effect of intonation on meaning must be mediated by syntax.[4]

Consequently, many authors from Halliday (1967) and Chomsky (1972) on have concluded that there are syntactic features and transformations which encode prosodic prominence. Chomsky (1977), for example, suggested that all focused phrases move outside their base position in syntax. Related ideas are present in more recent Minimalist work such as Kayne (1998). Many other authors also postulate some syntactic effect of prosodic prominence, though they might use features, transformations, or syntactic derivations in quite a different way; see e.g. Rooth (1985, 1992) von Stechow (1985/1989), Krifka (1992b, 2006), and Steedman (2000).

What all these accounts have in common is that they accept the premise that there is a grammatical interface between focus and meaning. Indeed, most accounts of this sort posit a combination of interfaces allowing information transfer first from phonology to syntax and then from syntax to semantics. Yet some authors have argued that the interaction between focus and meaning is not mediated syntactically at all; see e.g. Dryer (1994), Kadmon (2001), Martí (2003), Roberts (1996), Schwarzschild (1997), Vallduví (1990), and Williams (1997). These authors have suggested that many effects of focus on meaning are pragmatic.

Let us examine a little more closely how the phenomenon we will study here bears on the nature of grammatical interfaces, since this is an issue of potential interest across several linguistic subfields. In traditional architectures, interfaces between modules are presumed to be tightly constrained: we may think of interfaces metaphorically as narrow channels through which only certain types

---

[3] *Suprasegmental* features are so called because they are spread out across multiple segments (basic sound units), or even across multiple words.

[4] The architecture assumed in the Minimalist Program, e.g. Chomsky (2000), diverges from that in prior work, as does much of the terminology. It remains the case that the phonological processes at PF (PHONETIC FORM) and the meaning-related processes at LF (LOGICAL FORM) do not exchange information directly. Furthermore, if we take SYNTAX to refer collectively to all the processes occurring between the LEXICON and LF (rather than to a distinct level of representation), the architecture assumed by Minimalists can still be taken as a special case of that in Figure 1.1.

of information may pass. Specifically, it is common to think of the function of the syntax/phonology interface primarily in terms of segmental information, the information that determines which morphemes are present and how those morphemes are grouped. The place of suprasegmental information in a modular grammar is unclear and rarely discussed.

Pragmatic theories of focus could be seen as part of an enterprise of keeping the interfaces between phonology, morphosyntax, and semantics as narrowly circumscribed as possible. These pragmatic theories lean on extragrammatical mechanisms to make up the shortfall, much as in the model of Grice (1975).[5] If the interpretive effects of focus could be explained pragmatically, then the phenomenon of focus would provide us with little insight into how suprasegmental information is represented at the morphosyntax/phonology and semantics/morphosyntax interfaces. But if there is a grammatical, conventionalized connection between focus and meaning, then that places minimal constraints on the suprasegmental information that must be represented at the morphosyntax/phonology interface. It also places a lower limit on what information must be passed between syntax and semantics.

If the relationship between focus sensitive expressions and their associated focus is conventionalized as part of the meaning of those expressions, then compositional interpretation must have access to focus at some representational level. But if the purely pragmatic accounts of focus sensitivity are right, then natural language semantics needs no special component for focus. Thus people have proposed wildly different models of focus and focus sensitivity. In the coming chapters, we will try to show where the truth lies.

A Look Ahead

As we will see in Chapter 3, the set of expressions that apparently manifest focus sensitivity is a veritable Noah's ark:[6]

exclusives: *only, just, merely, . . . ;*
non-scalar additives: *too, also, . . . ;*
scalar additives: *even;*
particularizers: *in particular, for example, . . . ;*
intensives: *really, totally, . . . ;*
quantificational adverbs: *always, usually, . . . ;*
determiners: *many, most, . . . ;*
sentential connectives: *because, since, . . . ;*
counterfactuals: *if it were . . . ;*

---

[5] But note that it is controversial to what extent pragmatics may itself be conventionalized and possibly grammaticized – see e.g. Levinson (2000) for discussion.

[6] For prior discussion of the focus sensitivity of most of these expression types, see e.g. Kadmon (2001), Rooth (1996a) and Hajičová et al. (1998).

emotives: *regret, be glad, . . . ;*
superlatives: *-est;*
negation: *not, no, . . . ;* and
generics: *Mice eat CHEESE.*

As can be seen in this list, the menagerie of focus sensitive expressions includes both open and closed class items, and it includes both bound morphemes and independent lexical items. There are nouns, verbs, adverbs, and adjectives. Faced with the astonishing range of expressions that have been labeled *focus sensitive*, it is unclear whether there are limits. First, can just any expression be focus sensitive? And, second, is focus sensitivity really a homogeneous phenomenon at all?

Certainly, from a methodological point of view, one would prefer to explain all the observed effects of focus in terms of a unitary mechanism. But wishful thinking is not enough – the question of whether focus sensitivity results from one mechanism or many is surely an empirical one. Yet there has been a dearth of empirical work systematically comparing focus sensitivity across different expression types. A primary goal of this book is to show how data on focus sensitivity can be marshaled so as to enable such comparisons, and thence to derive conclusions about how focus sensitivity functions.

In case you cannot stand the suspense, here is a sneak preview. In answer to the first question, of whether just any expression can be focus sensitive, we argue that there are strict limits. In particular, there is only a narrow range of expression types, those with certain discourse functions, for which focus sensitivity can be conventionalized as part of the expression's lexical meaning. And in answer to the second question, of whether focus sensitivity really is a homogeneous phenomenon, it turns out that all focus sensitive expressions are not equal: there are multiple mechanisms at work. In Chapter 3, we present a new account of focus sensitivity, the QFC theory, which involves a three-way distinction between different effects of focus: QUASI ASSOCIATION, a special type of pragmatic inference; FREE ASSOCIATION, the resolution of a free variable; and CONVENTIONAL ASSOCIATION, a grammatical dependency on the current question under discussion. Yet we will also argue that these three effects of focus can be described in terms of a common core.

Thus, while we depart from, for example, Rooth (1985), Partee (1991), Krifka (1993a), von Fintel (1994), and Roberts (1996) in that we explicitly suggest differences across types of expressions that manifest focus sensitivity, we also build heavily on these predecessors' work. We will suggest that while some expressions are grammatically constrained to be focus sensitive, others are not. And yet we will argue, like all of those just cited, that focus itself can and should be interpreted quite uniformly, for example using Rooth's Alternative Semantics, to be discussed in gory detail in Chapters 2 and 4.

Chapter 2 provides background for the rest of the book. We begin by introducing the notion of focus and discuss the role it plays in information structure. Many of the claims about focus sensitivity that we attack in this book were made for English. For that reason, in Chapter 2 we spend some time examining the way in which information structure is marked through intonation in English, including aspects of intonational phonology and focus projection. The chapter ends with an overview of the semantic and pragmatic framework we adopt in this book and an outline of our account of focus sensitive expressions. Chapter 3 describes in detail the range of natural language expressions that appear to be focus sensitive and relates them to our three-way QFC classification of focus sensitivity.

Chapters 4 and 5 present semantic and pragmatic approaches to focus interpretation respectively. Though they primarily serve a preparatory function for the material in Chapters 6–10, they are also the most technically demanding chapters in the book. Our discussions of theoretical issues arising in prior work are more detailed and extensive than those to be found in any comparable work in this area, and will demand both logical acumen (first order logic and some lambda calculus) and significant graduate level training in formal semantics. However, some of the more technical subsections can safely be skipped, at least by those readers who are prepared to trust our formal claims, without overly compromising the broader argument of the book.

Taking as their primary object of study quantificational adverbs and exclusives, Chapters 6–8 explore a range of phenomena and diagnostics that demonstrate that the class of focus sensitive expressions is not monolithic. At a theoretical level, Chapters 6–8 adopt a simple events-based model drawn from Chapters 4 and 5, and in using this model we intentionally compromise the core meanings of exclusives and quantificational adverbs in order to bring out their semantic similarities. This is, we freely admit, a didactic trick. For it is by setting up the meanings of these expression types to be as similar as possible that we are able most effectively to highlight the differences that we are interested in, i.e. differences in their focus sensitivity.

Chapters 9 and 10 do away with our thin pretense that quantificational adverbs and exclusives are functionally similar, concentrating on the semantics and pragmatics of exclusives. We study in detail the large and controversy-laden literature in this area, take out of it what we need, and fashion a new proposal. This proposal puts the discourse function of exclusives at the heart of their meaning, and, we hope, explains both how and why exclusives manifest focus sensitivity. Finally, in Chapter 11, we consider the big picture, taking another look at our Noah's Ark of focus sensitive expressions, and seeing how what we have learned about exclusives and quantificational adverbs transfers to other expression types.

Chapter 2

Intonation and Meaning

The fact is that, given the clear importance of prosodic factors in pragmatics, the area is grossly understudied. There is disagreement even about the fundamentals of how such factors should be described ...

Levinson (1983: x)

2.1 Introduction

The notion of focus plays an important role in INFORMATION STRUCTURE, the ways in which information is organized at the sentence and discourse level. In the next section we introduce this notion and review some of the different manners in which it is realized cross-linguistically. In English, information structure is largely marked through intonation, and in §2.3 and §2.4 we look in more detail at the nature of this marking. §2.3 summarizes relevant aspects of the intonational phonology of English. §2.4 discusses so-called FOCUS PROJECTION, which relates intonational marking to information structure. After giving some background on how the interpretation of focus relates to the interpretation of questions (in §2.5) we introduce the semantic and pragmatic framework within which our own account is set. This framework is a development of Rooth's (1985, 1992) Alternative Semantics for focus (§2.6) and Roberts' (1996) question-based model of discourse structure (§2.7). In §2.8, we outline the main theoretical contribution of this book, an account of focus sensitive expressions which divides them into three separate categories only one of which involves conventionalized association with focus. We summarize the central points covered in the chapter in §2.9.

2.2 Focus

Summary: *We use the term* focus *to describe an information structural property that an expression may have which affects truth-conditional and non-truth-conditional meaning. Focus phenomena include the fact that prosodic prominence in* *an answer corresponds to the* wh-*phrase in a question. In many languages, word order and morphology can serve a similar function to focus in English.*

Previous work does not always cleanly separate phonological focus from information structure notions of focus such as discourse-new and/or hearer-new information. We use the term *focus* loosely to describe an information structural property that an expression may have which affects truth-conditional and non-truth-conditional meaning.[1] In English, focus is typically marked by a nuclear pitch accent; i.e. the last pitch accent in a phonological phrase (Cohan 2000; Ladd 1996: 45–46). We will discuss evidence in Chapter 6 that pitch accents are not required to mark focus.

As an illustration of focus phenomena, consider possible pairings of the questions in (2.1) with the answers in (2.2). (2.1a+2.2a) and (2.1b+2.2b) are appropriate question-answer pairs. (2.1a+2.2b) and (2.1b+2.2a) are not. In (2.2a), *teaching* corresponds to the *wh*-phrase *when* in (2.1a). In (2.2b), *bow tie* corresponds to the *wh*-phrase *what* in (2.1b). These examples illustrate the fact that in well-formed, or CONGRUENT, question-answer sequences, prosodic prominence in the answer corresponds to the *wh*-phrase in the question.

(2.1) a.   When does David wear a bow tie?

    b.   What does David wear when teaching?

(2.2) a.   David (only) wears a bow tie when TEACHING.

    b.   David (only) wears a BOW TIE when teaching.

In English, certain types of clausal constructions such as *it*-clefts convey similar, but not equivalent, information as focus. For example, the *it*-cleft in (2.3b) is akin to (2.3a) in the context provided in (2.3) (example from Ward et al. 2002: 1424).

(2.3) John only did the illustrations for the book . . .

    a.   MARY wrote the story.

    b.   It was MARY who wrote the story.

However, as Ward et al. (2002: 1424–5) point out, the foregrounded element in the *it*-cleft construction is not always equated with focus. For example, in (2.4), the focus *this* is located within the relative clause, contrasting one house with another.

(2.4)   Jill designed THAT house. It was Jill who designed THIS house too.

                                            (adapted from Ward et al. 2002: 1425)

---

[1] The literature on intonation and meaning makes reference to a range of phonetic, phonological, syntactic, and semantic notions of focus (Beaver et al. 2007). These notions of focus include *prominence* (a psychoacoustic notion), *phonological focus marking* (which is sometimes referred to as *prosodic* or *intonational* focus), *F-marking* (which is syntactic), and *semantic focus* (an aspect of the representation of meaning).

In many languages, special word orders play the same functional role as focus in English. In French, a range of clefting constructions are used much more commonly than English clefts (Lambrecht 1994), and these constructions have the effect of forcing the focus to be in a highly prominent post-verbal position. There are many other languages in which information structure is considered a primary determinant of word order, e.g. Hungarian, Czech, Mayan, and Catalan.

In Hungarian, immediately preverbal constituents correlate with the questioned position in *wh*-questions, just as focus does in English (Brody 1990; Roberts 1998; Szendrői 2003). In (2.5b) (from Szendrői 2003), the preverbal *egy könyvet* 'a book' is in what is usually described as a FOCUS POSITION, and corresponds to *mit* 'what' in (2.5a). By contrast, in our (2.6b) and (2.6c), the pre-verbal focus position is occupied by *a barátom* 'my friend', corresponding to *ki* 'who' in (2.5b).[2]

(2.5) a. Mit   vett   a   barátod?
        what-ACC bought the friend-yours
        'What did your friend buy?'

    b. (A barátom) egy KÖNYVET vett.
        the friend-my a   book-ACC bought
        'My friend bought a BOOK.'

(2.6) a. Ki   vett   (egy) könyvet?
        who bought (a)   book-acc
        'Who bought a book?'

    b. A barátom vett   (egy) könyvet.
        the friend-my bought (a)   book-ACC
        'My FRIEND bought a book.'

    c. Könyvet   a barátom vett.
        book-ACC the friend-my bought
        'As for books, my FRIEND bought some.'

In some languages, morphology serves a similar function to prosodic prominence in English. For example, Cuzco Quechua, like other varieties of Quechua, has several evidential focus enclitics (Faller 2002: 13). Example (2.7) (from Faller 2002: 150) contains the evidential focus enclitic *-mi* and the topic marker *-qa*.

(2.7) a. Law-ta-**mi**   pay-**qa** mikhu-rqa-n
        soup-ACC-**mi** (s)he-**qa** eat-PST1-3
        '(S)he ate soup.'

---

2 Hungarian is also usually described as having a TOPIC POSITION immediately before the focus position. Note that according to our informant it is somewhat unnatural, though possible, to front an indefinite like *egy könyvet* 'a book' into this position, which is why it remains in canonical post-verbal position in the answer in (2.6b). Fronting of the bare singular *könyvet* 'books' is reportedly somewhat easier, but with a contrastive interpretation, e.g. books as opposed to newspapers.

The Japanese nominative case marker *-ga*, which marks the grammatical subject of a sentence, is often used as a focus marker (Fry and Kaufmann 1998). Some languages, e.g. Japanese and Hindi, use word order, morphology, and prosody. To illustrate, Hindi has (i) a set of focus morphemes, (ii) a preverbal focus position, and (iii) phonetic reduction of words surrounding the focus (Sharma 2003). Word order and prosodic prominence do not necessarily function independently. For example, Szendrői (2001) argues that the special word order used to mark focus in Hungarian reduces to the way in which main stress is assigned in that language. An account of how such phenomena might form part of a cross-linguistic typology of focus realization is found in Büring (2006b).

2.3   Intonational Phonology

Summary: *We provide a brief introduction to the phonology of focus and look at ToBI, a system for transcribing English intonation.*

As we saw in the previous section, focus in English typically involves a certain type of prosodic prominence. In later chapters, we will discuss some of the phonological factors that have been claimed to be decisive for the theories of focus discussed in Chapter 1. In this section, we give a brief introduction to the phonology of prosody. For a more comprehensive introduction, see Ladd (1996) and Kadmon (2001). In the next section, we discuss the relationship between focus and pitch accent.

The prosody of an utterance involves three interrelated components: PHONOLOGICAL PHRASING, INTONATION, and STRESS. An utterance is divided up into phonological phrases. Each phonological phrase is characterized by an intonational melody and is usually marked by lengthening of the final syllable or syllables. Phonological phrasing is related to, but distinct from, syntactic phrasing; see Shattuck-Hufnagel and Turk (1996) for a review.

Intonation and stress both correlate with psychoacoustic prominence. They are marked using similar features, including pitch, intensity, duration, and vowel quality. Yet, they are typically treated as conceptually distinct: stress is largely morphosyntactically predictable, but intonation is pragmatic. In this book, we will take the naive view that stress assignment is a separate module, and assignment of the intonational melody just needs to see the output stress assignment, i.e. primary, secondary, or unstressed.[3]

There is extensive cross-linguistic variation in the phonology of prosody. Because of this, the field of prosody has not yet reached a stage where the range of variation has been captured in a detailed system, i.e. there is no suprasegmental IPA transcription system. In this section, we will look at the To(nes) and

---

[3] But see Selkirk (1996) and Ladd (1996): Chs. 5 and 6.

B(reak) I(ndices)[4] approach (ToBI) for English (Silverman et al. 1992). Similar systems for transcribing intonational melody for other languages have been developed (e.g. G(erman)ToBI, J(apanese)ToBI, etc.).[5]

In ToBI, intonation is represented as a string of tones (H, L), which determine the shape of the fundamental frequency (f_0) contour (see Pierrehumbert 1980; Beckman and Pierrehumbert 1986). We use T as a metavariable over the two tones H (high) and L (low). There are three kinds of tones: PITCH ACCENTS, PHRASE ACCENTS, and BOUNDARY TONES, defined in (2.8).

(2.8) a. **Pitch accents**: T* (are realized in the region containing a stressed syllable, e.g. H* indicates a high tone and comes out as a peak on the accented syllable)

b. **Phrase accents**: T– or T (mark (minor) phrase boundaries)

c. **Boundary tones**: T% (mark (major) phrase boundaries)

A pitch accent is "a local feature of a pitch contour – usually but not invariably a pitch change, and often involving a local maximum or minimum" (Ladd 1996: 45–6). In the ToBI system, pitch accents are represented as high or low tones (H*, L*) or combinations of tones (e.g. L+H*), and are annotated with an asterisk to distinguish them from phrase accents and boundary tones. Phrase accents include H- and L- and boundary tones include H% and L%. The ToBI system is based on the model of intonation developed in Pierrehumbert (1980). The inventories of pitch accents in Pierrehumbert's (1980) original system and in the ToBI system are given in Figure 2.1.

ToBI essentially gives the simple re-write grammar in (2.9) of possible intonational strings.[6] Pitch accents are grouped together and followed by a phrase

Pierrehumbert (1980): 7 pitch accents	ToBI: 5 pitch accents, downstep ("!")
H*	H*
L*	L*
H+L*	H+!H*
H*+L	L*+H
L*+H	L+H*
L+H*	
H*+H	

Figure 2.1 Pitch accents

---

[4] There are currently extensive introductions to ToBI, complete with tutorial material, at http://www.ling.ohio-state.edu/~tobi/ and http://anita.simmons.edu/~tobi/index.html.

[5] Other linguistic representations of intonation include the IPO model ('t Hart and Collier 1975) and the Tilt model (Taylor 2000).

[6] "|" in (2.9) is the disjunction operator, e.g. for the pitch accent rule, you get H* or L* or L+H* or etc. The "+" superscript means one or more times.

accent to make an INTERMEDIATE PHRASE; e.g. L+H* L-. Intermediate phrases are grouped together and followed by a boundary tone to make an INTONATIONAL PHRASE; e.g. L+H* L-H% (Jackendoff's (1972) B accent). While intonational phrase boundary tones are targets at the end of a phrase, intermediate tones fill in the space between the final pitch accent and the boundary.

(2.9)   **Pitch accent:** I → H* | L* | L+H* | H+L* | ...
             Intermediate phrase: I' → I⁺ [H-|L-]
             Intonational phrase: I'' → I'⁺ [H%|L%]

To illustrate how the system works, the sentence *This book is even sold at Wal-Mart* can be pronounced as a single phrase, as in (2.10a). Alternatively, the subject *this book* can be phrased separately from the rest of the sentence, as in (2.10b). In the latter case, the sentence-medial, intermediate phrase boundary is marked by a low boundary tone (L-).

(2.10) a.   Declarative with one intermediate phrase, multiple accents:
            This   book   is   even   sold at   Wal-Mart
            [H*   H* L-L%]
       b.   Declarative with an intermediate phrase break:
            This   book is   even   sold at   Wal-Mart
            [H* L-] [H* L-L%]

   In §2.2, we noted that, in English, focus is typically marked by a nuclear pitch accent; i.e. the last pitch accent in a phonological phrase (Cohan 2000; Ladd 1996: 45–6). Which ToBI label corresponds to focus? This is an area of ongoing research. Although focus is frequently marked by an H* accent (see, e.g., Hedberg and Sosa 2001 and Hedberg 2003), other accents are possible. For example, in yes–no questions, focus is often by marked by an L+H* (Hedberg and Sosa 2002). And to the extent that the marking of focus requires a nuclear accent, the pitch accent should be followed by an intermediate phrase boundary tone, and be the last accent before the next intonational phrase boundary.

2.4 Focus Projection

Summary: *We discuss the principles that govern the relationship between pitch accent and focus. Of central concern is the problem of focus projection, where a pitch accent is able to mark more than just the word it is placed on as focused. We provide an overview of two theories of focus projection, Selkirk (1996) and Schwarzschild (1999), and discuss their empirical and conceptual limitations. We propose a variant of Schwarzschild's theory that depends on the notion of activation.*

In the previous section we discussed the phonological representation of English prosody. In this section we consider the principles that govern the relationship between pitch accent and focus. We begin by considering some early accounts of the distributions of sentence accents in English. With that background, we turn to the problem of FOCUS PROJECTION, i.e. the observation that a pitch accent on an individual word can mark more than just the word that it is placed on as focused.

Chomsky and Halle (1968) argue that word stress plus syntactic structure fully determine the "stress contour" of the sentence.[7] They propose a cyclic algorithm for assigning sentential stress. The stress rules are given in (2.11):

(2.11)   **Compound Stress Rule:** add stress to the leftmost stressable vowel in nouns, verbs, or adjectives.
          Nuclear Stress Rule: add primary stress to the rightmost stressable vowel in a major constituent.

The effect of the Nuclear Stress Rule is illustrated in (2.12) (adapted from Truckenbrodt 2006). Following Truckenbrodt (2006), we use single and double underlines to indicate phrasal (as opposed to word) stress. In (2.12), there is no narrow focus. The Nuclear Stress Rule applies cyclically. In (2.12a), the Nuclear Stress Rule assigns rightmost stress in the NP and in the VP. In (2.12b), the Nuclear Stress Rule assigns rightmost, sentence-level stress.

(2.12) a.   NSR applies in the NP and VP:
            [$_S$ [$_{NP}$ The mayor of Evanston] [$_{VP}$ lost their support]]
       b.   NSR applies in S:
            [$_S$ [$_{NP}$ The mayor of Evanston] [$_{VP}$ lost their support]]

However, Bolinger (1972a) discusses data that suggests that the distribution of accents is not determined by syntactic or morphological structure. For example, relative semantic weight influences the assignment of sentential stress, as illustrated by (2.13)–(2.15).

(2.13) a.   My MOTHER is coming.
       b.   #My MOTHER is eating.
            (cf. My mother is EATING.)

(2.14) a.   He was arrested because he KILLED a man.
       b.   #He was arrested because he KILLED a policeman.
            (cf. He was arrested because he killed a POLICEMAN.)

(2.15) a.   In this class, there will be lots of ISSUES to resolve.
       b.   #In this class, there will be lots of ISSUES to ignore.
            (cf. In this class, there will be lots of issues to IGNORE.)

---

[7] See also Bresnan (1971).

On the basis of examples such as (2.13)–(2.15), Bolinger concludes that accent (his generalization of stress) is correlated with informational value. Thus, accent is affected by world knowledge, local context and speaker intentions, rather than by syntax. Later, Jackendoff (1972), Selkirk (1984), and Gussenhoven (1992) present accounts that combine stress principles like the Nuclear Stress Rule with constraints on intonational prominence.[8]

With this background, let's return to the question that we posed at the beginning of this section: What principles govern the relationship between pitch accent and focus? In the following examples, we adopt the convention of indicating a focused constituent with a subscripted "F", taken to indicate marking of focus at a syntactic level (Jackendoff 1972; Rooth 1992; Selkirk 1996). Thus, using what will be the standard notational convention adopted in this book, we have (2.16) for (1.1).

(2.16) a.   This book may even be sold at [Wal-Mart]$_F$.

     b.   This book may even be [sold]$_F$ at Wal-Mart.

We can restate our original question now in terms of F-marking: what principles govern the relationship between pitch accent and F-marking (Selkirk 1996)?

One major issue in the intonation-focus relation is *focus projection* (Chomsky 1972): a pitch accent is able to mark more than just the word it is placed on as focused. Gussenhoven (1999) discusses this phenomenon not only for English but also for related languages like German, Frisian, Dutch, and Afrikaans. Focus projection has been tackled by a number of different researchers.[9] Selkirk (1996: 554) presents the example in (2.17). Different F-markings are possible when the sentence *Mary bought a book about bats* is pronounced with a pitch accent on *bats*. The same sentence can be an appropriate answer to different *wh*-questions.

---

[8]   There is natural language processing work on automatically predicting default accentuation using information-theoretic measures. For example, Hirschberg (1993) uses given/new and contrast information. Pan and McKeown (1999) define information content using a simple measure of word probability, and predict about 70% of accents in their corpus. Yuan et al. (2005) combine information content with syntactic category, N-gram probability, number of constituent boundaries, sentence position, collocation effects, genre, and speaker variation. They correctly predict typical accentuation of a word over 80% of the time. Inter-speaker consistency is no better, meaning that there is a great deal of optionality in accenting, and suggesting that at around the 80% mark we reach a ceiling in terms of how accurately we can usefully predict the accents that would be produced by a particular speaker on a particular occasion of utterance. See Brenier et al. (2006) and Nenkova et al. (2007) for further discussion.

[9]   See, e.g., Büring (1997, 2006a), Chomsky (1972), Féry and Samek-Lodovici (2006), German et al. (2006), Gussenhoven (1983, 1992, 1999), Jackendoff (1972), Jacobs (1991a), Kadmon (2001), Ladd (1980), Lambrecht (1994), Reinhart (2006), Rochemont (1986), Schwarzschild (1993, 1999), and Selkirk (1984, 1996). Kadmon (2001) and Winkler (1997) contain recent major overviews of the literature on focus projection.

(2.17) a.   Mary bought a book about [BATS]$_F$.
              (*What did Mary buy a book about?*)

       b.   Mary bought a book [about BATS]$_F$.
              (*What kind of book did Mary buy?*)

       c.   Mary bought [a book about BATS]$_F$.
              (*What did Mary buy?*)

       d.   Mary [bought a book about BATS]$_F$.
              (*What did Mary do?*)

       e.   [Mary bought a book about BATS]$_F$.
              (*What's been happening?*)

A theory of focus projection should determine what constituents are possible foci. Typically the theory is stated in terms of an extra abstract level of marking, which we will notate as f-marking (*not* F-marking!): e.g. accents determine basic f-marking, f-marking is inherited by higher constituents, and foci are maximal f-marked constituents. These maximal f-marked constituents are marked with FOC to indicate their special status.[10]

Theories of focus-projection can be divided into top-down and bottom-up approaches (Winkler 1997). In top-down approaches (Gussenhoven 1983, 1992, 1999; Jacobs 1991a), the focus feature is assigned to the highest possible node and then percolates down to find an adequate exponent upon which accent is realized. In bottom-up approaches (Rochemont 1986; Selkirk 1984, 1996), the focus feature is assigned to a pitch-accented element and then projected up the tree to mark the range of focus. Both bottom-up and top-down approaches assume that argument structure is the decisive factor in determining the focus structure of the sentence. In what follows, we explore the bottom-up approach to focus projection presented in Selkirk (1996). Selkirk's approach is important because it attempts to pull together the meaning and phonology of focus.

Selkirk (1996) assumes that an SPE-like (Chomsky and Halle 1968) stress theory provides a default stress structure for each sentence. ToBI-style accents are then draped over the stress structure, boosting pitch accented words above all others. Selkirk's recursive definition of focus projection is given in (2.18).

---

[10]   There is an unfortunate notational clash in the literature on focus: in most of the literature, focused constituents in examples are labeled with an F, and this is the practice we follow through most of the current book. But in literature on focus projection, as we have just noted, foci may be annotated with FOC, and in this literature F-marking represents yet another abstract feature used to mediate between accenting and focus. We adopt a convention whereby f-marking with a small 'f' is used to indicate what in the focus projection literature is notated as F-marking, FOC is used as in the focus projection literature to indicate maximal f-marking, and F-marking is used to indicate that a constituent is focused.

(2.18)   **Basic Focus Rule:** An accented word is f-marked.
         Phrasal Focus Rules:
              i. f-marking of a constituent is licensed by f-marking of its
                 head, and
             ii. f-marking of an internal argument licenses f-marking of its
                 head.
         Sentence Focus Rule: A FOC is f-marked but not dominated by
              another f-marked constituent.

The application of Selkirk's (1996) system is illustrated in bottom-up fashion in
(2.19). In (2.19a), the accented word *bats* has been f-marked by the Basic Focus
Rule. In (2.19b), the Phrasal Focus Rules have been applied. In (2.19c), the Sentence Focus Rule has been applied, FOC-marking the S node.

(2.19) a.   An accented word is f-marked:

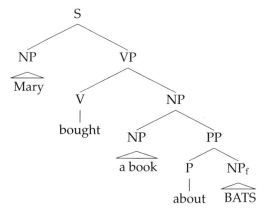

       b.   f-marking of a constituent is licensed by f-marking of its head, and
            f-marking of an internal argument licenses f-marking of its head:

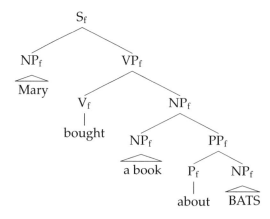

c. A FOC is f-marked but not dominated by another f-marked constituent:

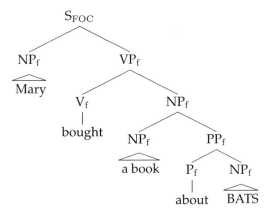

If f-marking served only to indicate FOC, Selkirk's system would overgenerate accent possibilities. So Selkirk suggests that her account of focus projection must also involve the distinction between *Given* and *New* information. Prince (1981) suggests that these notions subdivide into many subcategories, but current work on focus projection assumes a simple dichotomy. According to Selkirk (1996), the f-marking of syntactic constituents is constrained by their given or new discourse status according to the generalizations in (2.20).

(2.20) a. An f-marked constituent that is not a FOC must be NEW in the discourse.

b. A constituent without f-marking must be GIVEN.

Schwarzschild (1999: 145–7) notes several problems with Selkirk's notion of *Given* – e.g. it cannot apply to non-constituents – and attempts to spell out a more successful definition.[11] Schwarzschild does this by defining *Given* in terms of entailment. This is easy to do for constituents that express propositions, but tricky for non-propositional constituents, because entailment is normally defined as a relationship between propositions.[12] Consequently, he turns expressions of any type into propositions using EXISTENTIAL CLOSURE. Existential closure is "a type shifting operation that raises expressions to type t, by existentially binding unfilled arguments" (Schwarzschild 1999: 147). For

---

[11] Moreover, he shows that it is possible to do so with minimal syntactic stipulation: we refer the reader to Schwarzschild (1999) for full details, and will merely describe here aspects of his system most relevant to our purposes.

[12] In §2.7 we make use of a standard notion of entailment between questions rather than between propositions (Groenendijk and Stokhof 1984). It is natural to ask whether when one question entails a second, the second is *given* in the context of the first on Schwarzschild's notion of *given*. The answer, unfortunately, is no. For example, *Who likes who?* entails *Who likes Sam?*, but the first is *given* in the context of the second rather than the other way around.

example, $[\![happy]\!]^{13}$ becomes $\exists x \; happy'(x)$. Schwarzschild's definition of *Given* is presented in (2.21).

(2.21)   A constituent is *Given* if it is entailed by a salient antecedent modulo removal of any f-marked parts, and existential closure to produce a proposition.

Example (2.22) illustrates an application of Schwarzschild's entailment-based account of *Given* to the verb phrase *saw Mary*f.

(2.22) a.   In the context of *Fred saw John* is *saw Mary*f *Given*?

   b.   First, remove the f-marked part of *saw Mary*f to get *saw*.

   c.   Then existentially close $[\![saw]\!]$ to get $\exists x \exists y \; saw'(x,y)$.

   d.   This is entailed by $[\![Fred \; saw \; John]\!]$, so *saw Mary*f is *Given*.

Schwarzschild suggests that a sentence should have MINIMAL f-marking such that all non-f-marked constituents are *Given*. This allows us to check whether a particular f-marking is acceptable in a given context, by trying to remove f-markings. Schwarzschild defines the rules of focus projection in terms of ranked optimality-theoretic constraints. The two key constraints for focus projection are GIVENNESS and AVOIDF, presented in (2.23).

(2.23) a.   *Givenness*: Non-f-marked constituents are *Given*.

   b.   *AvoidF*: Minimize f-marking, without violating *Givenness*.

Givenness says that non-f-marked constituents are *Given*. *AvoidF* says that when f-marking is not needed, it is avoided. Schwarzschild suggests that a sentence should have MINIMAL f-marking such that all non-f-marked constituents are *Given*. This allows us to check whether a particular f-marking is acceptable in a given context, by trying to remove f-markings.

   Example (2.24) illustrates the application of *Givenness* and *AvoidF*. Examples (2.24a) and (2.24b) both satisfy *Givenness*: all the non-f-marked constituents are *Given* in the sense of (2.21). *AvoidF* rules out (2.24b), since it has more f-marking than its competitor (2.24a).

(2.24) {Who did John's mother praise?}

   a.   She praised HIM$_f$

   b.   *She [PRAISED$_f$ him]$_f$

Without f-marking on *him*, we would violate *Givenness* since *She praised him* is not entailed by the context.

---

13    $[\![\;\;]\!]$ is a function (the INTERPRETATION FUNCTION) that assigns meanings to linguistic expressions (Heim and Kratzer 1998: 15).

Schwarzschild formulates a variant of Selkirk's second Phrasal Focus Rule, in (2.18), above:

(2.25)   HEADARG: A head is less prominent than its internal argument(s).

This rule is motivated by an asymmetry in accenting possibilities between verbs and direct objects. For example, *What did Mary do?* can be answered with *She bought a BOOK*, with an H* pitch accent on *book*, or *She BOUGHT a BOOK*, with two H* pitch accents, realized with a sustained plateau between *bought* and *book*, but not with *She BOUGHT a book*, in which there is a pitch accent only on *bought*.

Exactly which arguments of a verb are internal for the purposes of (2.25) is a matter of theoretical debate. While this makes it difficult to make concrete predictions, it also provides the flexibility to account for some awkward cases in the literature. For example, one of Bolinger's examples, (2.13), repeated below in (2.26), could be accounted for if the subject of *is eating* was taken to be an external argument, but the subject of *is coming* was taken to be an internal argument.[14]

(2.26) a.   My MOTHER is coming.

     b.   #My MOTHER is eating.
        (cf. My mother is EATING.)

Theories of accent placement must be able to account for cases where a *Foc* constituent dominates only *Given* items (Schwarzschild 1999; Büring 2006a). In these cases, if there is more than one word in the *Foc*, the placement of accents within the *Foc* constituent is determined solely by the head-argument asymmetry noted above. The definition of *Foc* constituents, given above in (2.18), is repeated in (2.27).

(2.27)   A *Foc* is f-marked but not dominated by another f-marked constituent.

In (2.28) (Schwarzschild 1999: 172), the second occurrence of *the rising of the tides* must be f-marked because it is not *Given* that something depends upon the rising of the tides. Yet, all of the material in *the rising of the tides* (e.g. *tides*) is *Given*. Consequently, *Givenness* does not require any further f-marking within this NP. However, the placement of accent is still determined by argument structure: the argument *the tides* is more prominent than the head *rising*.

---

[14]   It is not implausible that *is eating* and *is coming* differ in this way, since the former is transitive with a clearly agentive subject, while the latter is plausibly unaccusative, and its translation equivalent is clearly so in, e.g., Romance languages. Closely related to the internal/external argument difference is the distinction between complements and adjuncts. Lambrecht (1994), for example, argues that complements, like direct object arguments, differ from adjuncts in their focus projection behavior.

(2.28)   {The rising of the TIDES depends on the MOON being full, and}
          [the BOAT$_f$ being empty$_f$]$_f$ depends upon [the rising of the TIDES]$_f$

In order to ensure that *Foc* constituents which consist only of *Given* material are accented, Schwarzschild proposes the constraint in (2.29), requiring that *Foc* constituents carry an accent.

(2.29)   *Foc*: *Foc*-marked phrases contain an accent.

Schwarzschild's theory of focus marking and projection incorporates several conceptual developments, notably (i) the way of calculating what must be f-marked as a process of optimization, (ii) a formalization of the given/new distinction, and (iii) an attempt to deal with the relationship between questions and the accenting of answers in terms of that distinction.

Thus, although questions have played an important role in the literature on focus, they are not given any privileged status in Schwarzschild's account. The effect of a question in establishing givenness of later mentioned entities depends on first applying existential closure, with the result that a *wh*-question plays exactly the same role in his account as would the same utterance but with all *wh*-words replaced by indefinites. However, questions play a central role in the account of focus sensitivity developed in this book, and Schwarzschild's model, in its original form, does not quite provide the supporting structure we need. Before going on to suggest some modifications to Schwarzschild's model, let us consider briefly some empirical issues that illustrate why the original version will not serve us adequately. We will return to all of these issues in Chapter 3.

By any reasonable definition, repeated material is *Given*. Yet in echoic utterances, such as direct denials, it is common to accent repeated material, as in *FIDo* in the second sentence (b) of the discourse in (2.30):

(2.30) a. SANdy fed FIdo this morning.
       b. Uhm, wait, she DIDn't feed FIdo,
       c. she fed BUTCH.

In (2.30b), Schwarzschild's model predicts that the negative auxiliary form *DIDn't* must be f-marked. If it were not f-marked, it would have to be *Given*, which would imply that prior discourse established that someone didn't do something, which is not the case. Furthermore, once the negative auxiliary form is f-marked, there is no need to f-mark anything else: the complement of *DIDn't* is given, and by existential closure over possible values of the auxiliary, the phrase *DIDn't$_f$ feed FIdo* is also *Given*, as is the whole clause *she DIDn't$_f$ feed FIdo*. Schwarzschild, therefore, predicts that *FIdo* should not be f-marked, and should not be accented. Example (2.30b) shows that Schwarzschild's prediction is false.

Here is what seems to be a way out for Schwarzschild: we can use (2.30c) as the 'antecedent' when calculating givenness of constituents of (2.30b).

This would produce the desirable result that *Fido* would be predicted to be f-markable. However, to make this move would be to undercut one of the main ideas behind Schwarzschild's proposal, the idea that accenting can be explained entirely in terms of the *Given/New* distinction. Suppose that some material appears for the first time in a text in some sentence S_1, and then appears again in the following sentence S_2. It would seem very odd, in such a case, to say that the material was *Given* in its occurrence in S_1. Yet that is what taking (2.30c) as an antecedent when calculating givenness of constituents of (2.30b) would amount to. Below, we will suggest an alternative approach to solving the problem of why *FIdo* is accented in (2.30b). But first, we turn to some other examples that illustrate the limitations of Schwarzschild's original proposal, starting with emotive factive verbs.

The discourse consisting of (2.31a+b) conveys different information than that in (2.31a+b'). Examples (2.31b) and (2.31b') involve the emotive factive *be glad*.[15] (2.31b) claims that the students preferred Brady teaching semantics to the counterfactual alternative of someone else teaching semantics. In contrast, (2.31b') claims that the students preferred Brady teaching semantics to the counterfactual alternative of him teaching, e.g., historical linguistics or syntax. The prior discourse in (2.31a) for (2.31b) and (2.31b') establishes that Brady taught semantics. Consequently, for both (2.31b) and (2.31b'), the subordinate clause *Brady taught semantics* is *Given*. As with the negative auxiliary example in (2.30b), Schwarzschild, therefore, incorrectly predicts that *Brady* and *semantics* should not be f-marked and should not be accented in (2.31b) and (2.31b') .

(2.31) a. Brady taught semantics and . . .

   b. the students were glad that BRADY taught semantics.

   b'. the students were glad that Brady taught SEMANTICS.

We give one last illustration of the challenges faced by Schwarzschild's givenness based theory of focus in (2.32), involving the focus sensitive expression *only*. Several issues arise with examples like this, one of which is the question of whether the word which *only* associates with in (2.32b), *semantics*, needs to be accented at all. In Chapter 6 we will show that, in a closely related type of example, the word with which *only* associates is indeed prosodically prominent, although the prominence may involve acoustic features other than pitch movement. But for current purposes, what matters is not whether or not the word *semantics* has to be focus marked, but the fact that it *can* be so marked. This much is uncontroversial, since it clearly is possible to produce (2.32b) with a pitch accent on *semantics*, so that it must be f-marked. On a natural analysis of (2.32b), the VP *taught semantics last year* would not be f-marked, so that *semantics* would in fact be *Foc*-marked. Yet, as with examples (2.30b) and (2.31b)/(2.31b'), marking here is clearly not a matter of givenness, since *semantics* is *Given*, as are

---

[15] We give the full story on emotive factives in Chapter 3.

all the constituents in the VP complement of *only*. So Schwarzschild's theory correctly predicts an accent on *only*, but incorrectly predicts that no accent should be allowed on *semantics*.

(2.32) a.   Brady taught semantics last year.

   b.   In fact, he ONLY taught SEMANTICS last year.

We have now discussed three types of example we consider problematic for Schwarzschild's model of focus projection. These are all cases involving focus sensitivity. We based the examples on three different expression types (negation, emotive factives like *be glad*, and exclusives like *only*). We will shortly place each of these expression types in different classes of focus sensitive expression. Our account of these three classes depends upon some model of focus projection, even though developing such a model is not our main aim in this book. We therefore suggest a way in which Schwarzschild's theory can be modified so as to ground our theory of focus sensitivity, while still accounting for the types of example that motivated him to develop his account in the first place.

Speakers use accenting to make expressions more prominent, and thus to draw attention to those expressions, as opposed to others. In what follows, we talk of the amount of attention being paid to a particular concept or discourse referent as the *activation* of that concept or referent.[16] Our strategy, then will be to allow the notion of (sufficient) *activation* to play the role of *Givenness* in our variant of Schwarzschild's theory, and to understand *Givenness* as a special case of *activation*. The intuition behind this is that even if something is *Given*, and thus activated, it may be that the speaker wishes to draw yet more attention to it, i.e. to increase its activation, for example because of a desire to contrast it with something else.

We define the set of expressions which are insufficiently activated as the minimal set satisfying the two following constraints, although we allow that in a more general model other factors (such as visual salience) would also be significant:

(2.33) a.   *New activation*: Constituents which are not *Given* are insufficiently *Activated*.

   b.   *Alternative activation*: Constituents for which the speaker wishes to evoke alternatives are insufficiently *Activated*.

---

[16]   For an introduction to the notion of *activation* of discourse referents, see Arnold (1998). Our use of this term is inspired by its use in (neuro-)psychology, though we do not pretend to have any evidence that our use of the term indicates a measurable brain state. Within linguistics, the term is known through the work of Chafe (1994): for critical discussion of his use of the term, see Lambrecht (1994). Our understanding of *activation* differs from Chafe's. For him *activation* is essentially a level of givenness but, for us, even a discourse referent which is established as the most salient entity from prior discourse, and which is thus as *Given* as anything ever can be, may require a boost in activation. This will be the case precisely when the speaker wishes to draw the hearer's attention to the fact that alternatives might have been used in place of the term picking out that referent.

We now replace Schwarzschild's *Givenness* constraint with one we term *Activation*, and make a concomitant change to Schwarzschild's *AvoidF*:[17]

(2.34) a. *Activation*: f-marked constituents are insufficiently *Activated*.

 b. *AvoidF*: Minimize f-marking, without violating *Activation*.

The theory of focus projection we have now described is conservative, in the sense that, in cases where no additional factors come into play, the predictions will be identical to Schwarzschild's. However, examples (2.30), (2.31), and (2.32) all involve additional accenting not predicted by Schwarzschild's theory. In all these cases, the speaker wishes to draw additional attention to already *Given* entities in order to evoke alternatives. This will be accounted for by the second clause of the definition of *activation*, i.e. *Alternative activation*.

Our theory is thus comparable to Selkirk's model, in that we assume that f-marking is not constrained by *Given/New* alone. But it is unlike Selkirk's model in three ways: first, it utilizes Schwarzschild's formalization of *Given/New*; second, the multiple factors we take to determine information status are related to f-marking via a single measure, i.e. *activation*; third, the actual calculation of what is f-marked follows Schwarzschild's optimization approach.[18]

Consider again example (2.24), repeated below:

(2.24) {Who did John's mother praise?}

 a. She praised HIM$_f$

 b. *She [PRAISED$_f$ him]$_f$

The theory of alternatives that we discuss in the next few sections establishes that an answer to *Who did John's mother praise?* must make alternatives of the form *she praised X* salient, implying that the constituent corresponding to the *X*, i.e. *him*, must be f-marked. We already saw that, in Schwarzschild's account, *givenness* establishes that *him* must be f-marked. Although *givenness* is mediated via *activation* in our account of focus projection, we can also capture the contrast between (2.24a) and (2.24b). In the context of *Who did John's mother praise?*, the speaker wants to evoke alternatives of the form *she praised X* in order to ensure congruence to the current question under discussion. However, (2.24b) only succeeds in evoking alternatives of the form *she Xed him*, *she Xed*, or maybe no alternatives at all, depending on which f-mark, if any, is interpreted

---

[17] The term *evoking alternatives* will be discussed in §2.6.

[18] It might be that a minor strengthening of the account we have proposed is required, for example by requiring that constituents which are insufficiently activated by virtue of evoking alternatives are not merely f-marked, but are Foc-marked. For, the theory as stated does not imply that expressions which are f-marked in order to induce alternatives are more prominent than those which are f-marked because they are discourse new. Yet the various types of focus in which we are interested in this book tend to be not merely prominent, but maximally prominent in their intonational phrase. We leave investigation of this issue for future work.

as being present to evoke alternatives. So, in a case like (2.24), considerations pertaining to the evocation of alternatives happily coincide with considerations of *givenness*, and the net effect is that we make exactly the same prediction as Schwarzschild.

Now let us turn to an example where the predictions of our variant model differ from Schwarzschild's, (2.30), repeated below:

(2.30) a.   SANdy fed FIdo this morning.

      b.   Uhm, wait, she DIDn't feed FIdo,

      c.   she fed BUTCH.

By the same argument that we used earlier with respect to (2.30), *DIDn't* is not given in (2.30b). Because of this, it is not sufficiently activated and must be f-marked. However, the speaker may also wish to evoke alternatives to *FIdo*, since it is being contrasted with *BUTCH*. In our new version of Schwarzschild's system, *FIdo* is also insufficiently activated, and requires f-marking. There is no need to f-mark anything else, so this is a minimal f-marking, and both *DIDn't* and *FIdo* are therefore not only f-marked, but also Foc-marked. They must then both be accented, producing the observed utterance.[19]

Summing up, in this section we explored the relationship between accent placement and focus. We have assumed, with Selkirk and Schwarzschild, that the relation between accent placement and information structure is regulated by rules or constraints that operate at the interface between syntax and interpretation.[20] We proposed a variant of an existing model (Schwarzschild's) that will support the developments in the rest of this book, and provide a backdrop to some of the arguments we discuss concerning the realization of focus, in Chapter 6 in particular.

---

[19]   Note that other accentuations are also predicted to be possible. For example, the speaker may wish to evoke alternatives not only to *Fido*, but also to the entire IP *didn't feed Fido*, so as to contrast properties of Sandy. In that case, that entire IP would be f-marked, and Foc-marked. It would follow that the auxiliary, while still f-marked, would not be Foc-marked, since it would be dominated by an f-marked node. This would then lead to the utterance *Uhm, wait, she didn't feed FIdo*, instead of (2.30b). This is a felicitous production in the context described, so we take the prediction to be correct. But note that it is very awkward for Schwarzschild's system. Quite generally, Schwarzschild's system is not good at predicting simple optionality of accents, i.e. cases where there are two legitimate productions differing only in that one of them has more f-marking than the other.

[20]   Recent work on the relationship between focus and pitch accents calls for a radical reevaluation of the prosody-meaning interface. For example, Büring (2006a) and Reinhart (2006) attempt to dispense with focus projection rules entirely. Similarly, Féry and Samek-Lodovici (2006) argue that the distribution of pitch accents follows from the interaction of constraints that govern the prosodic organization of the clause, and constraints that govern the prosodic expression of discourse status.

2.5   Questions and Focus

Summary: *We introduce the approach to the interpretation of questions that we adopt in this book, the* Rooth–Hamblin *semantics of questions. We contrast our approach with the questions-as-properties model.*

In the preceding sections we introduced the notion of focus and discussed the role it plays in information structure. We also examined the different ways information structure can be marked through prosody in English. With this background, we present, in the remaining sections of this chapter, the semantic and pragmatic framework we adopt in this book, and we outline our theory of focus sensitivity. The intepretation of focus divides the content of an expression into two parts: the meaning of the focus, and the meaning of the BACKGROUND, the part of the expression unmarked by prosodic prominence. Example (2.35) illustrates some of the different ways of focusing the sentence *Mary likes Sandy* and the resulting focus and background, notated as ⟨Background, Focus⟩.

(2.35) a.   [Mary]$_F$ likes Sandy ↦ ⟨$\lambda x.x$ *likes Sandy*, *Mary*⟩

   b.   Mary [likes]$_F$ Sandy ↦ ⟨$\lambda R.Mary\ R\ Sandy$, *like*⟩

   c.   Mary likes [Sandy]$_F$ ↦ ⟨$\lambda x.Mary\ likes\ x$, *Sandy*⟩

  The function of the focus-background distinction can be compared to that of question-answer pairs. We may think of the focus in (2.36) as saying that the utterance serves as an answer to the question in (2.37). Then the focus sensitive operator *only* in (2.38) can be thought of as saying that the sentence to which it is attached, i.e. (2.36), provides an exhaustive (strongest possible, or most complete) answer to the question indicated by the focus, i.e. an exhaustive answer to (2.37).[21]

(2.36)   Mary likes [Sandy]$_F$.

(2.37)   Who does Mary like?

(2.38)   Mary only likes [Sandy]$_F$.

But how do we analyze questions and answers? One approach, since Hamblin (1973), is to take the meaning of a question to be a set of alternative answers, thus a set of propositions. Opinion has varied as to whether this should be the set of true answers or a set of all possible answers, right or wrong. Hamblin took a set of true possible answers, Karttunen (1977) argued instead for sets of true answers, and Groenendijk and Stokhof (1984), while also making some other very significant changes, reverted to possible answers.[22] Thus, for Hamblin,

---

[21] Cf. the discussion of *exhaustification* in §3.2.
[22] Yet another approach influenced by Hamblin, though more syntactically oriented, is that of Higginbotham (1993, 1996).

the meaning of (2.37) may be thought of as the following set of propositions: $\{[\![\text{Mary likes Adam}]\!], [\![\text{Mary likes Bertha}]\!], [\![\text{Mary likes Casper}]\!], \ldots\}$. If $[\![\text{Mary likes Adam}]\!]$ is represented as $likes(m,a)$, then we may rewrite the meaning of the question as $\{likes(m, x) \mid person(x)\}$.

According to Groenendijk and Stokhof (1984), the denotation of a question, or, more properly, what they take to be the question's *sense* rather than its *reference*, is not just a set of possible answers, but a set of possible exhaustive answers. Thus, for them, (2.37) corresponds to the set of propositions: $\{[\![\text{Mary likes nobody}]\!],$ $[\![\text{Mary likes Adam and nobody else}]\!], [\![\text{Mary likes Bertha and nobody else}]\!], [\![\text{Mary likes Bertha and Adam and nobody else}]\!], \ldots\}$. Model theoretically, the meaning of a question for Groenendijk and Stokhof is a partition on the set of worlds, which means that alternatives share no worlds with each other. Put differently, on Groenendijk and Stokhof's picture, the propositions corresponding to alternatives never entail each other. However, for many focus examples it will be important for us that some alternatives entail others. We take the moral to be that while Groenendijk and Stokhof's account makes for an interesting semantics for questions, it does not provide us with exactly what we need for our account of focus.[23]

In this book, we adopt a semantics for questions that combines Hamblin's approach with the Alternative Semantics of Rooth (1985, 1992). Rooth developed an Alternative Semantics for focus along the same lines as Hamblin's Alternative Semantics for questions, giving focus sensitive expressions such as *only* in (2.38) access to a set of alternatives similar to those of the question in (2.37). There is a significant technical difference between Hamblin's alternatives and those which Rooth uses. In Hamblin's theory, propositions correspond to the alternative answers to a *wh*-question in which (modulo changes in word-order) the *wh*-word is replaced by the name of an individual. In Rooth's theory, alternative sets correspond to answers in which the *wh*-word is replaced by the name of an individual or a conjunction of such names. Accordingly, the meaning of (2.37) corresponds to the set of propositions: $\{[\![\text{Mary likes Adam}]\!],$ $[\![\text{Mary likes Bertha}]\!], [\![\text{Mary likes Casper}]\!], [\![\text{Mary likes Adam and Bertha}]\!],$ $[\![\text{Mary likes Adam and Casper}]\!], [\![\text{Mary likes Adam and Bertha and Casper}]\!] \ldots\}$. That is, Rooth builds the propositions in his focus alternatives using *sums* of individuals, and the meaning of (2.37) is $\{likes(m, x) \mid people(x)\}$, where we

---

[23] It should be noted that Groenendijk and Stokhof (1984) do cover the application of their framework to phenomena very closely related to those we consider here, in particular, the phenomenon of exhaustivity. Van Rooij (2001), and van Rooij and Schulz (2007) take the model of exhaustivity further, and the latter show explicitly how it might be applied in the case of the exclusive *only*. In the model that we eventually develop, in Chapter 10, the meaning of *only* turns out to go further than that of exhaustivity, as standardly conceived. In particular, we will make use of orderings between focal alternatives that do not equate naturally to orderings between the alternatives in Groenendijk and Stokhof's model. Nonetheless, we must make clear that our rejection of the Groenendijk and Stokhof framework for interpreting questions is not based on any absolute limits we have established to what can be achieved in that framework, but rather is based on our conclusion that the framework we actually do use better fits our purposes.

allow that the predicate *people* ranges over possibly empty sums of people. To the extent that the question presupposes that Mary likes at least somebody, the empty sum should be removed from this set, but this is an issue we leave unresolved.

We will refer to the modification of Hamblin's question semantics to use Rooth-style alternative sets as the ROOTH–HAMBLIN SEMANTICS of questions. We will frequently use Hamblin's original semantics to simplify the presentation, but the Rooth–Hamblin semantics is the *official* approach we adopt for the interpretation of questions in this book.

We have now considered various notions of alternatives, but we should point out that questions do not have to be analyzed using alternatives at all. Another standard way of dealing with questions is to treat them as properties. A *wh*-question would denote a function from individuals to propositions, or, extensionally, just a function from individuals to truth values. So the meaning of (2.37) might be represented as $\lambda x.likes(m,x)$, a function from individuals to truth values, true for just those individuals that Mary likes. This type of analysis has been pursued by e.g. Scha (1983), Hausser (1983), and Krifka (2001, 2004), and in a slightly different form by Ginzburg (1995a, 1995b) and Ginzburg and Sag (2000).

The analysis of questions as denoting properties has a couple of *prima facie* advantages over the Hamblin derived models. First, it is intuitively more direct, since it assigns as the meaning of a *wh*-question exactly what we might expect to be the Montagovian meaning of a sentence with a missing NP. The meaning of (2.37) will come out just the same as or closely related to the most natural meaning of the corresponding relative clause, *who Mary likes*. Second, the property approach gives a natural account of short answers, e.g. the answer *Sandy* to (2.37). In such cases, the information conveyed by the short answer is given simply by applying the meaning of the question to the meaning of the answer, whereas in a Hamblin derived model the information conveyed by the short answer can only be understood through a process of reconstructing a full sentence.

Nonetheless, with the notable exception of the work by Krifka and Ginzburg, Hamblin style approaches to the semantics of questions have largely had the upper hand in recent years, at least as judged by the number of published articles. Perhaps this relates to one of the main disadvantages of taking questions to be properties: if questions denote properties, and the type of these properties varies, then verbs which take interrogative complements (consider e.g. *knowing who* and *wondering whether*) need to be systematically polysemous across a range of different types that their interrogative complements might take.

Structured Meanings is an approach to focus developed by Jacobs (1983), Stechow (1991, 1985/1989), and Krifka (1991, 1992a, 1993), with developments in Categorial Grammar including Jäger (1999). It can be seen as a close cousin of the questions-as-properties model, as is made explicit by Krifka (2001, 2004). We just sketched how the short answer *Sandy* could be combined with (2.37), *Who does Mary like?* The Structured Meaning of the focused sentence (2.36) *Mary likes [Sandy]*$_F$ consists simply of the meanings of the corresponding question + short answer pair, i.e. $\langle \lambda x.likes(m, x), s \rangle$.

As we will see in Chapter 4, there is a clear relationship between Structured Meanings and Alternative Semantics (Rooth 1985, 1992), the approach to focus that we adopt in this book: both analyze a focused sentence as a pair of a question and an answer. However, the two approaches differ in that (i) they use differing models of questions, and (ii) Alternative Semantics uses a full answer, where Structured Meanings uses a short answer. In Chapter 4 we set out both approaches in more detail, and then consider some arguments that have been offered in the literature to suggest that Structured Meanings is to be preferred. For now, though, we restrict our attention to those aspects of Alternative Semantics that play a key role in our theory of focus sensitivity.

2.6   The Interpretation of Focus

Summary: *We provide an overview of Rooth's Alternative Semantics, the approach to the interpretation of focus that we adopt in this book. We discuss the similarities and differences between Alternative Semantics and Structured Meanings.*

The Alternative Semantics of Rooth (1985, 1992) is among the best known approaches to the interpretation of focus. Rooth takes focus to introduce sets of alternatives which are built up compositionally alongside the standard semantics. Rooth shows how this approach can be applied to model phenomena including question–answer congruence, reconstruction of elided VPs, focus on contrastive pairs, focus-triggered implicature, and the focus sensitivity of expressions like the exclusive *only*. In Chapter 4, we present a compositional grammar along the lines of Rooth's proposals. This serves as groundwork when, later in Chapter 4, we tackle some of the issues that have been claimed to make Alternative Semantics unworkable.[24]

In the previous section, we saw how the interpretation of the question in (2.37), *Who does Mary like?*, could be viewed as the set of propositions $\{likes(m, x) \mid person(x)\}$. This set of propositions corresponds to what Rooth terms the FOCUS SEMANTIC VALUE (henceforth, FOCAL MEANING) of (2.36), *Mary likes [Sandy]*$_F$.

We can use focal meanings to account for the focus sensitivity of expressions like *only*. Given both the focal meaning M and the regular meaning R of a sentence S to which *only* is attached, a meaning can be given for the corresponding sentence with an exclusive, e.g. (2.38), *Mary only likes [Sandy]*$_F$. Only (S) says that every true alternative to S is no stronger than S itself. In symbols we can render this as the formula in (2.39).

---

[24]   For another introduction to Alternative Semantics, see Kadmon (2001).

(2.39) $\forall p \in M, true(p) \rightarrow p = R.$

In the specific case of (2.38), *Mary only likes [Sandy]*$_F$, we derive a meaning which may be glossed as the claim that the set of true answers to the question *Who does Mary like?* contains no elements except *(Mary likes) Sandy*. A representation that does not refer directly to questions is given in (2.40a). Symbolically, this may be represented as in (2.40b).

(2.40) a.   *Every true proposition which says of someone that Mary likes them is the proposition that Mary likes Sandy.*

   b. $\forall p \in \{likes(m, x) \mid person(x)\}\, true(p) \rightarrow p = likes(m, s)$

The meanings in (2.40a) and (2.40b) involve quantification over propositions: logicians would describe this as HIGHER ORDER quantification. The semantics of Rooth (1992) is not given in terms of quantification over propositions, but over properties. Still, the intuitions driving the model are much the same as for the propositional case above, and quantification over properties is still higher order. Whether the Roothian model is described in terms of propositions or properties, it would be much easier to work with meanings that quantify over individuals, i.e. meanings that involve only FIRST ORDER quantification. Consequently, Rooth's Alternative Semantics for *only* would become much more attractive if we were able to reduce the higher order meaning in (2.40a) to the first-order meaning in (2.41a), corresponding to the formula in (2.41b).

(2.41) a.   *Everybody who Mary likes is identical to Sandy.*

   b. $\forall x\, (person(x) \wedge likes(m, x)) \rightarrow x = s$

In Chapter 4, we will turn to the question of what assumptions would have to be made so that this reduction is valid.

   So far in this section, we have treated the meanings of sentences with a focus sensitive expression as if they were determined entirely by lexical meaning, focus positioning, and syntax. However, the restricting effect that context has on the interpretation of focused sentences also needs to be built into Alternative Semantics. We have suggested that (2.38) gets the interpretation in (2.41), in which case it implies not only that Mary does not like Terry, but also that she does not like, e.g. Adam, Bertha and Casper. But now consider the dialogue in (2.42). When (2.38) is embedded in this dialogue, i.e. as (2.42B), it can be understood as saying nothing about Mary's preferences for people other than Sandy or Terry.

(2.42) A: Out of the people you introduced Mary to, does she like Sandy or does she like Terry?

   B: She only likes [Sandy]$_F$.

On this basis, Rooth (1992) proposes that focal meanings are used in combination with contextually available sets of alternatives. He takes the focal meaning

to be *presupposed*, although it is arguable that his use of this term is similar to
what others would term *given*: what is presupposed is that a set of alternatives
related to the focal meaning is salient in the context of utterance. Specifically,
he requires that the focal meaning is a subset of a set of salient alternatives. The
domain of quantification of *only* is not restricted by the focal meaning of the
sentence to which it is attached, but by the salient set of alternatives to which
the focal meaning is related. Thus, the meaning of *only* in terms of quantification
over propositions is captured by the definition in (2.43):

(2.43) $[\![only(S)]\!] = \forall p \in$ ALT $true(p) \rightarrow (p = S')$, where S' is the ordinary
           meaning of the sentence S, and ALT is a salient set of alternatives
           which is a subset of the focal meaning of S.

As regards (2.42), ALT could be the set containing two propositions, the
proposition that Mary likes Sandy and the proposition that she likes Terry.
Clearly, ALT is a subset of the focal alternative set, and we end up with an
appropriately restricted meaning for (2.42B).

What unites Structured Meanings, discussed in the previous section, and
Alternative Semantics is their use of semantic objects, focus-influenced semantic values, which can be manipulated by construction-specific rules. Take the
rules for *only* in (2.43) and (2.44) (from Rooth 1996a: 276). (2.44) is the semantic rule for *only* stated in terms of Structured Meanings. Both rules use focus-
influenced semantic values to account for the contribution of focus to the
meaning of *only*-constructions. For the Alternative Semantics rule in (2.43),
reference is made to ALT. For the Structured Meanings rule in (2.44), reference is
made to the focus-influenced structuring of the proposition denoted by the sentence: a pairing of a property (the background) and the meaning of the focused
phrase(s).[25]

(2.44)   *only* combining with the structured meaning $\langle R, \alpha_1 \dots , \alpha_k \rangle$ yields the
           assertion $\forall x_1 \dots \forall x_k [R(x_1 \dots x_k) \rightarrow \langle x_1 \dots , x_k \rangle = \langle \alpha_1 \dots , \alpha_k \rangle]$.

The rule in (2.44) says that the sentence *Mary only likes [Sandy]*$_F$ has the interpretation in (2.45b), where *only* combining with the structured meaning in (2.45a)
yields the assertion in (2.45b). The structured meaning in (2.45a) is a pair consisting of the property obtained by abstracting over the focused position *Sandy*
in *Mary only likes [Sandy]*$_F$ and the interpretation of *Sandy*.

(2.45) a. $\langle \lambda x.likes(m, x), s \rangle$

       b. $\forall x [likes(m, x) \rightarrow x = s]$

Given the types of rules in (2.43) and (2.44), it is the responsibility of
construction-specific rules to make use of focus-influenced semantic values.

---

[25] As noted in the previous section, we discuss Alternative Semantics and Structured Meanings in
much greater detail in Chapter 4.

Hence, neither Structured Meanings nor Alternative Semantics characterizes a notion of POSSIBLE FOCUS SENSITIVE CONSTRUCTION. An analysis which fails to address this issue says nothing about focus in general, while saying a lot about specific focus-sensitive constructions (Rooth 1996a: 278). By omission, a construction-specific account maintains that there is no uniform semantic or pragmatic phenomenon of focus.

This problem of restrictiveness is most severe for Structured Meanings (Rooth 1996a: 278). Structured Meanings, as characterized in Chapter 4, gives us access to all the information which could possibly be relevant to a focus sensitive construction including the semantics of the focused element and the semantics of the rest of the sentence. This lack of restrictiveness allows us to define quite implausible focus sensitive lexical items using Structured Meanings. For example, Rooth pointed out that one could define a focus-sensitive element like *tolfed* where *tolfed* ϕ amounts to 'told the focus (or foci) of ϕ that ϕ'. Rooth gives the paradigm in (2.46):

(2.46) a.   I tolfed [that [he]$_F$ resembles her] $\equiv$ I told him that he resembles her.

b.   I tolfed [that he resembles [her]$_F$] $\equiv$ I told her that he resembles her.

c.   I tolfed [that [he]$_F$ resembles [her]$_F$] $\equiv$ I told him and her that he resembles her.

While Alternative Semantics may not be subject to the same restrictiveness argument as Structured Meanings (Rooth 1996a: 278), if we maintain that grammars include construction-specific rules for focus sensitive constructions, as do both Alternative Semantics and Structured Meanings, we are still making a weak claim about focus sensitivity effects. Consequently, Rooth calls theories of this sort *weak theories of focus interpretation* (or, in our terms, semantic theories of focus sensitivity).

Rooth (1992) (see also Rooth 1996a) utilizes the restrictiveness argument just presented to argue for what he calls a *strong theory of focus interpretation* (or, in our terms, a pragmatic theory of focus sensitivity). In a strong theory there is no construction-specific reference to focus (Rooth 1992: 108). To this end, Rooth (1992) drastically reduces the repertoire of Alternative Semantics by having a single operator, the $\sim$ operator, handle the interface between focus sensitive constructions and F-marking. The definition of $\sim$ is given in (2.47).

(2.47)   Where ϕ is a syntactic phrase and C is a syntactically covert semantic variable, $\phi \sim C$ introduces the presupposition that C is a subset of $[\![\phi]\!]^f$ containing $[\![\phi]\!]^o$ and at least one another element.

(Rooth 1996a: (20))

Given that construction-specific rules are not available in the strong theory of focus interpretation, pragmatic factors alone link the interpretation of focus sensitive expressions to their focus associate. For example, in the strong account of von Fintel (1994: 49) the relationship between (the quantificational domain of) focus sensitive expressions and focus is mediated by the fact that both are anaphoric to the same discourse topic. As a consequence, association with focus effects are predicted to be optional in certain contexts. We present data that has been taken to support this prediction in Chapter 5.

Retaining the idea that *only* quantifies over properties, Rooth (1992: 89, 1996a: 277) argues that the domain of quantification of VP-*only* is a free variable *C* with the type of a set of properties the value of which is fixed pragmatically. (2.48) is the interpretation of VP-*only* given by Rooth (1992: 89). The key property of (2.48) is that focus may, but need not, be a source of information about the free variable *C*.

(2.48) $\lambda x[\forall P[P \in C \wedge {}^{\vee}P \rightarrow P = VP']]$

To illustrate, Rooth assumes the representation in (2.49) for a VP of the form *only introduced [Bill]*$_F$ *to Sue*. The variable *C* in the notation *only(C)* is an overt representation of the domain of quantification of *only* in (2.48). Focus interpretation on the argument of *only(C)* contributes a constraint on the value of the quantificational domain variable *C*. Crucially, however, focus need not be the only constraint on the value of *C*, since *C* in *only(C)* is just a free variable (Rooth 1992: 90).

(2.49)

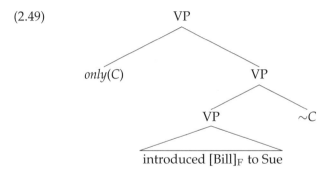

Rooth also considers the possibility of what he terms an *intermediate theory of focus interpretation*, which allows for lexical stipulation of focus sensitivity, but only of a very limited sort. For example, he suggests that the lexical entry for *only* might stipulate focus association, but does not suggest this for other focus sensitive expressions. The QFC theory of focus sensitivity that we present in §2.8 and discuss in detail in Chapter 3 is an intermediate theory in Rooth's sense, since focus can only affect meaning via a very specific channel: lexical stipulation of focus sensitivity is limited to dependency on what we will call the Current Question, and it is the choice of Current Question that constrains focus.

In sum, we have now made more precise what we meant when we utilized the notion of *evoking alternatives* in the definition of *activation* in §2.4, and in the coming chapters we will put even more meat on these bones. The idea that focus evokes a set of alternatives helps account for focus sensitivity. But compositionally derived alternatives are not the whole story. A crucial assumption of Rooth's account of focus sensitivity is that focus sensitive expressions such as *only* are anaphoric on a salient set of contextually available alternatives. Thus the context of utterance plays a central role in a comprehensive account of focus sensitivity. In Chapter 3, and more fully in Chapter 10, we lay out a uniform theory of exclusives that accounts for their meaning and focus sensitivity in terms of the function of exclusives in discourse, and uses both composition- ally derived alternative sets and context. In the next section, we present the question-based model of discourse structure (Roberts 1996, 2004) that forms the basis of that theory.

2.7   Structuring Discourse with Questions

Summary: *We present the question-based model of discourse structure that forms the basis of our theory of focus sensitive expressions.*

Hamblin (1971) was the first to offer a formal model of dialogue which focused on the dynamically evolving information states of interlocutors. He termed these information states *commitment slates*. The same decade gave us a plethora of further dynamic models of discourse, notably Stalnaker's (1972, 1974, 1978) model of assertion as update of the common ground, Karttunen's (1974) dynamic model of presupposition, and, at the end of the decade, the influ- ential work of Gazdar (1979) in linguistics, Lewis (1979) in philosophy, and Sidner (1979) in artificial intelligence. The flow of dynamic models of discourse became a flood in the 1980s and 1990s, with the current of work in so-called *dynamic semantics* beginning with Kamp (1981) and Heim (1982), and notably including Groenendijk and Stokhof (1991), being particularly vigorous. The direct antecedent of the model we develop in this book is found in the midst of this outpouring of work on dynamic approaches that has dominated the last few decades of formal and computational work on discourse and dialogue, the question-based model of discourse structure developed by Roberts (1996, 2004).

In Roberts' model, the ultimate goal of participants in a discourse is to answer the question *What is the way things are?*, or in more colloquial terms, *What's up?* She uses Stalnaker's notions of COMMON GROUND and CONTEXT SET. The common ground is the set of propositions taken for granted by the speaker and hearer(s) at a given point in a discourse.[26] The context set is the intersection of the set of propositions in the common ground, i.e. the set of pos- sible worlds compatible with what is taken for granted by the interlocuters.

Discourse involves the successive refinement of the context set. Refinement is updating the context set to incorporate the content of a new assertion by one of the discourse participants. In this model, each new assertion expresses

---

[26]   For a particularly clear discussion of how we should understand the notion of *common ground*, see Clark (1996: ch. 4).

a proposition, where a proposition is a set of worlds for which the proposition takes the value *true*. If a new assertion is accepted, the context set is updated by intersecting the current contents of the context set with the set expressed by the new assertion. The context set is updated until a single possible world is reached. That is, the question *What is the way things are?* has been answered.

Stalnaker's model is illustrated by the toy example in (2.50). Assuming that the set of possible worlds W is {w, w′, w″} (i.e. blissful ignorance: ☺)), at Stage (2.50:1) the common ground is empty and the context set is W. At Stage (2.50:2) interlocutor A asserts that Kim loves Sandy, which is true in w and w′. As a result, at Stage (2.50:3) the common ground contains the proposition KIM LOVES SANDY and the context set is {w, w′} (the intersection of W and {w, w′}). At Stage (2.50:4), speaker B asserts that Sandy hates Kim, which is true in w′ and w″. As a consequence, at Stage (2.50:5) the common ground contains both the proposition KIM LOVES SANDY and the proposition SANDY HATES KIM, and the context set is {w′} (the intersection of {w′, w″} and {w, w′}).

(2.50) 1.
$$\begin{bmatrix} \text{CG:} & \{\} \\ \text{CS:} & ☺ \end{bmatrix}$$

2. Speaker A: "Kim loves Sandy"
   (true in w and w′)

3.
$$\begin{bmatrix} \text{CG:} & \{\text{KIM LOVES SANDY}\} \\ \text{CS:} & \{w, w′\} \end{bmatrix}$$

4. Speaker B: "Sandy hates Kim"
   (true in w′ and w″)

5.
$$\begin{bmatrix} \text{CG:} & \{\text{KIM LOVES SANDY, SANDY HATES KIM}\} \\ \text{CS:} & \{w′\} \end{bmatrix}$$

One way to understand Stalnaker's model is in terms of a game (Stalnaker 1978: 88). The context set is the playing field. Different moves in the game (e.g. an assertion) are attempts to reduce the context set or rejections of moves made by others. All players have a common interest: reduce the size of the context set. Players diverge, however, on what strategies they use to reduce the context set.

Roberts (1996, 2004) elaborates on Stalnaker's view of discourse as a game. Roberts' model involves considering strategies for narrowing down the context set. However, rather than choosing arbitrary new sets of worlds to intersect with the context set, interlocutors set up strategies using sequences of questions. (2.51) illustrates the type of strategy Roberts has in mind. Every proposition that fully answers (2.51a), would also fully answer (2.51b). Likewise, every proposition that fully answers (2.51b) fully answers (2.51c).

(2.51) a. What is the way things are?

  b. Who does Sandy feed what?

  c. Who does Sandy feed Nutrapup?

There are two types of moves in Roberts' model, questions and answers to questions. The interpretation of any move involves two aspects: PRESUPPOSED CONTENT and PROFFERED CONTENT. Proffered content refers to what is asserted in an assertion and to the non-presupposed content of questions and commands.

Roberts draws upon Hamblin's (1973) theory of questions, whereby the question in (2.52a) introduces a set of possible answers corresponding to sentences of the form *Sandy feeds Nutrapup to X*. If only Fido, Clifford, and Rover are relevant, then (2.52a) has the question meaning in (2.52b). Note, though, that in our slight variant of Roberts' model, we use Rooth–Hamblin question semantics, so that the meaning of the question is that in (2.52c).

(2.52) a. Who does Sandy feed Nutrapup?

   b. {[Sandy feeds Nutrapup to Fido], [Sandy feeds Nutrapup to Clifford], [Sandy feeds Nutrapup to Rover]}

   c. {[Sandy feeds Nutrapup to Fido], [Sandy feeds Nutrapup to Clifford], [Sandy feeds Nutrapup to Rover], [Sandy feeds Nutrapup to Fido and Clifford], [Sandy feeds Nutrapup to Fido and Rover], [Sandy feeds Nutrapup to Clifford and Rover], [Sandy feeds Nutrapup to Fido, Clifford and Rover]}

The possible answers to a question are the proffered alternatives. A question that is proffered and mutually accepted by the interlocutors as the most immediate goal of the discourse becomes the Current Question (henceforth the CQ). We will call the sequence of unresolved questions in a discourse the *Open Questions* (henceforth, the OQ). As we will see in the next section, Roberts' notion of the CQ will play a key role in our theory of focus sensitivity.

In Roberts' model, discourse progresses by interlocutors continually raising and answering questions. Interlocutors choose strategies – sequences of questions – for narrowing down the set of possible worlds. Recall that the main goal of discourse is to answer the question *What is the way things are?*, as in (2.51a). The strategy that interlocutors use to address this goal is to develop subgoals. Thus, we can understand all three utterances in (2.51) as a sequence of successively more specific questions asked (at least implicitly) by the same speaker, with the questions related to each other in such a way as to enable the interlocutors to jointly reach their main goal.

The crucial relationship in sequences of questions that make up a strategy is one of ENTAILMENT (Groenendijk and Stokhof 1984: 16): a question Q_1 entails another Q_2 iff every proposition that gives a complete answer to Q_1 also gives a complete answer to Q_2. In terms of the Rooth–Hamblin alternative semantics for questions (and this applies equally to Hamblin's original semantics or to Groenendijk and Stokhof's semantics), a *complete*, or *total*, *answer* to a question is an utterance expressing a proposition which determines the truth value of every proposition in the alternative set. In (2.51), *Who does Sandy feed what?* entails *Who does Sandy feed Nutrapup*, i.e. a complete answer to *Who does Sandy feed what?* gives a complete answer to any other question of the form *Who does*

Sandy feed X? In contrast, *Who does Sandy feed Nutrapup?* does not entail *Who does Sandy feed what?*

Roberts relabels the notion of question entailment using the terms SUB-QUESTION and its inverse SUPER-QUESTION: Q_1 is a SUB-QUESTION of Q_2 just in case Q_2 entails Q_1. We can now say that *What is the way things are?* is a super-question of *Who does Sandy feed what?* which is a super-question of *Who does Sandy feed Nutrapup?* etc. A point in a discourse may be characterized in terms of a sequence of such Open Questions, of which the most recent is the Current Question. When the CQ is answered, it gets removed from the sequence, potentially to be replaced by a new sub-question.

Before going on, we must make explicit the principle that determines whether the CQ remains open, the CURRENT QUESTION RULE in (2.53), which we use in Chapters 3 and 10.[27]

(2.53)   **Current Question Rule:** The Current Question must contain at least one true alternative, and contain multiple alternatives which are not resolved as true or false in the common ground.

We now define a notion of RELEVANCE for questions and answers. For a move to be relevant it must address the CQ, which Roberts takes to mean either that the move introduces a partial or total answer to the CQ, or that it is part of a strategy to answer the CQ. We define a *partial answer* to be an utterance which is incompatible with one or more alternatives in the CQ, but which is compatible with more than one logically independent alternative. The idea here is that *Sandy fed Fido and Clifford Nutrapup* entails e.g. *Sandy fed Fido Nutrapup*, so the latter is not logically independent of the former. But consider the answer *Not Butch!* to the question *Who does Sandy feed Nutrapup?* While eliminating all alternatives in which Butch is fed Nutrapup, this answer is compatible with both the proposition that *Sandy feeds Fido Nutrapup*, and the proposition that *Sandy feeds Clifford Nutrapup*. Since neither of these two entails the other, more than one logically independent alternative remains. So the CQ is only *partially answered*, and remains *open*.[28]

---

[27] The Current Question Rule, in combination with the Focus Principle, establishes that at least one focal alternative is true, and thus covers the effects of the Background Presupposition Rule of Geurts and van der Sandt (2004), discussed in §5.2. We depend for this effect on the assumption that the empty set is not in the extension of any predicate, so that e.g. *Who laughed?* does not introduce as one of its alternatives the proposition that the empty group of people is in the extension of *laughed*. In order to cover answers like *Nobody laughed*, we would need a set of alternatives of the form Q(*laughed*) to be available. We assume that such alternatives are not part of the basic meaning of the question *Who laughed?*, but rather would have to be accommodated in a process involving revision of the assumed common ground, but we do not investigate the issue further here.

[28] We could also define what it means for one move to be *more* relevant than another: it must eliminate strictly more alternatives from the CQ, or suggest a more immediate strategy for answering the CQ. We will not pursue this notion of relative relevance here, though it is implicitly needed in our statement of the Discourse Principle. For a detailed exposition of what makes one answer more relevant than another, see van Rooij's (2003) development of the account of informativity developed by Groenendijk and Stokhof (1984).

We base our adaption of Roberts' model on two core principles, given in (2.54), the first of which refers to the above discussion of relevance, and the second of which links the discourse model, via Rooth's notion of focus alternatives, to our earlier discussion of focus projection:

(2.54)   **Discourse Principle:** Utterances should be maximally relevant to the CQ.

    Focus Principle: Some part of a declarative utterance should evoke a set of alternatives containing all the Rooth–Hamblin alternatives of the CQ.

Our Focus Principle is an adaption of principles Roberts uses, centering around what she terms *congruence*. Under her definition, a declarative statement is *congruent* to a question if its focal alternatives are identical to those in the question, and congruence is considered to be a presupposition induced by focus in the assertion of the declarative. The Focus Principle establishes the last link in the chain between what is accented in a declarative sentence, and what question the sentence can be used to answer. Specifically, what is accented is related to what is F-marked by our version of Schwarzschild's account of focus projection, an account which itself uses a separate abstract of f-marking, a feature indicating insufficiency of activation. We stated constraints, (2.33) and (2.34), implying that this condition will be satisfied (thus requiring F-marking) if the speaker intends to evoke alternatives to the F-marked expression. Rooth's model of focus then tells us how the alternatives thus induced enter into the compositional calculation of the alternative set for the sentence. The Focus Principle, in turn, relates these alternatives to the current question.

Following Rooth, we demand not equality between the alternative set and the CQ denotation, as is demanded by *congruence*, but a subset relation. This is essential to developing the right anaphoric relationship between answers and questions. For example, the question *Which of her three dogs did Sandy feed?* can be answered by *She fed [Fido]*$_\mathrm{F}$, but the alternative set of the latter contains extra alternatives which are not in the denotation of the question, for example, the proposition that Sandy fed Brady.

There is another respect in which the Focus Principle is weaker than the corresponding principles in Roberts' account. She requires that when a declarative sentence is asserted, the complete sentence is *congruent* to the CQ, whereas we require only that a part of it is congruent. This relaxation simplifies the analyses of sentences in which a sentential clause is embedded under a propositional operator. For example, in our model the sentence *I think [Mary]*$_\mathrm{F}$ *laughed* can answer the CQ *Who laughed?*, whereas for Roberts this sentence would be congruent to the CQ *Who do you think laughed?*, so that extra accommodation would be required when only the first question was salient in prior discourse. More discussion of this point follows in Chapters 3 and 5.

The diagram in (2.55) illustrates how these principles fit into the model of discourse. At Stage (2.55:1), the common ground is empty and the context set contains every possible world, i.e. the interlocutors are in a state of blissful ignorance. Since no questions have been proffered, the list of open questions OQ is empty as well. At Stage (2.55:2), speaker A proffers the question *Who does Sandy feed what?* As a consequence, the OQ list at Stage (2.55:3) contains the (content of) the question *Who does Sandy feed what?* and that question becomes the current open question CQ. At Stage (2.55:4), speaker A proffers another question, *Who does Sandy feed Nutrapup?*, that is a sub-question of the previous question, satisfying Roberts' Discourse Principle. Thus at Stage (2.55:5), *Who does Sandy feed Nutrapup?* is the new CQ. At Stage (2.55:6) speaker B answers the CQ with the assertion *Sandy feeds [Fido]$_F$ Nutrapup*. Importantly, B's assertion satisfies Roberts' Focus Principle: the set of focal alternatives to *Sandy feeds [Fido]$_F$ Nutrapup* is identical to the Hamblin semantics of the question *Who does Sandy feed Nutrapup* {SANDY FEEDS CLIFFORD NUTRAPUP, SANDY FEEDS FIDO NUTRAPUP, SANDY FEEDS ROVER NUTRAPUP}. The proposition denoted by speaker B's answer is true in worlds w and w′. Hence at Stage (2.55:7), the *Who does Sandy feed Nutrapup* has been popped off the OQ list and the context set has now been reduced to {w, w′}.

(2.55) 1.
$$\begin{bmatrix} \text{CG:} & \{\} \\ \text{OQ:} & <> \\ \text{CQ:} & \\ \text{CS:} & ☺ \end{bmatrix}$$

2. Speaker A: "Who does Sandy feed what?"

3.
$$\begin{bmatrix} \text{CG:} & \{\} \\ \text{OQ:} & <\text{WHO DOES SANDY FEED WHAT?}> \\ \text{CQ:} & \text{WHO DOES SANDY FEED WHAT?} \\ \text{CS:} & ☺ \end{bmatrix}$$

4. Speaker A: "Who does Sandy feed Nutrapup?"

5.
$$\begin{bmatrix} \text{CG:} & \{\} \\ \text{OQ:} & <\text{WHO DOES SANDY FEED WHAT?,} \\ & \text{WHO DOES SANDY FEED NUTRAPUP?}> \\ \text{CQ:} & \text{WHO DOES SANDY FEED NUTRAPUP?} \\ \text{CS:} & ☺ \end{bmatrix}$$

6. Speaker B: "Sandy feeds [Fido]$_F$ Nutrapup."
    (true in w and w′)

7.
$$\begin{bmatrix} \text{CG:} & \{\text{SANDY FEEDS FIDO NUTRAPUP}\} \\ \text{OQ:} & <\text{WHO DOES SANDY FEED WHAT?}> \\ \text{CQ:} & \text{WHO DOES SANDY FEED WHAT?} \\ \text{CS:} & \{\text{w, w}'\} \end{bmatrix}$$

The model of discourse we use in this book, grafted from Roberts' work, provides the structure we need to talk about how focus sensitivity operates in at least certain types of discourse. But it is limited. First, it deals only with discourses where the primary goal is to exchange information about the world, and deals only with aspects of the discourse that are geared to that end. Thus there is no mention of speech acts other than requesting information and making assertions. Even within the bounds of such informational discourse, the model does not explicitly cover a very wide range of discourse moves. In this regard, Roberts' model, and our variant of it, share some of their shortcomings with a closely related question-based model, that of Büring (2003), who deals with many of the same phenomena as Roberts' model.

Though clearly much work remains to be done, we take it that the limitations we have mentioned are not insuperable, for there is a rich literature on how discourse and dialogue may be structured, much of it originating at the same well-spring (Hamblin, Stalnaker, and so on) as Roberts' (and Büring's) model. Of particular note is the work of Carlson (1985) and van Kuppevelt (1994, 1995, 1996), which, while taking (possibly implicit) questions and answers to structure discourse, attends to a wide range of features of dialogue and discourse that have not entered the current discussion. Van Kuppevelt, for example, allows for a more sophisticated organization of text than we have discussed, whereby declarative statements that do not directly answer existing OQs can function as *feeders*, suggesting future lines of questioning. But it should be noted that much of the literature on text organization allows for a far richer panoply of discourse relations than is found in any of the question–answer based literature: see e.g. the recent work on discourse structure of Asher and Lascarides (2003), or, for the most profligate array of discourse relations, the literature on Rhetorical Structure Theory starting with Mann and A. Thompson (1987).

One critical issue for all of the question-based accounts we have mentioned is that in real discourse, only a small minority of declarative sentences directly follow utterances of appropriate questions. So if these accounts are to be seen as modeling real discourse, they must allow for the possibility of implicit questions. In some cases, we can say that though the question is not explicitly uttered in prior discourse, it is made salient by that prior discourse: extending Grice's terminology we can say that the question is *conversationally implicated* by the prior text. But in other cases, the fact that a speaker thinks that a certain question is of interest becomes evident only when the answer is given. In these cases, we cannot say that the prior text implicates the question. Instead, we must say that interlocutors *accommodate* the question when they hear the answer, and that it is only after such accommodation that the Discourse Principle and Focus Principle are satisfied.   *Prima facie*, the possibility of such accommodation raises problems: how can a question based model be predictive if we allow that whenever a sentence does not fit into a discourse, hearers may simply accommodate? The answer is that the model only becomes predictive once the possibilities for accommodation are constrained. Here are two such constraints, the first based on Roberts' own proposals, and the second by analogy with a constraint that Grice (1975: 31) imposed on implicatures, namely that they should be *calculable* by hearers:

(2.56)   Q-accommodation 1. A question may be accommodated (i.e. added to the list of OQs) if the resulting structure involves only moves satisfying the Discourse Principle.

           Q-accommodation 2. A question may be accommodated only if it is part of a strategy that is jointly identifiable by speaker and hearer as a means to common discourse goals.

We make no attempt here to develop a full model of the constraints on question accommodation: it is undeniably a huge project. However, a good start has been made in a study of accommodation of questions in naturally occurring texts by Cooper et al. (2000). We can also refer the reader to the excellent review both of the use of implicit dialogue moves, and of the literature on dialogue structure more generally, provided by Zaenen et al. (2001).

2.8 The Quasi/Free/Conventional (QFC) Model

Summary: *We outline our theory of focus sensitivity, the QFC theory, which involves a three-way distinction between different effects of focus: Quasi association, a special type of pragmatic inference; Free association, the resolution of a free variable; and Conventional association, a grammatical dependency on the current question under discussion.*

Now that we have introduced our semantic and pragmatic framework for focus interpretation, we can outline our theory of focus sensitivity. Recall the examples in (1.1), repeated below in (2.57). Examples (2.57a) and (2.57b) have different interpretations. The source of the difference between (2.57a) and (2.57b) is the scalar additive *even*.

(2.57) a.   This book is even sold at [Wal-Mart]$_F$.

       b.   This book is even [sold]$_F$ at Wal-Mart.

We would like to explain the correlation between the differing placement of focus in (2.57) and the differing interpretations. But we would also like to explain similar effects for all the other types of focus sensitive expressions listed in Chapter 1 and discussed in detail in Chapter 3. It is by no means clear that there is a unitary explanation. We will suggest not.

We alluded in Chapter 1 to a debate that has been central to the literature on the focus interpretation for the last 30 years, a debate we would summarize as follows:

(2.58) Is focus sensitivity

     a.   lexically encoded as part of the meaning of expressions which have been identified as focus sensitive, *or*

     b.   an epiphenomenon resulting from independent pragmatic forces which make sure presuppositions are satisfied and texts are coherent?

Our answer to this question is: yes. Focus sensitivity is either lexically encoded or a non-conventionalized epiphenomenon, depending on which focus sensitive expression you consider. Note that in clarifying our glib "yes", we shifted wording slightly: we do not contrast *semantic* with *pragmatic*, though the dichotomy is so ingrained in the minds of linguists and philosophers of language that it is hard to resist. Rather, we oppose *lexically encoded* with *non-conventionalized epiphenomenon*.

Can we now flesh out the notion of a NON-CONVENTIONAL EPIPHENOM-ENON? Non-conventional association with focus results because the focal structure of a clause containing a focus sensitive expression is tied to the context of utterance in the sense described in the previous section. There are, we suggest, two different phenomena involved: *quasi* association with focus and *free* association with focus.

The first, *quasi* association, covers a broad swathe of expressions, e.g. just about any propositional operator such as negation and *either . . . or*. But the effect is correspondingly weak: the interaction between focus and the operator produces cancelable implicatures rather than indefeasible truth conditional effects. A classic case, discussed by Jackendoff (1972: 254), is negation.

The second type of non-conventional focus sensitivity, *free* association, affects a narrower, though still quite broad class of operators, namely all those that perform quantification over, or comparison within, an implicit domain. This class includes, for example, quantificational adverbs, many modal operators, and also superlatives. To illustrate, the examples in (1.4), repeated below in (2.59), illustrate the interaction of the quantificational adverb *always* and focus marking.

(2.59) a.   Kim always serves Sandy COURVOISIER.
         'Whenever Kim serves Sandy something it's Courvoisier.'

     b.   Kim always serves SANDY Courvoisier.
         'Whenever Kim serves Courvoisier to someone, it's Sandy.'

Focus marking relates both to what is said and to what is being presupposed. In a well-regulated conversation involving an utterance of an operator like *always* with an implicit domain, the domain of the operator should be such that the meaning expressed is both relevant to the issues under discussion, and compatible with whatever is presupposed. As a result, the choice of domain is tightly correlated with what is focus marked.

Furthermore, since the truth conditions of operators in this class are affected by their domain of quantification or comparison, the placement of focus often correlates with relatively robust truth conditional differences. It is precisely because of the relative robustness of these effects that free association with focus is easily confused with lexical association with focus. Chapters 6–8 of this book are taken up with establishing ways to draw a line between the two phenomena empirically. But we have some work to do before we even attempt to draw that line.

It is essential to our proposal that when association with focus is conventional, that does not make the phenomenon non-pragmatic. On our view, CONVENTIONAL ASSOCIATION WITH FOCUS is found in expressions such as exclusives (e.g. *only*) whose meaning and function is primarily pragmatic. The function of these expressions is not to describe what is the case in the external world, but to modulate the flow of information in the discourse in which they appear. We claim that the primary function of any lexically focus sensitive expression is information structural, by which we mean that the expression is used to comment on the CQ, or on how a proffered answer relates to an expected answer.

There are many ways in which this idea could be worked out. One possibility would be that lexically focus sensitive expressions in a language like English (in which information structure is marked through intonation) encode a grammatical dependence on intonation. Another would be that they encode a dependence on some abstract level of focus marking. Yet another would be that they encode a dependence on a special compositionally derived component of meaning that itself reflects what is focused. We will adopt none of these. Rather, we will analyze conventionally focus sensitive expressions as encoding a dependence on the CQ, the (possibly implicit) question answered by the clause in which the expression is situated.

Note that Roberts (1996) claims that a focus sensitive expression *may* be anaphoric on the CQ. Von Fintel (1994) similarly claims that a focus sensitive expressions *may* be anaphoric on the discourse topic. We differ in saying that it is part of the lexical meaning of some expressions such as *only* that they *must* comment on the CQ. That is: all focus sensitivity has to do with pragmatics, but lexically focus sensitive expressions have an intrinsically pragmatic function. Thus, to take the class of expressions we will study in most detail, we claim that the function of exclusives like *only* is to say that the strongest true answer to the CQ is weaker than some expected answer. Contrarily, the function of the scalar additive *even* is to say that the strongest true answer is stronger than expected. An additive, like *too*, says that its argument parallels a previous answer to the CQ. In the next chapter, we will consider these examples in more detail, as well as some other cases where it seems appropriate to say that focus sensitivity of an expression is intrinsic to the pragmatic function of that expression.

2.9 Summary

Let's take stock. We defined focus as an information structural property that an expression may have which affects truth-conditional and non-truth-conditional meaning. This property is typically marked in English by prosodic prominence. In other languages morphology and word order can play the same functional role as prosodic prominences in English. Then we gave a brief introduction to the phonology of focus in English and the principles that govern the relationship between pitch accent and focus. With that background, we then turned to the framework for focus interpretation that we adopt in this book. This framework involves two central ideas. First, focus introduces a set of alternatives. Second, the focal structure of a clause is tied to the context of utterance. Lastly, we introduced our account of focus sensitive expressions. Expressions that manifest sensitivity to focus are divided into three classes: quasi-association with focus, free association with focus, and conventional association with focus. In the next chapter, we describe each of these classes in detail.

Chapter 3

Three Degrees of Association: Quasi, Free, and Conventional

Focus particles like only, also, too, even, *and* just *and their equivalents in other languages have long been considered a real challenge for linguistic description and theory.*

Krifka (1993b)

3.1 Introduction

Our task now is to describe in more detail the range of expressions that manifest focus sensitivity, and to relate them to the three way classification of focus sensitivity – quasi, free, and conventional (QFC) – that we described at the end of the previous chapter.

§3.2 of this chapter discusses quasi-focus sensitive expressions like negation. §3.3 discusses expressions, such as quantificational adverbs, which, while they have no conventionalized dependency on focus, interact by free association with focus so as to produce robust truth-conditional effects. §3.4 discusses conventionalized dependency on focus, and we wrap-up in §3.5 with a short discussion clarifying which of the many questions that the current chapter raises we intend to answer in the remainder of the book.

3.2 The First Degree: Quasi-Association

Summary: *We discuss* quasi-association with focus, *a special type of pragmatic inference. Quasi-associating expressions are non-veridical, propositional operators such that the alternatives evoked within their syntactic scope form a set of propositions that can be congruent to the Current Question. We examine expressions of this type, including negation, sentential connectives such as* either, *possibility modals, verbs of appearance, and belief operators.*

Negation

We begin this section with an extended study of negation, and then move to show how our treatment of negation applies to other cases.

Jackendoff (1972: 254)[1] observes that there is a relationship between focus and the interpretation of negation. For example, in (3.1a), with focus on *linguistics*, the speaker denies that Kim studies linguistics. In (3.1b), with focus on *Northwestern*, the speaker denies that the place where Kim studies is Northwestern.

(3.1)   a.   Kim doesn't study [linguistics]$_F$ at Northwestern.

      b.   Kim doesn't study linguistics at [Northwestern]$_F$.

In both (3.1a) and (3.1b), the negation applies to only the focused part of the entire sentence. In an intuitive sense, the remainder is not negated. For (3.1a) the speaker does not deny that Kim studies at Northwestern, and for (3.1b) the speaker does not deny that Kim studies linguistics.

It is clear that (3.1a, b) have different functions, in that they would serve their purpose in different contexts. But the fact that sentences differing in focus marking can appear in different contexts already follows from the Focus Principle in (2.54), repeated below in (3.2).

(3.2)   **Focus Principle:**
             Some part of a declarative utterance should evoke a set of alternatives containing all the Rooth–Hamblin alternatives of the Current Question.

Focus determines information structure, which for us means that focus determines the Current Question. But to claim that some expression is focus sensitive would require that focus has an effect on the interpretation of an expression that goes beyond information structure. In the case of negation, there are indeed such effects: variation in focus placement in negated sentences produces different inferences. For example, (3.1a) suggests that Kim does study something other than linguistics, which could not be inferred from (3.1b). In contrast, (3.1b) suggests that Kim studies linguistics somewhere other than Northwestern, which could not be inferred from (3.1a).

To explain these inferences, we must start by considering what question or claim an utterance of (3.1a), for example, might help answer:[2]

---

[1] On the interaction of negation and focus, see also Fischer (1968), Karttunen and Peters (1979: 46–8), Jacobs (1991b), McCawley (1998: 612–22), Herburger (2000: 28ff.), and Wagner (2007).

[2] Note that in some accounts of the semantics of questions, notably that of Groenendijk and Stokhof (1984), the semantics of (3.3) and (3.4) would be identical. In the Groenendijk and Stokhof (1984) model, this is because any complete answer to one of the two questions is also a complete answer to the other, and the sense of a question in their framework is just the set of all (propositions

(3.3)   What doesn't Kim study at Northwestern?

(3.4)   What does Kim study at Northwestern?

(3.5)   Kim studies [linguistics]$_F$ at Northwestern.

Let us assume that at the level of representation at which alternatives are calculated, negation is a propositional operator taking wide scope over the subject, at least in cases where the subject is not itself a quantificational phrase that is raised to an even higher level. Then, the argument of the negation operator in (3.1a) would be the clause *Kim does study [linguistics]$_F$ at Northwestern.*

By the principles of Alternative Semantics we laid out in §2.6, sets of alternatives will be evoked at various levels in the compositional build-up of the sentence meaning. There will be a set of alternatives at the level immediately under the negation consisting of propositions corresponding to sentences of the form *Kim does study X at Northwestern.* And there will be another set of alternatives at the level of the full sentence consisting of propositions corresponding to sentences of the form *Kim does not study X at Northwestern.*

Now consider how the Focus Principle applies. It requires that *some* part of the sentence matches the Current Question. Since alternatives matching both questions (3.3) and (3.4) are evoked, the Focus Principle allows (3.1a) to answer either. Furthermore, (3.1a) could provide a partial answer to either question, since whichever of the two questions has been asked, (3.1a) would eliminate at least some alternatives. So, therefore, the Discourse Principle from §2.7, which requires that a declarative statement partially answers the Current Question, allows that either of the two questions could be under discussion.

Nonetheless, there are certainly some further intonational factors which constrain when (3.1a) is appropriately taken to answer the questions in (3.3) and (3.4), and thus when the inferences occur. The type of focus sensitivity we see in cases like (3.1) involves not only the issue of which expression is focused, but the details of how that focus is marked. We now briefly consider the issue

---

corresponding to) complete answers. The inability of Groenendijk and Stokhof's system to distinguish between positive and negative questions might be seen as an advantage as regards the current application, for it implies, correctly we believe, that negative statements can be congruent to positive questions (as well as negative ones). However, it is not clear how the same property would help analyze some of the cases considered later in this section, involving, e.g., modal operators rather than negation.

The inability of Groenendijk and Stokhof's system to distinguish positive and negative questions has often been considered a drawback, but to the extent that it is a problem at all, it is not insurmountable. In a development of their work, van Rooij (2003) allows that alternatives in a question partition are associated with a probability distribution. On this view, (3.3) and (3.4) may differ in that they are associated with different expectations (the first presumably suggesting that she studies more subjects than the second).

In our account, the use of Rooth–Hamblin semantics means that positive and negative questions have completely different denotations. Specifically, (3.4) picks out a set of alternatives of the form *Kim studies X at Northwestern*, and (3.3) picks out alternatives of the form *Kim does not study X at Northwestern.*

of how focus can be marked in negative sentences, before returning to the inferences.

In (3.6), three possible intonational contours for (3.1a) are given:[3]

(3.6)   Kim   doesn't study [linguistics]$_F$ at Northwestern

a)			H*	L-L%
b)			L+H*	L-H%
c)		L*	L*	L-H%

The H* L-L% countour in (3.6a) is what is sometimes called a *neutral declarative intonation*, perhaps the most obvious intonational contour for a sentence with a single focus used to make an assertion. However, it is not the first intonational contour that comes to mind for a sentence with a negation like (3.6a). Answers to questions given with this intonation (in particular, the low L-L% boundary contour) suggest neither uncertainty nor a need for further clarification, and so are naturally taken to provide complete answers.

The type of intonational contour in (3.6b), a 'wiggly' rise-fall-rise, can suggest contrast, uncertainty, incompleteness, or even incredulity (Pierrehumbert and Steele 1987). The complex L+H* pitch accent is not always clearly distinguishable from an H* accent, but it may be heard as having a more acute initial pitch rise. The final rise associated with the L-H%, a low phrase accent between the focused word and the end of the sentence, and a final rise at the end, is more readily identifiable. Sentence finally, it is often taken to imply a lack of commitment by the speaker, or to signal that further information ought to follow. As an answer to a question, this boundary combination would plausibly signal that the answer was at best partial.

Finally, production (3.6c), is intended to correspond to what Liberman and Sag (1974) termed a *contradiction contour*: a low trough occupies the central portion of the utterance. The focus on *linguistics* is not necessarily distinguished with a markedly lower f0 value than the rest of this trough, but should still be acoustically prominent, e.g. through increased intensity and duration. As the term *contradiction contour* indicates, this intonation would most naturally be taken to indicate that the speaker was involved in a speech act of denial. Note that the pitch accented negation would also be considered a FOC, in the sense of §2.4, since, in the terminology of that section, it is f-marked and not dominated by an f-marked node. But we are now using the F subscript to indicate elements that we take to evoke alternatives, rather than those made prominent to indicate lack of givenness.[4]

---

[3] In thinking about intonation in negative sentences and other denials, we found the discussions of Swerts and Krahmer (2007) and Hedberg and Sosa (2003) useful, and both are very well grounded empirically. Our discussion of the significance of the various pitch accents and boundary tones in these impressionistic transcriptions also leans on the interpretations given by Pierrehumbert and Hirschberg (1990).

[4] It is relevant here that *linguistics* is the final pitch accented expression in the sentence, and thus would typically be perceived as the most prominent. Though we stop short of a full theory

With this background on the pragmatics associated with the three contours in (3.6), which question could an utterance of (3.1a), *Kim doesn't study
[linguistics]*F *at Northwestern*, with each of the three contours answer? Given
that the transcription in (3.6a) is appropriate for a complete answer, it would
be singularly inappropriate as a response to the positive question in (3.4), *What
does Kim study at Northwestern?* The negative statement in (3.1a) only hints at a
partial answer to that question, and does not determine which, if any, alternatives in the question denotation might be true.

However, (3.1a) does determine that at least one alternative in the denotation of the negative question (3.3), *What doesn't Kim study at Northwestern?*, is
true. This does not in itself make (3.1a) a complete answer to that question,
but it does allow the speaker to implicate a complete answer via the inference
known in the literature as *exhaustification*. We can think of exhaustification as a
special case of a *scalar implicature*.[5] For example, the answer *Mary laughed* to the
question *Who laughed?* would be drawn from alternatives of the form *X laughed*,
where *X* is an individual or a conjunction of individuals. Of these answers, any
of them for which *X* is a conjunction containing Mary and at least one other
individual would be logically stronger than the answer *Mary laughed*. So, if
we assume that the speaker actually knows the answer to the question, then
by Grice's Maxim of Quantity the speaker would have produced one of these
stronger answers if it were true. Since the speaker did not do so, we reason that
the speaker was not in a position to do so, and thus to the implicature that all
stronger answers than *Mary laughed* are false. Thus, we derive the implicature
that the answer *Mary laughed* exhausts what can be said in answer to the question, and derive, pragmatically, a complete answer, even though semantically
the given answer is only partial.

Exhaustification allows (3.1a) to be understood as a complete answer to
the negative question (3.3), though not to the positive question (3.4). Since
the tune in (3.6a) suggests completeness of the answer, this tune should only
be appropriate when (3.1a) is taken to answer (3.3). Since this is a somewhat
odd question in the first place (because it suggests that there are relatively few
subjects which Kim does not study), this also gives an explanation why the tune
in (3.6a) is not the first that comes to mind for (3.1a).

The tune in (3.6b) is naturally taken to be associated with a partial answer.[6]
But since (3.1a) could be a partial answer to either (3.3) or (3.4), the intonation

---

of how alternative evoking expressions differ acoustically from merely non-given expressions, we
would suggest that, other things being equal, alternative evoking expressions are typically more
prominent.

[5] For discussion of exhaustification, and critical discussion of whether this really is best thought
of as a scalar implicature, see Groenendijk and Stokhof (1984), Zeevat (1994), van Rooij and Schulz
(2003), and Spector (2007).

[6] There is extensive literature on the interpretation of intonation like that in (3.6b), e.g. Ward and
Hirschberg (1985, 1988), Hendriks (2002), and Büring (1997, 1999, 2003).

allows, in principle, for both possibilities. Since the positive question (3.4) is inherently more natural, this is perhaps more likely to be the question which we take (3.1a) to answer with this intonation.

Finally, use of the contradiction contour in (3.6c) would normally be taken to imply that the speaker was denying some positive statement, presumably the one in (3.5). Since this is an answer to the positive question (3.4), it follows that (3.4) will be taken to be the Current Question for which (3.1a) provides an answer with the melody in (3.6c).

To summarize: of the three ways of producing (3.1a) that we have considered, one, (3.6a), would be appropriate for an answer to the negative question (3.3). The other two, (3.6b) and (3.6c), are most naturally taken to relate to the positive question (3.4). We now suggest that it is only when (3.1a) is taken to answer the positive question (3.4), and this only for the intonation contours in (3.6b) and (3.6c), that the inference arises that Kim studies something other than linguistics. It is now straightforward to explain this inference.

(3.4) is the Current Question, so the *Current Question Rule* of (2.53) implies that there is some subject which Kim studies at Northwestern. Given what is directly entailed by (3.1a), it follows that Kim studies something other than linguistics at Northwestern. Similar reasoning would apply *mutatis mutandi*, to (3.1b) to produce the inference that Kim studies linguistics somewhere other than Northwestern. In either case, we can derive the inference without positing that negation has any conventionalized sensitivity to focus. The most that needs to be said is that negation acts as a propositional operator such that the alternatives evoked within its syntactic scope form a set of propositions that can be congruent to the Current Question. This congruence between the set of propositional alternatives and the Current Question gives rise to quasi-association with focus.

Let us note in passing that the inferences considered in the above discussion have the character of implicatures rather than entailments. Thus (3.1a) can coherently be followed by the claim *In fact, she doesn't study anything at Northwestern!* The cancelability of the existential inference might be understood in several ways. First, as we have shown, (3.1a) is not necessarily congruent to (3.4), so that in contexts where the rather marked question (3.3) is present or can be accommodated, the only existential presupposition is the proposition that Kim does not study something at Northwestern, which is anyway entailed by (3.3). A second way to account for the defeasibility of the inference to the proposition that Kim studies something at Northwestern would be to say that the *Current Question Rule* is only a preference, e.g. arising as a consequence of general maxims of conversation, and expected to hold unless it is explicitly denied. In that case the defeasibility of the inference that Kim studies something other than Linguistics would be predicted, although the inference would remain whenever there was no explicit denial of the existential assumption.

Other quasi-associating operators

Just as negation quasi-associates with focus, so does any other lexicalized propositional operator, such as, for example, sentential connectives like *either*. To illustrate, someone who uttered example (3.7a) would seem to take it for granted that Kim studied something at Texas, and to be questioning whether it was linguistics or something else she studied there. As a result, an implicature arises that among all the things you can study at Texas, only studying linguistics leads to black belt-like prowess at lambda calculus. On the other hand, (3.7b) generates the implicature that among different schools where you can study linguistics, only Texas yields the relevant abilities.

(3.7) a. Either Kim studies [linguistics]$_F$ at Texas, or else she just happens to be a lambda calculus black belt.

  b. Either Kim studies linguistics at [Texas]$_F$, or else she just happens to be a lambda calculus black belt.

Similar examples are easily constructed with various intensional propositional operators, such as possibility modals like *perhaps* (3.8), verbs of appearance like *seem* (3.9), and belief operators like *think* (3.10). We infer from (3.8a), (3.9a) and (3.10a) that Mary fed some dog Nutrapup, but not from (3.8b), (3.9b) and (3.10b), although in the last case the inference does go through if we take the speaker to trust Jane's opinion.

(3.8) a. Perhaps Mary fed [Fido]$_F$ Nutrapup.

  b. Perhaps Mary fed Fido [Nutrapup]$_F$.

(3.9) a. Mary seems to have fed [Fido]$_F$ Nutrapup.

  b. Mary seems to have fed Fido [Nutrapup]$_F$.

(3.10) a. Jane thinks Mary fed [Fido]$_F$ Nutrapup.

  b. Jane thinks Mary fed Fido [Nutrapup]$_F$.

We can account for all of the cases in (3.8)–(3.10) without demanding anything special of the operators in each case. The same explanation works for possibility modals, verbs of appearance, and belief operators as for negation and disjunction. In each case, it is sufficient to say that the argument of the operator (if we allow that *seems* is a raising verb which takes a propositional argument) is associated with a set of alternatives that is congruent to the Current Question. The *Current Question Rule* then guarantees that for the (a) cases it is accepted that Mary fed some critter Nutrapup. This would not follow from the *Current Question Rule* in the corresponding (b) cases.

The five cases we have considered in this section all involve an operator interacting with focus to produce variable inferences. In none of these cases are the inferences we observe easily explicable in terms of standard pragmatic reasoning. Consider the first example (3.1a). Since *linguistics* is not part of a conventional scale, nor part of a scale salient in this particular case, we do not expect any scalar implicature to arise. What about the exhaustification inference explored in the discussion of negation above? If we apply a standard theory of focus interpretation (e.g. Rooth 1992) blindly, we might expect focus to yield the exhaustivity implicature that there is no subject other than linguistics which Kim doesn't study at Northwestern, i.e. that Kim does study every subject other than linguistics at Northwestern.[7] This inference is not generated. Similarly, the exhaustivity implicature predicted for (3.7a) would be that there is no subject other than linguistics such that either Kim studies it at Texas or she happens to be a lambda calculus black belt. Again, this is not the desired inference. Thus, neither scalar implicature nor exhaustivity implicature can explain the inferences in (3.1a) and (3.7a), and we leave it to the reader to confirm that the same is true for the examples in (3.8–3.10).

The implicature that we need in all of the cases discussed in this section is derived from the assumption that the argument of the propositional operator (rather than the entire sentence including the operator) is congruent to the Current Question, and the default requirement that the Current Question must contain at least one true alternative.

There is one further property that the operator must have for quasi-association to occur: the operator must be *non-veridical*, meaning that a sentence $op(S)$, where op is the operator and S is its argument, does not entail S. If the operator were veridical, then the existential proposition following from non-triviality of the Current Question would be a proposition that was entailed by the entire sentence. In that case, the inferential effects of changing what was focused would be masked by the entailments of the sentence as a whole, so the principles we have considered up to now would not yield any interesting interaction between focus placement and inference.

Consequently, the properties that an expression must have to produce quasi-association with focus are just (i) that the expression is a propositional operator, and (ii) that the expression is non-veridical. All five cases we have considered, i.e. negation, disjunction, possibility modals, verbs of appearance, and belief operators, have both of these properties.

---

[7] We are not claiming that quasi-association is not analyzable in Rooth's (1992) system. On the contrary, we take our inspiration from his proposal, and everything needed for this part of our analysis can be found there, though in slightly different form. To make a Rooth-style analysis work, we would have make sure that for a sentence like (3.1a) *Kim doesn't study [linguistics]$_F$ at Northwestern*, the alternatives are calculated at a level underneath the negation. Thus, Rooth might use the structure *[not [[Kim does study [linguistics]$_F$ at Northwestern] $\sim$C]]*. One difference between such an analysis and our own proposal is that for Rooth the relation to an earlier question is enforced by the $\sim$ operator, whereas in our proposal the relation to the Current Question arises from general principles of discourse which are not encoded directly in the representation of the sentence.

3.3   The Second Degree: Free Association

Summary: *We discuss* free association with focus, *the resolution of a free variable. Free association affects operators which perform quantification over, or comparison within, an implict domain. We examine expressions of this type, including quantificational adverbs, quantificational determiners, generics, modals, superlatives, counterfactuals, statements of reason, emotive factives, and verbs of desire.*

Speakers tend to omit or reduce much of what is predictable or obvious, and devote proportionately more effort to what is new or unexpected. This is reflected in the use of accenting and deaccenting, in the use of pronouns, and in various forms of ellipsis, but it is also reflected in the lexicon and elsewhere in the grammar. For example, many linguistic expressions have *implicit arguments*, meaning that the semantic interpretation of these expressions makes reference to a non-overt argument. A standard way to analyze expressions with implicit arguments is to say that compositional semantics yields a logical form that includes a free variable, and pragmatics ties that variable to a contextually relevant value. Since the free variable reflects recoverable material, and since focus tends to mark material which is unrecoverable, it is expected that there will be at least a correlation between what is marked as focused and what value is taken by the free variable. Of course, this tends to be a negative correlation, in the sense that the value of the free variable is likely to relate to material *not* marked as focused.

A number of prior authors explained focus sensitivity effects using argumentation of this sort. This is what we termed, in the last chapter, *free association*. Rooth (1992) discussed it as one of several mechanisms that might explain focus effects, and von Fintel (1994) develops a detailed theory of how pragmatic restriction of free variables can explain the focus sensitivity of quantificational adverbs, as well as applying the same technique to other expression types. Our goal is to circumscribe more clearly than these prior authors which cases of focus sensitivity should be explained as free association, and which should be explained using other mechanisms.

We have already seen that many operators apparently manifesting focus sensitivity are best seen as producing only *quasi-association* with focus. In such cases, observed inference effects result from the fact that the argument of the operator may be understood as congruent to the Current Question. And in the next section we will consider yet another class, those cases where association with focus is not free but conventionalized.

Nevertheless, there remain a diverse set of expressions where we believe that free association effects can be observed, including:

- quantificational adverbs
- some quantificational determiners
- generics

- superlatives
- counterfactuals
- *because*-clauses
- modals (which also exhibit quasi-association effects, as we have seen)
- emotive factive verbs
- verbs of desire.

In the remainder of this section we will discuss the focus sensitivity effects seen in these cases.

Quantificational adverbs

We start with quantificational adverbs (Lewis 1975; Kamp 1981; Heim 1982; de Swart 1993), e.g. *always, usually, mostly*, and *8 out of 10 times*, all of which exhibit clear truth conditional focus effects in their non-temporal interpretations (von Fintel 1994, 1995; Rooth 1995). The effects of focus for adverbs of quantification were seen in example (1.4), repeated in (3.11), For example, in a situation where Kim serves Pat and Sandy Johnnie Walker, and serves nobody anything else, (3.11a) is true while (3.11b) is false.

(3.11) a. Kim always serves Sandy [Johnnie Walker]$_F$.

b. Kim always serves [Sandy]$_F$ Johnnie Walker.

An adverb of quantification, like any quantifier, has a restrictor argument and a scope argument. The scope argument is the clause containing the adverb, and the restrictor, if it is realized at all, is a subordinate clause, e.g. an *if*-clause or a *when* clause. But when the restrictor can be recovered from context, it may be omitted, leaving what we may view as a free variable. So now the question is, how does focus affect the resolution of that free variable?

In Chapters 6–8 we present data from a range of Germanic and Romance languages that shows that quantificational adverbs such as *always* have no grammaticalized dependency on focus. Thus while many examples witness the effects of focus on the meaning of sentences involving quantificational adverbs, the effects are not robust.

What quantificational adverbs do have is an argument position that can be filled in by a salient set of occurrences, such that quantification is over the given set. This argument is filled in pragmatically in a couple of different ways. It may be resolved anaphorically to a previously mentioned set of occurrences. Alternatively, the argument position may be resolved to a set that is salient, but not yet made explicit. This resolution process identifies sets of occurrences such that coherence of the discourse is maximized, and in order to maximize coherence both information structure and presupposition must be respected.

So far, what we have said about resolution of the restrictor of *always* is true of *any* resolution process. The same point could have been made with regard to the setting of a standard for a vague adjective – how big is *big*? Or it could have been made with respect to the resolution of a lexical ambiguity – is it more plausible that the speaker meant the *bank* of a river or the *bank* that has a big door and lots of money? But we don't want to say that *big* or *bank* are in any way focus sensitive. There is a crucial further feature which distinguishes the resolution of the restrictor of *always* from these other types of resolution: *always* is a propositional operator.

Consider, once more, (3.11a), *Kim always serves Sandy [Courvoisier]*$_F$. We take *always* to quantify over a set of events, which we will write as σ, so we may approximate the meaning of (3.11a) as: $\forall e \in \sigma$ (*Kim serves Sandy Courvoisier in e*). The argument of *always* is then the open proposition (i.e. proposition with a free variable): *Kim serves Sandy Courvoisier in e*. Focus on *Courvoisier* means that the focal meaning of the argument of *always* is a set of propositions corresponding to glosses of the form *Kim serves Sandy X in e*, for different choices of X. The alternative set would be congruent to a question like: *what does Kim serve Sandy in e?* Since this question contains a variable bound by *always*,[8] we cannot expect the question to be explicitly present in prior discourse.

Instead, a question like this must be added locally, i.e. added to the context under the quantificational adverb, the process known as LOCAL ACCOMMO-DATION, and about which we will have more to say later. At this point, non-triviality of the locally accommodated question requires that e is an event in which Kim served Sandy something. This yields a condition on discourse coherence: (3.11a) will be felicitous in a discourse context in which there is a salient set of events of Mary serving Kim something. In such a context, the restrictor of *always*, i.e. the free variable σ, can be identified with this set of events. It follows that (3.11a) expresses the proposition that in each of some salient set of events of Kim serving Sandy something, she served her Courvoisier.

Similar considerations apply to (3.11b). But this sentence will be felicitous only in a discourse context where there is a salient set of events of Sandy serving individuals Courvoisier. (3.11b) will then express the proposition that in each one of those events, she served Sandy Courvoisier. So we predict not only that (3.11a) and (3.11b) will be felicitous in different discourse contexts, but also that they must express different propositions. And so we have accounted for the focus sensitivity of *always*.

As noted above, in Chapters 6–8 we present many further arguments to the effect that quantificational adverbs display free, as opposed to conventionalized, association with focus. These arguments will be based primarily on universals, i.e. *always* and its cross-linguistic cognates. It seems natural to suggest that the same analysis extends to the full range of quantificational adverbs. However, it should be noted that for any quantificational adverb which is symmetric in the sense that Q(A)(B) has the same truth conditions as Q(B)(A), we do not expect such strong effects. *Never* and *sometimes* have this symmetry property,

---

8   Cf. the discussion in Chapter 5 of van der Sandt's TRAPPING.

and consequently for these operators there is not even any apparent focus sensitivity to explain. For example, (3.12a) and (3.12b) would be used to make truth conditionally identical assertions, albeit that they answer different questions.

(3.12) a. Officers never dance with [ballerinas]$_F$.

     b. [Officers]$_F$ never dance with ballerinas.

Nonetheless, let us stick with the idea that all quantificational adverbs exhibit free association with focus, and ask the question: what other expression types which the literature suggests are focus sensitive share this property? The most obvious examples are quantificational determiners and generics, since both involve quantification over a domain which may not be fully specified by the sentence in which they appear.

Quantificational determiners

Let us consider quantificational determiners first, a case for which focus sensitivity might not be immediately apparent. In the crucial examples, it appears that deaccented material in the scope argument of quantifiers such as *every* may be interpreted in the restrictor (Büring 1999; Krifka 1990; Cohen 1999; Herburger 2000; Hendriks and de Hoop 2001; Eckardt 1999; Partee 1991, 1999). Thus for (3.13) and (3.14), the interpretation of (a) is as in (b).

(3.13) a. Every ship passed through the lock [at night]$_F$.
        (Every [ship]$_{restrictor}$ [passed through the lock [at night]$_F$]$_{scope}$)

     b. Every ship which passed through the lock did so at night.

(3.14) a. Mary reads every book [twice]$_F$.
        (Every [book]$_{restrictor}$ [Mary reads [twice]$_F$]$_{scope}$)

     b. Every book that Mary reads, she reads twice.

Note that focal material in the restrictor of quantifiers, as in (3.15a), stays there (Partee 1991). Consequently, (3.15a) cannot mean (3.15b).

(3.15) a. Most [graduate]$_F$ students are auditing Ling 100.

     b. Most students who are auditing Ling 100 are graduate students.

The effects seen in examples (3.13) and (3.14) are naturally analyzed as free association with focus, and the analysis of quantificational determiners is almost exactly parallel to the analysis of quantificational adverbs. The two differences are, first, that for quantificational determiners the restrictor is usually explicit, and, second, that quantificational determiners are not so clearly propositional operators as are quantificational adverbs.

    With regard to the restrictor, focus sensitivity is only observed for strong determiners such as *every*, Strong determiners are precisely the class of determiners standardly analyzed as quantifying over a contextually given set

(Diesing 1992), meaning that even though the NP which is the sister of the determiner restricts the domain of quantification, the NP does not uniquely specify that domain. So while, for example, an utterance of the DP *every book* can be used to quantify over the set of all books, it can also be used to quantify over some salient set of books, such as those on your bookshelf. It is natural, then to say that the LF of *every book was dusty* incorporates a free variable, say C, which, in this case, would pick out a set of books.

Concerning the observation that quantificational determiners are not propositional operators, for the type of analysis given for adverbs of quantification to work we do not require that quantificational determiners are propositional operators. Rather, we require that propositions are embedded somewhere in the LF in the scope of a quantificational determiner. This is a property which is common to any theory of quantification which explains scope ambiguity in terms of QUANTIFYING-IN or QUANTIFIER RAISING: for a standard text taking such an approach, see Heim and Kratzer (1998).

Based on these considerations, we gloss (3.13a) as: *for every ship x in C, x passed through the lock [at night]*$_F$, with C picking out a salient set of ships, and *x* corresponding to a trace. Now the clausal argument *x passed through the lock [at night]*$_F$ has a focus semantic value consisting of a set of propositions *x passed through the lock during interval y* for various intervals *y*. This set could be congruent with the question: *When did x pass through the lock?* But since *x* is bound by the quantifier, we cannot expect that question to have been given explicitly in the discourse. As with our analysis of quantificational adverbs, we assume that the question is locally accommodated, inducing the existential requirement: *x passed through the lock during some interval.*

We then predict that a discourse containing (3.13a) will only be felicitous if there is a salient set of ships each of which passed through the lock, and the sentence as a whole will express the proposition that every one of those ships which passed through the lock did so at night. Thus we derive free association with focus in this case: deaccented material appears to restrict the quantifier, though what deaccenting actually does is determine the conditions which have to be met by a contextually salient set over which the determiner quantifies.[9]

Why, then, do we not see such effects when the focus is in the NP complement of a quantificational determiner, as in (3.15a), *Most [graduate]*$_F$ *students are auditing Ling 100?* For this to happen, focused material in the NP complement of a quantifier (e.g. *graduate* in (3.15a)) would have to restrict the scope argument of the quantifier, but quantificational determiners have two properties that preclude this, or preclude it from being detectable.

---

[9] Note that the truth conditions we derive for (3.13a) allow that some ships passed through the lock both at night and during the day. This certainly corresponds to a reading of the sentence, but there may be a further reading which implies that no ships passed through the lock during the day. To account for this reading may require a more radical revision of the semantics of nominal quantification than we have proposed – see Krifka (1990).

First, the scope argument of a quantificational determiner has no additional free domain variable, so there is nothing to mediate the effects of free association with focus as regards restriction of the scope argument.

Second, quantificational determiners are generally taken to denote CONSER-VATIVE quantifiers, in the sense that for quantifier Q, restrictor set R, and scope set S, $Q(R)(S) = Q(R)(R \cap S)$ (Westerståhl 2005). As a result, quantificational sentences are always interpreted as if material in the NP complement of the determiner semantically restricts both the restrictor and the scope argument. Thus, allowing focus to cause material in the restrictor to also restrict the scope would have no effect.[10]

We now turn to the quantificational determiners *many* and *few*, operators with apparently non-logical properties that have lead to much name calling. They have been described as *vague* (Altham and Tennant 1975; Bennett 1980), *non-conservative* (Westerståhl 1985), *intensional* (Bennett 1980; Keenan and Stavi 1986), and even *focus affected* (Herburger 1997, 2000). Of course, it is the last property which interests us here, but, as we will see, the others are all connected.

The vagueness of *many* is memorably illustrated by (3.16), which can be understood as indicating a much larger cardinality for the set of men involved than for the sets of women each of them is involved with. So *many* is vague insofar as its lexical entry does not fully determine what counts as *many*. We may state this in terms of the semantics of *many* having a free variable, a contextually determined *amount* parameter, such that the value of this variable sets the lower bound for how many counts as *many*. *Few* is understood similarly, except with a contextually determined upper bound.

(3.16)   Many men date many women.

(Bennett 1980)

To see why it has been suggested that *many* is intensional, suppose that you are teaching a class which, as luck would have it, happens to contain every single person in the world with an IQ of 210 and nobody else. Of the two dozen students in the class, seven attempted the current assignment. In that situation, you might view (3.17) as false, but (3.18) as true. But here we have a failure of substitutivity, since *students in the class* cannot be replaced by the extensionally identical *people with an IQ of 210* while preserving truth value – *salva veritate*, to use the standard Leibniz-derived terminology.

(3.17)   Many students in the class attempted this assignment.

(3.18)   Many people with an IQ of 210 attempted this assignment.

---

[10] It is perhaps significant that it is precisely the non-conservative quantificational operators on NPs which exhibit conventional association with focus effects in their NP argument, *only* and other exclusives, and perhaps also *mostly*, as in *Kim gave mostly women with [dark]$_F$ hair chocolates*, which means that most of the women Kim gave chocolates had dark hair.

Mathematical statements of the property of conservativity, following Barwise and Cooper (1981), generally assume that the determiner is not intensional, so that on such definitions it follows from the contrast between (3.17) and (3.18) that *many* is non-conservative. Westerståhl illustrates the non-conservative interpretation of *many* with (3.19). The claim is that there is a reading of this sentence which says that the proportion of prize winners who are Scandinavian is large.[11] If conservativity held, we would expect that the truth conditions could equally be rendered as the claim that the proportion of Scandinavian prize winners who are Scandinavian is large, but this latter seems to be a different claim (indeed, quite an odd one).

(3.19)   Many Scandinavians have won the Nobel Prize in literature.

                                                              (Westerståhl 1985)

Herburger notes that the reading Westerståhl observed is only available with focus in the NP complement of *many*, as in (3.20a), and not with focus in the VP, as in (3.20b). Similar comments apply to Herburger's (3.21). The claim she makes is that, *contra* a generalization we discussed above, focal material can restrict the scope argument of the quantifying determiners *few* and *many*:

(3.20) a.   Many [Scandinavians]$_F$ have won the Nobel Prize in literature.
            (can mean 'Many who have won the Nobel Prize in literature are Scandinavian')

      b.   Many Scandinavians have won [the Nobel Prize in literature]$_F$.
            (cannot mean 'Many who have won the Nobel Prize in literature are Scandinavian')

(3.21)   Few [incompetent]$_F$ cooks applied.

                                                              (Herburger 1997)
            (can mean 'Few cooks that applied were incompetent')

Herberger analyzes these cases as involving what we term *conventional association* with focus in the next section, as does Cohen (2001). But we suggest, loosely mirroring the analysis of Büring (1996), that the focus sensitivity of *many* and *few* can be explained entirely in terms of the free amount parameter, the standard interpretational effects of focus, and pragmatic reasoning. As a result, the apparent intensionality and non-conservativity of these determiners can be explained in terms of vagueness, i.e. in terms of the pragmatic process by which the amount parameter is set.

We can describe this pragmatic process in the following way. The vague statement that a certain amount is *high* becomes informative only to the extent that that amount could have been expected to be lower, and *vice versa* for

---

[11]   Since (3.19) was first given, the percentage of Scandinavian Nobel prize winners in literature has dropped from nearly 15% to under 12%. Here we follow standard practice by disregarding the Finn, Sillanpää.

the statement that an amount is *low*. Thus *many* and *few* convey the information that some amount is abnormal, i.e. higher or lower than expected, respectively (Fernando and Kamp 1996). A natural way of determining whether some group has a property to an abnormal extent is to compare with some other similar group. For example, we can compare the group of Scandinavians to other similarly sized groups of people, perhaps even drawn from geopolitically similar units.[12] Or we can compare incompetent cooks to competent cooks, as in (3.21).

We suggest, and this much is completely standard, that (3.20a) is true for some amount α if and only if the proportion (or number) of Scandinavians who have won the prize is significantly greater than α. The sentence then evokes a set of alternatives of the form *the proportion (or number) of Xs who have won the prize is significantly greater than α*, where the Xs are comparable groups, perhaps Latin Americans, Slavs, or people whose first name begins with 'D'. For the claim in (3.20a) to be informative, which for us is enforced by the Discourse Principle, there has to be a choice of α that verifies the sentence, but eliminates alternatives. Thus, we need an α lower than the proportion of Scandinavians who won, but higher than e.g. the proportion of Latin Americans, Slavs, or people whose first name begins with 'D' that won.

Sticking to a proportional reading, we estimate that setting α anywhere between 1/2,000,000 and 1/20,000,000 would do the trick. Since it is easy to find a choice of α, (3.20a) is determined to be both true and informative. For the nonproportional, so-called *cardinal* reading, setting $\alpha = 11$ would at least eliminate the Latin American and people whose first name begins with 'D' alternatives, so we predict that there are possible choices of α that would make the sentence true.[13] But the choice of alternatives, and hence of an appropriate α, is crucial for making this reading true, and hence that the sentence should not be felt to be so robustly true under this reading as it is under the proportional reading.

By contrast, (3.20b) seems more clearly false, though it would be true in a context which already makes appropriate alternatives salient. The compositionally derived truth conditions are identical to those for (3.20a), except that pragmatics leads to a different choice of α. In this case, the alternatives all have the form: *the proportion (or number) of Scandinavians who have property X is significantly greater than α*. Here X might be, e.g. the property of wearing rimless glasses, the property of being blonde, the property of working in the oil industry, or the property of being able to speak Arabic. For such alternatives, there will be no choice of α which allows the sentence to be both informative and true.

---

[12]   Sentences involving *many* or *few* can also be understood as making comparisons between the performance of the same group over time, as in *Recently, few Scandinavians have won Nobel prizes*, in which *few* itself might be accented.

[13]   The Nobel prize for literature has been won by five Latin Americans, twelve from Slavic nations, and two whose first name begins with a 'D'.

The analysis of (3.21) proceeds along the same lines. We take the sentence to favor a cardinal reading, and need a choice of α such that the number of incompetent cooks who applied is well below α. The alternatives are propositions that *the number of cooks with property X who applied is well below* α. If we assume just the two alternatives where X is set to be the property of being competent (as a cook), and where X is set to be the property of being incompetent (as a cook), then it will be possible to make the sentence true just in case the number of competent cooks who applied is significantly higher than the number of incompetent cooks who applied.

Our conclusion is that there is no need to postulate any conventional focus sensitivity lexicalized in the meaning of *many* and *few*: the completely standard assumption that these expressions have a free amount parameter is all that is needed to explain the effect of focus on meaning for these expressions.

Furthermore, there is no need to postulate that *many* and *few* denote intensional operators, or that they denote non-conservative quantifiers. Their apparent intensionality arises because the choice of alternatives is, completely generally, sensitive to intensions and not merely extensions. And the lexical semantics we assumed for *many* and *few* makes them into ordinary conservative quantifiers, just the same ones you would expect on the basis of Barwise and Cooper (1981). It is in this latter work that a language universal was offered to the effect that all quantificational determiners are conservative: we have shown that *many* and *few* do not counter-exemplify that universal.

More generally still, all the quantificational determiners we have looked at, including also *every* and *most*, seem to us to follow the strictures of Barwise and Cooper's generalized quantifier approach. The apparent bad behavior of these determiners results in every case from the pragmatic effects of focus in setting a free parameter, either for the quantificational domain, or for an amount that counts as high or low.

Generics and modals

In the case of generics, the quantificational structure is standardly taken to be very similar to that for quantificational adverbs. Generics are often analyzed in terms of an implicit quantificational operator, though the quantificational force of this operator is vague or supplied by context (Carlson and Pelletier 1995).

Consider the naturally occurring example in (3.22). If the expression *bare plurals* is taken as focused, there is a reading of the sentence that says it will be argued that generically, when something is ambiguous, that thing is a bare plural. But a much more plausible reading (and surely the intended one) is obtained with focus on the word *ambiguous*. In that case the sentence says it will be argued that generically, when something is a bare plural, that thing is ambiguous.

(3.22)   It will be argued that bare plurals are ambiguous [. . .]
*(Sentence drawn from abstract of: Oosterhof, Albert, Dutch Bare Plurals,
Faded Partitives and Subject–Object Asymmetry, Belgian Journal
of Linguistics, Volume 19, Number 1, 2005, pp. 59–91(33))*

Analyzing (3.22) by analogy with quantificational adverbs, and representing the implicit generic operator as *gen*, the LF of the clause *bare plurals are ambiguous* becomes: *gen(x, x ∈ C, x is a bare plural and x is ambiguous)*, where the restrictor set C is a free variable that must pick out a set of objects. Focus on the word *ambiguous* triggers local accommodation of the question *x is a bare plural with what property?*. This, in turn, leads to the existential requirement *x is a bare plural with some property*. This requirement can be met if C is the set of entities that are bare plurals, thus producing the reading: generically, if something is a bare plural, then that thing is ambiguous.[14]

In the next example (see Halliday 1970: 38; cited in Partee 1991: 169 and Ladd 1996: 199), the sign in Figure 3.1, we also see focus sensitivity, though it is unclear whether this results from an implicit generic operator, or from the explicit modal *must*. The desired reading is that if dogs are present (on the escalator next to which the sign is affixed in a London Underground station) then those dogs must be carried. If read aloud, this reading would be obtained with focus on *carried*. But if *dogs* is focused instead, the implausible reading that results is that anyone riding the escalator must carry a dog.

We could analyze Figure 3.1 in exactly the same way as (3.22), assuming that there is a generic operator outscoping the deontic modal *must*, and that the effects of focus are mediated via a free variable in the restrictor of the generic. But an alternative is to take the relevant variable to be directly constraining the modal itself, along lines suggested by Kratzer (1977).

The claim then would be that although *must* appears to combine with a single propositional argument, it also has a second implicit argument, what Kratzer calls a MODAL BASE. If the modal base is M, and we analyze the modal as saying that all situations compatible with M are situations obeying the carrying requirement, then Figure 3.1 would have a logical form: *must(s, s is a minimal situation compatible with M, s is a situation in which dogs are carried)*. Focus sensitivity would then result from free association with the variable M. Later in this section we will consider another case where a modal is thus restricted.

---

[14] Note that typically the restrictor set of a generic is not identified with an already salient set, but with the maximal set that satisfies the existential requirement. We offer no explanation of this, but take it to be a feature to be explained in a more complete theory of generics, rather than a more complete theory of focus. Note, relatedly, that while it has been argued that presuppositions in the scope of a quantifier cannot be accommodated directly into the restrictor (Beaver 2001), it is not clear that the same arguments apply to generics. That is, in the case of generics, there may be reason to say that presuppositions directly constrain the domain of quantification (if indeed generics are quantifiers at all).

Figure 3.1 Focus sensitivity of *must*

Superlatives

What we have looked at so far in this section are what we might call the *easy* cases of free association, all involving the relatively well-studied phenomenon of restriction of a domain of quantification. We now turn to some which are harder to analyze, but for which we nonetheless sketch suggestive analyses. The hard cases of free association that we will examine in the remainder of this section are superlatives, counterfactuals and statements of reason, emotive factives, and verbs of desire.

Superlatives are the first *hard* case we will consider, and are yet another case where truth conditional effects result from what we believe is free association with focus.[15] If *Mary* is focused in the superlative example (3.23), then we naturally understand the claim as a comparison of the sizes of boxes from all of the people who gave boxes to John. In contrast, if *John* is focused, then we are to compare the sizes of all of the boxes that Mary gave to different people.

(3.23) a. [Mary]$_F$ gave John the biggest box.

b. Mary gave [John]$_F$ the biggest box.

---

[15] On the interaction of superlatives and focus, see Ross (1964), Bowers (1969), Jackendoff (1972: 254), Heim (1985, 1999), Szabolcsi (1986), Gawron (1992, 1995), Sharvit and Stateva (2002), and Stateva (2002).

Once again, the key to explaining focus sensitivity is to identify an implicit free variable, in this case, a variable for the class of objects to which the present in question is compared. There is a *prima facie* case for regarding superlatives as a case of free association, since association with focus is not compulsory. Specifically, both (3.23a) and (3.23b) have a reading where there is an independently salient set of boxes, say a set of stacking boxes in a child's toy. Then *the biggest box* simply refers to one of these boxes, (3.23a) answers the question of who gave John that box, and (3.23b) answers the question of who Mary gave that box.

But the question of who gave John the biggest box, the question to which (3.23a) is congruent, is itself congruent to the question: *who gave John a box?* This question evokes a set of propositional alternatives 'X gave John a box', which in turn makes the set of all boxes given to John salient. It is when this comparison set is plugged in as the value of the free variable introduced by the superlative that we derive the reading for (3.23a): *Mary gave John a bigger box than anyone else gave him.*

In contrast, (3.23b) is congruent to the question: *who did Mary give the biggest box?* This, in turn, is congruent to the question: *who did Mary give a box?* That question makes the set of boxes Mary gave to people salient, and plugging this in as the comparison set yields the desired reading for (3.23b), that is: *Mary gave John a bigger box than she gave anyone else.*[16]

Counterfactuals and statements of reason

We now turn to a varied group of constructions that we class together as *counterfactuals and statements of reason*. Dretske (1972) observed that focus often affects truth conditions in such cases. Consider the following scenario (Rooth 1999: 233):

> Pat had two daughters, one named Bertha; the other was named Aretha and was indispensable to him in his business. He had made a commitment to marry one of the daughters to one of the sons of a man who once saved his life. There were two such sons, the elder son Clyde and the younger son Derek. According to a custom of the society and period, an elder son had to marry before his younger brothers; this was known as seniority. Given the contract, seniority, and the desirability of leaving Aretha free to run his business for him, he figured out that the best thing to do was to marry Bertha to Clyde, and that is what he did.

---

[16] Taking the definite determiner *the* that occurs in the superlative construction to be semantically vacuous, we might analyze *biggest* as a predicate which takes three arguments: the noun complement, a comparison class C, and a property given by the remainder of the sentence. So the compositionally derived LF of (3.23a) and (3.23b) can be represented as: *biggest(present)(C)(λx Mary gave John x)*. The intended meaning might be glossed as: *the biggest present in the set of presents C was something Mary gave to John*, with the readings described in the main text derived by plugging in different values for C.

Focus sensitivity is now observed in the counterfactual examples in (3.24) (Rooth 1999: 233). Given the preceding scenario, (3.24a) and (3.24d) are true and (3.24b) and (3.24c) are false.

(3.24) a. If he hadn't married [Bertha]$_F$ to Clyde, Aretha couldn't have continued to run the business.
            (true)

        b. If he hadn't married Bertha to [Clyde]$_F$, Aretha couldn't have continued to run the business.
            (false)

        c. If he hadn't married [Bertha]$_F$ to Clyde, seniority would have been violated.
            (false)

        d. If he hadn't married Bertha to [Clyde]$_F$, seniority would have been violated.
            (true)

The statements of reason in (3.25) display the same truth-conditional effect of focus.

(3.25) a. The reason he married [Bertha]$_F$ to Clyde was that Aretha was indispensable in the business.
            (true)

        b. The reason he married Bertha to [Clyde]$_F$ was that Aretha was indispensable in the business.
            (false)

        c. The reason he married [Bertha]$_F$ to Clyde was that he wanted to obey seniority.
            (false)

        d. The reason he married Bertha to [Clyde]$_F$ was that he wanted to obey seniority.
            (true)

We get the same effects with *because* clauses (3.26) and also bouletic modals such as *had to* in (3.27):[17]

(3.26) a. He married [Bertha]$_F$ to Clyde because Aretha was indispensable in the business.
            (true)

        b. He married Bertha to [Clyde]$_F$ because Aretha was indispensable in the business.
            (false)

---

[17] Dretske and Rooth did not consider bouletic modals in such contexts.

(3.27) a. (Given that Arethra was indispensable in the business ...)
He had to marry [Bertha]_F to Clyde.
(true)

  b. (Given that Arethra was indispensable in the business ...)
He had to marry Bertha to [Clyde]_F.
(false)

We can analyze all of these cases (counterfactuals, *reason that* constructions, *because* clauses, and bouletic modals) following the discussion of counterfactuals by Rooth (1999), itself building on the analysis of counterfactuals of von Fintel (1994). For each case, the idea is that the focus sensitive operator has a free variable for an implicit comparison set, though this set may be thought of as a set of worlds rather than a set of individuals. Lewis (1973) analyzed a counterfactual conditional *if A then B* as being true if and only if in all the most similar worlds to the real world where *A* is the case, *B* also holds.

But there is a twist: in deciding which worlds are most similar, all propositions are not equal. There may be a set of propositions which the speaker wishes to hold constant while considering alternatives to the real world. We may make such propositions explicit. For example the *given* clause in (3.28) signals that only worlds where you are reading this book are to be considered, and it says that in all the most similar such worlds where the book is burning, your eyebrows get singed. So here we rule out certain worlds explicitly, and then rule out yet further worlds (like those where you are reading the book while wearing a fire resistant mask) as being insufficiently similar to the real world. The conditional can be thought of as involving an implicit free variable ranging over the set of worlds under consideration, although we could also think of this variable as ranging over sets of propositions, i.e. the propositions to be held constant.

(3.28)   Given that you are reading this book, if the book were burning, it would singe your eyebrows.

Let us say that C is the free variable for the set of worlds under consideration, if you will the *modal base* of the counterfactual, and now consider a counterfactual with a negative antecedent *if not A then B*. By the same logic, this should be true if and only if in all the most similar worlds in C to the real world where *A* is the not case, *B* also holds. But then what if *A* has presuppositions?

It turns out that we understand counterfactual conditionals as being relative to a modal base C where the presuppositions of the antecedent are satisfied.[18] Thus in (3.29), C includes only worlds where the presupposition triggered by the factive *realize* is satisfied, i.e. worlds where the book is burning. The example says that in all worlds where the book is burning but you did not realize it, you do not drop the book.

---

[18] Cf. Heim (1992: 204–5) (also Ippolito 2003) on presupposition projection from the antecedent of counterfactuals.

(3.29)   If you didn't realize the book was burning, you would not drop it.

Now we are ready to analyze focus sensitivity in counterfactuals. Take (3.24a), repeated below in example (3.30), which has focus on *Bertha*. The antecedent is congruent to the question: *who did he marry to Clyde?* The Current Question Rule in (2.53) produces the requirement that he (i.e. Pat) married someone to Clyde. This requirement is typically presupposed by the speaker, and so respected by the modal base of the counterfactual.

(3.30)   If he hadn't married [Bertha]$_F$ to Clyde, Aretha couldn't have continued to run the business.

Therefore in all worlds in C, Pat married someone to Clyde, and the truth conditions of the example amount to the claim: *if Pat had married someone other than Bertha to Clyde, Aretha couldn't have continued to run the business.* This is true in the given scenario. By contrast, similar argumentation for (3.24b), repeated below in example (3.31), where *Clyde* is focused, predicts that it has the truth conditions: *if Pat had married Bertha to someone other than Clyde, Aretha couldn't have continued to run the business.* This is false, as required.

(3.31)   If he hadn't married Bertha to [Clyde]$_F$, Aretha couldn't have continued to run the business.

Let us turn briefly to the focus sensitivity effects found in *statements of reason* constructions, *because* clauses, and bouletic modals. We take each of these to have meanings that can be glossed as in (3.32). Free association effects parallel to those observed for counterfactuals will then be predicted in each case provided non-triviality requirements of salient questions are met in all worlds in the modal base C.

(3.32) a. *The reason for B is A* means that in all worlds in C where A happens, that causes B, or creates a need for B.

  b. *B because A* means that in all worlds in C where A happens, that causes B, or implies that B is the case.

  c. *had-to(A)* means that in all worlds in C, A was necessary to achieve certain goals.

Emotive factives

The last case we will consider as involving free association is that of attitudinal verbs such as *be glad* and *hope*.

Example (3.33a) and (3.33b) involve the emotive factive *be glad*. The first may be glossed as the claim that the students preferred Brady teaching semantics to the counterfactual alternative of someone else teaching semantics. Similarly, we gloss the second as the claim that the students preferred Brady teaching semantics to the counterfactual alternative of him teaching something else (e.g. historical linguistics).

(3.33) a.   The students were glad that [Brady]$_F$ taught semantics.

b.   The students were glad that Brady taught [semantics]$_F$.

It is tempting to try to analyze these as cases of quasi-association with focus. But that would not work since quasi-association, at least of the form we have described, applies only to non-veridical operators, and factive verbs are, by definition, veridical. What we suggest is that emotive factives are intrinsically interpreted relative to a set of counterfactual alternatives: one is glad of something because one prefers it to certain alternative outcomes that did not occur; cf. Heim (1992) and von Fintel (1999).

Once again, it suffices to assume that emotive factives are interpreted relative to a modal base C, undetermined by compositional semantics, which we take to be a set of worlds. Recall that the Current Question Rule says that the Current Question must contain at least one true alternative. In order to analyze examples like (3.33a), we can then fall back on the existential requirement associated with the question to which the propositional complement of the operator is congruent. If C respects this requirement, then what (3.33a) says is that in all worlds where someone taught semantics, the preferred worlds, among them the real world, are those where Brady taught it. And (3.33a) says that in all worlds where Brady taught something, the preferred worlds, among them the real world, are those where he taught semantics.

The same argument would explain focus sensitivity of any emotive factive, e.g. *regrets*, *be happy that*, *be unhappy that*, *be sad that*, *be annoyed that*, *be surprised that*, *be impressed that*, *be unimpressed that*, and so on. But the argument would also apply to non-factive emotives, such as verbs of desire. Thus, e.g., (3.34a), with the verb *hope*, implies that the students prefer Brady to teach semantics than for someone else to, while (3.34b) implies that the students prefer Brady to teach semantics than for him to teach something else.

(3.34) a.   The students hope that [Brady]$_F$ will teach semantics.

b.   The students hope that Brady will teach [semantics]$_F$.

Again, this behavior can be explained if there is a free variable for a modal base which is constrained by the existential requirements of the question to which the complement of the verb is congruent. Note, however, that for the non-factive *hope* we might also explain focus sensitivity as mere quasi-association, without any assumption of an implicit modal base. For (3.34a), quasi-association would produce the implicature that there is nobody other than Brady who the students hope will teach semantics.

We find the free association analysis of *hope* more attractive, but this is based primarily on uniformity with the analysis of emotive factives, rather than direct evidence for the free association account over the quasi-association account. For all the other expression types we have considered in this section, i.e. quantificational adverbs, quantificational determiners, generics, deontic modals, superlatives, counterfactual conditions, *reason* constructions, *because* clauses, bouletic

modals, and emotive factives, we believe that nothing less than free association can explain the focus sensitivity observed in examples like those we have
presented.

3.4 The Third Degree: Conventional Association

Summary: *We discuss* conventional association with focus, *a grammatical
dependency on the Current Question. We examine expressions of this type, including exclusives, additives, scalar additives, intensifiers, downtoners, and particu
-larizers.*

As we show in Chapters 6–8, only some expressions that have been labeled
focus sensitive have a lexically-encoded, conventionalized dependency on focus.
In this section we discuss some of these types of expressions, including exclusives, additives, scalar additives, intensifiers, downtoners, and particularizers.
These types of expressions are challenging to describe using the standard tools
of formal semantics. For that reason, we only attempt in this book to provide a
detailed case study of one class of conventionally focus sensitive expression, the
exclusives (e.g. *only*). Developing a theory that accounts for the complex behavior of exclusives, and does justice to the many insights of previous scholars, will
take two full chapters (9 and 10).

We start this section by previewing the theory of exclusives to be developed
in those later chapters, and then illustrate how similar ideas could be applied
to other expressions we take to conventionally associate with focus.

Exclusives

'Only just merely for the sake of the costs?' one naturally asks.
                        Punch, Or the Lord Charivari. Vol. 1. November 27, 1841.

The prototypical English exclusive is *only*, but there are others including *just*,
merely, *but* (archaic/dialectal), *exclusively*, *solely*, and, perhaps, *purely* and
uniquely. Languages typically have multiple exclusives, often derived from
expressions referring to the number one, like *only*, or purity, like *just* (but cf. *but*
from *bout* 'outside').

As Nevalainen (1991) makes clear, in a detailed study of the historical development of exclusives, the prototypicality of *only* as an exclusive in modern
English (filling a role once held by *but*) is reflected in at least three properties: it occurs with highest frequency of the exclusives, it can occupy the widest
range of syntactic positions of any exclusive, and it has a full range of uses, both
NON-SCALAR and SCALAR, notions to which we will now turn.

We already saw apparently non-scalar uses of *only*, as in (3.35), in which *only*
can be seen as modifying the proposition *David wears a bow tie when teaching*.
This underlying proposition is commonly termed the PREJACENT.

(3.35)   David only wears a bow tie when [teaching]$_F$.

A scalar use of *only* is illustrated in (3.36a) – a scale based on army rank. As we will argue in Chapter 10, some exclusives are always non-scalar, e.g. *exclusively*. *Merely*, as in (3.36b), is primarily scalar, as is *just*.

(3.36) a.   At the time of the battle of Shiloh, MacPherson had only been a lieutenant colonel.

[web example]

    b.   The first, which he merely observed as a junior official, took Ireland from its policy of official wartime neutralism, embarrassing after 1945, to one of broad support for a US-led anti-communist West.

[web example]

Faced with examples such as (3.36) and (3.35), the following question arises: should we regard exclusives that have both scalar and non-scalar uses as being ambiguous, or can both uses be understood as special cases of a single meaning? We will argue, in Chapter 10, for the latter position, maintaining the same truth conditional semantics for both scalar and non-scalar uses of exclusives.

To understand this, we need to start with the idea of a scale. We take a scale to be a salient partial ordering of propositions from weaker to stronger. In the simplest case, the notion of strength is just standard entailment, an ordering which is salient in all contexts. It is when the ordering is standard entailment that we get the uses which are commonly termed *non-scalar*.

We maintain, further, that the scalar uses also respect entailment, but use a scale in which the entailment relation has been supplemented with additional pairs of propositions. For example, the ordering relation in (3.36a) includes the pair ⟨*MacPherson had been a general, MacPherson had been a lieutenant colonel*⟩, since the first is contextually understood as a stronger claim than the second, even though the first does not standardly entail the second.[19] The exclusive *exclusively* would then simply be more constrained than *only*, lexically restricted to entailment scales.

The view we will develop hinges on the scalar nature of exclusives. We claim that the function of exclusives is to comment on an overly strong expectation regarding the answer to the Current Question, and to say that the strongest true answer is the prejacent. Normally, the relevant expectation is an expectation of the addressee, but this is not necessarily the case.

For example, (3.37), *David only wears a bow tie when [teaching]$_F$*, comments on the question of when David wears a bow tie, and combats an expectation that his wearing of a bow tie is a common occurrence. In fact, in considering situations in which the example might arise, it becomes natural to understand even this case as involving supplementation of the basic entailment scale.

---

[19]   Other authors who unify scalar and non-scalar uses of exclusives include Jacobs (1983), Schwarzschild (1997), van Rooij (2002), van Rooij and Schulz (2007), Beaver (2004), and Klinedinst (2004).

On a non-scalar interpretation, the hearer would already accept that David wears a bow tie when teaching, but would also believe that he wears one at other times. On a scalar interpretation, a natural way to supplement the entailment scale would be by allowing that a proposition that David wears a bow tie on many occasions is stronger than a proposition that he wears one on a small set of occasions. In that case the addressee of (3.37) would not necessarily be taken to believe prior to the utterance that David wears a bow tie when teaching, but would be taken to believe that David's bow tie wearing is relatively widespread.

On our account, the focus sensitivity of exclusives arises as a direct consequence of their intrinsic discourse function, which is to comment on the current question. Since we take focus to mark which part of a clause answers the Current Question, a particle which comments on alternative answers to the Current Question is necessarily focus sensitive. If an expression is not focus sensitive, then that expression does not comment on the Current Question.

For (3.37), focus on *teaching* signals that the Current Question is *When does David wear a bow tie?* So (3.35) says that the strongest true answer to the question of when David wears a bow tie is the proposition that he wears a bow tie when teaching. On the other hand, if *bow tie* had been focused instead of *teaching*, the example would instead say that the strongest true answer to the question of what David wears when teaching is the proposition that he wears a bow tie when teaching. Thus focus produces a truth conditional effect. Whereas the meaning we gave for (3.35) entails, for example, that David does not wear a bow tie when clubbing, this would not be entailed by the meaning we specified for the variant of (3.37) with focus shifted to *bow tie*.

Scalar additives

We now turn from exclusives to SCALAR ADDITIVES, of which the lone exemplar in English is *even*. The literature on scalar additives is almost as large as that on exclusives,[20] and we will not even attempt to do the scalar additives literature justice in this book. But we will comment that the moves we make in analyzing exclusives, while a major shift from other analyses of exclusives, would be right at home in the recent literature on scalar additives.

It is now the standard view (a view with which we agree wholeheartedly) that scalar additives comment on expectations that addressees have relative to a salient ordering of propositions. The developments in this book allow us to resolve two open issues regarding scalar additives: first, we can clarify their

---

[20] Accounts of scalar additives, including much cross-linguistic work, can be found in: Horn (1969, 1972/1976), Karttunen and Peters (1979), Kay (1990), Tancredi (1990, 1997), Barker (1991), König (1991), Lycan (1991), Wilkinson (1996), Krifka (1999), Schwenter and Vasishth (2001), Iten (2002), Oshima (2002), Schwenter (2002), Herburger (2003), Giannakidou (2003, 2005), Schwarz (2005), and Tovena (2005).

relation to scalar exclusives, and second, we can explain why scalar additives are focus sensitive, or at least push the explanation one level deeper.

In considering the meanings of *only* and *even*, one is tempted to say that they are, in some sense, opposites. Yet it is hard to put one's finger on the nature of this intuitive antonymy. From a purely truth conditional perspective, they do not appear to be antonyms at all, since it has been argued since Horn (1969), that whereas *only* has a significant truth conditional effect, *even* does not contribute to truth conditional meaning at all. We suggest that *only* and *even* might best be labeled PRAGMATIC ANTONYMS, and that their peculiar semantic difference (one has a truth conditional effect, the other apparently does not) simply mirrors their pragmatic functions.

If the function of exclusives is to comment on an overly strong expectation regarding the answer to the Current Question, the function of a scalar additive is to comment on an overly weak expectation. Thus whereas exclusives are inherently downward oriented in the sense that they declare a strong answer to be false in favor of something weaker, scalar additives are upward oriented, suggesting something stronger than what has been assumed or stated.

Let us consider an example, in (3.37), to be contrasted with the *only* sentence in (3.35), *David only wears a bow tie when [teaching]*$_F$, above.

(3.37)   David even wears a bow tie when [teaching]$_F$.

Someone uttering (3.35) seems to regard wearing a bow tie when teaching as a harmless enough little quirk, whereas someone uttering (3.37) might be taken to regard David as worryingly eccentric. So exclusives and scalar additives place quite different constraints on the scale of answers to the Current Question, and this can be exploited by speakers in order to convey what scale they think appropriate.

But ignoring such cases of exploitation, the basic observation illustrating the opposition between *only* and *even* is the following: whereas (3.35) is appropriate if wearing a bow tie when teaching is less, e.g., eccentric than had been expected or previously indicated, (3.37) is appropriate if wearing a bow tie when teaching is regarded as significantly more, e.g., eccentric than has been expected or previously indicated. It is this contrast that explains the feeling that *only* and *even* are opposites.

But now we might ask how come *even*, in contrast to *only*, does not have any truth conditional import? This difference relates directly to the fact that *even*, unlike *only*, is upward oriented. That is, *only* is inherently antagonistic, denying a proposition some would have thought true, and denying that such propositions should ever be added to the discourse record. On the other hand, because *even* is upward oriented, it adds monotonically to what is already assumed, and does not place any upper bound on what further answers to the Current Question might be true. That is not to say that a sentence with *even* does not contradict anything: *au contraire*, a sentence with *even* strongly conflicts with expectations. But what a sentence with *even* contradicts is a false belief about a putative upper bound to the Current Question. So it is upward monotonic in the sense that it allows for still stronger answers to the Current Question, and antagonistic only to the extent that it removes upper bounds.

Upward monotonicity is the unmarked case in natural language semantics: though a non-circular explanation of this fact is hard to come by, it seems clear that sentences are by default upward monotonic, and only downward monotonic when some special element is introduced, like negation. So the upward monotonicity of a sentence with *even* comes for free: there is no need for the operator *even* to convert the prejacent into an upward monotone proposition, since it is taken to be upward monotone by default.

And here is where the difference with *only* arises. The function of *only* is precisely to specify the type of upper bound that *even* removes, and that function can only be achieved by performing a semantic operation that converts an upward monotone proposition into a downward monotone proposition. Hence while *even* and *only* are opposites pragmatically, they are not opposites semantically: *even* has the trivial semantic effect of preserving the existing upward monotonicity of the prejacent, whereas *only* reverses it.[21]

Additives

While English has only one scalar additive, it has several NON-SCALAR ADDITIVES, including *too*, *also*, *as well*, *additionally*, *in addition*, as well as what we might term VAGUE ADDITIVES, such as *similarly*, *likewise* and *analogously*.[22] Consider (3.38a) and (3.38b), the former being taken from Kripke (1991):

(3.38) a. Tonight [Sam]$_F$ is having dinner in New York, too.

　　　b. Tonight Sam is having dinner in [New York]$_F$, too.

Additives have often been analyzed as carrying an existential presupposition, i.e. the proposition obtained by replacing the focused item with an existential. But as Kripke (1991) pointed out, this is not right. The relevant existential presupposition in this case would be that someone is having dinner in New York. However, this proposition is surely uncontroversial, so it might be expected that (3.38a) would be felicitous out of the blue. This is not the case: (3.38a) seems

---

[21] Much of the literature on *even* concerns the issue of whether *even* has the same sense when appearing in negative contexts as when appearing in positive contexts, or is ambiguous, and it is relevant here that many languages (e.g. German) use separate items in contexts corresponding to positive and negative uses of English *even*. Though this certainly relates to our discussion of the relationship between *only* and *even*, we will not pursue it here. For recent discussion, the reader is referred to Schwarz (2005).

[22] English *either* might also be considered an additive, though it would be better termed a NEGATIVE ADDITIVE. Also related to this class is *instead*, which could be labeled a MIXED ADDITIVE: if an ordinary non-scalar additive combines two positive propositions, a negative additive combines two negative propositions, then *instead* combines a negative proposition with a later positive proposition. We know of no reverse case, a particle which is found in a negative context, but which must have a positive antecedent.

to have a stronger requirement, a requirement that there is a specific salient instance of someone other than John having dinner in New York tonight. Similarly, (3.38b), with the focus marking shifted, presupposes that there is some place other than New York such that it is salient that Sam is having dinner there tonight.

Our framework provides a promising basis for explaining both the focus sensitivity of additives and the requirements they place on discourse. We propose that additives mark that the Current Question has already been partially answered, with the additional requirement that the pre-existing partial answer is not entailed by the prejacent. Additives, then, conventionally associate with focus, since the position of the focus is dependent on the Current Question.

For example, (3.38a) is congruent to the question *Who is having dinner in New York tonight?* The additive then says that this has been partially answered, i.e. there is a salient proposition in the common ground (typically because that proposition has just been expressed) which says of some individual that the individual is having dinner in New York tonight. Note that the requirement is intrinsically stronger than an existential, since the existential in question would not count as an answer to the Current Question at all: knowing that someone is having dinner in New York tonight does not imply knowing anything about *who* is having dinner in New York tonight.

Our analysis of the contribution of a non-scalar additive includes a requirement that the pre-existing partial answer is not entailed by the prejacent. The logic behind this can be seen from the oddity of the two following discourses:[23]

(3.39)   Sam is [happy]$_F$. # He's [ecstatic]$_F$ too.

(3.40)   Sam is happy. # [Sam and Jane]$_F$ are happy too.

Particularizers

Closely related to the additives, at least insofar as being generally non-scalar, are the PARTICULARIZERS, which include *such as, e.g., i.e., for example, for instance, in particular,* and *specifically,* and perhaps also *primarily,* and *predominantly,* though these have an additional INTENSIFYING function (see below). Focus sensitivity of these expressions is illustrated by (3.41a), which implies that Mary gave Fred something in addition to pizza, and (3.41b), which implies that Mary gave someone other than Fred pizza.

---

[23]   The requirement that the pre-existing partial answer is not entailed by the prejacent is implicit in the analysis of additives of Asher (2000) and Asher and Lascarides (1998). They take additives to mark a *parallel* discourse relation. If entailment was allowed, this would be hard to distinguish from the discourse relation they term ELABORATION. For further recent discussion of the presuppositions of additives, see Beaver and Zeevat (2007) (§3.3) and references therein.

(3.41) a.   For example, Mary gave Fred [pizza]$_F$.

   b.   For example, Mary gave [Fred]$_F$ pizza.

Use of a particularizer indicates that the speaker has already given reason to believe that he or she is in possession of an answer to the Current Question. Specific particularizers may then provide further information: e.g. the phrase *for example* indicates that the Current Question has multiple answers, and *specifically* indicates that the prejacent provides a precise, total answer to the Current Question.

Intensives

As discussed in the introduction to this book, intonation commonly conveys affect, e.g. uncertainty, deference, irony, and intensity. Intensity can be conveyed by, for example, increased pitch movements. There are also corresponding intensifying particles called INTENSIVES (e.g. Stoffel 1901; Bolinger 1972b; Quirk et al. 1985; Labov 1985; Ito and Tagliamonte 2003; and Potts 2006), e.g. *(most) importantly, significantly, especially, really, truly, fucking, damn, well*, and *totally*. We suggest that the function of an intensive is to indicate that the prejacent is a particularly notable answer to the Current Question by comparison with other alternatives. The naturally occurring examples in (3.42) illustrate the interaction with focus: in each case the writer has used capital letters to make explicit a focus in an intensive's scope:

(3.42) a.   "5 minutes away" aint a place mark ass. go read the other thread i fuckin gave the EXACT spot im gonna be ... shit man ...

   [web example]

   b.   OMG .. this fuckin video is hilarous .. everything about it ,, him being a drunk fuck , and tryn to resist ,, and then how he fuckin falls like a LOG .. omg

   [web example]

   c.   WHAT THE HECK!?!?! this post is apalling!! but hilarious!!!!!!! lol he fuckin gave ALL his info yo thats hysterical hahahaha WOA THERE BUDDY

   [web example]

   d.   MTV like totally gave us TWO episodes back to back! It was like so random. The more the merrier, but it's like waay too much for one recap.

   [web example]

   e.   I totally saw a guy get his head CUT RIGHT OFF out front of Chapters! Swear to God, man!

   [web example]

But are intensives really focus sensitive? This is a challenging question partly because the affect conveyed by intensives is difficult to gauge systematically, and partly because many of the intensifiers are very marked stylistically, as will be clear from the examples in (3.42), often having considerable social significance beyond their information structural effects.

Nonetheless, it is possible to test for the focus sensitivity of intensives. First, observe that (3.43a), which has no intensive, can be followed by either (3.43b) or (3.43c), and this would still be the case if the focus was shifted to *the purple vase* in this example.

(3.43) a. Mary gave [my mother]$_F$ the purple vase.
   b. Obviously, she had to give the purple vase to someone, but I can't believe it was my mother she gave it to.
   c. Obviously, she's always giving stuff to my mother, but I can't believe it was the purple vase she gave her.

Now we add the intensive *fucking* to the example, and manipulate the position of focus. In (3.44a) the intensive associates with the focus on *my mother*, indicating that it is particularly notable that she gave it to the speaker's mother, as opposed to someone else. The (c) answer now becomes marked, since it indicates, contrary to the (a) sentence, that there is nothing special about Mary giving stuff to the speaker's mother, but rather something notable about her giving the vase. By contrast, in (3.45a) the intensive associates with the focus on *the purple vase*. Now it is the (b) sentence that becomes marked, since it indicates that involvement of the speaker's mother was the notable part of the transaction, not the fact that it involved the purple vase.

(3.44) a. Mary fucking gave [my mother]$_F$ the purple vase.
   b. Obviously, she had to give the purple vase to someone, but I can't believe it was my mother she gave it to.
   c. # Obviously, she's always giving stuff to my mother, but I can't believe it was the purple vase she gave her.

(3.45) a. Mary fucking gave my mother [the purple vase]$_F$.
   b. # Obviously, she had to give the purple vase to someone, but I can't believe it was my mother she gave it to.
   c. Obviously, she's always giving stuff to my mother, but I can't believe it was the purple vase she gave her.

Downtoners

The last class we consider are the DOWNTONERS (e.g. Stoffel 1901; Bolinger 1972b; Quirk et al. 1985), which we split into two groups, MINIMIZING DOWN-TONERS and MAXIMIZING DOWNTONERS.

The minimizing downtoners include, e.g., *kind of, barely, hardly, at the very minimum, to say the least, at the very least,* and *scarcely*. The minimizing downtoners indicate that although the prejacent is not a very strong answer to the Current Question on the salient scale, it is compatible with what the speaker knows, i.e. that a stronger answer may hold. The interaction with focus can be illustrated using the same approach that we used above for intensives. While example (3.46a), which lacks a downtoner, can be felicitously followed by (3.46b) or (3.46c), the variant with a downtoner in (3.47a) is much more naturally followed by the (a) sentence than the (b) sentence. But shifting the focus, as in (3.48) reverses this pattern.

(3.46) a.   Kim fed [Fido]$_F$ Nutrapup.

       b.   And there's no way she fed Fido anything else.

       c.   And there's no way she fed it to any other dogs.

(3.47) a.   At the very least, Kim fed [Fido]$_F$ Nutrapup.

       b.   And there's no way she fed Fido anything else.

       c.   # And there's no way she fed it to any other dogs.

(3.48) a.   At the very least, Kim fed Fido [Nutrapup]$_F$.

       b.   # And there's no way she fed Fido anything else.

       c.   And there's no way she fed it to any other dogs.

Related to the minimizing downtoners are maximizing downtoners, a class we take to include *at the very most*, *at most*, *at a maximum*, *at best*, and a family of phrasal idioms like *the most you can say is* … These are downtoners insofar as they suggest that the prejacent they combine with is not a strong proposition: something stronger might have been the case, although in fact it is claimed that S is the strongest true answer to the Current Question. And it comes as no surprise that the maximizing downtoners display focus sensitivity, as in (3.49):

(3.49) a.   Kim at most fed [Fido]$_F$ Nutrapup (# and maybe Butch too).

       b.   Kim at most fed Fido [Nutrapup]$_F$ (and maybe Butch too).

We will not lay out in detail the explanation for the focus sensitivity of the maximizing downtoners, since it is not significantly different to that for other downtoners, or, for that matter, to the explanation for exclusives and additives. With regard to exclusives in particular, it is notable that the maximizing downtoners have a very similar truth-conditional effect, and it is appropriate to ask how exclusives and maximizing downtoners are related. Like exclusives, it is natural to use a maximizing downtoner when there is an expectation that something stronger than the prejacent is true on a salient scale, and, like an exclusive, a maximizing downtoner is used to deny that anything stronger than the prejacent is true. This parallelism is shown in (3.50).

(3.50) a.   Everyone thinks Kim earns 100K, but she only earns 90K.

b.   Everyone thinks Kim earns 100K, but at the very most she earns 90K.

However, there are subtle differences between exclusives and maximizing downtoners. While both classes are compatible with a prior expectation of something stronger than the prejacent, this is only a requirement of exclusives. As the contrast in (3.51) shows, a maximizing downtoner can be felicitous even when the most salient expectation is that the maximal true answer to the current question is weaker than the prejacent.

(3.51) a.   #Everyone thinks Kim earns 90K, and she only earns 100K.

b.   Everyone thinks Kim earns 90K, and at the very most she earns 100K.

Relatedly, the prejacent follows from a sentence with an exclusive, but not from a use of a maximizing downtoner. Indeed, it will be argued in Chapter 10 that exclusives presuppose that something at least as strong as the prejacent is true. Maximizing downtoners have no such presupposition. Thus from *she only earns 100K* in (3.51a), we would normally conclude that whoever is under discussion does earn 100K, but we would not conclude this from *at the very most she earns 100K* in (3.51b). The overall message is that exclusives and maximizing downtoners are semantically related, but that exclusives seem to impose stronger constraints on context, and carry stronger implications. So it would be reasonable to analyze exclusives as a subclass of maximizing downtoners which have some additional lexical specifications.

At this point, it is worth briefly returning to our claim of how *only* and *even* relate to each other. We want to observe that pairs of minimizing and maximizing downtoners like *at least* and *at most* stand in a precisely analogous relationship. It would seem completely unsurprising to informally label this pair *opposites*, but in that case we would not be describing a relationship between the truth conditional effects of the two operators. For, once again, while one of them (*at most*) has a significant truth conditional effect, the other (*at least*) has no discernable truth conditional effect as regards description of the world outside the conversation. In fact, looking at the effects on truth conditional semantics is misleading, for the *raison d'être* of downtoners is their discourse function. Whereas *at least* indicates that the Current Question remains open, *at most* indicates that it is closed. The pair are not opposites in a standard sense, but rather what we termed above *pragmatic antonyms*.

Moving up to a more general level, while we saw in the previous two sections that focus sensitivity does not imply conventional association with focus, what we have seen in this section is that a huge array of English expressions do manifest conventional association with focus. And the reason we find conventional association with focus in these cases is that they have a particular pragmatic function, namely to comment on the relationship of the prejacent to the Current Question.

3.5 Summary

This chapter has introduced at a superficial level an immense range of focus
sensitive expressions, which we have organized into a three way taxonomy
based on the mechanisms that produce the observed focus sensitivity. This taxonomy is summarized in Table 3.1.

The taxonomy has implications for the taxonomy of focus sensitive expressions cross-linguistically. For example, for Dutch, we would anticipate a similar
breakdown (see Foolen 1993). Thus the conventional association expressions
would include exhaustifiers (*alleen maar, slechts, maar, alleen, net*), the additive
scalar *zelfs*, non-scalar additives (*nog, ook*), and intensives (*vooral, zeker, wel,
zelfs*). It should be noted here that Dutch is very rich in these expressions, and
is also more liberal than English in allowing combinations of particles, so that
there are many more complex expressions which may conventionally associate
with focus on our analysis. The Dutch free association expressions would once
again include a range of quantificational adverbs (*altijd, gewoonlijk, zelden, nooit*,
etc.), generics, as well as various truth functional or rhetorical connectives
(*maar* as a conjunction, *omdat, als*).[24] Expressions for the quasi-association
category include *niet* ('not'), *of* ('or'), *scheinen/lijken* ('seem') and *geloven*
('believe').

It is now time to get more specific about focus interpretation and focus
sensitivity. Chapter 4 presents the compositional approach to focus interpretation, Alternative Semantics, on which the QFC theory is based. That approach
is compared to two other semantic theories of focus interpretation, Structured
Meanings and an events-based account. Chapter 5 discusses in detail two pragmatic accounts of focus sensitivity and contrasts them with the pragmatic

Table 3.1 The QFC taxonomy of focus sensitive expressions

Quasi-association	*Free association*	*Conventional association*
negation	q-adverbs	exclusives
disjunction	q-determiners	scalar additives
verbs of appearance	generics	non-scalar additives
modals	counterfactuals	particularizers
	reason clauses	minimizing downtoners
	emotive factives	maximizing downtoners
	verbs of desire	intensifiers
	modals (*via modal base*)	

---

[24] Perhaps *niet eens* ('not at all') and *gewoon* ('as usual'), which are common in colloquial Dutch
and distributed similarly to the conventional association expressions listed above, belong in the
conventional association class.

framework that we adopt in this book. In Chapter 6, we show that the most substantive argument against grammaticalized dependency on focus, the argument from Second Occurrence Focus, is bogus.

In Chapters 6–8 we also present a great deal of positive evidence showing that the dependency of exclusives on focus is very robust. If you take a sentence which has an exclusive with a focus in its scope, and you manipulate the sentence by reducing or removing the focus, you immediately lose readings or produce infelicity. And where the restrictor of an exclusive is at stake, presupposition never trumps focus: for exclusives, there simply is no phenomenon of association with presupposition. In Chapter 8 we show that the fact that Negative Polarity Items (NPIs) are licensed in non-focal positions in the scope of exclusives, but not in focal positions, demonstrates that non-focal material is grammatically constrained to limit the restrictor of the exclusive, while focal material only affects the scope. Furthermore, the lexicalized focus sensitivity of exclusives is not a peculiarity of English: our data shows that it extends at least to a range of Germanic and Romance languages.

Having painstakingly marshalled the evidence that exclusives, unlike quantificational adverbs, have a conventionalized dependency on focus, in Chapters 9 and 10 we develop in more detail an account of their meaning and function. We will argue that this account of exclusives provides a significant empirical improvement over its predecessors. What we cannot argue is that the detailed account of exclusives in and of itself justifies the explanations we have given for all the other expression types discussed in this section. But we hope, at the very least, that the evidence we will present in the remainder of this book will give both the taxonomy and the explanations we have given in this chapter considerable plausibility.

Chapter 4

Compositional Analysis of Focus

"[rational discourse] is composed of words, and each word is a thought-symbol."
Aristotle, 350 BC, *On Sense and the Sensible*, translated by J. I. Beare

4.1 Introduction

Rooth's (1985, 1992) Alternative Semantics provides the mechanism for interpreting focus on which the QFC theory is based. In this chapter, we elaborate on the presentation of Alternative Semantics in Chapter 2, stating precisely how it can be incorporated in a compositional grammar, comparing Alternative Semantics to two other compositional accounts of focus interpretation, and defending Alternative Semantics in the face of some seemingly damning objections.

The compositional presentation of Alternative Semantics, for which the reader will need some background in lambda calculus, and in possible worlds semantics, is presented in §4.2. The two alternatives to Alternative Semantics we will discuss are Structured Meanings (e.g. Jacobs 1983; von Stechow 1991; Krifka 1991) in §4.3, and an events-based account (e.g. Bonomi and Casalegno 1993 and Herburger 2000) in §4.4. We show in §4.5 that the frameworks are closely related, though there are subtle differences in expressivity, Alternative Semantics in its standard form being slightly less expressive (or, equivalently, more restrictive) than the other frameworks.

However, of greater importance for the QFC theory is the natural way that Alternative Semantics lends itself to a theory of the pragmatics of questions and answers: we suggest that in an account of the role of focus and focus sensitivity in discourse, this provides a clear motivation for using Alternative Semantics rather than the other frameworks.

Empirical arguments that Alternative Semantics cannot adequately model focus sensitivity are discussed in §4.6. We show that these arguments do not hold up to scrutiny.

4.2 Compositional Alternative Semantics

Summary: *We present Alternative Semantics, the approach to focus interpretation that we adopt in this book. We give compositional analyses of sentences in which focus does and does not affect truth conditions.*

We will now fill in some of the details of the Alternative Semantics model, and show how it can be used within a compositional grammar.

From the examples that Rooth (1992) gives, he takes proper names simply to pick out individuals, and transitive verbs to map pairs of individuals to propositions. Rooth does not say what a proposition is, a point to which we will return, but for the sake of concreteness, let us take propositions to correspond to (characteristic functions of) sets of worlds, and give them the standard Montagovian type $\langle s, t \rangle$. Taking e as the type of individuals, a transitive verb has as its intension (and here we depart from Montague 1973) something of type $\langle s, \langle e, \langle e, t \rangle \rangle \rangle$.

As a warm up exercise let us consider the compositional analysis of a sentence in which focus does not affect the truth conditions, (4.1).

(4.1)   Sandy met [Bush]$_\text{F}$.

In the intensional semantics we adopt, every constituent α in a syntactic tree has an intension $[\![\alpha]\!]^I$. Suppose that for some constituent we would expect the ordinary extensional meaning to be in some domain. For example, the extension of a proper name might be an individual, and the extension of a sentence is standardly a truth value. Then, again quite standardly, the intension is a function from possible worlds to that domain. For example, if the name *Bush* picks out the same individual B in all worlds, i.e. it is a rigid designator in the sense of Kripke (1980), then the intension $[\![Bush]\!]^I = \lambda w.B$.[1]

In the case of a complex phrase, we must use a form of function application that operates on intensions. Since we are not interested in intensional predicates *per se*, in most cases we will assume that the predicate is underlyingly extensional, and so combine a predicate α and an argument β as follows: $[\![\alpha\,\beta]\!]^I = \lambda w.[\![\alpha]\!]^I(w)([\![\beta]\!]^I(w))$. (4.2), then, is the derivation of the meaning of (4.1).

(4.2)   *Intension of "Sandy met [Bush]$_\text{F}$":*

$$[\![met]\!]^I = meet$$
$$[\![[Bush]_\text{F}]\!]^I = \lambda w.B$$
$$[\![met\ [Bush]_\text{F}]\!]^I = \lambda w\ [[\![met]\!]^I(w)(B)]$$
$$[\![Sandy]\!]^I = \lambda w.S$$
$$[\![Sandy\ met\ [Bush]_\text{F}]\!]^I = \lambda w\ [[\![met]\!]^I(w)(B)(S)]$$

---

[1] Making names into rigid designators is an oversimplification, since Kripke's arguments only show that names behave rigidly under considerations of metaphysical possibility, not under epistemic modalities. That is, while Kripke may be right in saying that Bush could not have been Kerry (a metaphysical assertion), it may well be the case that somebody mistakenly believes that Bush and Kerry are the same person.

We adopt a convention that the intension of a predicate is written as the italicized base-form of the predicate, as in the first line of (4.2). Also, for any verbal predicate we will adopt a further notation convention according to which the arguments are written as a tuple, the first element of which is a world parameter, and the remaining elements of which are presented in the standard order of arguments in English, so $\lambda w[[\text{met}]^I(w)(B)(S)]$ can be rewritten as $\lambda w.\text{meet}(w, S, B)$.[2]

Although focus does not affect the truth conditions of (4.1), focus still has interpretational significance. On Rooth's account, the positioning of focus determines for each constituent an alternative set. We will write the alternative set of a given phrase α as $[\![\alpha]\!]^A$, and calculate alternatives as follows:

(4.3) a.   The alternative set for an unfocused atomic constituent is the singleton set containing the intension of that constituent.

  b.   If a constituent is focused, then the alternative set will be a set of objects that have the same type as the intension of the focused constituent.

  c.   If an NP having intension $\langle w, e \rangle$ is focused, the alternatives will be all the constant functions from worlds to individuals, i.e. the functions that behave like rigidly designating names.

  d.   If a phrase α with extensional predicate β and argument γ is not itself focused, then $[\![\alpha]\!]^A = \lambda P[\exists a \in [\![\beta]\!]^A, b \in [\![\gamma]\!]^A \ P = \lambda w.a(w)(b(w))]$

We can apply these rules in the case of (4.1) as in the following derivation:

(4.4)   *Alternative set of "Sandy met [Bush]_F":*

$$[[\text{Bush}]_F]^A = \lambda X[\text{rigid}(X)]$$
$$[\![\text{met}]\!]^A = \lambda P[P = [\![\text{met}]\!]^I]$$
$$[\![\text{met } [\text{Bush}]_F]\!]^A = \lambda P[\exists X \ \text{rigid}(X) \wedge$$
$$P = \lambda w[[\text{met}]^I(w)(X(w))]]$$
$$[\![\text{Sandy}]\!]^A = \lambda P[P = \lambda w[S]]$$
$$[\![\text{Sandy met } [\text{Bush}]_F]\!]^A = \lambda \phi[\exists X \ \text{rigid}(X) \wedge$$
$$\phi = \lambda w.\text{meet}(w, S, X(w))]$$

So the alternative set for *Sandy met [Bush]_F* is a set of propositions corresponding to sentences of the form *Sandy met X*, where each X is a rigidly designating name, and there is one such name for every individual in the domain. We can simplify this one stage further. To do so, we use that fact that by definition the rigid individual concepts of type $\langle s, e \rangle$, i.e. functions from worlds to individuals, stand in one-to-one correspondence with the individuals of type e.

---

[2] We simplify by ignoring the semantic contribution of tense morphology.

This means that the alternative set in the last line of (4.4) can be simplified to: $\lambda\phi[\exists x\ \phi = \lambda w.meet(w, S, x)]$.

We now consider a derivation in which focus does affect truth conditions, that for (4.5).

(4.5)   Sandy only met [Bush]$_F$.

Whereas other predicates in the fragment operate on the extensions of their arguments, a focus sensitive operator needs to get ahold of its argument's intension, and not only that, it also needs to get ahold of its argument's alternative set. For this we use a special semantic rule:

(4.6) $[\![\text{op VP}]\!]^I = \lambda w[op(w, [\![\text{VP}]\!]^I, [\![\text{VP}]\!]^A)]$, where op is, e.g., *only*

We will also need a special rule for the alternative set, and will adopt one of several possibilities:

(4.7) $[\![\text{op VP}]\!]^A = [\![\text{VP}]\!]^A$

This rule says that the alternative set of a sentence with a focus sensitive operator is the same as the alternative set for the same sentence minus the operator. Given that the alternative set is used to determine which questions a sentence can answer, this rule could explain why a sentence with *only* can be used to answer the same questions as the same sentence without *only*.

For the analysis of (4.5), the intensions and alternative sets of everything up to the level of the VP *met [Bush]*$_F$ are as for (4.1), shown in (4.2) and (4.4), above. Furthermore, since the VP with the focus sensitive operator simply inherits the alternative set of the VP the operator modifies, the alternative set of the whole sentence is also the same as that for (4.5). It remains only to calculate the intension of the VP with *only*, and the intension of the whole sentence:

(4.8)   *Intension of "Sandy only met [Bush]$_F$":*

$$[\![\text{only met [Bush]}_F]\!]^I$$
$$= \lambda y.\lambda w.\forall P\ [\![\text{met [Bush]}_F]\!]^A(P) \wedge P(y)(w) \rightarrow$$
$$P = [\![\text{met [Bush]}_F]\!]^I$$
$$[\![\text{Sandy only met [Bush]}_F]\!]^I$$
$$= \lambda w.\forall P\ [\![\text{met [Bush]}_F]\!]^A(P) \wedge P(S)(w) \rightarrow$$
$$P = [\![\text{met [Bush]}_F]\!]^I$$
$$= \lambda w.\forall P\exists X\ \text{rigid}(X) \wedge P = \lambda y.\lambda w[[\![\text{met}]\!]^I(w)(X(w))(y)]\wedge$$
$$P(S)(w) \rightarrow P = \lambda y.\lambda w[[\![\text{met}]\!]^I(w)(B)(y)]$$
$$= \lambda w.\forall x\ [meet(w, S, x) \rightarrow$$
$$\lambda y.\lambda w\ [meet(w, y, x)] = \lambda y.\lambda w\ [meet(w, y, B)]]$$

In the derivation in (4.8), it can be seen that a compositional analysis based on Rooth's proposals yields meanings a step away from the intuitive first order meanings we would expect. However, by placing constraints on the possible denotations of transitive verbs, we can derive more palatable meanings. In the case of (4.5) what we require is that the property of meeting one individual is identical to the property of meeting another individual if and only if the individuals are identical. This boils down to the MEETING IDENTITY POSTULATE in (4.9):

(4.9)   *Meeting identity postulate*:

$$\forall y, z \ (\lambda x.\lambda w[meet(w, x, y)] = \lambda x.\lambda w[meet(w, x, z)]) \leftrightarrow (y = z)$$

By applying the meeting identity postulate we can simplify the meaning in (4.8), and this gives us the intuitively correct first order meaning relative to a world, w:

(4.10)   *Simplified intension of "Sandy only met [Bush]$_F$"*:

$$[\![\text{Sandy only met [Bush]}_F]\!]^I (w) = \forall x \ meet(w, S, x) \rightarrow x = B$$

Summing up, in this section we gave a compositional presentation of Alternative Semantics, the approach to focus interpretation that we adopt in this book. We considered compositional analyses of sentences in which focus does and does not affect the truth conditions. In the next section, we describe another major semantic approach to focus interpretation, Structured Meanings.

4.3   Structured Meanings

Summary: *We present the Structured Meanings approach to focus interpretation. The interpretations involved in Structured Meanings involve two components, a background and foreground. As in the previous section, we consider compositional analyses of sentences in which focus does and does not affect the truth conditions.*

Structured Meanings, like the interpretations involved in Alternative Semantics, involve two components. But, as we described in Chapter 2, Structured Meanings cut the pie differently.

In Alternative Semantics one meaning component is the standard meaning, and the other component is a special focus value. But neither component of a Structured Meaning individually carries the complete content of the standard meaning. Rather, the two components represent a question and a short answer, or, as we will now refer to them, a *background* and a *foreground* (usually referred to as *background/focus*).

The standard meaning is obtained by applying the background to the foreground. For example, we can represent the Structured Meaning of *Mary kissed [the boy scouts]*$_F$ extensionally (i.e. ignoring possible worlds) as (4.11), where the background is the property of being kissed by Mary $\lambda x.kiss(m, x)$, and the foreground is the largest plurality of boy scouts in the domain $\iota\ boy-scouts$ (Chierchia 1998: 346).

(4.11) $\langle \lambda x.kiss(m,x), \iota\ boy\text{-}scouts \rangle$

Applying the first member of the pair in (4.11) to the second generates the standard meaning, i.e. $kiss(m, \iota\ boy-scouts)$.

It should be obvious how focus is interpreted here: anything marked as focal ends up in the foreground component of meaning, and everything else ends up in the background. There are two main complications. First, it might be that a focused expression is a predicate which has a non-focal expression as an argument, as in *Mary [kissed]$_F$ the boy scouts*. In this case the Structured Meaning should be $\langle \lambda P.P(m, \iota\ boy-scouts), kiss \rangle$. The interpretation procedure needs to be set up in such a way that backgrounded arguments, here *Mary* and *the boy scouts*, are type raised so as to become predicates.

The second complication is that there may be multiple (and possibly discontinuous) foci, as in:

(4.12)   Mary introduced [Bill]$_F$ to [Sam]$_F$.

In Alternative Semantics, this sentence would yield the set of propositions P involving two individuals such that P is the proposition that Mary introduced the first to the second. To deal with this type of example with Structured Meanings, Krifka (1991) adds compound objects to the formalism. In our notation, the list $\langle b, s \rangle$, i.e the pair of Bill and Sam, will denote such an object. We then add abstraction over lists, e.g. formulae $\lambda \langle x, y \rangle.P(x, y)$, so that (4.12) may be represented as follows:

(4.13) $\langle \lambda \langle x, y \rangle.introduce(m, x, y), \langle b, s \rangle \rangle$.

We now need a way to combine Structured Meanings compositionally. It is helpful to have a way of putting lists together, so we will assume that $\sqcap$ concatenates lists in the obvious way:

(4.14) $(\langle x_1, \ldots, x_i \rangle \sqcap \langle y_1, \ldots, y_j \rangle = \langle x_1, \ldots, x_i, y_1, \ldots, y_j \rangle.)$

Now suppose that we have two sister phrases A and B which in a standard grammar would have combined by application of the meaning of A to that of B, and suppose that they have Structured Meanings $\langle \alpha_b, \alpha_f \rangle$ and $\langle \beta_b, \beta_f \rangle$, respectively. Then the structured meaning of the phrase AB will be: $\langle \lambda[x, y].\alpha_b(x)(\beta_b(y)), \alpha_f \sqcap \beta_f \rangle$. This will be the method of combination for all expressions which are not focus sensitive.

We will assume that vacuous abstraction and application have no effect. So $\lambda \langle\ \rangle \phi = \phi$, meaning that abstracting over an empty list of variables has the same effect as not abstracting at all. Similarly, applying a function to an empty list will also have no effect: $\phi(\langle\ \rangle) = \phi$. We will also adopt an idiosyncratic bracketing abbreviation that makes derivations run in a visually appealing way: "$\langle \phi$" will abbreviate the pair of ϕ and the empty list, "$\langle \phi, \langle\ \rangle \rangle$", a Structured Meaning with a background but no focus. Similarly "$\phi\rangle$" will abbreviate "$\langle\lambda X.X, \phi\rangle$", in which the background is trivial (X having the same type as ϕ). These conventions enable us to represent a purely focus object as "$\phi\rangle$", and a purely background object as "$\langle\phi$".

In (4.15), *Butch* has a purely background meaning $\langle b$ but focus converts this to a purely foreground meaning $b\rangle$. The predicate *fed* again has a purely background meaning $\langle fed$, and this combined with the meaning of [Butch]$_F$ in the obvious way to form $\langle fed, b\rangle$, with the background predicate *fed* and the foreground b. The rest of the derivation proceeds by the addition of extra background material.

(4.15)   *Structured Meaning of "Sam fed [Butch]$_F$ Nutrapup":*

$$\text{Butch} \mapsto \langle b$$

$$[\text{Butch}]_F \mapsto b\rangle$$

$$\text{fed} \mapsto \langle fed$$

$$\text{fed [Butch]}_F \mapsto \langle fed, b\rangle$$

$$\text{Nutrapup} \mapsto \langle n$$

$$\text{fed [Butch]}_F \text{ Nutrapup} \mapsto \langle \lambda\beta.fed(\beta)(n), b\rangle$$

$$\text{Sam} \mapsto \langle s$$

$$\text{Sam fed [Butch]}_F \text{ Nutrapup} \mapsto \langle \lambda\beta.fed(\beta)(n)(s), b\rangle$$

Having seen how we can compositionally derive the Structured Meaning of a focused sentence, next up is an analysis of focus sensitivity. Once again, we will use VP *only* as an illustration. To simplify, we will temporarily assume that the meaning of a phrase *only VP* is completely backgrounded, as if *only* used up the focus so that it was not available for further focus sensitive operators.[3]

The interpretation of *only* proceeds just as might be expected. It takes as arguments a Structured Meaning (α) corresponding to a VP, and an individual (x) corresponding to the subject. After combining with these arguments, the result says that anything you can apply the background (B) to, so as to create a property holding of the subject, must be identical to the foreground (F):[4]

---

[3] Krifka (1991: 131) discusses cases where two focus sensitive operators such as *even* and *only* share the same focus associate, as in (i), and shows how Structured Meanings can account for these cases compositionally:

  (i) [At yesterday's party, people stayed with their first choice of drink. Bill only drank WINE, Sue only drank BEER, and]
       John even$_1$ only$_2$ drank [WATER]$_{F1, F2}$

[4] Note that strictly speaking in a standardly typed lambda calculus, the meaning given for VP *only* is not a single meaning but a template, since the type of the variables (e.g. γ) in the definition is not fixed.

(4.16)   A Structured Meaning for VP *only*
$$\lambda\langle B, F\rangle.\langle\lambda x.\forall\gamma B(\gamma)(x)\rightarrow\gamma = F$$

We can now slot the meaning of *only* into the derivation above to get the interpretation of *Sam only fed [Butch]*$_F$ *Nutrapup* in (4.17):

(4.17)   *Structured meaning of "Sam only fed [Butch]*$_F$ *Nutrapup":*

$$only \mapsto \lambda\langle B, F\rangle.\langle\lambda x\forall\gamma\ B(\gamma)(x)\rightarrow\gamma = F$$
$$only\ fed\ [Butch]_F\ N \mapsto \langle\lambda x\forall\gamma\ [\lambda\beta.fed(\beta)(n)]\,(\gamma)(x)\rightarrow\gamma = b$$
$$= \langle\lambda x\forall\gamma\ fed(\gamma)(n)(x)\rightarrow\gamma = b$$
$$Sam \mapsto \langle s$$
$$Sam\ only\ fed\ [Butch]_F\ N \mapsto \langle\forall\gamma\ fed(\gamma)(n)(s)\rightarrow\gamma = b$$

In sum, in this section we described the Structured Meaning approach to focus interpretation. Like Alternative Semantics, the interpretations involved in Structured Meanings consist of two components, a background and foreground. In contrast to Alternative Semantics, neither component of a Structured Meaning is the standard meaning. Rather, the standard meaning is obtained by applying the background component to the foreground. As in the previous section, we considered compositional analyses of sentences in which focus does and does not affect the truth conditions. In the next section, we describe a third semantic approach to focus interpretation, an events-based account.

4.4   Focus with Events

Summary: *We present the events-based account of focus interpretation. As in the previous two sections, we examine compositional analyses of sentences in which focus does and does not affect the truth conditions.*

Bonomi and Casalegno (1993) and Herburger (2000) model focus sensitivity in neo-Davidsonian frameworks which make essential use of a semantic type of *events*. There are two main advantages to using events. First, events allow fine-grained distinctions to be made between the meanings of expressions that might be equivalent in a traditional Montagovian account which distinguishes propositions in terms of possible worlds. Second, as Davidson (1967) first showed, use of an event argument can simplify the syntax–semantics interface: this becomes even clearer when focus is involved. The presentation we now give is loosely modeled on that of Bonomi and Casalegno (1993), though we simplify somewhat.

Let us start with a model including events, and a distinguished type of events in our semantic representation language with helpfully named variables like *e*. We use the word *events* in a broad sense which includes both states and events, a combined class some authors refer to as *eventualities* (e.g Bach 1981,

1986; Parsons 1990). A verb provides a predication over events, so that in the sentence *Sandy met Bush*, the semantic contribution of the verb, *met*, is an *event description*. An event description can be thought of as a set of events, but strictly, it is the characteristic function of a set of events, i.e. a function from events to truth values. We can equivalently write $\lambda e.met(e)$ to make the eventive nature of the verb explicit.

The connection between verbs and arguments is mediated by thematic predicates, so that in the same example (*Sandy met Bush*) *Sandy* contributes another event description AGENT(s), or, equivalently $\lambda e.$AGENT(s)(e), and *Bush* contributes THEME(b). So the thematic predicates AGENT and THEME are functions from individuals to event descriptions. We assume that in some way the syntax decides what the appropriate thematic predicate is.

Thus, like many prior authors working in event frameworks, we skirt over one of the toughest issues in event semantics, the process that identifies the right thematic relation, and thus differentiates between the thematic predicate assigned to the subject of *met* (AGENT), and the thematic predicate of the subject of an unaccusative verb like *arrive* (say, THEME).

As in Heim and Kratzer (1998), we assume two basic compositional rules, one for function application, and a second rule for putting together two set-like objects of the same type by the lambda analogue of set intersection. It is this latter rule that is used to combine event descriptions. As is standard, we assume that existential closure takes place at a clausal level to bind off the event description, and we will treat tense as performing this function (as well as adding further temporal information, which we omit). We then have the derivation in (4.18), in which $[\![E]\!]^O$ is the ordinary semantic value of E:

(4.18)   *An eventful ordinary semantic value of "Sandy met [Bush]*$_F$*"*:

$$[\![\text{Sandy}]\!]^O = \lambda e.\text{AG}(e, s)$$
$$[\![[\text{Bush}]_F]\!]^O = \lambda e.\text{TH}(e, b)$$
$$[\![\text{meet}]\!]^O = meet$$
$$[\![\text{meet } [\text{Bush}]_F]\!]^O = \lambda e.meet(e) \wedge \text{TH}(e, b)$$
$$[\![\text{Sandy meet } [\text{Bush}]_F]\!]^O = \lambda e.\text{AG}(e, s) \wedge meet(e) \wedge \text{TH}(e, b)$$
$$[\![\text{Sandy met } [\text{Bush}]_F]\!]^O = \exists e\,\text{AG}(e, s) \wedge meet(e) \wedge \text{TH}(e, b)$$

How do we add focus to an events-based grammar like that we have just described? Potentially, we might use either Alternative Semantics or Structured Meanings, but Bonomi and Casalegno do not exactly do either: their system has some properties of each of those approaches.

Like these two frameworks, the Bonomi and Casalegno proposal includes two meaning components, and, as in Alternative Semantics, one of these components is the ordinary (though event-based) meaning of the expression. The other component, however, is not a set of alternative propositions, since it is given the same type as the main meaning. Rather, the second component is a less specified variant of the main meaning, a variant which only carries semantic information corresponding to the backgrounded part of the sentence. So we will refer to it as the background meaning, denoted $[\![E]\!]^B$ for an expression E.

For the cases we will consider, it suffices to assume that background meanings are propagated exactly like ordinary meanings, except that (i) focused expressions which normally denote an event description instead contribute a trivial event description $\lambda e.T$,[5] and (ii) modifiers contribute only the identity function of an appropriate type, i.e. $\lambda X.X$. As should be clear from the derivation in (4.19), in effect the contribution of focused elements is simply missing from the background meaning:

(4.19)   *An eventful background semantic value of "Sandy met [Bush]$_F$":*

$$[\![Sandy]\!]^B = \lambda e.\text{AG}(e,s)$$
$$[\![[Bush]_F]\!]^B = \lambda e.T$$
$$[\![meet]\!]^B = meet$$
$$[\![meet\ [Bush]_F]\!]^B = \lambda e.meet(e) \wedge T$$
$$= \lambda e.meet(e)$$
$$[\![Sandy\ meet\ [Bush]_F]\!]^B = \lambda e.\text{AG}(e,s) \wedge meet(e)$$
$$[\![Sandy\ met\ [Bush]_F]\!]^B = \exists e\text{AG}(e,s) \wedge meet(e)$$

We can now apply this type of analysis to *only*. In the following definition VP *only* first takes two arguments. The first is a pair α consisting of an ordinary VP meaning and a background VP meaning, and the second is an event description corresponding to the denotation of the subject. The result is an event description, true of an event if (i) it satisfies the backgrounded and subject material, and (ii) any event that satisfies the subject and backgrounded material also satisfies the focal material.

(4.20)   *An eventful meaning for VP "only" (v.1)*
$$\lambda\langle O, B\rangle.\lambda P.\lambda e.P(e) \wedge \alpha_B(e) \wedge \forall e'(P(e) \wedge B(e)) \rightarrow O(e)$$

The ordinary meaning for *only meet [Bush]$_F$* is (4.21):

(4.21)   *An eventful ordinary semantic value of "only meet [Bush]$_F$":*

$$[\![only\ meet\ [Bush]_F]\!]^O = \lambda P.\lambda e[P(e) \wedge [\![meet\ [Bush]_F]\!]^B \wedge$$
$$\forall e'[(P(e') \wedge [\![meet\ [Bush]_F]\!]^B(e'))$$
$$\rightarrow [\![meet\ [Bush]_F]\!]^O(e')]]$$

---

[5] T is a tautology along the lines of $X = X$.

In (4.22), the ordinary semantic value of *Sandy* is combined with the ordinary meaning of *only meet [Bush]*$_F$.

(4.22)   *An eventful ordinary semantic value of "Sandy only meet [Bush]$_F$":*

$$[\![\text{Sandy only meet [Bush]}_F]\!]^O$$
$$= \lambda e[[\![\text{Sandy}]\!]^O(e) \wedge [\![\text{meet [Bush]}_F]\!]^B \wedge$$
$$\forall e'[([\![\text{Sandy}]\!]^O(e') \wedge [\![\text{meet [Bush]}_F]\!]^B(e'))$$
$$\rightarrow [\![\text{meet [Bush]}_F]\!]^O(e')]]$$
$$= \lambda e[\text{AG}(e, s) \wedge meet(e) \wedge$$
$$\forall e'[(\text{AG}(e', s) \wedge meet(e'))$$
$$\rightarrow (\text{AG}(e', s) \wedge meet(e') \wedge \text{TH}(e', b))]]$$
$$= \lambda e[\text{AG}(e, s) \wedge meet(e) \wedge$$
$$\forall e'[(\text{AG}(e', s) \wedge meet(e'))$$
$$\rightarrow \text{TH}(e', b)]]$$

As noted above, tense performs the function of binding of the event description. This is shown in (4.23).

(4.23)   *An eventful ordinary semantic value of "Sandy only met [Bush]$_F$":*

$$[\![\text{Sandy only met [Bush]}_F]\!]^O = \exists e[\text{AG}(e, s) \wedge meet(e) \wedge$$
$$\forall e'[(\text{AG}(e', s) \wedge meet(e'))$$
$$\rightarrow \text{TH}(e', b)]]$$

Summing up, in this section we explored the events-based approach to focus interpretation. The model that we presented was loosely based on the approach of Bonomi and Casalegno (1993). Like the other two approaches to focus interpretation we have considered in this chapter, the events-based approach includes two meaning components. As in Alternative Semantics, one of these components is the standard meaning. However, unlike Alternative Semantics, the other component is a less specified variant of the standard meaning which only carries the semantic information corresponding to the backgrounded part of the sentence. As in the previous two sections, we considered compositional analyses of sentences in which focus does and does not affect the truth conditions. In the next section, we show that the three approaches to focus interpretation that we have examined in this chapter are closely related, and argue that Alternative Semantics is more restrictive than the other two frameworks and provides a better framework for describing how focus functions in discourse.

4.5 Relating the Frameworks

Summary: *We show that the three frameworks for focus interpretation that we have considered in this chapter are closely related. Though there are subtle differences in expressivity, Alternative Semantics in its standard form is slightly more restrictive than the other two frameworks. Once we get to the discourse level, Alternative Semantics has major advantages over Structured Meanings and events-based approaches to focus interpretation. In particular, Alternative Semantics provides an algebraic, model-theoretic measure of information.*

We have now shown how focus sensitivity can be modeled compositionally in three frameworks. Which is best? Both Rooth (1992) and Krifka (2006) have observed that Alternative Semantics is more restrictive than Structured Semantics, and both endorse the view that if two frameworks are both capable of accounting for the data at hand, then the more restrictive framework is to be preferred on methodological grounds. Let us consider in what sense Alternative Semantics is more restrictive.

First, and as e.g. Krifka (2006: 110) remarks, it is simple to recover the Alternative Semantics meaning pair from the Structured Meanings pair, though this assumes that the Structured Meaning is intensional. Assume all predicates in the Structured Meaning representation have an argument place for a possible world, and that this is filled by a free variable w. If we have a Structured Meaning $\langle B(w), F(w)\rangle$, then the intensional ordinary meaning is $\lambda w.B(w)(F(w))$, and the Alternative Semantics focus meaning is $\lambda p\,[p = \lambda w \exists X B(w)(X(w))]$, as in (4.24), where X has the same type as F:

(4.24)   *Mapping from Structured Meaning to Alternative Semantics representation:*

$\langle B(w), F(w)\rangle \mapsto$
Ordinary meaning: $\lambda w.B(w)(F(w))$
Focus meaning: $\lambda p\,[p = \lambda w \exists X B(w)(X(w))]$

So, we can get from a Structured Meaning to an Alternative Semantics representation of the meaning of the same expression. But can we go the other way? No, not with full generality: the above function to Alternative Semantics meanings does not have an inverse. Consider, e.g., the rather artificial Structured Meaning $\langle \lambda x.P(w,a), b\rangle$. Mapping this to Alternative Semantics as above gives the ordinary meaning $\lambda w.P(w,a)$ and the focal meaning $\lambda p\,[p = \lambda w.P(w,a)]$. Since neither the ordinary meaning nor the focal meaning include the constant b, clearly the original Structured Meaning cannot be recovered from the Alternative Semantics representation.

Furthermore, the mapping from Structured Meaning to Alternative Semantics that we used in (4.24) was not arbitrary: for a given expression, taking the Structured Meaning and applying the mapping does take us to what we would expect to get by applying Alternative Semantics directly, so we conclude that the Structured Meaning representation for an expression conveys strictly more information than an Alternative Semantics representation of the meaning of the same expression.[6]

How does the event semantics model compare? To answer this question fully would require a mapping between meaning representations with events and meaning representations without, and this is too tall an order for the current book. However, we can compare the models from an architectural level, and identify several similarities and differences.

First, for all three models the analysis of focus requires access to a fine-grained notion of proposition. In Alternative Semantics propositions are distinguished using possible worlds, in Structured Meanings propositions are distinguished using a special level of function argument structure, and in the events-based model propositions are distinguished (obviously) by event structure. (4.25)–(4.27) give the meaning of *Sandy met [Bush]*$_F$ in all three approaches. (4.25a) is the ordinary meaning in Alternative Semantics; (4.25b) is the representation for the alternatives. (4.26) is the Structured Meaning representation. (4.27a) is the ordinary semantic value in the events-based model; (4.27b) is the background semantic value.

(4.25) *Alternative Semantics meaning of "Sandy met [Bush]*$_F$*":*
    a.   Ordinary meaning: $\lambda w.meet(w, S, B)$
    b.   Alternative set: $\lambda\phi[\exists X \text{ rigid}(X) \wedge \phi = \lambda w.meet(w, S, X(w))$

(4.26) *Structured Meaning of "Sandy met [Bush]*$_F$*":*
    $\langle\lambda\beta.meet(\beta)(s), b\rangle$

(4.27) *Eventful meaning of "Sandy met [Bush]*$_F$*":*
    a.   Eventful ordinary semantic value: $\exists e\text{AG}(e, s) \wedge meet(e) \wedge \text{TH}(e, b)$
    b.   Eventful background semantic value: $\exists e\text{AG}(e, s) \wedge meet(e)$

Second, all three models use two meaning components. In Structured Meanings these correspond to the background and foreground, as illustrated in (4.26). Alternative Semantics and the events-based model both take as one component the ordinary meaning, which (assuming other aspects of the semantics are held constant) is recoverable from a Structured Meaning by combining the Background and Foreground (see (4.25a) and (4.27a), respectively). Ignoring context, Alternative Semantics and the events-based model both take as their second

---

[6] A proof of this would require rigorous statement of Alternative Semantics and Structured Meaning translation functions over the same syntactic fragment, but we attempt no such proof here. Let us note one further reason to be cautious: it may seem that we have shown that Alternative Semantics representations are inherently less expressive than Structured Semantics representations, but this is not in fact what we have shown. We have merely shown that one mapping from Structured Semantics to Alternative Semantics does not have an inverse. An infinite number of meaning representations are possible in each framework, and from a mathematical perspective simply knowing that there exists an inverse-less function from one infinite set to another does not reveal much about the relative nature of the two sets. The reason the mapping we used is significant is that it is not just an arbitrary function between two sets of representations. Rather it is intended to map the Structured Meaning of an expression onto the Alternative Semantics of *the same* expression.

component something derived from background material alone, and thus comparable to the second component of the Structured Meaning model (see (4.25b) and (4.27b), respectively).

Third, the three models differ in their intertranslatability. In general, we would not expect Structured Meanings to be recoverable from the representations in the two other frameworks, because the actual focus meaning cannot necessarily be recovered from the ordinary meaning and the background meaning. In this sense, Structured Meanings is the least restrictive of the three frameworks as regards the possible interactions with focus it could be used to describe (Rooth 1996a: 278; see Chapter 2). If we ignore inherently intensional phenomena, such as belief and modality, and stick to extensional phenomena an events-based model will typically allow more distinctions to be made between propositions than a possible worlds model. Thus in principle we might expect to be able to derive Alternative Semantics representations from events-based representations, but not the other way around. We tentatively conclude that, as regards restrictiveness, Structured Meanings is the least restrictive, Alternative Semantics is the most restrictive, and the events-based model is somewhere in the middle.

Lastly, Alternative Semantics differs from the events-based model in that the alternative set (i.e. the background meaning) in Alternative Semantics is generated by considering alternative values of the ordinary meaning achieved by plugging in every possible value for the focus, whereas the background meaning in the events-based model is the ordinary meaning that would result from plugging in a trivial meaning in place of the focus. This difference can be seen by comparing (4.25b) and (4.27b). In (4.25b), the alternative set contains alternative values of the ordinary meaning of *Sandy met [Bush]*$_F$ obtained by plugging in every alternative to *Bush*. In (4.27b), the background meaning is the ordinary meaning that results from replacing the focus $\text{TH}(e, b)$ with a trivial event description $\lambda e.T$.

These considerations suggest that the space of possible models of focus is far from complete. For example, one could consider a model in which the two components were the ordinary meaning and a second value derived from the ordinary meaning of the focused element, rather than being derived from the meaning of the backgrounded material. Also, one could consider a variant of Alternative Semantics in which we simply replaced worlds by events. Then the two components would be an ordinary event-based proposition and a set of event-based propositions, those derived by filling in for the focus every possible (events-based) semantic value which something with the same syntactic category as the focus could take.

Yet another alternative would be to take the Bonomi and Casalegno model but use worlds instead of events. Then both meaning components would be propositions, i.e. sets of worlds, one component being the ordinary meaning, and the other component being derived by plugging in a trivial value instead of the focus. Thus, for example, *Sandy met [Bush]*$_F$ would pick out a pair consisting of the set of worlds where Sandy met Bush, and the set of worlds where Sandy met someone or something. There are doubtless many other possibilities, for example any of the above architectures but with (partial) situations used instead of (total) worlds or events. Then again, if what the theories need is a fine-grained notion of proposition, property theory (Chierchia and Turner 1988) could also be applied to the problem: one might take as one component the ordinary property theoretic meaning, and for the other component e.g. a set of such alternative fine-grained meanings.

Given such a plethora of possible frameworks for interpreting focus, which is the best suited to our purpose? Simply to describe a compositional mechanism whereby focus can affect truth conditions, all of the frameworks are adequate. We will, in fact, use the events-based analysis in Chapters 6–8 of this book, since it yields probably the simplest derivations of any of the three frameworks, and since quantification over events provides a good starting place for analyzing quantificational adverbs. But our wider ambitions are greater. We do not merely seek to describe a mechanism whereby focus can affect truth conditions, but to describe a theory of how focus functions in discourse.

Despite the close relationships between the three frameworks, once we get to the discourse level, Alternative Semantics has major practical and theoretical advantages. At a practical level, the advantage is simply that predecessors have done so much of the work for us. We think here in particular of the landmark dissertation of Groenendijk and Stokhof (1984), but also later work such as Roberts (1996), Groenendijk (1999), and van Rooij (2003). These authors provide a natural way to model the relative information content of different answers to a question, formalizations of the notions of partial and total answer, and a logic of interrogation which makes explicit the relative specificity of different questions. These are exactly the tools that are needed to make a development of Roberts' structured questions model of discourse (introduced in Chapter 2) precise.

There is also a theoretical reason why Alternative Semantics (or close variants on it) have enabled such developments, namely that it provides an algebraic, model theoretic measure of information. Certainly such a measure could in principle be recovered from Structured Meanings, since, as we have pointed out, the Alternative Semantics meaning can itself be recovered from the Structured Meaning. But there would be no point in employing Structured Meanings in the compositional build-up of the sentence only to translate later into Alternative Semantics to deal with issues of discourse coherence: it makes more sense to use Alternative Semantics all the way down.

As for the events-based model, we do not see how this helps us specify useful question–answer relations at all. The events model as we have described it involves quantification over sets of actual events in the model. Questions certainly do not denote sets of actual events. Presumably it would be possible to model questions in terms of some abstract, intensional notion of event type, but we know of no attempt to formulate such a model, and will not attempt to do so here. Rather, while we frequently use events to illustrate what is happening at the sentential level, we use Alternative Semantics whenever we want to combine sentence and discourse levels.

4.6   The President, the Boy Scouts, and a Trip to Tanglewood

Summary: *We discuss empirical arguments that Alternative Semantics cannot adequately model focus sensitivity. These arguments do not hold up to scrutiny.*

Bonomi and Casalegno (1993), in motivating their model, argue that Alternative Semantics is fundamentally flawed. This section provides a detailed reaction to Bonomi and Casalegno, via a treatment of the single putative counterexample they offer against Alternative Semantics. This does not in and of itself lessen the attractiveness of the elegant proposal that Bonomi and Casalegno develop, or indeed the attractiveness of many other proposals for interpreting focus that we consider in this chapter and the next. It merely establishes that Alternative Semantics remains a contender.

A problem: association with the president

It may seem arbitrary that in the text above the alternative set of a focused name is restricted to range over rigid individual concepts. Indeed, there is a certain arbitrariness in the choice, but some such choice must be made.

To appreciate this, consider what the consequences would be of letting the alternatives to a focused name be the set of all individual concepts, i.e. all functions from worlds to individuals. In that case, a sentence like (4.5), repeated in (4.28), would never be true in a non-trivial model, for it would claim that there was exactly one individual concept such that the reification of that concept in the actual world (i.e. the object the concept corresponds to in the actual world) was met by Sandy. Suppose there are just two individuals in the domain, and just two worlds. Then there are a total of four individual concepts. And for any individual, world pair there are two concepts which correspond to the individual in that world. So already in a model with two individuals and two worlds, (4.28) would be false, and the same is true for all other models with at least two individuals and at least two worlds.

(4.28)   Sandy only met [Bush]$_F$.

It seems, then, that *only* does not quantify over the complete domain of individual concepts: there are just too many individual concepts for uniqueness to be achievable under such an approach.[7] The solution taken above was to keep quantifying over individual concepts, but heavily restrict the domain of quantification. Specifically, a subset of the individual concepts was taken, namely those that behave like rigid designators, uniform functions that map

---

[7]   The problem is reminiscent of issues that beset the development of quantified modal logics for many years, and indeed we will soon consider a solution which was targeted at those very same problems.

every world to the same individual. This subset of individual concepts has a nice property: for every individual there is exactly one such concept, and *vice versa*. So quantifying over the rigid individual concepts can act as a proxy for quantifying over the individuals themselves. However, the approach is not yet fully general, as is easily seen.

Consider (4.29), which involves an occurrence of a definite description within the syntactic scope of the exclusive *only*.

(4.29)   Sandy only met [the president]$_F$.

Suppose that (for some contextually salient nation) the intension of *the president* is a function from possible worlds to a unique individual who is the president in that world. Such a function is an individual concept, but, at least in a democracy, it is not rigid. In particular, it may well be that in the real world this concept picks out the same individual as that given by *Bush*, but the two concepts are obviously not identical: there are attractive neighboring worlds in which the concepts pick out different individuals.

Furthermore, since *the president* is not a rigid function, it is not even a member of the alternative set we have up to now been using for focused NPs, for that alternative set contains only rigid individual concepts. As a result, using the same type of analysis for (4.29) as we used for (4.5) would be disastrous. Cutting the story short, it would yield the proposition that every rigidly individual concept such that Sandy met its instantiation is identical to the individual concept for *the president*. But since the latter is not a rigid individual concept, this would be equivalent to saying Sandy met nobody, which is obviously not the meaning of (4.29).

Clearly the interpretation of non-rigid terms in the scope of *only* presents a problem. Furthermore, this problem seems to be an artifact of Alternative Semantics. That is, we have a problem involving intensionality because we have chosen to analyze *only*, and focus sensitivity more generally, intensionally. Yet it is far from obvious that the intensionality problem has anything to do with the meaning of *only*. In fact, we can argue to the contrary.

Here is an observation: knowing that George W. Bush is president tells us that if either of (4.5) or (4.29) is true then the other is true too. To use standard terminology, within the scope of *only* (and absent other relevant operators) referentially identical noun phrases are substitutable without altering the truth value of the statements in which they occur. So *only* does not create a referentially opaque context. Standardly this would lead a semanticist to avoid treating *only* as an inherently intensional operator. But in Rooth's Alternative Semantics, intensionality is not being used for its own sake, but as a means to an end, so we must keep the intensionality, or drop Alternative Semantics.

The question now arises: is the problem of non-rigid terms fatal to Alternative Semantics, or can we work around it? What we need is just enough intensionality to let Rooth's semantics do its work, but not so much intensionality that we end up with substitution failures in cases like (4.29) and (4.5).

Moving the president

In each of the next three sections we will consider a different way to solve the intensionality problem. Here we consider an approach involving movement: by interpreting the NP *the president* non-locally, we make sure that the intensional properties that *only* has access to are not sensitive to the fact that the denotation of *the president* varies from world to world.

The movement solution involves interpreting not the surface structure of (4.29), but a variant in which the object has been moved out of the scope of *only* leaving a trace behind. We will argue in Chapters 6–8 that *only* needs a focused constituent in its syntactic scope, so we allow, as a working assumption in order to develop the movement account in this section, that the trace left behind by covert movement may be F-marked.[8] This is the tree which we use for interpretation:

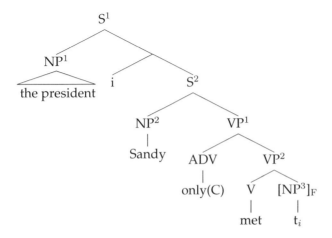

To interpret the above tree we require rules for the abstraction operation involved when a constituent is moved, one rule for the constituent [i S^2], and one for the trace t_i. To express these rules, we need to assume, as is standard, that the intension is calculated relative to an assignment function, for which we use g, or $g[i/x]$ to mean the assignment function differing from g by mapping the variable i to the entity x. The following two rules are intensional versions of the rules used by Heim and Kratzer (1998):

(4.30)   *Abstraction rules:*

$$[\![\text{i } S]\!]^I{}_g = \lambda w.\lambda x.[\![S]\!]^I{}_{g[i/x]}$$
$$[\![t_i]\!]^I{}_g = \lambda w[g(i)]$$

---

[8] It is significant that we allow only that a trace left by *covert* movement can be F-marked. This is consistent with data we will consider in Chapter 7 which indicates that traces left by *overt* movement are not F-marked.

On the assumption that a focused trace has the same alternative set as any other focused NP that denotes an individual, calculation of the alternative set below the level of VP[1] is not affected by the introduction of movement.[9] Thus $[\![\text{met } [t_i]_F]\!]^A{}_g = [\![\text{met } [\text{Bush}]_F]\!]^A$, which was calculated above. The intension of *Sandy met* $[t_i]_F$ also mirrors that of *Sandy met* $[\text{Bush}]_F$, and in the following we assume all the simplifying steps made in that earlier derivation (i.e. in (4.8) and (4.10)):

(4.31)   *Intension of "Sandy only met* $[t_i]_F$*"*

$$[\![\text{met } [t_i]_F]\!]^I{}_g = \lambda w \, [[\![\text{met}]\!]^I(w)(g(i))]$$

$$[\![\text{only met } [t_i]_F]\!]^I{}_g = \lambda y.\lambda w.\forall P \, [\![\text{met } [t_i]_F]\!]^A{}_g(P) \wedge P(y)(w) \rightarrow$$
$$P = [\![\text{met } [t_i]_F]\!]^I{}_g$$

$$[\![\text{Sandy only met } [t_i]_F]\!]^I{}_g = \lambda w.\forall P \, [\![\text{met } [t_i]_F]\!]^A(P) \wedge P(S)(w) \rightarrow$$
$$P = [\![\text{met } [t_i]_F]\!]^I{}_g$$
$$= \lambda w.\forall y \; meet(w, S, y) \rightarrow y = g(i)$$

The final stage of the derivation is to abstract over the value of the trace, and then apply to *the president*:

(4.32)   *Intension of "the president$_i$: Sandy only met* $[t_i]_F$*"*

$$[\![\text{the president}]\!]^I{}_g$$
$$= \lambda w.\lambda Q.\exists u[president(w, u) \wedge$$
$$\forall v[president(w, v) \rightarrow u = v] \wedge Q(u)]$$
$$[\![\text{i Sandy only met } [t_i]_F]\!]^I{}_g$$
$$= \lambda w.\lambda v[\![\text{Sandy only met } [t_i]_F]\!]^I{}_{g[i/v]}$$
$$= \lambda w.\lambda z.\forall y \; meet(w, S, y) \rightarrow y = z$$
$$[\![\text{the president i: Sandy only met } [t_i]_F]\!]^I{}_g$$
$$= \lambda w.\exists u[president(w, u) \wedge \forall v[president(w, v) \rightarrow u = v] \wedge$$
$$\forall y \; meet(w, S, y) \rightarrow y = u]$$

This is the meaning we want: in any world where there is one and only one president, and that president is Bush, the claim that Sandy only met the president

---

[9]   It is difficult to formulate a compositional rule for the alternative set of abstracts [i S]. For example, the rule in (i) is problematic because of rebinding of the variable i in β. However, a rule of this sort is not needed to establish the truth conditions of the examples at hand, and we leave it as an exercise for the interested reader.

(i) $[\![\text{i S}]\!]^A{}_g = \lambda \alpha.\exists \beta \in [\![\text{S}]\!]^A{}_g[\lambda i.\beta] = \alpha$

will be true iff Sandy only met Bush.[10] However, the movement of the object NP may seem *ad hoc*. Before considering a much more general approach, let us consider how presupposition can be used to derive the same effects as movement.

Presupposing the president

Rather than raising the object, we could have left it *in situ*, and relied on the fact that the NP *the president* is presuppositional, requiring that some individual is uniquely identifiable as the president. Presuppositional expressions are semantic Houdinis: their interpretations are able to escape from the scope of any operators that embed them. On the basis of this motivation, we could take *the president* to be interpreted relative to the utterance context, rather than relative to the local context of the sentence.

One way to cash this idea out without introducing yet further complications is to treat *the president* as individual denoting, and assume that the context of utterance provides a world w_0 relative to which the extension of the predicate *president* is obtained. Using Russell's iota notation for the unique individual picked out by a property, we can represent the intension of *the president* as: $\lambda w \iota x[\text{president}'(w_0, x)]$, provided there is a unique object satisfying the description in w_0.[11] Without going into details, and following the derivational method above, this would yield the following:

(4.33) $[\![\text{Sandy only met [the president]}_F]\!]^I$

$$= \lambda w. \forall y \; meet(w, S, y) \rightarrow y = \iota x[president(w_0, x)]$$

Provided Bush is the president in the world of evaluation w_0, again *Sandy only met [the president]*$_F$ will be predicted true iff she met Bush and nobody else, which is the result we desire.

---

[10] Note also that by quantifying in *the president* we have side-stepped the issue of what the alternatives to a focused generalized quantifier should be, and only had to deal with calculating alternatives to a focused individual denoting expression, albeit in an intensional setting.

[11] Kai von Fintel (p.c.) notes that the presuppositional analysis we describe in this section could equally well be thought of as an INDEXICAL analysis. It is indeed true that in cases where the presupposition of *the president* is satisfied, the analysis we propose has precisely the same effect as one in which the reference of *the president* is indexed to the unique entity who is the president in the context of utterance. However, in more complex cases, not considered in the main text, it could be that the presupposition was not satisfied in the global context, or had to be accommodated. Consider e.g. (i). This is a case in which the existence of a butler of the King is accommodated into the hearer's model of Sandy's belief set, and the global context does not provide a referent for the description *the King's butler*. Such behavior is more naturally treated in presupposition theory than in standard models of indexicals.

(i) Young Sandy, who thinks the US is a monarchy, believes that Sandy only met [the King's butler]$_F$.

Covering the president

We have shown that the problem posed by association with a focused definite description can be solved. The basic problem is that a definite description is non-rigid, while NP alternatives, as we have defined them, consist entirely of rigid individual concepts. The solutions offered above, using movement and presupposition, avoid the problem by ensuring that the focused NP behaves as if it were rigid. The movement solution uses the fact that traces behave locally like names, while the presuppositional approach uses a global context parameter to locate a particular individual corresponding to the description, and then treats the NP locally as if it were a rigid designator picking out this object. These methods solve the basic problem, but the solutions raise yet further issues.

If the correct interpretation of a sentence involving association with a focused definite involves interpreting the definite as having wide-scope over the focus sensitive operator, then it might be expected that there would also be another reading in which the definite takes narrow scope. Similarly, the presuppositional approach described above produces the effect of a wide scope object through what amounts to global accommodation of the definite's presupposition. But presupposition theory allows for local accommodation as well, which would have a similar effect to interpreting the definite quantificationally and giving it narrow scope. Yet on the narrow scope or local accommodation readings, the sentence (4.29) would falsely imply that Sandy did not meet anyone. This is not a reading of the sentence.

Why, then, are the narrow scope or local accommodation readings unavailable? One could argue that there are pragmatic preferences against these readings. First, a speaker who intended to say that Sandy met nobody could just say "Sandy met nobody" which is simpler than (4.29), so the more complex sentence should not be uttered with that intended meaning. Secondly, in presupposition theory it is standardly recognized that local accommodation readings are systematically less common than global accommodation readings: on some accounts the local reading is available only when the global reading is blocked (Sandt 1992). While these pragmatic explanations of the absence of extra readings are plausible, we would surely prefer an account in which they were not needed, an account in which a focused NP denoting a non-rigid individual concept could be interpreted *in situ*. We will now outline such an account.

We observed earlier that the alternative set for an NP cannot consist of the set of all individual concepts, and this led us to use a smaller set, the rigid individual concepts. But this in turn produced problems as soon as the focused NP was non-rigid. The scopal and presuppositional solutions avoid the problem, but we can instead confront it head on, provided we are prepared to adopt the following two desiderata:

(4.34)   *Desiderata for NP alternative sets*

   1.   If an NP is focused, the NP's alternative set must include the intension of the NP.

2. For any individual and for any world, the basic alternative set of an NP (i.e. absent any additional contextual restriction) should contain exactly one concept which picks out the individual in that world.

The first of the criteria seems implicit in the very notion of *alternative*. Loosely, we can take the alternatives to represent the meanings of expressions that could have occupied the place of the focused NP. Clearly the focused NP could occupy that space, since it actually does. Therefore we expect the meaning of the focused NP to be amongst its own alternatives.

The second criterion is a special case of the constraints imposed by Aloni (2000) in defining her notion of a *conceptual cover*, a solution to a range of long-standing problems concerning quantification in modal contexts. This criterion is needed to avoid double-counting of individuals in the alternative set. For example, we do not want both the intension of *Bush* and the intension of *the president* in the same alternative set, because that would mean that in some worlds (e.g. the real world) we would include the same individual twice in the alternative set under two different guises. For our purposes, one Bush suffices.

Let us now see how these considerations affect the interpretation of (4.29), assuming that the definite *the president* is interpreted *in situ*, at an individual level rather than quantificationally, and relative to the local world of evaluation rather than a global parameter provided by the utterance context. The basic derivation proceeds along what should now be familiar lines:

(4.35)   *Intension of "Sandy only met [the president]$_F$":*

⟦the president⟧^{I}
    $= \lambda w.\iota x[president(w, x)]$
⟦met the president⟧^{I}
    $= \lambda w⟦\text{met}⟧^I(w)(\iota x[president(w, x)])$
⟦only met the president⟧^{I}
    $= \lambda y.\lambda w.\forall P$ ⟦met [the president]$_F$⟧$^A(P) \wedge P(y)(w) \rightarrow$
       $P = \lambda w⟦\text{met}⟧^I(w)(\iota x[president(w, x)])$
⟦Sandy only met [the president]$_F$⟧^{I}
    $= \lambda w.\forall P$ ⟦met [the president]$_F$⟧$^A(P) \wedge P(S)(w) \rightarrow$
       $P = \lambda w⟦\text{met}⟧^I(w)(\iota x[president(w, x)])$

In order to simplify the meaning arrived at in (4.35), we need to analyze the alternative set ⟦met [the president]$_F$⟧^{A}. Using the standard rule above for calculating the alternative set of a complex expression, this can be expressed in terms of the alternative set of *[the president]$_F$* and the intension of *met* as: $\lambda P[\exists X$ ⟦the president⟧$^A(X) \wedge P=\lambda w[⟦\text{met}⟧^I(w)(X(w))]]$. Using this variant together with the meeting identity postulate allows us to replace quantification over properties in the last line of (4.35) with quantification over individual concepts. Combining with our notation convention for $[\![met]\!]^I$ produces:

(4.36)   *Simplified intension of "Sandy only met [the president]$_F$":*

$[\![Sandy\ only\ met\ [the\ president]_F]\!]^I$
$= \lambda w.\ \forall X\ ([\![the\ president]\!]^A(X) \wedge meet(w, S, X(w))) \rightarrow$
$X = \lambda w.\iota x[president(w, x)]$

Now the question arises as to just what $[\![the\ president]\!]^A$ is: there are many alternative sets that would satisfy the desiderata listed above, i.e. that would both include the intension of *the president*, and provide exactly one individual concept for each individual in the model. We assume, as does Aloni in her discussion of conceptual covers, that language users would have to determine the relevant alternative set pragmatically.

Although it is not clear how the process of completely identifying the correct alternative set could be modeled, this is not problematic. For we can determine the truth conditions of the example at hand without knowing which alternative set is in the speaker's mind, if, indeed, any particular such set is fully determined. It suffices that whatever the alternative used, it obeys the above desiderata. Given that we know that $[\![the\ president]\!]^A$ includes $[\![the\ president]\!]^I$, and given also that it contains exactly one individual concept for each individual, the higher order quantification over concepts in (4.36) can be reduced to first order quantification over individuals:

(4.37)   *Further simplified intension of "Sandy only met [the president]$_F$":*

$[\![Sandy\ only\ met\ [the\ president]_F]\!]^I$
$= \lambda w.\forall x\ [meet(w, S, x) \rightarrow x = \iota x[president(w, x)]]$

We have now shown that the problem of referentially identical focused NPs can be solved in three different ways. We now turn to a more complicated case, Bonomi and Casalegno's counterexample to Alternative Semantics.

The boy scout problem

Bonomi and Casalegno discuss (4.38) in the context of two worlds. In world W, the set of boy scouts is identical to the set of those kissed by Mary: John, David, and Peter. In world V, the set of those kissed by Mary is as in W, but the set of boy scouts is now just John and David. Intuitively, (4.38) is true in W but false in V.

(4.38)   Mary only kissed [the boy scouts]$_F$.
                                    (Bonomi and Casalegno 1993, example 17)

Bonomi and Casalegno make the following assertion:

> it can be proved that there is absolutely no way of accounting for a sentence like [(4.38)] in the framework of Rooth's theory ... For an analysis of [(4.38)] in the style of Rooth to be possible, we should be able to define the extension of *only kissed [the boy scouts]*F in terms of the intension of *kissed the boy scouts* and of the set of alternatives determined by *kissed [the boy scouts]*F. But it turns out that such a definition does not exist. The actual proof is a bit tedious ...

We will now show that, on the assumption that our extensions to Rooth (1992) can be seen as being "in the style of Rooth", examples like (4.38) are completely unproblematic. But before considering how to remedy the problem, let us examine more carefully why Bonomi and Casalegno think (4.38) presents difficulties for Alternative Semantics.

Bonomi and Casalegno assume that the extension of *Mary kissed the boy scouts* is the same in both worlds (i.e. it is true), the intension of *kissed the boy scouts* remains constant across worlds, and the alternative set, which is itself a set of intensions, also remains constant across all worlds. Since these are the only objects which Rooth's *only* has access to, Rooth's definitions must predict the same truth value in V and W. Or so Bonomi and Casalegno think. And it is not surprising that they think this, because there are various assumptions that might make it true.

For example, suppose we (i) generalized the system above to deal with plurals, (ii) interpreted *the boy scouts in situ*, (iii) ignored the fact that *the boy scouts* is presuppositional, and (iv) made the alternative set for *the boy scouts* into the set of all *plural concepts* (functions from worlds to sets of individuals). In that case, and by analogy with the case of *the president* discussed above, it is easily seen that (4.38) would end up with the same truth value in both U and V. Consider: Whatever set *the boy scouts* picks out in one of these worlds, there will be other plural individual concepts that also pick out this set; so it will not be the case that there is exactly one individual concept such that Mary kissed the set picked out out by the concept in that world; therefore the sentence would be predicted false independently of whether it is actually false in that world.

Given our treatment of *the president*, it is not difficult to deal with Bonomi and Casalegno's putative counterexample. We simply need to extend Alternative Semantics to deal with plurals, and then discard one of the other three assumptions (ii–iv) in the paragraph above. We will drop the fourth assumption, and use conceptual covers, but it would be unproblematic to solve the problem instead using movement or presuppositionality.

How to kiss the boy scouts

Let us assume that the type we have up to now been using for individuals, e, is not basic. Rather, e is an abbreviation for $\langle \epsilon, t \rangle$, such that ϵ is the type of atomic individuals, and e corresponds to sets of individuals. Then the constant M, representing the extension of *Mary*, corresponds to the characteristic function of a singleton set. If the constant m is the individual in that set, and α is a variable of type ϵ, then $M = \lambda\alpha[\alpha = m]$.

We now need to change the meaning of *the* to allow for plural NPs. We let nouns (including the compound noun *boy scout*) take simple individuals (of type ϵ) as arguments, and take a definite to pick out (the characteristic function of) the set of all objects satisfying the nominal predicate, as in (4.39):

(4.39) $[\![\text{the boy scouts}]\!]^I{}_g = \lambda w.\lambda x[boy{-}scout(w, x)]$

Aloni set up her conceptual covers for ordinary individuals, and did not consider plurals. So we need to generalize the notion slightly, and impose desiderata on alternative sets that are appropriate to a plural domain. In doing so, we will deal with a problem that arises in any attempt to allow an exclusive like *only* to associate with plurals.

To understand the problem with plurals and *only*, observe that if Mary kissed the boy scouts, then, assuming kissing is distributive, it must also be true that she kissed every subset of the boy scouts. So if there are multiple boy scouts, then there is no way that someone could uniquely have the property of kissing the boy scouts and not have also various related properties, like the property of kissing the tallest boy scouts.

In response to this problem, we could reformulate the meaning of *only* such that X *only* VP allows for X having properties weaker than that expressed by the VP. For example, the property of having kissed the tallest boy scouts is weaker than the property of having kissed the boy scouts because any individual that did the latter in a given world must have also done the former.

However, there is a second solution: the problem can be solved by restricting plural NP alternative sets so as not to include subsets of the focused NP. Since we are already committed to placing restrictions on the alternative set, it makes sense to use the second solution, which saves us from having to tinker with the semantics of *only*.[12]

(4.40)   *Desiderata for plural NP alternative sets*
   1. If an NP is focused, the NP's alternative set must include the intension of the NP.

   2. For any world w, there must be no alternative that is mapped onto a strict subset of the focused NP's extension in that world.

---

[12] However, if we were instead to tinker with the semantics of *only*, the result would look like this:

$P \sqsubseteq Q \equiv \forall x, w\ [P(w, x) \rightarrow Q(w, x)]$

$[\![\text{only VP}]\!]^I = \lambda y.\forall P[[\![\text{VP}]\!]^A(P) \wedge P(y)(w_0) \rightarrow [\![\text{VP}]\!]^I \sqsubseteq P]$

Von Fintel (1997) discusses the choice between placing restrictions on the alternative set or refining the meaning of *only*.

3. For any world and for any other set of individuals (i.e. not a strict subset of the focused NP), the basic alternative set should contain exactly one concept which picks out the set in that world.

We use $X \supseteq Y$ in the obvious way to mean $\forall \alpha Y(\alpha) \rightarrow X(\alpha)$, and similarly for $X \supset Y$. We further assume two postulates on the meaning of *kiss*: (a) a form of distributivity, that if someone kisses a set of individuals then they kiss any subgroup of that set, and (b) distinctness, as for *meet*, that kissing one set is the same property as kissing another iff the two sets are identical. In the formalization of these postulates, the variables X, Y, Z have type $\langle s, e \rangle$, i.e. they range over plural concepts:

(4.41)   *Constraints on kissing*:

(i) $\forall X, Y, Z, w[(kiss(w, X, Y) \wedge Y \subseteq Z) \rightarrow kiss(w, X, Z)]$
(ii) $\forall Y, Z.(\lambda X. \lambda w.[kiss(w, X, Y)] = \lambda X. \lambda w[kiss(w, X, Z)]) \leftrightarrow Y = Z$

It is now straightforward to derive the meaning of (4.38). Following the same pattern as for the derivation of the meaning of (4.29) in §4.6, we first derive a meaning in terms of quantification over properties. Using the above constraints on the meaning of the predicate *kiss*, we convert this to a meaning that involves quantification over plural concepts:

(4.42)   *Intension of "Mary only kissed [the boy scouts]$_F$"*

$[\![$Mary only kissed [the boy scouts]$_F]\!]^I$
$= \lambda w. \forall X \, [(([\![$the boy scouts]$_F]\!]^A(X) \wedge kiss(w, M, X(w)))$
$\rightarrow X = [\![$the boy scouts$]\!]^I]$

Using the desiderata on plural alternative sets, we can further simplify, first replacing quantification over plural concepts by quantification over ordinary sets of individuals, and then rearranging:

(4.43)   *Simplified intension of "Mary only kissed [the boy scouts]$_F$"*

$[\![$Mary only kissed [the boy scouts]$_F]\!]^I$
$= \lambda w. \forall S \, [(S \not\subseteq \lambda x[boy-scouts(w, x)] \wedge kiss(w, M, S))$
$\rightarrow S = \lambda x[boy-scouts(w, x)]]$
$= \lambda w. \forall S \, [kiss(w, M, S) \rightarrow S \subseteq \lambda x[boy-scouts(w, x)]$

It is clear that this proposition contains world W but not world V, i.e. the infamous boy scouts example is correctly predicted to be true in the first world, and false in the second.

Bonomi and Casalegno claimed that there is "absolutely no way" of dealing with their boy scout example "in the framework of Rooth's theory." Bonomi and Casalegno's claim appears to be false. Whatever its flaws, Alternative Semantics is not so easily dismissed as some have imagined.

Oh, what a Tanglewood web

Over a decade before Bonomi and Casalegno introduced their boy scout argument, Kratzer had pointed out what appeared to be a major flaw in Alternative Semantics (Kratzer 1991). But Kratzer's problem has nothing to do with intensionality: it depends on variable binding, or, more generally, the difficulty of encoding dependencies between the focus and other parts of the meaning.

Suppose that you've accused David of following you around to various places, but he wants to maintain that in every case but one it was just a coincidence that he went to the same place as you. He defends himself by saying:

(4.44)   I only went to [Tanglewood]$_F$ because you did.

(Kratzer 1991)

Suppose that VP ellipsis in this example is analyzed by assuming deletion of duplicated material, so that we can reconstruct the underlying form as:

(4.45)   I only went to [Tanglewood]$_F$ because you did [go to [Tanglewood]$_F$]

Kratzer observes that Alternative Semantics now produces incorrect predictions. If the entire VP *went to [Tanglewood]$_F$ because you did [go to [Tanglewood]$_F$]* is under the scope of *only*, then the two foci may vary independently. The predicted interpretation of (4.44) is then (from Jäger 1999) 'The only pair of places $\langle x, y \rangle$ such that I went to x because you went to y is $\langle$Tanglewood, Tanglewood$\rangle$'. So the sentence comes to imply e.g. that the speaker did not go to London because the addressee went to Paris.

But intuitively the sentence in (4.44) says nothing of the sort. Rather, it says that there's only one value of X that makes *I only went to X because you went to X* true, i.e. the value X = Tanglewood. There is a dependency between the two focus values and Alternative Semantics appears not to capture that dependency.

The Tanglewood example is commonly used to advance alternatives to Alternative Semantics. Kratzer herself suggested a semantics which, instead of keeping track of alternative propositions, keeps track of special variable assignments, assignments which provide values to each of the focal elements. Thus (4.44) would get, in addition to it's regular meaning, a focus meaning consisting of the set of variable assignments which assign to X a value which makes *I only went to X because you went to X* true.

The resultant model is not exactly Alternative Semantics or Structured Meanings, though it resembles both. Krifka (2006) uses the Tanglewood example, amongst other phenomena, to motivate a quite different hybrid of

Alternative Semantics and Structured Meanings, saying about a related example: "Pure [Alternative Semantics] cannot express this restriction on paired foci [. . .] The [Structured Meanings] approach, on the other hand, can identify [the paired foci] and combine them [. . .]." Kadmon (2001) also discusses the Tanglewood example at length, concluding that [p. 366]: "the VP deletion examples provide evidence for choosing [Kratzer's] substitution method over [Rooth's] recursion method." *Contra* Kratzer, Krifka and Kadmon, we do not take the Tanglewood examples to be any more decisive than the boy scout examples considered above, and we will now explain why.[13]

We might start to approach this problem by wondering whether a reconstructed VP ought to bear the same focus features as its antecedent. Indeed, in Chapter 7 we will consider examples like that in (4.46a), below. The oddity of this example contrasts with the felicity of the corresponding example (4.46b) in which the elided material has been made explicit, and the difference between the examples shows that focus cannot be freely reconstructed within ellipsis sites:

(4.46) a.   *Kim only SALUTES because Sandy only does.
            (cannot mean: 'Kim salutes (and does nothing else) because Sandy salutes (and does nothing else)')

       b.   Kim only SALUTES because Sandy only SALUTES.

---

[13]   The approach developed by Kratzer (1991) to deal with Tanglewood examples was later extended by Wold (1996). However, Wold's main quarry was cases of multiple foci, as discussed by Krifka (1991), in particular examples involving multiple focus sensitive operators combining with different foci, as in the following:

> (i)   I only gave Fred [a tiny peck on the cheek]$_F$, and I only gave [Mary]$_F$ [a tiny peck on the cheek]$_F$ too.

These data can only be analyzed in Alternative Semantics if we allow that multiple alternative sets are calculated simultaneously, and then allow different focus sensitive operators to be constrained by different alternative sets. However, simply adding the possibility of multiple parallel alternative sets would not capture what seems to us an important generalization: cases like these, of what we might call "overlapping alternatives", only occur when at least one of the foci is repeated. Furthermore, when there are two foci present in an English sentence, and these two foci associate with different operators, the foci are realized differently from each other. One is typically produced with what we take to be a L+H*L-H% accent – Jackendoff's B accent. This suggests that it may be a misnomer to term both prominent expressions *foci*, since one may be better thought of as a contrastive topic. In (i), it is *[a tiny peck on the cheek]$_F$* that is repeated, and it is *Mary* that is most naturally given a B accent: this is the expression which might be considered a contrastive topic. We suggest that these examples are best understood in terms of the hierarchy of questions under discussion postulated by Roberts (1996), and at the heart of the QFC model. So, in (i), we might have a super-question: *what form of kiss did the speaker give to which people?* There would then be two sub-questions *what form of kiss did the speaker give to Fred?*, and *what form of kiss did the speaker give to Mary?* One of the foci corresponds to a *wh*-expression in the super-question, and the other to the *wh*-expression in the sub-question. Roberts (1996) in fact analyzes discourses of this general form, though her examples do not involve multiple focus sensitive operators. We will not attempt an analysis of such cases in this work.

Yet the fact that ellipsis cannot be freely reconstructed does not take us any-where with the Tanglewood example. For if the elided VP in (4.44) is recon-structed without focus, Alternative Semantics will predict that the example is true in case there is only one X such that the speaker went to it because the hearer went to Tanglewood. This is clearly not the desired meaning, since it would allow that the speaker went to any number of places other than Tangle-wood because the hearer went to those places.

As suggested above, what the Tanglewood example really shows is that a theory of focus sensitivity has to be able to deal with dependencies between focus and other elements. As a prelude to showing a couple of ways to deal with the Tanglewood example, let us consider another sort of dependency, that between an anaphoric NP and its antecedent. Example (4.47a), which is of a type familiar in the literature (Heim and Kratzer 1998: 257) has two readings, as in (b) and (c):

(4.47) a.   Mary only gave [Fido$_i$]$_F$ his$_i$ dinner.

       b.   'There's no X except Fido such that Mary gave X Fido's dinner.'

       c.   'There's no X except Fido such that Mary gave X X's dinner.'

How can we analyze this case in Alternative Semantics? There are many ways, depending on how anaphoric links are analyzed in the first place. The two most obvious approaches are (i) movement, and (ii) dynamic seman-tics (Groenendijk and Stokhof 1991). In the remainder of this section we give a proof-of-concept demonstration that Alternative Semantics can handle the example using a movement-based approach, once again allowing movement to work in the style of Heim and Kratzer (1998). In the next section, we will show how dynamic semantics can be applied to the problem, though we will treat a simplified variant of the Tanglewood example.

In the tree in (4.48) we allow movement of *only*, movement of the focal NP, and movement of the focus marked trace that this NP leaves behind – in for a penny, in for a pound! We treat *only* as a sentential operator in this example: to keep it as an operator over properties rather than propositions would require subject movement, but we leave this as an exercise for the reader. The tree in (4.48) is really two different trees, depending on whether the index on *his* in NP^4 is set to j or k. If it is set to j, then the possessive pronoun will be firmly anchored to Fido, the focal meaning will consist of propositions of the form *Mary fed X Fido's dinner*, and the ordinary mean-ing of the sentence will be as in (4.47b). On the other hand, if the posses-sive pronoun is coindexed with k, then its contribution to the focal meaning will covary with the focus. The alternative set will then consist of proposi-tions of the form *Mary fed X X's dinner*, and we derive the sentence meaning in (4.47c).

(4.48)

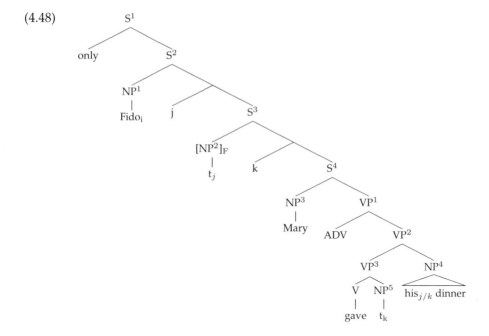

We now return to Tanglewood, i.e. a case of focal dependency involving VP ellipsis rather than NP anaphora. Recall that the problem arose within the context of a combination of Alternative Semantics with a syntactic reconstruction approach to ellipsis. But reconstruction is not the only possible approach to ellipsis, an alternative being to treat it as being a special case of anaphora. In that case, there are still plenty of options, since anaphora can be analyzed in many different ways. As with nominal anaphora, a dynamic semantic model would be an option (see e.g. Gardent 1991.)

We adopt a movement-based approach to VP ellipsis which runs parallel to the treatment of anaphora in example (4.47). Such an account cannot cover all cases of VP ellipsis, since the phenomena allows cross-sentential dependencies, but the account will cover intra-sentential cases of the Tanglewood type, and so is sufficient for current purposes. Of course, the fact that movement cannot naturally cover the full range of VP ellipsis cases once again parallels the fact that movement cannot naturally treat the full range of nominal cases. Adopting parallel terminology, one might say that the analysis we present accounts for cases of bound VP ellipsis, but not discourse VP ellipsis, though we make no claim that there is a linguistically interesting empirical distinction between the two.

Allowing then that we have adopted a syntactically non-standard account of ellipsis, the tree in (4.49), by mirroring the above analysis of (4.47a), provides us with the desired reading. The variable u ranges over (intensional but untensed) properties, and we assume that both the VP trace t_u and the anaphoric element PRO_u are bound by abstraction over u. Note that it would have required only a minor variant of this analysis to make the anaphoric element into a second VP trace rather than a VP PRO: we offer no empirical or theoretical considerations which might decide the matter either way.

(4.49)

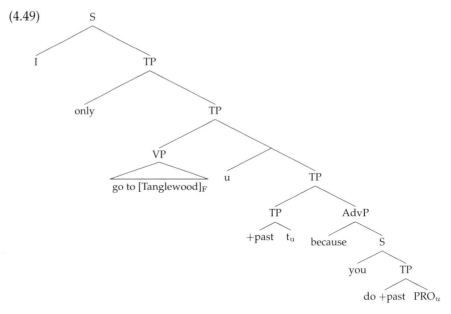

Interpreting (4.49) using the same Alternative Semantics apparatus as we deployed above, will yield a focal meaning corresponding to the set of propositions of the form *I went to X because you went to X*, and will produce the desired truth conditions, i.e. no value of X except Tanglewood yields a true alternative.

The tree in (4.49), of course, is not particular to Alternative Semantics. Precisely the same syntactic analysis would work for the Structured Meanings approach. In that case *only* will have as its argument a background/foreground pair such that the background is the property of being an X such that the speaker went to X because the addressee did, and the foreground will be Tanglewood. Applying *only* will then produce the desired truth conditions.

Treating Tanglewood sentences using movement is viable, but the large amounts of covert movement required leave a clutter of crossing dependencies that may be felt to make the analysis unattractive, and may be felt to lack independent empirical motivation.[14] For that reason, we think it worth making clear that the account of focus sensitivity we develop in this book, building

---

[14] As Kai von Fintel (p.c.) points out, a stronger complaint could be leveled at a movement solution to the Tanglewood example, i.e. that it presents empirical difficulties. Specifically, and as Kratzer herself realized, Tanglewood-type examples can be constructed in which the focus is in an island to movement. Thus, in a situation where you are accusing the speaker of saying of several locations that they are nice just because you said the same thing of those places, the speaker might defensively say:

(i) I only said that [Tanglewood]_F was nice because you did.

on work of Rooth and others, is in no way dependent on syntactic movement. We demonstrate this in the next section by sketching how a similar example to the Tanglewood case can be accounted for without movement, instead using dynamic semantics.

Getting out of Tanglewood without moving

The problem with the sentence *I only went to [Tanglewood]*$_F$ *because you did* is that a non-focused element is dependent for its meaning on the focused element, so that when focal alternatives are calculated we need to make sure that the dependent element covaries with the focus. In Kratzer's example, the dependent element is an elided VP, but the type of problem she discovered could equally well be illustrated with any construction that involves a single element affecting interpretation in two different places.

In principle, a copy theory of control (Hornstein 1999, 2000) might combine with Alternative Semantics to produce similar problems. For example, the sentence *I only think [Mary]*$_F$ *tried to leave* must be interpreted so that the implied agent of *leave* covaries with the subject of the control verb *tried*. The Tanglewood phenomenon can also be seen with propositional anaphors (4.50) and reflexives (4.51, 4.52):

(4.50)   Mary only said she loved [Bill]$_F$ because it was true. (She said she loved those other guys in order to make them feel good).

(4.51)   I only think [John]$_F$ shaved himself.

(4.52)   Mary only showed [Butch]$_F$ himself in the mirror.

Note that there is a different range of interpretative options available with reflexives than with bound pronouns. Example (4.51) has no reading whereby the sentence is claiming that the speaker does not think people other than John shaved John. And (4.52) has no reading whereby it claims that Mary didn't show people other than Butch Butch in the mirror.

However, (4.53) has two readings in which the pronoun is interpreted as picking out John. The first, what we might call the *bound* reading, is analogous to the reflexive case in (4.50): it says that there's no x other than John for which I think that x shaved x's head. The second might be called a coreferential reading, and says that there's no x other than John for which I think x shaved John's head. Similar comments apply to (4.54).[15]

In this example, the subject *Tanglewood* follows the complementizer *that*. Consequently, (covert) movement of *Tanglewood* to a position in a higher clause is problematic (i.e. the so-called *that*-trace effect). However, the solution we propose in this section would involve moving the complete phrase *said that [Tanglewood]*$_F$ *was nice*, and would not be subject to this objection.

[15]   See Heim and Kratzer (1998: 257–8) and Büring (2005: 105–9) for discussion of the interaction between the exclusive *only* and binding, although commonly discussed examples have the form

(4.53)   I only think [John]$_F$ shaved his head.

(4.54)   Mary only showed [Butch]$_F$ his head in the mirror.

On our judgments, the control case patterns with reflexives. More surprisingly, both Kratzer's VP ellipsis example and the propositional anaphora example in (4.50) seem to us to pattern with reflexives rather than individual denoting pronouns. That is, the Tanglewood sentence does not, for us, have a reading whereby it denies of any place that the speaker went there because the addressee went to Tanglewood. On the other hand, a pronominal variant, like that in (4.55), gets both the reading of the original sentence and this further reading:

(4.55)   I only went to [Tanglewood]$_F$ because you went there.

The conclusion this data suggests is that individual denoting pronouns are the only type of intrasentential dependency allowing a non-bound but coreferential reading in addition to the bound reading.

These observations, that some Tanglewood-type sentences have more readings than others, are of interest for theories of anaphora, control, and binding, but are only indirectly germane to the current project. What is relevant for us is the fact that a bound reading is available at all, a reading where a dependent element covaries with the focus in each alternative. And since examples involving bound pronouns exhibit this reading, it suffices to demonstrate how an analysis might work using an example with a pronominal dependency rather than the more complex VP ellipsis dependency in Kratzer's original example. We will consider (4.56), on the reading where it implies that Mary did not give any other dogs *their* dinners.

(4.56)   Mary only gave [Butch$_i$]$_F$ his$_i$ dinner

In the remainder of this section we sketch a treatment of this simplified Tanglewood type example of a dependency on a focused constituent using a combination of Dynamic Semantics (Groenendijk and Stokhof 1991) and Alternative Semantics. We should warn the reader that for the purposes of this sketch we assume a working knowledge of Dynamic Semantics, and do not attempt a gentle introduction.

Let an assignment function f be a function from indices (represented as integers) to individuals in the domain of the model. We write $f = g + \langle i, b \rangle$ to indicate that f and g denote mappings which are identical except possibly for the index i, which g maps onto the individual b.

A dynamic proposition maps an input assignment and an output assignment to (the characteristic function of) a set of worlds. E.g. *A woman$_i$ is singing* would have as its meaning the dynamic proposition:

---

of (4.47a), above: the exclusive is adjacent to the focus, and no account of (long-distance) focus sensitivity is required.

(4.57) $\lambda f \lambda g \lambda w \exists x woman(w)(x) \wedge g = f + \langle i, x \rangle \wedge singing(w, x).$

The sentence *She$_i$ is happy* would be interpreted as:

(4.58) $\lambda f \lambda g \lambda w f = g \wedge happy(w, f(i)).$

The discourse consisting of the sequencing of these two sentences is then derived by using the output assignment of the first as the input of the second. The discourse *A woman$_i$ is singing. She$_i$ is happy* ends up with the meaning:

(4.59) $\lambda f \lambda g \lambda w \exists x \, woman(w)(x) \wedge g = f + \langle i, x \rangle \wedge singing(w, x) \wedge$
           $\quad happy(w, f(i)).$

Let us say that a sentence or discourse is true relative to an input assignment and a world just in case there is some output relative to this pair. Thus, for example, *A woman$_i$ is singing. She$_i$ is happy* will be true relative to input assignment f and world w just in case $\exists g \exists x woman(w)(x) \wedge g = f + \langle i, x \rangle \wedge singing(w, x) \wedge happy(w, f(i))$. This reduces to the condition: $\exists x \, woman(w)(x) \wedge singing(w, x) \wedge happy(w, x)$, as would be expected.

We define the meaning of *Butch$_i$* as taking a property as an argument to yield a dynamic proposition. But crucially the dynamic potential of *Butch$_i$* is accounted for: the argument property is interpreted relative to an assignment which maps the index i onto Butch:

(4.60) $[\![Butch_i]\!]^I = \lambda P \lambda f \lambda g \lambda w \exists h \, h = f + \langle i, b \rangle \wedge P(w)(b)(h)(g)$

A pronoun is interpreted as the value the assignment function gives to the pronoun's index. Possessive pronouns are more complicated because they are part of a larger definite NP, the definiteness can only be interpreted relative to further contextual parameters, and the NP they are part of may itself introduce a new referent. We ignore these complications. We will simply assume that for the NP *his$_i$ dinner*, there is a function *dinner-of* mapping individuals to a unique dinner of that individual relative to a world, and that *his$_i$ dinner* does not introduce any new discourse referent:

(4.61) $[\![his_i \ dinner]\!]^I = \lambda P \lambda f \lambda g \lambda w P(dinner\text{-}of(w)(f(i)))(f)(g)$

Modulo some additional type shifting needed when NPs are in non-subject positions, we can now give the ordinary meaning of *gave [Butch$_i$]$_F$ his$_i$ dinner*:

(4.62) $[\![gave \ [Butch_i]_F \ his_i \ dinner]\!]^I =$
           $\quad \lambda y \lambda f \lambda g \lambda w \, g = f + \langle i, b \rangle \wedge gave(w)(y)(b)(dinner\text{-}of(w)(f(i)))$

We will assume that alternative meanings are calculated in the standard way. That is, non-focused constituents become (characteristic functions of) singleton sets, and focused constituents become (characteristic functions of) larger sets of meanings, each of which has the same type as the ordinary meaning.

So the alternative set corresponding to *Mary gave [Butch$_i$]$_F$ his$_i$ dinner* corresponds to a set of dynamic propositions:

(4.63) $[\![$Mary gave [Butch$_i$]$_F$ his$_i$ dinner$]\!]^A =$
$$\lambda\phi\exists y[\phi = \lambda f\lambda g\lambda w \; g = f + \langle i,y\rangle \wedge gave(w)(m)(y)(dinner\text{-}of(w)(f(i)))]$$

Suppose that *only* took a sentential argument. In that case we could understand it in terms of an operator *d-only* (i.e. *dynamic only*) which maps a set of alternative dynamic propositions and a single dynamic proposition to a new dynamic proposition. We simplify by assuming that the resulting dynamic proposition does not have any effects on assignment functions:

(4.64) $d\text{-}only(\alpha)(\beta) = \lambda f\lambda g\lambda w f = g \wedge \forall\phi \in \alpha\exists h\phi(f)(h)(w) \rightarrow \phi = \beta$

When this dynamic exclusive operator *d-only* is applied to an alternative set α and a dynamic proposition β, the new dynamic proposition that results will be true if and only if any alternative in α which is itself true (for the same world and input assignment) is equal to the proposition β.

The meaning of VP modifying *only* is a slight variant on *d-only*, since it must abstract over the value of the subject:

(4.65) $[\![$only$]\!]^I = \lambda X\lambda f\lambda g\lambda w f = g \wedge \forall P \in \alpha\exists hX(P)(f)(h)(w) \rightarrow \phi = \beta$

Using this meaning for VP *only*, we get the same effect as if *only* was a sentential operator, with the meaning of *d-only*, but without needing to move *only* to a sentence modifying position syntactically. So we can now proceed as if *only* was in fact a sentential operator, and calculate the meaning for our pronominal variant of a Tanglewood sentence by combining the meaning of *d-only* with the alternative set and ordinary meaning of *Mary gave [Butch$_i$]$_F$ his$_i$ dinner*:

(4.66) $[\![$Mary only gave [Butch$_i$]$_F$ his$_i$ dinner$]\!]^I =$
          $d\text{-}only([\![$Mary gave [Butch$_i$]$_F$ his$_i$ dinner$]\!]^A)$
          $([\![$Mary gave [Butch$_i$]$_F$ his$_i$ dinner$]\!]^I)$

To simplify the truth conditions of this formula, it helps to assume a meaning postulate constraining the interpretation of *give*, by analogy with the *meeting* identity postulate (4.9) used earlier: the dynamic proposition that A gave B C is the same as the dynamic proposition that D gave E F iff A = D, B = E, and C = F. Formally:

(4.67) $\forall A,B,C,D,E,F[\lambda wgave(w)(B)(C)(A) = \lambda wgave(w)(E)(F)(D) \leftrightarrow$
          $(A{=}D \wedge B{=}E \wedge C{=}F).$

We can now show that the truth conditions derived for (4.56) are exactly what we would expect:[16]

---

[16] The derivation in fact depends upon yet another assumption: that the focal alternatives to *Butch* each introduce exactly one referent. This would be satisfied if e.g. all the alternatives correspond to the meanings of proper names.

(4.68)   *Mary only gave [Butch$_i$]$_F$ his$_i$ dinner* is true relative to w, f

$$iff\ \exists g\ d\text{-}only([\![Mary\ gave\ [Butch_i]_F\ his_i\ dinner]\!]^A)$$
$$([\![Mary\ gave\ [Butch_i]_F\ his_i\ dinner]\!]^I)(f)(g)(w)$$
$$iff\ \forall \phi \in [\![Mary\ gave\ [Butch]_F\ his\ dinner]\!]^A \exists h \phi(f)(h)(w) \rightarrow$$
$$\phi = [\![Mary\ gave\ [Butch_i]_F\ his_i\ dinner]\!]^I$$
$$iff\ \forall y\ gave(w)(m)(y)(dinner\text{-}of(w)(y)) \rightarrow y = b$$

This completes our demonstration that Tanglewood type examples can be treated in Alternative Semantics without invoking movement, provided that an adequate account of binding is used. We do not attempt to analyze Kratzer's original Tanglewood example in a dynamic framework, but see no reason why the same methods we applied for (4.56) would not transfer to a VP ellipsis case. But for such an analysis, it would be necessary to assume that *went to [Tanglewood]$_F$* created a (dynamic) property-type discourse referent, and that this property was then used to interpret the elided VP after *you did*. Thus, in effect, we would be treating ellipsis as a special case of anaphora, and analyzing it semantically. We make no attempt to defend such a semantic account of VP ellipsis over the perhaps more prevalent accounts which explain the phenomenon in terms of syntactic reconstruction.

We take it that at present the framework of Dynamic Semantics offers the most adequate and general account of binding, and would favor an integrated Dynamic Alternative Semantic account of focus and anaphora over an account which rescued Alternative Semantics by positing large amounts of covert movement. However, in order to keep the meanings we use manageable, and because we can get most of the same effects using movement operations that are relatively easy to follow for most linguists, we restrict ourselves to a classical static semantics for the remainder of this book.

4.7 Summary

We considered the three major compositional approaches to focus that have been developed. It was argued that of the three, Structured Meanings is the least restrictive, Alternative Semantics the most restrictive, and (under further assumptions about how we relate the event framework to the possible worlds framework) the events-based model falls in between.

The question then arises as to whether the extra restrictiveness of Alternative Semantics means that it is incapable of describing the relevant linguistic phenomena. We considered two apparently knock-down arguments that have been used against Alternative Semantics. In both cases, Alternative Semantics stood back up: we were able to show that there are various ways to patch up Alternative Semantics so as to deal with the problems.

For someone working at the sentence level, the choice between major compositional approaches to focus appears to be a matter of personal preference. But we have argued that at the discourse level only Alternative Semantics naturally captures the notions of information content that we need. The moral of this chapter, then, is that despite the existence of alternative frameworks, and despite objections that have been raised against it, Alternative Semantics is not merely defensible: it is also the only natural foundation for the discourse based model of focus that we develop in this book.

Chapter 5

Pragmatic Explanations of Focus

Wittgenstein, Philosophische Untersuchunqen, par. 22:

> *"Wir könnten sehr gut auch jede Behauptung in der Form einer Frage mit nachge-*
> *setzter Bejahung schreiben; etwa: 'Regnet es? Ja!'. Würde das zeigen, dass in jeder*
> *Behauptung einer Frage steekt?"*

Ja!

From the *Stellingen* of Jeroen Groenendijk, in Groenendijk and Stokhof (1984).[1]

5.1 Introduction

Suppose that focus sensitivity of some operators is a conventionalized part of
lexical meaning, as is the case in what Rooth 1992 terms *weak* theories of focus.
In that case, focus-marking of elements with which those operators associate
should not be optional, but should rather be grammatically required. Specifically, focus-marked elements should be required in the syntactic scope of focus
sensitive expressions like *only* and *always*.[2] A number of analysts (Vallduví 1990,
1992; Rooth 1992; Roberts 1996; Schwarzschild 1997) have questioned this prediction. Notably, it has been claimed (see Kadmon 2001: 316) that sometimes the
interpretational effects normally attributed to focus sensitivity are found even
without focus marking. We will call this class of phenomena 'accentless focus.'

---

[1] Translation: "Wittgenstein, Philosophical Investigations, par. 22: 'We could very well write each
statement in the form of a question with an affirmation placed after it; for example: 'Is it raining?
Yes!' Would that show that a question hangs on every statement?' Yes!"

   The Stellingen are statements that a Dutch PhD candidate takes to be irrefutably true. In this
unusual case of a joint dissertation, separate Stellingen were offered by each candidate, and the
dissertation's co-author, Martin Stokhof, offered a twin claim: "Het inzicht dat veel van de vragen
in Wittgenstein's Philosophische untersuchungen rethorische vragen zijn, bevordert het begrip van
deze tekst aanzienlijk." ("The insight that many of the questions in Wittgenstein's Philosophical
Investigations are rhetorical greatly eases the comprehension of the text.")

[2] This assumption is explored in great detail in Chapters 6 and 7.

Purported cases of accentless focus have been the main phenomenon cited against theories in which focus sensitivity is treated as a conventionalized part of lexical meaning. Another phenomenon cited in this regard is so-called *association with presupposition*. In this phenomenon, an intonationally marked focus is available, but somehow presuppositions come to 'trump' focus, apparently showing that the dependency on focus is optional. Given cases of accentless focus and association with presupposition, or so it is sometimes argued, the link between operators like *only* and foci with which they associate cannot be conventionalized. Instead, the link must be pragmatically mediated. Instead of the relationship between an operator like *only* and its focus being established in the compositional build-up of sentence meaning, the relationship is established via some sort of inferencing based on general principles of conversational coherence.

Purely pragmatic approaches to focus sensitivity share the property that the lexical semantics of focus sensitive expressions cannot make reference to focus-influenced semantic values incorporated in the compositional semantics. In these approaches, focus sensitivity is typically explained as an effect of free variables in the interpretation of focus sensitive expressions becoming bound to salient sets, where the salience of these sets might itself be correlated with focus by pragmatic mechanisms. These theories have been postulated to account for accentless focus and association with presupposition effects.

In §2.6 and §3.3, we discussed one type of purely pragmatic theory, the anaphoric account of Rooth (1992) and von Fintel (1994), which is essentially the free association portion of the QFC model. In that account, focus does not automatically establish the value of the free variable which is an implicit argument of a focus sensitive expression. At most, von Fintel and Rooth see the focus as constraining the free variable, with the actual value of the variable picked up contextually. Consider the example in (5.1).

(5.1)   Kim, Sandy, and Max were approaching. I could only see what [Kim]$_F$ was wearing.

Crucially, this example does not entail that I could not see, for example, what Jan (who isn't previously salient) was wearing, although this would follow if we equated Rooth's focal meaning directly with the free argument of the focus sensitive expression *only*, and did not allow context to intercede.[3]

To be clear: the idea of a pragmatic theory of focus sensitivity would not merely be that some odd cases of association with focus are explained pragmatically, but that all such cases are explained pragmatically. So the QFC theory does not count as a purely pragmatic theory in this sense, because there is a class of operators which we suggest have a conventionalized dependency on focus.

---

[3]   This issue is discussed in §2.6 with respect to example (2.42), and is what leads to the Focus Principle of (2.54) in §2.7 being defined (following Rooth 1992) so that the set of focal alternatives contains the CQ rather than being identical with it.

Are there, then, pragmatic mechanisms that might explain a complete range of cases of focus sensitivity without postulating any conventionalized dependency on focus? That is the issue we will explore in this chapter.[4] We start off by reviewing the evidence for purely pragmatic theories: first, in §5.2, cases of accentless focus, and second, in §5.3, cases of association with presupposition.

We then turn, in §5.4, to Roberts' pragmatic account of focus sensitivity (Roberts 1996; Kadmon 2001; Martí 2003), which provides the model of discourse that is at the heart of the QFC theory. It should be borne in mind that Roberts applies the model in a slightly different way than we do, and suggests an explanation of the focus sensitivity of exclusives that involves only free association, and no conventionalized dependency on focus. In §5.5 we consider an alternative approach to explaining focus sensitivity, the presuppositional model of Geurts and Van der Sandt (1999; 2004). Our conclusion is that neither Roberts' model nor van der Sandt and Geurts' model is capable of explaining a full range of focus sensitivity effects without stipulating any conventional dependency on focus.

5.2 Accentless Focus

Summary: *We introduce the phenomenon of* second occurrence focus, *in which an expression which is the associate of a focus sensitive operator is repeated, and appears not to be prosodically prominent in its second occurrence. We then consider other example types in which the associate of a focus sensitive operator is apparently not prominent.*

One well-known type of accentless focus is SECOND OCCURRENCE FOCUS. A second occurrence focus is an expression which is in the scope of a focus sensitive operator, is the semantic focus of that operator, and which is a repeat of an earlier focused occurrence. It has often been claimed that second occurrence foci lack any intonational marking, e.g. pitch accent.[5] (5.2) (adapted from Partee 1999) is a classic example of second occurrence focus. In Speaker A's turn, *vegetable* – the associated focus of *only* – is focus-marked. In Speaker B's turn, *vegetables* is repeated but is not focus-marked, at least impressionistically, yet *vegetables* is still interpreted as the focus associate of *only*.[6]

(5.2) A: Everyone already knew that Mary only eats [vegetables]$_F$.

B: If even [Paul]$_F$ knew that Mary only eats [vegetables]$_{SOF}$, then he should have suggested a different restaurant.

---

[4] Some early pragmatic approaches to focus sensitivity not discussed here are those of Dretske (1972) and Taglicht (1984).

[5] For discussion, see Rooth (1996b), Bartels (1997), and Partee (1999).

[6] In discussion of examples like (5.2), it has been generally assumed that lack of pitch accent implies lack of focus-marking. However, focus could be marked by other means. In Chapter 6, we discuss the prosodic correlates of second occurrence focus.

Note that in Speaker B's utterance in (5.2), the second occurrence focus *vegetables* follows the nuclear accent (on *Paul*). The majority of examples in the literature on accentless focus phenomena likewise involve an expression which semantically one would expect to be accented but occurs in post-nuclear position.

Consider (5.3), from Rooth (1992). Here, we have another example of a mismatch between the intonational focus following a focus sensitive expression and the semantic focus of the expression. The intonational focus, looking only at pitch movement, is *eat* while the semantic focus of *only* is *rice*.[7]

(5.3)   People who [grow]$_F$ rice generally only [eat]$_F$ rice.

(5.2) and (5.3) both illustrate cases where the semantic focus of *only* follows a nuclear accent.

Are there any cases where the semantic focus lacks accent, but does not follow a nuclear accent? Dryer (1994) presents an example of this sort.[8] In the final sentence of (5.4) the semantic focus *a book* of *only* precedes the nuclear accent on *many people*.

(5.4)   A: I hear that John only gave [a book]$_F$ to Mary.

        B: True, but John only gave [a book]$_{SOF}$ to [many people]$_F$.

Examples (5.2)–(5.4) involve a repeat of some earlier focused occurrence of an expression.

Another logically possible accentless focus type is one in which the associate of a focus is both not explicitly mentioned in the previous discourse and is not intonationally prominent. An example of this sort is illustrated in (5.5), from Vallduví (1990; 1992: 150).[9]

(5.5)   [A last-minute guest arrives at host's house. The host has known the guest's family for years.]

        A: I'm glad you could come for dinner. Had I known before, I wouldn't have made pig's feet.

        B: I love pig's feet. It's my SISTER who *only* eats *prime cuts*.

---

[7] There is another reading of this string in which *only* associates with intonationally prominent *eat*. For the purposes of the discussion in this section, we are interested in the reading suggested by the continuation in (i), from Kadmon (2001: 316).

   (i) ... They don't eat [meat]$_F$ or [bread]$_F$.

[8] Rooth (1996b: 220) discusses the importance of the relative position of second occurrence foci and nuclear accented foci. We return to this issue in Chapter 6.

[9] In this example, capital letters indicate intonational prominence and italics indicate *only* and its semantic focus.

There are two key things to note about (5.5). First, the example is felicitous only in a context where the host knows that one of the guest's family members eats only prime cuts. Second, it is claimed that *prime cuts* is nonfocal (i.e. is not intonationally prominent) in (5.5).

As noted above, semantic theories of focus sensitivity predict focus-marked elements in the syntactic scope of focus sensitive expressions. Examples like (5.2)–(5.5) suggest that this prediction is false, at least in the case of *only*.

In Chapter 6, we show that this argument is unjustified on empirical and conceptual grounds. For example, we demonstrate that, at least for cases like (5.2), the semantic focus is indeed prosodically marked. For now, though, we will take it that examples like (5.2)–(5.5) are, on the surface, problematic for semantic theories of focus sensitivity. In the next section, we turn to the second empirical argument that is taken to favor pragmatic theories of focus sensitivity.

5.3 Association with Presupposition

Summary: *We introduce the phenomenon of* association with presupposition, *in which purportedly focus sensitive expressions seem to be less affected by focus than by presupposition. We present examples of the phenomenon involving quantificational adverbs and counterfactual conditionals.*

This next type of phenomenon also suggests that focus sensitive expressions do not associate with stressed material in their syntactic scope, contrary to what semantic theories of focus sensitivity would predict. Rather, the restrictor of these expressions is determined contextually, producing an effect that has been described as ASSOCIATION WITH PRESUPPOSITION (Rooth 1999).

Perhaps the best known evidence that focus sensitive constructions can associate with presupposition is due to Schubert and Pelletier (1987, 1989). They offer examples like (5.6), in which the restrictor of the adverb of quantification *always* does not correspond to material explicitly present in the sentence, but to material related to the presuppositions of what is in the adverb's scope (here, the presupposition that there is an appropriate professor available for admiration):

(5.6)   A student always admires a fair professor.
         'When a situation occurs allowing a student to perceive that a professor is fair, the student always admires the professor.'

Rooth (1999) and Cohen (1999) discuss similar data. Both suggest that presupposition might play a central role in the analysis of focus sensitivity effects. Rooth develops, and eventually rejects, a strong hypothesis: that all focus sensitivity is mediated by association with presupposition. In this view, taken up in different form by Geurts and van der Sandt (1997, 2004) (see below), there is no mechanism of association with focus. Rather, all focus is associated with presuppositions, and certain operators are sensitive to these presuppositions.

Rooth (1999) discusses cases where the interpretation of a counterfactual conditional is affected by presupposition.[10] To illustrate, Rooth (1999: 236) observes that focus sensitive particles like *too* interact with counterfactual conditionals in an interesting way. Consider a context in which Mary is in the elevator and John is in the snack bar. Is (5.7) true or false? As Rooth points out, the answer to this questions depends on, for example, whether Mary always avoids being in confined spaces with other people.

(5.7)   If John were in the elevator, Mary and John would be in the same place.

In contrast, for Speaker B's utterance (with *too*) in the exchange in (5.8), we are to consider counterfactual situations in which John and Mary are both in the elevator.

(5.8)   A: Mary is in the elevator.

         B: If John were in the elevator too, Mary and John would be in the same place.

Rooth assumes that *too* in Speaker B's utterance has a covert pronominal argument referring to the proposition denoted by Speaker A's utterance (i.e. Mary is in the elevator) and that *too* introduces the presupposition that this proposition is true. The key thing to note about Speaker B's utterance is that this presupposition is true both in the global context and in the counterfactual situations we are being asked to consider in evaluating the truth of Speaker B's utterance. That is, the *if*-clause in (5.8) presupposes that Mary is in the elevator.

Cohen (1999) considers cases in which there is both a clear focus and a separately induced presupposition, and in which it is the presupposition rather than the focus that ends up restricting a quantificational adverb. Notably, he does not consider focus sensitive expressions other than adverbs of quantification. To illustrate, the implicative verb *manage* normally carries the presupposition that the subject of the verb attempted to accomplish what is specified by the verb's infinitival complement. Hence, *Mary managed to complete her exams* presupposes that Mary tried to complete them.

Now consider how *manage* interacts with quantificational adverbs like *always*. Example (5.9) involves both a presupposition and a focus in the argument to the quantificational adverb *always*. Theoretically, we might conceive of two readings, as shown in (a) and (b). In the (a) reading, the restrictor clause contains the material presupposed by the verb *managed* (that Mary took exams), and in the (b) reading the restrictor contains all non-focal material.

(5.9)   Mary always managed to complete her [exams]$_F$.

        A: 'Whenever Mary took exams, she completed them.'

        B: ?'Whenever Mary completed something, it was invariably an exam.'

---

[10]   We discussed the focus sensitivity of counterfactuals in Chapter 3, §3.3.

On the basis of examples like (5.9), Cohen observed that, contrary to the predictions of semantic theories of focus sensitivity like Rooth (1985) and von Stechow (1985/1989), the (a) reading is the preferred one.

In Chapter 8, we return to the phenomenon of association with presupposition. In that chapter, we argue that the data does not support a general move to a pragmatic approach to focus sensitivity. We show instead that, with respect to association with presupposition, there are differences between the behavior of exclusives (like English *only*) and adverbs of quantification.

Having presented some of the empirical evidence against semantic accounts of focus sensitivity, we now turn to two prominent pragmatic theories of focus sensitivity, both closely related to the QFC model we presented in Chapters 2 and 3. Our goal is to show that, as yet, there is no satisfactory way of explaining association with focus effects that is purely pragmatic, in the sense that there are no expressions which encode a conventionalized dependency on focus as part of their lexical meaning. The absence of a viable alternative provides at least weak support for the QFC model. But note that the primary support for the QFC model comes later in the book, in the form of direct empirical evidence that there is conventionalization of association with focus effects for at least some operators.

5.4 Roberts' Account of Focus Sensitivity

Summary: *Roberts' (1996) explanation of association with focus differs from that in the QFC theory because she postulates that exclusives and other focus sensitive expressions have no conventionalized dependency on focus. We show how she explains association with focus effects for exclusives using a simple constructed example. We then discuss problems that her account faces as a general explanation of focus sensitivity, and suggest some simplifications that would bring her model closer to the QFC account.*

The QFC account developed in Chapters 2 and 3, although based on Roberts' (1996) pragmatic account of focus, differs from it in an important respect. Whereas we adopt the position that some expressions conventionally associate with focus, Roberts claims that all focus sensitive expressions freely associate. That is, she sets herself the difficult objective of explaining why certain expressions give rise to association-with-focus effects without postulating that any of those expressions have special access to focus. She considers one case in detail, the exclusive *only*, an expression which we claim conventionally associates with focus.

Consider (5.10a). Roberts takes the restrictor of the exclusive *only* to be a free variable. For simplicity, let us treat *only* as if it were a sentential operator, and take the restrictor to be a set of propositions R, so that the meaning of (5.10a) is (5.10b). What is needed is a mechanism that will fill in the value of R appropriately, i.e. as the set of alternatives in (5.10b). Let us see how Roberts derives the value of R, and then consider some issues arising.

(5.10) a. Sandy only feeds [Fido]$_F$ Nutrapup.

     b. $\forall p \in R$ $(\text{true}(p) \rightarrow p = feeds(s, f, n))$

     c. $R = \{feeds(s, x, n) \mid x \in D\}$

Transferring Roberts' discussion to the example at hand, what she attempts to show is that in the context set up by the question in (5.11a), resolving R as in (5.11b) would produce a felicitous discourse.

(5.11) a. Who does Sandy feed Nutrapup?

     b. Who does Sandy only feed Nutrapup?

     c. Which thing is such that Sandy only feeds [that thing]$_F$ Nutrapup?

Her argument has two stages. First, constraints similar to the Focus Principle and Discourse Principle of (2.54) force (5.10a) to be congruent to the question formed by replacing the focus with a WH-element, i.e. the question in (5.11b). For reasons to be discussed in §5.4, that is not quite the right question: example (5.11c), with the occurrence of *only* still restricted by R, expresses the meaning Roberts intends.

The second stage is to relate (5.11c) to (5.11a). Under the semantics for questions Roberts adopts, these two questions have slightly different meanings. (5.11a) denotes the set of propositions which say of some individual (possibly a plural individual) that the individual is fed Nutrapup by Sandy, whereas (5.11c) denotes the set of propositions which say of some individual (i) that the individual is fed Nutrapup by Sandy, and also (ii) that there is no other such individual.

Despite this difference, the two questions are mutually entailing in the sense of question entailment given above, in §2.5: any complete answer to one question is also a complete answer to the other. On this basis, (5.11c) is *relevant* to (5.11a). It then follows that in a situation where (5.11a) had been asked, (5.11c), with the restriction to R, could be freely accommodated, and this establishes the felicity of the discourse (5.11a+5.10a) with the desired restriction to R.

In §5.4, we will discuss several problems with Roberts' account. These problems relate to the fact that while the model works in some specific cases, it is not (yet) a general model of association with focus. But before looking at these problems, let us observe that we might have expected the theory to be of great breadth of application.

Take a case where nobody suggests a connection with focus: resolution of a lexically ambiguous word form. Ambiguity resolution is surely affected by the type of pragmatic consideration Roberts mentions. Consider the sentence *The bank is nearby* in the context of the question *Where is a bank?* Here interpretation of the homophone *bank* is surely constrained by pragmatics of the type Roberts mentions such that it gets the same interpretation in both question and answer. But there is nothing very magical about this: it is not an example of *bank* manifesting special association with focus effects.

Echoing a point we made in Chapter 3 with respect to the QFC model, the question then arises: according to Roberts, is *only* in any sense more focus sensitive than *bank*? The answer appears to be negative: resolution of the restrictor of *only* and resolution of the lexical ambiguity between *bank* (river) and *bank* (financial institution) are presumably analogous processes in so far as they are both constrained by general pragmatic principles, but neither type of resolution involves a grammaticized connection with focus.

Problems for Roberts' topical questions model

Kadmon (2001) observed a weakness in Roberts' argument. What Roberts shows is that under the assumption that R is set in the desired way the discourse (5.11a+5.10a) is felicitous. Kadmon's point is that what we really want to show is what the limits are on how R can be chosen. This is because association with focus in discourses like this is obligatory, meaning that *only* has to be restricted by R or some subset of the R-alternatives. So we need to show that if any non-R alternatives are in the restrictor set for *only*, infelicity will result.

What would happen if the restrictor of *only* was some R', which includes not only all the members of R, but also the proposition that Sandy fed Fido a competing dog food brand, say Doggotreats? In that case, the question in (5.11c) would come to be equivalent to:

(5.12)   What is the thing such that either Sandy feeds only that thing Nutrapup, or else she feeds nothing Nutrapup and feeds Fido Doggotreats?

This is a very strange question, and perhaps could be ruled out on some independent grounds. It would suffice for Roberts' argument if the question was in some way barred from being used as part of a strategy for answering (5.11a). However, every total answer to (5.12) would determine a total answer to (5.11a), so nothing in Roberts' theory explains what is wrong with R' as a restrictor.

To deal with the problems with Roberts' account, Kadmon makes a suggestion based on the double-edged nature of Grice's Maxim of Informativity. The maxim says not only that a speaker should provide enough information, but also that a speaker should not provide excessive information. An answer to (5.12) would provide strictly more information than is needed to determine a total answer to (5.11a), and this, Kadmon seems to be suggesting, is what makes (5.12) inappropriate. Kadmon is perhaps implicitly invoking a principle that questions cannot be accommodated if they would *strictly* entail their superquestions.

Finally, what if the restrictor consisted of a subset of R combined with some other extraneous proposition? In that case, (5.11c) would neither entail (5.11a) nor be entailed by it. So here it is clear that Roberts correctly predicts that such a restrictor would lead to an infelicitous discourse.

Suppose we accept what Roberts claims, that in the context of an explicit appropriate question, general pragmatic principles allow a sentence with *only* to get the right interpretation. So *Craige only ate [beans]*$_F$ will come to mean that she didn't eat anything else in the context of the question *What did Craige eat?*

This is good news, but is it enough? In a survey of all 35 Google hits on the string *only ate beans*, we found not one following a question. For example, the sentence in (5.13), on a website entitled *Funny Deaths*, has no relevant context that would make salient the question of what the man ate.

(5.13)   There once was a man who only ate beans and cabbage.

[web example]

The fact that a sentence with *only* can be understood out of the blue is not in and of itself damning for pragmatic models. The fact that we know what to focus when we read *only ate beans and cabbage* in the previous example shows quite clearly that pragmatics often is sufficient to determine the interpretation of *only*, even without explicit intonational marking. But the fact that in principle a pragmatic model might be able to solve the problem does not mean that Roberts has done the job. For it is far from obvious that Roberts' model introduces the right pragmatics.

What we will now show is that the model needs to be heavily constrained before it can do the job Roberts requires of it. Recall that Roberts' goal is to show that the effects of association with focus can be derived in a pragmatic model. And the little web survey reported above suggests that sentences involving *only* typically occur without explicit question contexts, so that, if Roberts is to be believed, we must rely on accommodation of questions most of the time before we can fill in the restrictor of *only*. But Roberts' model allows all sorts of questions to be accommodated which produce incorrect results.

Take example (5.14), which can be understood without the question *What did Craige eat?* being explicit.

(5.14)   Craige only ate [beans]$_F$

Roberts should be able to demonstrate the following: that for every question that could be accommodated so as to yield a coherent discourse, the answer ends up being interpreted with a meaning equivalent to that resulting from association with focus. But this is not the case. This is because Roberts' single constraint on accommodation is that discourse coherence is preserved or enhanced, and this can be satisfied if the hearer accommodates absolutely any question with the form *What X is such that Craige only ate X?*, with some choice of the restrictor for *only*.

For example, the restrictor might be:

(5.15) $R = \{[\![Craige\ ate\ beans]\!], [\![Craige\ ate\ caviar]\!]\}$.

In that case, (5.14) would be correctly predicted to entail that Craige did not eat caviar. But it would not entail, e.g. that Craige did not eat guacamole, which seems worrying for an out of the blue utterance of (5.14).

Even more worryingly, suppose the restrictor R in the accommodated question had been $\{[\![Craige\ ate\ beans]\!], [\![Craige\ grew\ beans]\!]\}$. Now the accommodated question is equivalent to *What X is such that Craige ate it but didn't grow it?* This seems *prima facie* a legitimate question, and there is no obvious reason why a hearer could not accommodate it. The discourse consisting of this question followed by (5.14) appears to be coherent according to Roberts' model, provided the same restrictor R is used in the accommodated question and (5.14) itself.

But the meaning derived for (5.14) is completely wrong: it is the meaning that you might get with focus on *ate*, plus some contextual restriction to the actions *eat* and *grow*. This is not an available interpretation for an out of the blue utterance of (5.14). Indeed, we doubt whether it is a possible interpretation in any context at all.

In addition to the preceding problems for Roberts' theory, there is a further issue that we find even more problematic. Roberts provides an analysis of the focus sensitivity of (non-scalar) exclusives, but it is unclear how her analysis might be applied to other operators that some might take to manifest conventionalized association with focus, as in (5.16a, b):

(5.16) A: Sandy always/usually/also/even/totally feeds Fido [Nutrapup]$_F$.

   B: In particular/for example, Sandy feeds Fido [Nutrapup]$_F$.

   C: R = $\{feeds(s, f, x) \mid x \in D\}$

Roberts gives no indication of whether she expects the argumentation she develops to explain focus sensitivity of exclusives to generalize to the operators in the above examples, quantificational adverbs, additives, scalar additives, intensifiers, and particularizers. In fact, it seems clear that her approach would not generalize to any of them without significant modification.

Consider first the case of quantificational adverbs. Roberts' argument for exclusives relates a sentence with *only* to a question which lacks *only*. This is what we would expect her account to achieve for a quantificational adverb like *usually*.

For example, (5.16), with the adverb *usually*, is congruent to the question *What did Sandy usually feed Fido?* We can assume that the restrictor of *usually* is some set of occasions S, so that we may paraphrase the meaning of the question as: *What (food) is such that for most occasions in S, Sandy fed that (food) to Fido on that occasion?* But this question is not related in any helpful way to a question without *usually*.

Presumably the question to aim for would be *What did Sandy feed Fido?* But this question is either understood as referring to a single occasion, or as a generic. If it refers to a single occasion, then it neither entails nor is entailed by the same question with *usually* added, except in the case where S is a trivial restrictor involving only one occasion. In that case, Roberts' pragmatic argumentation either fails, or produces an unwanted result.

On the other hand, the question minus *usually* could be understood generically. But in that case, we are presumably no nearer to understanding where the restrictor of *usually* comes from, since the generic itself would require a restrictor, presumably the same set of occasions S. Roberts' argumentation does not help us understand why association with focus is observed for quantificational adverbs.[11]

Let us consider the remaining cases in (5.16) (i.e. additives, scalar additives, intensifiers, and particularizers) as a group. Suppose that Roberts would take each of these operators to include an implicit argument on analogy with her treatment of exclusives. The aim of the pragmatic theory of association with focus is then to explain how the value of that argument comes to be correlated with the position of focus.

This group of expressions consists entirely of operators that are standardly claimed not to influence truth conditions.[12] Instead, they all have some pragmatic effect involving presupposition, discourse structure, or intensity. This makes them all plausible targets for the type of pragmatic account Roberts advocates, but unfortunately completely inappropriate targets for the specific argument she develops.

The trouble is that Roberts' explanation of association with focus effects depends on congruence of a sentence to an underlying question. Congruence is defined semantically, in terms of the truth conditions of the sentence and the question to which it is related. But as we have just noted, the group of operators now under consideration has no effect on truth conditions. So there is no way that altering the hidden argument of one of these operators could affect whether or not the sentence was congruent to an underlying question.

Based on the above arguments, we conclude that Roberts' congruence-based account does not yet adequately explain focus sensitivity of exclusives. We also conclude that the same account does not, in its original form, fare any better with other classes of focus sensitive operators than it does with exclusives. These negative conclusions should come as no surprise: we already argued in Chapters 2 and 3 that while something like Roberts' model makes an excellent

---

[11] Roberts is obviously aware of the fact that the argumentation she developed for exclusives does not apply directly to quantificational adverbs. She refers to Calcagno (1996) (in the same volume as her paper), who provides a detailed analysis of domain restriction in quantificational adverbs which takes Roberts' model as a starting point. We are sympathetic with the developments in Calcagno's paper, but will not pursue the approach here.

[12] Note that additives, scalar additives, intensifiers, and particulars are all conventional in the QFC taxonomy of focus sensitive expressions introduced in Chapter 2 and discussed in detail in Chapter 3.

foundation for a theory of focus sensitivity, additional apparatus is needed. And much of that apparatus, we claim must be tailored to the needs of the different classes of expression that manifest focus sensitivity.

Modifying Roberts' account

If we have harped on the problems with Roberts' account, it is because her model forms the main foundation of our own, and it is essential for us to subject it to close scrutiny. We believe that all the problems we have described can be avoided with two adaptations, both of which are made in the QFC model in Chapters 2 and 3.

First, many of the above problems with Roberts' model can be avoided by weakening her congruence requirement. Rather than insisting that a sentence uttered is congruent to the Current Question, our Focus Principle only requires that some part of a sentence is congruent to the Current Question. In typical examples we have considered involving focus sensitivity of propositional operators, it is the argument of the operator which is congruent to the Current Question.

An entirely independent simplifying adjustment we make to Roberts' theory is to claim that implicit restrictors of certain focus sensitive operators are lexically stipulated to be dependent on the Current Question. That is, we convert her model from a free association model to a conventionalized association model with respect to operators which can be independently argued to be discourse functional. This is one change that runs very strongly counter to the spirit of Roberts' original work. Roberts, in her discussion of *only*, argues that the implicit restrictor of *only* should be set to whatever value is pragmatically optimal.

A mid-way point between Roberts' proposal and ours would involve taking advantage of the fact that some potential values of the restrictor of *only* are more salient than others. If we allow that *only* tends to be anaphoric to the most salient question, then basic association with focus effects are explained straightforwardly.

For example, (5.10a), even if uttered in a relatively out of the blue context, makes salient the question in (5.11a). The alternative set corresponding to this question is then also salient, and a prime candidate for the value of the restrictor of *only*. On this picture, association with focus effects for exclusives would involve a happy confluence of two pragmatic forces: first, the need to fill in a free variable with a salient value of the right type, and second the pressure to choose a value for that variable which is optimal from the point of view of relevance and informativity.

As was noted above, Roberts' congruence analysis cannot work for operators which have a free variable but which do not contribute to truth conditional meaning (e.g. additives, particularizers, intensifiers). We might then argue that in these cases anaphoricity to a salient question is the primary force governing their interpretation. That is, discourse is structured by questions and these are discourse operators, so, not surprisingly, they act anaphorically on previously mentioned (or else implicit) questions. [13]

Let us draw together some of the themes from this section. We saw that while Roberts provides an intuitively appealing account of how a sentence with an exclusive gets its meaning when an appropriate question is already in the context, she does not constrain sufficiently what questions can be accommodated when there is no appropriate question explicit in prior discourse. Furthermore, we saw that Roberts' model, as stated, does not generalize easily from exclusives to other expressions that manifest association with focus effects. Our own reaction, in Chapter 2 and Chapter 3, was to modify Roberts' model somewhat, and use it as the basis of the QFC theory. In doing so, we have made at least one assumption which is antithetical to the spirit of Roberts' analysis: we have assumed that at least some operators are conventionally focus sensitive. But perhaps, as we have suggested in the last few paragraphs above, there remains some middle ground to be found between Roberts' theory and our own, an adaption of Roberts' model that is not quite so extreme. But we now leave further consideration of this possibility, and turn to an alternative attempt to explain association with focus in a purely pragmatic theory.

5.5 A Presuppositional Account of Focus Sensitivity

Summary: *We discuss how Geurts and van der Sandt (2004) attempt to explain some cases of association with focus in terms of the theory of presupposition first presented as van der Sandt (1992). In the proposed model, focus triggers an existential presupposition. An independently motivated account of presupposition accommodation then explains why this presupposition can end up restricting the domain of certain operators, producing the appearance of association with focus. We show that many unanswered questions remain regarding how the model would apply to cases in which the apparently focus sensitive operator is not a quantifier.*

Geurts and van der Sandt (2004) (hence GvdS) analyze a wide range of focus phenomena by combining a detailed theory of presupposition with a single interpretative rule for focus. This rule, the Background Presupposition Rule (BPR) states that focus generates existential presuppositions. This existential presupposition is logically equivalent to the disjunction of the Roothian alternative set, but because GvdS operate in the setting of Discourse Representation Theory (henceforth, DRT; Kamp 1981; Kamp and Reyle 1993), details of the

---

[13] The model we are proposing here has much in common with that proposed by von Fintel (1994). First, he assumes that focus operators do not contribute to the alternative set corresponding to a sentence with focus, a stipulation which is analogous to the stipulation we suggest that these operators do not affect the congruence calculation. Second, he assumes that these operators are primarily anaphoric. Like Roberts, he proposes (von Fintel 1994: 42, 49–52) that a large class of focus operators is anaphoric to (possibly implicit) salient questions.

representation of the focal presupposition could potentially make a difference, e.g. for accessibility of discourse referents.[14] But at least for NP focus we can think of the presupposition as equivalent to the clause containing the focus but with the focal element replaced, so that *Mary likes [Sam]*$_F$ presupposes *Mary likes somebody*.

GvdS discuss *always*, which is standardly analyzed as being focus sensitive. Their analysis proceeds via a combination of the BPR, a mechanism for ACCOMMODATION of presuppostions and a useful principle called TRAPPING. Accommodation and trapping are both components of the model of presupposition originally laid out in van der Sandt (1992).

In our formulation of van der Sandt's model of presupposition, we assume that presuppositions are uniformly represented using a type of complex condition, a special Discourse Representation Structure (DRS) marked with a ∂ operator. Consider the following example involving the factive verb *know*:

(5.17)   If Butch is barking, then Mary knows that Butch is awake.

Assuming some drastic simplifications (such as representing proper names with a *constant* discourse marker) we arrive at the initial DRS as shown in Figure 5.1.

There are two strategies available for *resolving* a presupposition, and each application of a strategy reduces by one the number of ∂-marked DRSs. The first strategy is BINDING, which requires that the presuppositional DRS has some pre-existing antecedent DRS in an *accessible* position (in the standard DRT sense of the word *accessible*). After identification of variables in the presupposition with those of the antecedent, the conditions in the antecedent DRS must be compatible with those in the presuppositional DRS. The binding operation consists of: (i) removing the presuppositional DRS; (ii) adding the markers and conditions of the presuppositional DRS at the site of the antecedent; (iii) adding

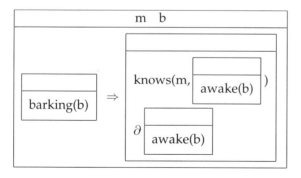

Figure 5.1 Initial DRS for (5.17)

---

[14]   In this section we presume familiarity with the basics of DRT. For what is intended as a quick and accessible introduction available on the web, see Geurts and Beaver (2007).

for each marker X from the universe of the presuppositional DRS a condition of the form X = Y, where Y is some marker of the antecedent DRS.

Binding would apply, for example, in an example like *A bird had flown in, and Mary realized that a bird had flown in.* Here the second instance of *a bird* occurs within the factive construction *realized that.* To resolve the presupposition, the discourse marker for the presuppositional *a bird* and for the first mentioned *a bird* are simply identified.

If only some of the discourse markers and conditions in the presuppositional DRS are present at the site of the antecedent, we obtain what is known as a *partial match.* For example, consider a newspaper-style text *Yesterday a man was shot in Utrecht. The Amsterdam father of four . . .* Here binding occurs by adding to the global DRS (there being here no local contexts) an equation identifying the discourse marker for *a man* and that for *the Amsterdam father of four*, and further adding the relevant conditions (that the marker corresponds to an Amsterdam father of four).

The second strategy is ACCOMMODATION, an operation for adding information required to resolve a presupposition lacking any explicit linguistic antecedent. For instance, to process the sentence *Her Ladyship regrets that she will be unable to attend*, the presupposed information that her Ladyship will not attend must be accommodated. In van der Sandt's model, accommodation can be thought of as *move-α* at the level of DRS, whereby presuppositional material moves from its trigger site to some other position in the DRS, and loses its special marking as *presupposed*. In the formulation here, this means that the ∂ operator is eliminated in the process of the move.

The move must be to an *accessible* site. Thus the 'arrival' site may be the global DRS, the local DRS of the trigger, or some intermediate DRS. Note that it is common for authors to term all non-global instances of accommodation *local*, whereas we find it more useful to reserve the word *local* for accommodation at the site of the trigger, and to name all remaining non-global cases *intermediate*.

Accommodation may itself be seen as a collection of strategies, depending on the exact accommodation site. For (5.17) above, there would be three ways of accommodating the presupposition that Butch is awake (Figures 5.2–4):

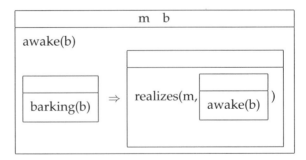

Figure 5.2 Global accommodation (Gloss: Butch is awake, and if he is barking Mary realizes he is awake.)

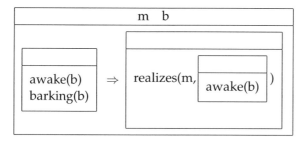

Figure 5.3 Intermediate accommodation (Gloss: If Butch is awake and barking, Mary realizes he is awake.)

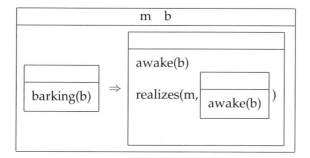

Figure 5.4 Local accommodation (Gloss: If Butch is barking, he is awake and Mary realizes he is awake.)

We now have a number of ways that a presupposition may be resolved. But how are we to choose between them in a particular case? There are a number of constraints in van der Sandt's model, most of which have a Gricean character, e.g. a preference for accommodation that preserves informativity. Only two of van der Sandt's constraints are relevant to our purposes, however (see Beaver and Zeevat 2007 for discussion):

The Trapping Principle: If a presupposition containing a variable x is triggered in an environment where x is bound by a quantifier Q, the presupposition will be accommodated in such a way that x remains bound by Q.

Generalized Globality Principle: One accommodation alternative is preferred to another if the first is more global (i.e. further from the site of the trigger, and nearer to the global context).

For example (5.17), the second of these two constraints wins the day, so the prediction of the theory is that the preferred reading of the example is the first of those above, the Global Accommodation reading. But in the cases we will now consider, the Global Accommodation Preference is overruled by Trapping.

GvdS analyze the focus sensitivity of *always* by claiming that the BPR generates presuppositions that include an event variable, and trapping forces the presupposition to be accommodated in the restrictor of *always*, binding the event variable. This is illustrated by (5.18), which (modulo a simplified treatment of names and tense) gets the initial representation in Figure 5.5. Intermediate accommodation of the presupposition generated by the BPR results in the representation in Figure 5.6: any event of Mary helping some x is an event of Mary helping Jim.[15]

(5.18)   Mary always helped [Jim]$_F$.

It seems that for the case of *always*, the BPR gives us a good start.

How about other cases? GvdS never state explicitly that the BPR accounts for all cases of focus sensitivity. Furthermore, as regards the two focus sensitive particles they discuss most, *only* and *too*, they never discuss how the focus sensitivity of the particles arises. Indeed, in the case of *only* they stick exclusively to examples in which the particle is left-adjoined to its focus (e.g. *Mary only [danced]$_F$, Only [Wilma]$_F$ guessed the secret word*), a subclass of cases for which focus sensitivity is not manifest. Can the analysis of focus

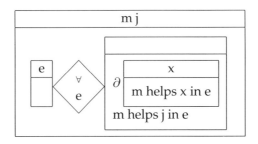

Figure 5.5 Initial DRS for (5.18)

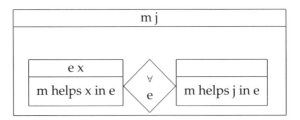

Figure 5.6 Intermediate accommodation (Gloss: Any event of Mary helping some x is an event of Mary helping Jim.)

---

[15]   The effect of *trapping* in this type of example is the same as what is achieved by Berman's (1991) *Presuppositionality Hypothesis*, which states that quite generally "presuppositions of the nuclear scope become part of the restrictive term." As stated, Berman's hypothesis is too broad. Consider e.g. *People rarely realize that Donald is older than Mickey*: here we want the presupposition (that Donald is older) to project globally, and not to end up in the restrictor of *rarely*. The advantage of *trapping* is that it would not apply in a case like this, since the presupposition contains no free variable.

sensitivity which GvdS apply to *always* be applied in general? Could the technique they apply in the case of *always* be used for *only* and other focus sensitive
particles?

The representations GvdS choose for *only* differ in several respects from
those we have considered, and we return to the issue of the lexical semantics
of *only* in Chapters 9 and 10. We do observe, however, that the representation
they use for *only* would not permit the same approach to focus sensitivity as
that given for *always*. The problem is that their representation of the meaning of
only does not include any quantification over events. This means that the focal
presupposition would not be 'trapped', and could be globally accommodated.[16]

Let us assume that by default event variables are existentially bound at the
top-level of the DRS, which is what one would expect in a DRT implementation
of a neo-Davidsonian event semantics. The initial representation of (5.19) would
be that shown in Figure 5.7, and global accommodation followed by binding
of the event variable would yield Figure 5.8. Under reasonable assumptions
about the meaning of *only*, for example, the assumptions GvdS make, Figure 5.8
would have the same truth conditions as *Mary helped Jim*, surely not the right
result.

(5.19)   Mary only helped [Jim]$_F$.

Based on the problem shown by (5.19), and Figures 5.7, 5.8, let us simply
add an event to the representation of *only*. In that case, trapping will have the
same effects as in the analysis of *always*, above, and we derive the desired representation as shown in Figure 5.9.

Having *only* bind events in this way is not in and of itself unreasonable: as
discussed in the last chapter, it is the mainstay of Bonomi and Casalegno (1993),
Herburger (2000), and, indeed, ourselves (Beaver and Clark 2003), and we will
make heavy use of events in Chapters 6–8 of this book. But some further work
is needed to make events do the job GvdS require if they are to account for a
wide range of focus sensitivity effects.

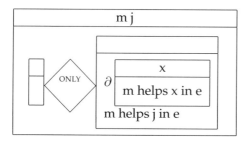

Figure 5.7 Initial DRS for (5.19)

---

[16]   What we represent as [A]⟨ONLY⟩[B] would for GvdS be ¬[A ¬B], but this difference does not
bear upon the discussion in this section.

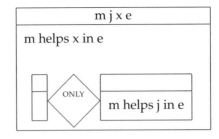

Figure 5.8 Global accommodation (Same truth conditions as *Mary helped Jim*.)

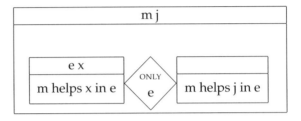

Figure 5.9 Intermediate accommodation

An assumption that GvdS make and that compromises the potential of their approach to explain the focus sensitivity of *only* is that *only* lacks an existential presupposition. The existential presupposition of *Mary only ate chocolate*, as defended recently by Horn (1996), would be *Mary ate something*. GvdS support there being such a presupposition, but claim that it derives not from the lexical meaning of *only*, but from the BPR. This is an interesting proposal.

However, it is not compatible with an analysis of the focus sensitivity of *only* based on trapping of the BPR presupposition. A supporter of the GvdS model has a choice: either the BPR is used to explain the existential presupposition of *only*, or it is used to explain the focus sensitivity of *only*, but not both. Since our main goal at the moment is to consider possible explanations of focus sensitivity, let us assume that this is what the BPR is used for, and suppose that the existential presupposition of *only* is explained by an independent lexical stipulation on the meaning of *only*.

There may still be some technical issues involved in assuming both that *only* has a lexically specified existential presupposition and that focus sensitivity is explained by trapping of the BPR presupposition. The problem is that the presupposition of *only* would have to be affected by the accommodation of the BPR presupposition.

For example, the sentence *Mary only ate [chocolates]*$_F$ would be analyzed by first accommodating in the restrictor of *only* the presupposition that Mary ate something, and then creating a secondary presupposition that the restrictor holds of some object, i.e. once again presupposing that Mary ate something. From a purely technical point of view, it is not clear how the GvdS framework allows for accommodation into a site that is itself a presupposition.

We suggest that in order to implement this in DRT, a new type of structure is needed, something like that pictured in Figure 5.10. What we see here is a type of duplex (i.e. two box) condition in which the antecedent box, depicted with double thick edges, is presupposed: we will call this a quantificational presupposition.

The resolution and accommodation algorithm used by GvdS would have to be revised in order to make such a structure work appropriately, but the required modifications are not complex. First, there is already a rule saying that more deeply embedded presuppositions are evaluated before less deeply embedded presuppositions. We extend this by stipulating that if a presupposition K is accessible from a presupposition K', then K' must be processed first.

Second, a quantificational presupposition is understood existentially. It is satisfied if copies of the conditions in the box are accessible modulo replacement of the names of locally bound variables. This condition that quantificational presuppositions are existential is needed, because without replacement of variable names, the presupposition would remain trapped in the duplex condition rather than being able to gain existential force in the global DRS.

To see how this works, consider the derivation illustrated in Figures 5.10, 5.11, and 5.12. First, the BPR induced presupposition in the righthand box in Figure 5.10 is subject to intermediate accommodation, as a result of trapping, to form the structure in Figure 5.11. Next, the quantificational presupposition is globally accommodated, modulo renaming of the variables x and e, to form the final structure in Figure 5.12.

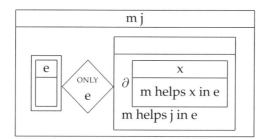

Figure 5.10 Initial DRS (for 5.19) with BPR induced presupposition

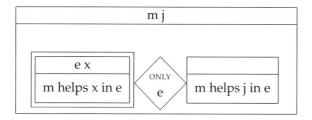

Figure 5.11 Intermediate accommodation

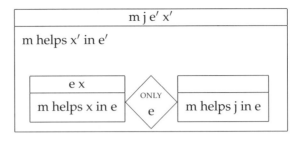

Figure 5.12 Global accommodation of quantificational presupposition

It is not obvious how GvdS would choose to analyze the focus sensitivity of additives like *too*. They give an example that is similar to (5.20) with a representation along the lines of Figure 5.13. But this represents a meaning in which the dependency of *too* on focus has already been computed.

(5.20)   If the boss comes to the party, [Barney]$_F$ is coming too. (variant on GvdS (61a))

The question is: what produces the representation in Figure 5.13? An answer would require more than just adding an event variable and relying on trapping to do the work, because the representation of *too* that GvdS assume does not include any good places for event variables to hide, ready to capture and transform focal presuppositions.

In addition, it remains unclear how the transformation of the standard existential BPR presupposition to the peculiar double-embedded presupposition GvdS propose for *too* would occur. However, if we use the double thick box technique above, it at least becomes technically possible to generate the desired effect. We would have to use an initial representation like that in Figure 5.14, in which we assume that the duplex condition introduced by *too* is understood purely conjunctively and existentially. The BPR induced presupposition on the right hand side is accommodated in the lefthand box of the complex *too* condition, as in Figure 5.15. The existential presupposition of *too* can then be resolved to the proposition in the antecedent of the implication (that the boss is coming to the party), discharging the presupposition of *too* with no further accommodation, as in Figure 5.16.[17]

---

[17]   Note that whereas GvdS assume an extra presupposition $x \neq v$, we do not incorporate this, but instead assume it will be generated by a neo-Gricean principle forcing non-redundancy of DRS. Such principles form the mainstay of the GvdS accommodation theory, although we have not described their application here. See Beaver and Zeevat (2007) for discussion.

Another issue arising is that the representation for *too* we use would appear to suggest that indefinites in the scope of *too* are not later available for anaphoric reference. This is problematic. For the moment all we can suggest is a further *ad hoc* modification to the accessibility conditions of DRT to say that material inside a *too* duplex condition is accessible from the outside. However, this issue seems to suggest that a more radical modification might be needed, for example a move to treating *too* at a higher level of DRS, as in the work of Asher and Lascarides (2003).

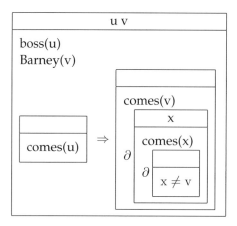

Figure 5.13 Geurts and van der Sandt representation for (5.22)

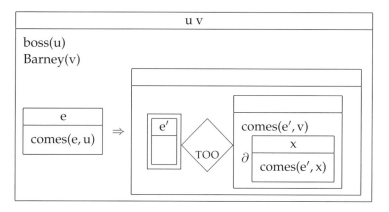

Figure 5.14 Initial DRS for (5.22)

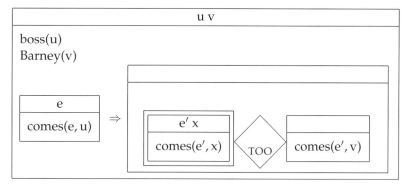

Figure 5.15 Accommodation of BPR induced presupposition

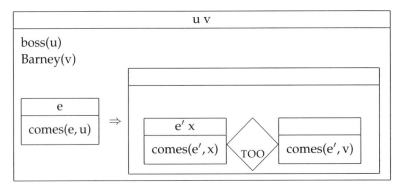

Figure 5.16 Existential presupposition of *too* resolved

5.6 Summary

We began this chapter with some of the data motivating pragmatic accounts of presupposition, starting with some methodological arguments offered by Rooth, and then moving on to evidence, including the argument from second occurrence focus and association with presupposition. We discussed in detail two types of pragmatic theory that might potentially explain association with presupposition effects.

The first was Roberts' application of her topical questions model of discourse to *only*. We noted that while there are some operators (e.g. exclusives, additives, scalar additives) to which this type of theory seems to have potential, there are others (e.g. quantificational adverbs) for which it is not at all clear how the theory might be applied.

Further, we argued that considerable extensions to the theory are needed to fully account for association with focus effects involving *only*, and even greater modifications would be needed to account for a wider range of operators. Of course, these are just the modifications we already included in the QFC model presented in Chapters 2 and 3 as applied to the conventional association class of focus sensitive expressions.

The second type of pragmatic theory we considered was the presupposition based model of Geurts and van der Sandt. Again, the original theory had only been applied to one example of association with focus effects, in this case the quantificational adverb *always*. It is, of course, interesting to note that the cases for which Roberts' theory is most obviously difficult to apply is precisely the case that Geurts and van der Sandt chose to analyze.

However, we showed that with some extensions to the theory, the presupposition based model could potentially be applied to a wider range of operators, including those that Roberts' model applies to, so this is not a case where the theories necessarily have mirror image domains of application.

Geurts and van der Sandt's proposal is an obvious inspiration for our treatment of free association cases in the QFC model. The main differences are: first, that we derive existential presuppositions by a slightly more roundabout path (using a principle we termed the Current Question Rule in Chapters 2 and 3, and discuss in detail in Chapter 10) than they do, and second, that we take intermediate accommodation of presuppositions to be a far more constrained process than Geurts and van der Sandt do. In many cases where Geurts and van der Sandt use intermediate accommodation of material, we take it that discourse coherence requires the material to be previously salient.

We have now detailed how conventionalized compositional theories of focus sensitivity work (in Chapter 4), and how pragmatic theories work. Seeing how these monolithic accounts of focus are supposed to work should have set into sharp relief the QFC model and its attendent three way classification of focus sensitivity. In the coming three chapters we will look at the data which motivates our move away from monolithic accounts of focus sensitivity.

Chapter 6

Soft Focus: Association with Reduced Material

I am convinced that there is a vast deal of inconsistency in almost every human character.
Jane Austen, 1811, *Sense and Sensibility*

6.1 Introduction

This chapter discusses the apparent optionality of focus sensitivity effects. We show that the main empirical argument put forward in favor of pragmatic theories of focus sensitivity is empirically flawed. In Chapter 5, we discussed a class of phenomena we called ACCENTLESS FOCUS. Accentless focus phenomena involve interpretational effects normally attributed to focus sensitivity but apparently without focus marking on the focus associate. On the basis of acoustical production and perception studies, we argue that for at least one type of accentless focus, second occurrence focus, the claim that there is no focus marking is wrong.

We are left with a lingering question. Can focus sensitive expressions ever associate with material that lacks prosodic prominence? To answer this question, we look at the distribution of unstressed pronouns in the scope of focus sensitive expressions and show that some, but not all, focus sensitive expressions can associate with material that completely lacks prosodic prominence.

This result supports the idea that some focus sensitive expressions obligatorily associate with prosodically marked material in their syntactic scope, contrary to pragmatic theories of focus interpretation which predict that prosodically marked elements are not required in the syntactic scope of focus sensitive expressions. We suggest that two different mechanisms explain the differences between focus sensitive expressions: some focus sensitive expressions such as *only* lexically encode a dependency on focus marking, whereas others such as *always* do not.

6.2   Second Occurrence Focus: Background

Summary: *We review the argument from second occurrence focus that has been used to support purely pragmatic theories of focus sensitivity.*

In Chapter 5 we introduced the core empirical argument against semantic theories of focus sensitivity, the ARGUMENT FROM SECOND OCCURRENCE FOCUS. In this section, we provide evidence against the claim that second occurrence foci are prosodically unmarked. Our understanding of second occurrence focus phenomena is grounded in production and perception experiments (Beaver et al. 2007; Ishihara and Féry 2006).[1] The results of these experiments show that second occurrence foci are prosodically marked, and that this marking is perceptible. On the basis of this result, we argue that second occurrence focus phenomena are compatible with semantic theories of focus interpretation.

The argument from second occurrence focus originates in a disagreement about how grammaticized the relationship between focus sensitive expressions and their associated focus is (Partee 1999: 215ff). Do the lexical entries of focus sensitive expressions stipulate association with a prosodically prominent element in their syntactic scope (as in the semantic analyses of focus presented in Chapter 4), or are there contexts in which the interpretational effects of focus sensitivity occur without focus being present either phonologically or syntactically (as predicted by the pragmatic analyses of focus presented in Chapter 5)?

As discussed in Chapter 5, second occurrence foci involve an apparent dislocation between the interpretation of focus sensitive expressions and the position of prosodic prominence. The exchange in (5.2), repeated here as (6.1), illustrates second occurrence focus. The two sentences are to be read as a dialogue. We represent the second occurrence focus with a subscripted "SOF". The focused element *vegetables* in Speaker A's turn is repeated in Speaker B's turn. In both turns, *vegetables* is the focus associate of *only* ('Mary eats vegetables and nothing else'), yet focus marking appears to be absent on *vegetables* in Speaker B's turn.

(6.1)   A: Everyone already knew that Mary only eats [vegetables]$_F$.

      B: If even [Paul]$_F$ knew that Mary only eats [vegetables]$_{SOF}$, then he should have suggested a different restaurant.

Partee (1999: 215–16) summarizes the problem succinctly:

> If "only" is a focus-sensitive operator, then it would seem that the two occurrences of "only eats vegetables" should have the same analysis, but if there really is no

---

[1]   The work reported in this and the following section was first presented at the 2003 LSA Annual Meeting (Beaver, Clark, Flemming, and Wolters, *Debunking the Argument from Second Occurrence Focus*) and the 2004 LSA Annual Meeting (Beaver, Clark, Flemming, and Jaeger, *The Perception of Second Occurrence Focus*). For more detail see Beaver et al (2007) and Jaeger (2004).

phonological reflex of focus on the second occurrence, then that leads to the notion of "phonologically invisible focus," which at best would force the recognition of a multiplicity of different notions of "focus" and at worst might lead to a fundamentally incoherent notion of focus.

The argument from second occurrence focus has the form in (6.2).[2]

(6.2)   a.   Semantic theories of focus sensitivity (e.g. Rooth 1985) require focus marked elements in the syntactic scope of focus sensitive expressions.

      b.   In the case of second occurrence focus there is no such element.

      c.   Therefore focus sensitivity is optional and requires a pragmatic account.

Many semanticists (a notable exception being Rooth 1996b) have assumed that lack of pitch accent correlates with lack of focus marking. This is the key assumption underlying (6.2b). Analyses of focus sensitivity which encode sensitivity in the lexical meanings of focus sensitive expressions have been taken to predict that there are no environments in which the focus associate of such an expression is not focus marked.

But if the observations underlying (6.2b) are correct, interpretational effects normally attributed to focus are found in second occurrence focus contexts even without focus marking on the focus associate of a focus sensitive expression (e.g. *vegetables* in Speaker B's utterance in (6.1)). This runs directly contrary to what semantic or otherwise conventionalized analyses of focus sensitivity are normally taken to predict.

Drawing on the production and perception studies of second occurrence focus presented in Beaver et al. (2007) and Ishihara and Féry (2006), we are now going to see how (6.2b), and thus the argument from second occurrence focus, cannot be used as an argument in favor of pragmatic theories of focus sensitivity. Before we turn to these acoustical studies, we review two earlier experimental studies on the phonetics and phonology of second occurrence focus.

The argument from second occurrence focus would be undermined if it could be demonstrated that second occurrence focus has prosodic correlates, contrary to (6.2b). Rooth (1996b) presented suggestive acoustical evidence indicating just that, and Rooth's observations provided the impetus for the more systematic experimental studies which we discuss in §6.3.

Rooth (1996b) made recordings of himself uttering two minimal pairs of second occurrence focus dialogues, as in (6.3) and (6.4). The VPs containing the second occurrence foci (e.g. *name Manny today* in (6.3)) were identical in all the examples he discussed. This allowed Rooth to compare second occurrence foci (e.g. *Manny* in (6.4)) to controls where the same NPs were not in focus at all (e.g. *Manny* in (6.3)).

---

[2]   Most arguments in the literature have basically the same structure; see e.g. Rooth (1996b: 206).

(6.3) a. Do you want Sue to only [name]$_F$ Manny today?

b. No. I only want [Eva]$_F$ to only [name]$_{SOF}$ Manny today.

(6.4) a. Do you want Sue to only name [Manny]$_F$ today?

b. No. I only want [Eva]$_F$ to only name [Manny]$_{SOF}$ today.

Rooth found that the pitch track was flat for second occurrence foci such as the words *name* and *Manny* in (6.3b) and (6.4b), but he could hear the marking of second occurrence focus in his own productions. Further, this marking of second occurrence focus is visible in the sample of his productions for which he presents waveforms and spectrograms. In these productions, although no major pitch movement is visible on second occurrence focus expressions, these expressions are longer and have greater absolute intensity than their non-focused counterparts.

In related work, Bartels (1997) examined various correlates of prosodic prominence (relative syllable lengthening and amplitude) on second occurrence expressions in a multi-subject production study. She found that second occurrence foci differed from ordinary foci not only with regard to pitch, but also with regard to amplitude and duration.

Bartels was the first to adopt a systematic experimental approach to focus phenomena, but her conclusions concerned the different realization of second occurrence focus from ordinary focus. Since she did not compare second occurrence foci to non-foci (Bartels 1997: 24), her experiment does not provide evidence as to whether expressions in second occurrence have any prosodic marking that makes them prominent, or which might be interpreted as marking focus. It merely establishes that if second occurrence focus is marked, then, on multiple acoustic dimensions including fundamental frequency, relative syllable lengthening and amplitude, second occurrence focus is marked differently from ordinary focus.

Rooth's work suggests that second occurrence foci are acoustically distinguished from non-foci. If this hypothesis is correct, and under the reasonable assumption that focus marking can be operationalized in terms of these acoustic correlates, the argument from second occurrence focus unravels. In the next section we discuss two production studies that confirm that second occurrence foci are indeed acoustically distinguished from non-foci. Further, we discuss a perception experiment that shows that hearers can distinguish between the acoustic realizations of second occurrence foci and those of non-foci.

6.3 Second Occurrence Focus: Experiments

Summary: *We discuss production and perception experiments reported by Beaver et al. (2007), with supporting evidence from Ishihara and Féry (2006). We show that the main empirical argument put forward in favor of pragmatic theories of focus sensitivity – the argument from second occurrence focus – is empirically flawed.*

Beaver et al. (2007) and Ishihara and Féry (2006) examine the hypothesis that second occurrence foci are acoustically distinguished from non-foci. This hypothesis competes with the null hypothesis assumed by the argument from second occurrence focus (cf. (6.2b)) that second occurrence focus is not prosodically marked. Both of the production experiments we discuss here test this null hypothesis.

Beaver et al. (2007) performed a multi-speaker, multi-discourse experiment. The goal of the experiment was to examine whether words in second occurrence focus are acoustically distinct from non-focal occurrences of the same words in the scope of focus sensitive expressions such as *only* and *always*. A number of acoustic correlates were looked at, including:

(6.5) a. maximal (f_0) pitch,

     b. pitch range,

     c. word duration,

     d. r.m.s. intensity in decibels,

     e. a pseudo-energy measure ($=$ r.m.s. intensity $\times$ duration)

An example of a minimal pair of discourses used as stimuli in the study is given in (6.6) and (6.7). In this pair, the relevant focus sensitive expression is *only*. Note that another focus sensitive expression *even* is also present in (6.6c) and (6.7c). In (6.6b), *Sid* is the focus of the focus sensitive expression *only*, whereas in (6.7b), *court* is the focus, and *Sid* is non-focal. Sentences (6.6c) and (6.7c) contain a textually identical VP (*only named Sid in court today*) to the (b) sentences, but the VP in (6.6c) and (6.7c) follows an earlier phrase *even the state prosecutor* containing what we take to be the nuclear accent of the sentence (presumably on *state prosecutor*). This is a configuration in which second occurrence foci, such as the focus in the VP in each of the (c) sentences below, have been reported to be unmarked prosodically.

(6.6) a. Both Sid and his accomplices should have been named in this morning's court session.

     b. But the defendant only named [Sid]$_F$ in court today.

     c. Even [the state prosecutor]$_F$ only named [Sid]$_{SOF}$ in court today.

(6.7) a. Defense and Prosecution had agreed to implicate Sid both in court and on television.

     b. Still, the defense attorney only named Sid in [court]$_F$ today.

     c. Even [the state prosecutor]$_F$ only named Sid in [court]$_{SOF}$ today.

Beaver et al. (2007) found significant effects for duration and energy: second occurrence focus expressions average 6 msecs longer than their non-focal counterparts and receive more energy. In contrast, there was no overall significant effect for various pitch measures such as maximum and mean pitch.

These results confirm that there are indeed prosodic correlates of second occurrence focus involving duration and energy. Further, the results show that second occurrence focus is marked differently than ordinary (first occurrence) focus, which is typically marked by pitch accent. In §6.4, we discuss evidence that suggests that *always*, but not *only*, can associate with material that completely lacks prosodic prominence. The experiment did not yield significant effects supporting a distinction between *only* and *always*, but this may be because the experimental design was not intended to reveal a distinction between the two.

Ishihara and Féry (2006) investigated second occurrence focus in German, as in (6.8). In (6.8c), *Peter* is the second occurrence focus and *einen Anzug* 'a tie' is the ordinary (first occurrence) focus.

(6.8) a. Die meisten unserer Kollegen   waren beim Beriebsausflug
           The most   of-our colleagues were   at   work-trip
           lässig   angezogen.
           casually dressed
           'Most of our colleagues were dressed casually at the staff outing'

       b. Nur [Peter]$_F$ het eine Krawatte getragen.
           Only Peter   has a   tie   worn
           'Only Peter wore a tie.'

       c. Sogar   [einen Anzug]$_F$ hat nur [Peter]$_{SOF}$ getragen.
           Actually a   suit   has only Peter   worn
           'Only Peter actually wore a suit.'

Ishihara and Féry (2006) show that second occurrence foci are generally longer in duration than their nonfocal counterparts, confirming for German the results of the production study conducted by Beaver et al. (2007). They also show that there is typically not a contrast between second occurrence foci and their nonfocal counterparts with respect to pitch.

In the production experiment presented in Beaver et al. (2007), the second occurrence focus was always preceded by a nuclear pitch accent, marking the focus associated with *even*. The great majority of examples in the literature on apparent disassociation between focus and pitch accent have this form: an expression which semantically one would expect to be accented occurs in postnuclear position.

For example, this is true of Rooth's (1992: 109) classic rice farmer example. In (6.9), the second occurrence of *rice* follows the nuclear pitch accent on *eat*.

(6.9)   People who [grow]$_F$ rice generally only [eat]$_F$ rice.

This observation raises the following question. Is there a prosodic correlate of prenuclear second occurrence focus? Example (6.10) (from Dryer 1994) illustrates the relevant configuration. In (6.10), the second occurrence focus *a book* in Speaker B's utterance precedes a nuclear accent on *many people*.

(6.10) A: I hear that John only gave [a book]$_F$ to Mary.

   B: True, but John only gave [a book]$_{SOF}$ to [many people]$_F$.

In contrast to Beaver et al. (2007), Ishihara and Féry (2006) looked at both postnuclear and prenuclear second occurrence foci. Example (6.8) illustrates a case where the second occurrence focus in (6.11) *Peter* is located in prenuclear position. Ishihara and Féry found that prenuclear second occurrence foci were typically marked with a pitch accent, unlike postnuclear ones. On the basis of this result, Ishihara and Féry conclude that if a second occurrence focus precedes, rather than follows, the ordinary (first occurrence) focus, it will get a pitch accent.

(6.11) a. Die meisten unserer Kollegen waren beim Beriebsausflug
    lässig angezogen.
    'Most of our colleagues were dressed casually at the staff outing.'

   b. Nur [Peter]$_F$ het eine Krawatte getragen.
    'Only Peter wore a tie.'

   c. Nur [Peter]$_{SOF}$ hat sogar [einen Anzug]$_F$ getragen.
    Only Peter has actually a suit worn
    'Only Peter actually wore a suit.'

Summing up the discussion so far, Beaver et al. (2007) and Ishihara and Féry (2006) conducted production experiments yielding significant effects. There is a prosodic correlate of second occurrence focus in prenuclear and postnuclear position. However, for English the effects are small – post-nuclear second occurrence focus expressions are on average only 6 msecs longer than their non-focal counterparts. Are the effects large enough to be perceptible? If they are not, then the marking of second occurrence focus could not influence interpretation, and the argument from second occurrence focus might survive.

Jaeger (2004) (see also Beaver et al. 2007) conducted a multi-speaker perception experiment in which speakers were asked to judge the prominence of words in sentence pairs differing only in the position of second occurrence focus. The pairs were spliced from the production data in Beaver et al. (2007) in such a way that no discourse context was available, i.e., only the last sentence in the discourse was given. A possible pair would be (6.6c) and (6.7c), repeated in (6.12). The production pairs used were chosen randomly to establish balance of conditions, discourse and speakers, but without regard to the acoustic measurements (e.g., duration) discussed above.

(6.12) a. Even [the state prosecutor]$_F$ only named [Sid]$_{SOF}$ in court today.
    (= (6.6c))

   b. Even [the state prosecutor]$_F$ only named Sid in [court]$_{SOF}$ today.
    (= (6.7c))

Jaeger's (2004) perception experiment confirmed that second occurrence foci are indeed distinguishable from non-foci. Subjects distinguished second occurrence expressions from non-foci significantly above chance. Consequently, although the effects found in the production experiments are small, they are perceptible.

The acoustical studies discussed in this section have demonstrated that the argument from second occurrence focus is invalid. The argument has been taken to imply a need for pragmatic theories of focus interpretation rather than semantic theories. The argument took as its empirical foundation the claim that in second occurrence focus contexts the interpretational effects typically attributed to focus sensitivity are found without focus marking. Beaver et al. (2007), Ishihara and Féry (2006), and Jaeger (2004) show that there are no grounds for denying that second occurrence foci are focus marked: second occurrence foci have acoustic properties, which in the absence of focus marking, would be unexplained. Consequently, the argument from second occurrence focus fails.

6.4 Leaners: a Contrast

Summary: *We look at the distribution of unstressed pronouns in the scope of focus sensitive expressions and show that some, but not all, focus sensitive expressions can associate with material that completely lacks prosodic prominence.*

In the previous section we showed that there is a prosodic reflex of focus on second occurrence foci such as *vegetables* in (6.1), repeated below in (6.13). This suggests that association of *only* with ordinary foci and the association of *only* with second occurrence foci have the same analysis. Consequently, the two occurrences of *only eats vegetables* in (6.13) are explained by the same mechanism.

(6.13) A: Everyone already knew that Mary only eats [vegetables]$_F$.

B: If even [Paul]$_F$ knew that Mary only eats [vegetables]$_{SOF}$, then he should have suggested a different restaurant.

This leaves us with the following question. Can focus sensitive expressions associate with material that is completely lacking prosodic prominence? In this section we examine whether the focus associate of focus sensitive expressions can be an element which is prosodically dependent (henceforth, *leaners*; Zwicky 1982).

We focus our attention on unstressed personal pronouns such as *'im* 'him'. We show, on the one hand, that *only* and its counterparts in other languages such as Dutch cannot associate with unstressed pronouns. On the other hand, for variant sentences with *always* and its counterparts in other languages, readings are available where the unstressed pronoun is realized in the semantic scope, but not the restrictor, of *always*.

This contrast, paired with the interactions discussed in Chapter 7, suggests that *only* and its morphemic counterparts are directly sensitive to prosodic prominence in their syntactic scope, while the interpretation of *always* and its counterparts is determined by a less syntactically constrained pragmatic mechanism. In §6.5, we present an analysis that captures the differences between these two types of focus sensitive expressions.

Examples (6.14) and (6.15) illustrate the interaction between the interpretation of English focus sensitive expressions and leaners, in this case the prosodically dependent pronoun *'im*. While *always* is able to associate with *'im*, *only* fails to get the equivalent reading.

> **Context**: You had many discussions with Sandy, but what I want to know is the extent to which you talked about Fred. Of all the times you talked with Sandy, how often was Fred the person you talked about?

(6.14)   I [always]$_F$ discussed'im with Sandy.
          'Whenever I discussed someone with Sandy, I discussed Fred.'

(6.15)   I [only]$_F$ discussed'im with Sandy.
          Cannot mean: 'I only discussed Fred (and no one else) with Sandy.'

Note that the intonation suggested in (6.14), with nuclear stress on *always*, is natural and is easy to explain theoretically: apart from *always*, all the other elements of the sentence were given in the context – the speaker, discussions, Fred, and Sandy had already been mentioned explicitly in the prior discourse. So it is unsurprising that the nuclear stress should have fallen on *always*, which was not previously mentioned, and which provided the most important part of the answer to the question *how often*.

A similar argument might lead one to expect that nuclear stress in (6.15) could felicitously be placed on *only*, but it cannot. In order for the sentence to answer the given question, *only* must associate with the NP denoting Fred, and since in (6.15) this NP is a leaner which cannot carry focus, the sentence is infelicitous in the specified context. Indeed, we cannot find any context such that there is a placement of focus in (6.15) which produces the reading 'I discussed Fred and no one else with Sandy.'

Note here that the infelicity of (6.15) is independent of the placement of focus. *I only discussed Fred with Sandy* is itself felicitous in the given context with stress on both *only* and *Fred*. Therefore, the infelicity of (6.15) does not result from sentences with *only* being fundamentally ill-suited to answering *how often* questions. Rather, it results from the fact that *'im* cannot be focused, whereas *Fred* can.

Dutch shows a similar contrast between *alleen maar* 'only' and *altijd* 'always.' Assume that (6.16a, b) appear in a Dutch context equivalent to the English context for (6.14) and (6.15). (6.16a) fails to have the reading where *alleen maar* associates with the reduced pronoun *'m* 'him'. In contrast, (6.16b) allows this reading, i.e., 'Whenever I discussed someone with Sandy, I discussed Fred.'

(6.16) a.   ?Ik had't   alleen maar over'm   met Sandy, en ook had
              I   had+it only   about+him with Sandy and also had
              ik't alleen maar over'm   met Kim.
              I+it only   about+him with Kim

              'I only discussed'im with Sandy and also only discussed'im with
              Kim.'
              (cannot mean: 'I only discussed Fred (and no one else) with Sandy,
              and I also only discussed Fred (and no one else) with Kim.')

      b.   Ik had't   altijd   over'm   met Sandy, en ook had ik't
              I   had+it always about+him with Sandy and also had I+it
              altijd   over'm   met Kim.
              always about+him with Kim

              'I always discussed'im with Sandy and also always discussed'im
              with Kim.'
              (can mean: 'Whenever I discussed someone with Sandy, I discussed
              Fred, and whenever I discussed someone with Kim, I discussed
              Fred.')

Other authors have also observed that certain focus sensitive expressions
fail to associate with unstressable pronouns. In the Dutch example (6.17) (from
Hoeksema and Zwarts 1991: 67), the focus sensitive expression *alleen* 'only' can
associate with the pronoun *mij* 'me' but not its weak variant *me*.

(6.17)   Ze   toonden Piet en   mij de Amazone, maar <u>alleen</u> mij/*me
            They showed Piet and me the Amazon   but   only   me
            toonden ze   ook de STEDEN.
            showed they also the cities

            'They showed Piet and me the Amazon, but it was only me they also
            showed the CITIES.'

The English example in (6.18a) and the German example in (6.18b) (from
Bayer 1999: 59–60) show that *only* and *nur* 'only' can associate with the prosodically independent pronouns *him* and *ihn* 'him', respectively, but not unstressable *it* and *es* 'it'; see also Krifka (1997).

(6.18) a.   Sally likes only HIM/*it

      b.   Sabine liebt nur IHN/*es
              Sabine likes only him/it
              'Sabine likes only him/it'

Example (6.19) (also from Bayer 1999: 59–60) shows the same contrast with *even*
and *sogar* 'even'/'actually'.

(6.19) a.   Sally likes even HIM/*it

  b.   Sabine liebt sogar IHN/*es
       Sabine likes even him/it
       'Sabine likes even him/it'

The interaction of leaners and the interpretation of focus sensitive expressions poses a problem for both semantic and pragmatic theories of focus.[3] The semantic theories discussed in Chapter 4 predict that focus-marked elements are required in the syntactic scope of focus sensitive expressions. Consequently, semantic theories incorrectly disallow *always* from associating with material such as leaners completely lacking prosodic prominence.

Recall that in the pragmatic approaches to focus interpretation discussed in Chapter 5, the lexical semantics of focus sensitive expressions such as *only* and *always* cannot make reference to focus-influenced semantic values. Consequently, all focus sensitivity effects are explained in these approaches as an effect of free variables in the interpretation of focus sensitive expressions becoming bound to salient sets.

Consider the example in (6.20) (from von Fintel 1994: 45).[4] If the NP *the graduate students* in A's utterance is replaced by the unaccented pronoun *them*, as in B's response, the discourse is odd. The pragmatic approach to focus sensitivity incorrectly predicts that the quantificational domain of *only* in B's response can be fixed by the focus *the graduate students* in A's utterance and, consequently, doesn't need a focus associate of its own.

(6.20) A: Eva only gave xerox copies to [the GRAduate students]$_F$.

   B: ?? (No.) [PETR]$_F$ only gave xerox copies to them.

Notice that the variant of (6.20) with *the graduate students* in (6.21) is perfectly acceptable: *only* can associate with *the graduate students* in B's response. Similarly, Krifka (1997) observes that a variant of (6.20) with a secondary accent on *them* is acceptable, as in (6.22).

(6.21) A: Eva only gave xerox copies to [the GRAduate students]$_F$.

   B: No, [PETR]$_F$ only gave xerox copies to the graduate students.

(6.22) A: Eva only gave xerox copies to [the GRAduate students]$_F$.

   B: No, [PETR]$_F$ only gave xerox copies to THEM.

Along the same lines, von Fintel (1994: 48) presents the variant of Rooth's classic rice farmer example, with *rice* replaced by *it*, in (6.24). Rooth's original example was presented in (6.9) and is repeated below in (6.23). (6.23) means that people who grow rice eat nothing but rice. In example (6.24), *only* cannot

---

[3]   See Krifka (1997) and Rooth (1996b) for previous discussion.
[4]   Von Fintel attributes this example to Susanne Tunstall.

associate with unstressed *it*, contrary to what the pragmatic theory of focus sensitivity would predict. Compare (6.24) with (6.25), substituting *always* for *only*. Association with *it* is possible in this case; the sentence in (6.25) can mean that whenever people who grow rice eat, they eat rice.

(6.23)   People who [GROW]$_F$ rice generally only [EAT]$_F$ rice.
            (means 'people who grow rice eat nothing but rice')

(6.24)   ??People who [GROW]$_F$ rice only [EAT]$_F$ it.
            (cannot mean 'people who grow rice eat nothing but rice')

(6.25)   People who [GROW]$_F$ rice always [EAT]$_F$ it.
            (can mean 'whenever people who grow rice eat, they eat rice')

Summing up, we have shown that *only* and its morphemic counterparts in Dutch and German cannot associate with prosodically unmarked pronouns. In contrast, *always* and its counterparts can.

This result is problematic for any theory of focus interpretation, semantic or pragmatic, that treats focus sensitive expressions as a homogeneous class. Semantic approaches require focus-marked elements in the scope of focus sensitive expressions. But *always* can associate with material in its syntactic scope that completely lacks prosodic prominence. Pragmatic approaches to focus interpretation predict that, in principle, all focus sensitive expressions can associate with material that is completely lacking prosodic prominence. This is false for *only*.

Von Fintel (1995: 174) presents an example, given in (6.26), that appears problematic for our conclusion that *always* is able to associate with leaners.

(6.26) A: John always takes [MARY]$_F$ to the movies.

       B: No, ??[Peter]$_F$ always takes her to the movies.

However, we think judgments of the felicity of Speaker B's utterance in (6.26) are affected by context prior to Speaker A's utterance. Consider (6.27), where *always* felicitously associates with leaner *'er*. In Speaker B's utterance in (6.27), *Mary* is in the scope of *always*. Speaker C's denial of Speaker B's claim can mean that whenever Peter takes someone to the movies it is Mary.

(6.27) A: Is there a guy who takes Mary to the movies whenever he goes?

       B: Yes, [John]$_F$ always takes Mary to the movies.

       C: No, [Peter]$_F$ always takes'er to the movies. (not John)

Now contrast (6.27) with (6.28), where *only* has been substituted for *always*. Crucially, Speaker C's utterance is infelicitous in this context. Speaker C's denial of Speaker B's claim cannot mean that Peter takes nobody but Mary to the movies.

(6.28) A: Is there a guy who takes Mary to the movies whenever he goes?

B: Yes, [John]$_F$ only takes Mary to the movies.

C: No, # [Peter]$_F$ only takes'er to the movies. (not John)

While further empirical study would be appropriate, we provisionally conclude that this type of example supports our position rather than refuting it.

6.5 Leaners: an Events-based Analysis

Summary: *We provide an events-based analysis of the descriptive component of the meanings of* only *and* always. *We show how the analysis captures the differences between exclusives and quantificational adverbs with respect to unstressed pronouns.*

According to the QFC model developed in Chapters 2 and 3, the focus sensitivity of *only* arises through a lexical dependency on the Current Question, and the Current Question is constrained by the Focus Principle to be related to the compositionally derived focal alternatives. Thus, *only* has a conventionalized, though indirect, sensitivity to focus. But in the QFC theory, *always* has no such conventionalized sensitivity.

Rather, the focus sensitivity of *always* arises through a combination of factors. First, as in the pragmatic approaches to focus interpretation reviewed in Chapter 5, an implicit argument of *always* is typically dependent on what is salient in the context of utterance. Second, there is a strong tendency for what is focused not to be previously salient in the context. This combination of factors produces *free* association, a type of non-conventionalized focus sensitivity.

A distinction of this sort between *only* and *always* can explain the type of data we just saw in §6.3.1, but to show this clearly it will be helpful to make some simplifying assumptions about the meanings of exclusives and quantificational adverbs.

The meaning of an exclusive in the QFC model can be broken into two parts, a discourse functional component, and a descriptive component. As sketched in 3.4, and detailed later, in Chapter 10, the discourse functional component consists in lowering expectations as regards the answer to the Current Question. The descriptive component is a universal, i.e. that every true alternative is no stronger than the one selected. Quantificational adverbs have no discourse functional component to their meaning, and are purely descriptive. To facilitate comparison of exclusives and quantificational adverbs for the remainder of this chapter, and also in Chapters 7 and 8, we will ignore the discourse function of exclusives altogether, and spell out the meanings of *only* and *always* entirely in terms of their descriptive function.

One impediment to describing even the descriptive component of the meaning in a way that makes comparison between *only* and *always* easy is that previous researchers have varied considerably in the ontology and formal tools they have used to describe each of the expressions. In what follows, we draw on ideas from both event semantics and situation semantics, borrowing from work of Bonomi and Casalegno (1993) described in §4.4, and von Fintel (1994), amongst others. This allows us to give relatively simple and uniform statements of the descriptive component of the meanings of a wide range of examples.

We analyze sentences of the form *NP always VP* and *NP only VP* as having the truth conditions in (6.29) and (6.30) respectively:

(6.29)   Truth conditions of *NP always VP*:
$$\forall e \; \sigma(e) \rightarrow \exists e' \; \rho(e, e') \wedge q(e')$$

(6.30)   Truth conditions of *NP only VP*:
$$\forall e \; p(e) \rightarrow q(e)$$

In the above, e and e' are understood to range over what we term EVENTU-ALITIES, which are happenings or states of the world, or may be thought of as situations or partial models. Eventualities are like the events of Krifka (1989), used in Bonomi and Casalegno's (1993) analysis of *only*:

1 there are basic eventualities and complex eventualities;
2 simple eventualities involve individuals in different roles, for instance you are currently the agent in an eventuality of reading;
3 complex events have parts which are basic, and may be compared to the situations of von Fintel (1994) in his analysis of *always*;
4 the relation ρ must be determined contextually, and maps eventualities to eventualities, for instance it could be a function which maps an eventuality e to the set of eventualities which immediately follow e and share the same agent.

It is the contextual identification of σ which gives *always* the anaphoric proper-ties we are interested in in this book, and ρ, which we will term the DOMAIN RELATION, will play little role in the analysis. In both (6.29) and (6.30), q is understood simply to be the ordinary meaning that the sentence *NP VP* (i.e., with *always* or *only* removed) would have, a property of eventualities. (6.30) also makes reference to a variable p: this represents the meaning of *NP VP*, but minus content related to any focused parts of the VP. We will term q the *under-lying (sentence) meaning*, and p the *VP-defocused (sentence) meaning*.

What does all this mean for simple cases of focus sensitivity such as exam-ples (6.31) and (6.32)?

(6.31) a.   Sandy always feeds [Fido]$_F$ Nutrapup.
       b.   Sandy only feeds [Fido]$_F$ Nutrapup.
       c. $\forall x \; feed(sandy, x, nutrapup) \rightarrow x = fido$
            "Everything Sandy feeds Nutrapup to is Fido"
       d. $\forall e(feeding(e) \wedge \text{AG}(e, sandy) \wedge \text{TH}(e, nutrapup)) \rightarrow \text{GO}(e, fido)$
       e.   Key: AG = AGENT, TH = THEME, GO = GOAL.

(6.32) a.   Sandy always feeds Fido [Nutrapup]$_F$.

   b.   Sandy only feeds Fido [Nutrapup]$_F$.

   c. $\forall x\, feed(sandy, fido, x) \rightarrow x = nutrapup$
       "Everything Sandy feeds to Fido is Nutrapup"

   d. $\forall e(feeding(e) \land \text{AG}(e, sandy) \land \text{GO}(e, fido)) \rightarrow$
       $\text{TH}(e, nutrapup)$

In our version of the Bonomi/Casalegno/Krifka neo-Davidsonian analysis of events, thematic roles such as AGENT are relations between events and individuals. Thus, for all of the examples in (6.31) and (6.32) we would analyze the underlying meaning of the sentence, in which neither focus nor the focus sensitive expressions have any effect, as follows:

(6.33) $q = \lambda e[feeding(e) \land \text{AG}(e, sandy) \land \text{GO}(e, fido) \land$
       $\text{TH}(e, nutrapup)]$

The VP-defocused meaning is simply the same formula minus one or other conjunct; e.g. minus the conjunct specifying GOAL for (6.31a). After performing simple lambda reductions and using a classical equivalence $(a \rightarrow (a \land b) \equiv a \rightarrow b)$, we arrive at (6.31d) for the meaning of (6.31b), and (6.32d) for the meaning of (6.32b). Note here that under natural assumptions (6.31d) is logically equivalent to (6.31c) and (6.32d) is logically equivalent to (6.32c). In particular, we need only assume that every event of feeding has an agent, a goal and a theme, and that the following holds in all models:

(6.34) $\forall x, y, z(\exists e\, feeding(e) \land \text{AG}(e, x) \land \text{GO}(e, y) \land$
       $\text{TH}(e, z)) \leftrightarrow feed(x, y, z)$

What of *always*? If we simply plug the value of q into the template in (6.29), and do nothing to resolve the free variables σ and ρ, we derive an identical meaning for (6.31a) and (6.32a), namely that in (6.35):

(6.35) $\forall e\, \sigma(e) \rightarrow \exists e'\, \rho(e, e') \land feeding(e') \land \text{AG}(e', sandy) \land$
       $\text{GO}(e', fido) \land \text{TH}(e, nutrapup)$

We must then settle how the contextual variables σ and ρ are to be resolved for each of the examples. Here it is important to realize that there is no unique correct resolution for these decontextualized single sentence examples. By definition, contextual variables only get a value in a particular context, so we would need to consider particular utterances of the sentences in particular contexts.

An utterance of (6.31a) would be felicitous in a context when we were discussing occasions on which Sandy fed some animal Nutrapup.[5] In that case, σ might get set to:

---

5   For example,

   A: Does Sandy ever feed any of her dogs Nutrapup?
   B: Yes, Sandy always feeds FIDO Nutrapup.

(6.36) $\lambda e[\exists x\ animal(x) \wedge feeding(e) \wedge \text{AG}(e, sandy) \wedge \text{GO}(e, x) \wedge$
            $\text{TH}(e, nutrapup)]$

Suppose we assume that ρ is resolved to the identity relation, which we will term *id*. Assume further a constraint on models that the only things that get fed Nutrapup are animals. In that case, it is easily seen that the truth conditions in (6.35) would be identical to those in (6.31d), which in turn, by assumption, are equivalent to the original truth conditions in (6.31c). Note that these are quite stringent requirements on context, so that there may well be other contexts in which (6.31a) could be felicitously uttered.

Similarly, an utterance of (6.32a) would be felicitous in a context in which we were discussing occasions on which Sandy fed Fido. Then σ might get set to the following:

(6.37) $\lambda e[feeding(e) \wedge \text{AG}(e, sandy) \wedge \text{GO}(e, fido)]$

Assuming once again that ρ is resolved to *id*, (6.35) would be equivalent to (6.31d), and hence (6.32c).

We will now see how examples (6.14a) and (6.15a) can be analyzed in the framework discussed in this section. For examples (6.14a) and (6.15a), we index pronouns as in (6.38) and (6.39), respectively. Let us suppose that *discuss* has thematic roles AGENT, THEME (the person or thing under discussion), and COPARTICIPANT, so that the underlying meaning would be given by q in (6.40).

(6.38)   I always discussed'im$_i$ with Sandy.

(6.39)   I only discussed'im$_i$ with Sandy.

(6.40) $q = \lambda e\ [discuss(e) \wedge \text{AG}(e, speaker) \wedge \text{TH}(e, x_i) \wedge$
            $\text{CO}(e, sandy)]$

For *only* the lack of a reading corresponding to association with the leaner follows from the fact that, since the leaner cannot be focused, focus must be either on the subject, or on some other element in the VP. In the case of subject focus, the VP-defocused meaning will be identical to the ordinary meaning, and we derive the trivially true meaning for (6.39): $\forall e\ q(e) \rightarrow q(e)$. We suppose that some pragmatic or grammatical mechanism blocks this derivation.

On the other hand, if the focus is in (or on) the VP c-commanded by *only*, various readings are available, none of which correspond to association with *'im*. As an illustrative example of a possible reading we predict for (6.39), suppose the entire VP *discussed'im$_i$ with Sandy* is in focus. The VP-defocused meaning of the sentence would then be AG($e, speaker$), and the reading that would result would be as shown in (6.41), not the impossible reading that would correspond to association with the leaner, as shown in (6.42):

(6.41) $\forall e\ \text{AG}(e, speaker) \rightarrow (discuss(e) \wedge \text{TH}(e, x_i) \wedge$
            $\text{CO}(e, sandy))$

(6.42) $\forall e \ (\text{AG}(e, speaker) \wedge discuss(e) \wedge \text{CO}(e, sandy)) \rightarrow \text{TH}(e, x_i)$

As regards (6.38), involving apparent association of *always* with *'im*, the context given earlier for the example would make salient a set of occasions when the speaker was involved in a discussion with Sandy. Thus the quantificational domain σ might be as given in (6.43).

(6.43) $\sigma = \lambda e \ [\text{AG}(e, speaker) \wedge discuss(e) \wedge \text{CO}(e, sandy)]$

Merely by identifying the domain relation ρ with the identity relation, and using the standard template for sentences involving *always* ($\forall e \ \sigma(e) \rightarrow \exists e' \ \rho(e, e') \wedge q(e')$), we would then derive (6.42), the meaning that was unavailable for the parallel example with *only*.

6.6 Summary

In this chapter we demonstrated that the standard empirical argument from second occurrence focus used to show that focus association is optional fails. We also considered a diagnostic, leaners, to probe for the optionality of focus association. Our application of this diagnostic provided evidence of a split between focus sensitive expressions. Exclusives such as *only*, unlike adverbs of quantification such as *always*, cannot associate with expressions completely lacking prosodic prominence.

Given that the QFC model covers many more types of expression than just exclusives and quantificational adverbs, the reader may be wondering how these other expression types behave as regards association with reduced material. For the most part the territory remains unexplored, but to the extent that we have examined this question, we would note the following: aside from exclusives and quantificational adverbs, it is generally hard to set up minimal pairs. So the task of drawing up a complete map of the extent to which different focus sensitive expressions associate with reduced material will be a difficult one.

Of those we have considered, however, we do find for most expressions that we take to be *conventionally* sensitive that the focus cannot easily be reduced, whereas for *quasi* and *free* associators, such reduction does not generally produce infelicity, except for independent reasons of discourse coherence.

The following examples give preliminary data showing interaction of various expressions with the leaner *'im*:

(6.44) You can see Bush, but do you see Cheney?

    a.   Yes, I see'im/see #HIM. *(No focus sensitive expression)*

    b.   Yes, I ALways see'im/see HIM. *(Quantificational adverb)*

    c.   I can ONly #see'im/see HIM. *(Exclusive)*

    d.   I can EVen #see'im/see HIM. *(Scalar additive)*

e. Yes, I can ALso #see'im/see HIM. *(Additive)*

f. No, I can't (?)see'im/see HIM speCIFically. *(Particularizer)*

g. No, I CAN't see'im/see HIM. *(Negation)*

h. I can TOtally see'im/see HIM. *(Intensive)*

i. I can KINda' see'im/see HIM. *(Downtoner)*

In accord with what we have already shown in this chapter, we see that the leaner is acceptable with no focus sensitive expression (a) and with a quantificational adverb (b), but that it is not acceptable as the focus of an exclusive (c). Cases (d, e, f) show that scalar additives, additives and particularizers behave, as the QFC theory would predict, like exclusives, though for us the judgement in (f) depends on getting the right interpretation, hence our bracketed question mark. Case (g) shows that negation, from our *quasi* associating class, does not seem to require a clearly distinguished focus in its scope (the negation itself might be accented here), again in accordance with the theory.

Cases (h) and (i) are potentially problematic: intensives and downtoners do not seem to require a clear focus in their scope, although on our classification they associate *conventionally*, and so should require one. Whether this is a fault of the diagnostic or of the theory, we leave open. One possibility is that for many of the other cases a Current Question *Who can you see?* is accommodated, but for (h) and (i) the explicit polar question *Do you see Cheney?* suffices. In that case, the sentences may have a corresponding *polarity* focus, which perhaps can just be marked on the intensive or downtoner itself.

We end with another example of *free* association, this time involving superlatives (c.f. §3.3):

(6.45) a. The Hilton in Chicago gave David the biggest room of anyone in the party and ...

b. the Hilton in Austin gave'im/gave HIM the biggest room too.

Example (6.45b) has an interpretation where it means that the Hilton in Austin gave David a bigger room than it gave anyone else in the party, and this interpretation is available whether the pronoun *him* is accented or reduced. This, of course, is just what we would expect of a construction like the superlative, for which the focus sensitivity is not conventionalized.

In this chapter, we first showed that second occurrence focus does not provide a valid argument against conventionalized models of focus sensitivity. We then provided direct evidence that the focus sensitivity of exclusives actually is conventionalized, but also that the focus sensitivity of quantificational adverbs is not. This is just as the QFC model predicts. As we have indicated in this section, there remain fruitful avenues of inquiry involving what happens when a focus is reduced, but we will not pursue them any further here. Instead, we move on: in the next chapter, we discuss two further effects which support the QFC model.

Chapter 7

Lacking Focus: Extraction and Ellipsis

At my time of life opinions are tolerably fixed. It is not likely that I should now see or hear anything to change them.

Jane Austen, 1811, *Sense and Sensibility*

7.1 Introduction

In this chapter we discuss the interaction of extraction and ellipsis constructions with the interpretation of focus sensitive expressions. Extraction and ellipsis afford us obvious ways of testing how applicable certain structural conditions on association with focus are to the whole class of focus sensitive expressions.[1]

For example, it has been observed that the associated focus of *only* cannot be extracted (Jackendoff 1972: 247; Krifka 1992a: 234; Aoun and Li 1993: 206; Kayne 1998: 159). The topicalization example in (7.1) (from Aoun and Li 1993: 206) cannot mean 'He likes nobody but Mary', the reading where *only* associates with the extracted element *Mary*.

(7.1)   *Mary$_i$, he only likes x_i.

---

[1]   Anderson (1972), Jackendoff (1972: 247–54), and Ross and Cooper (1979: 371) provide early discussions of structural conditions on the relation between focus sensitive expressions and their associated focus. For example, Jackendoff (1972) observed a contrast between *even* and *only*. (i) and (ii) illustrate the different positions from which *even* and *only* can associate with a subject. *Even*, but not *only*, can associate with the focused subject *John* following the first auxiliary *will*.

  (i) JOHN (even) will (even) have (*even) given his daughter a bicycle.
  (ii) JOHN (only) will (*only) have (*only) given his daughter a bicycle.

This constrast remains open for further investigation.

On the basis of observations like (7.1) it has been claimed that focus sensitive expressions must be associated with a prosodically prominent element in their c–command domain.[2] For example, Tancredi (1990) proposes the principle in (7.2): (cited in Aoun and Li 1993: 206).[3]

(7.2)   *The Principle of Lexical Association*
         An operator like *only* must be associated with a lexical constituent in its c–command domain.

Notably, previous analysts have not pursued the implications of data like (7.1) for focus sensitive expessions other than *only* and *even*.[4]

   In what follows, we devote our attention primarily to English, with supporting data from Dutch, Italian, Spanish, and Swedish. We provide evidence suggesting that in all of these languages, exclusives (e.g. *only*) systematically *fail* to associate with extracted and elided elements while adverbs of quantification (e.g. *always*) can do so.

   If this observation is correct then a structural principle such as (7.2) applies to some but not all focus sensitive expressions. This observation, paired with the evidence from second occurrence focus and weak pronouns in Chapter 6, suggests that some expressions that have been classified as focus sensitive involve obligatory dependence on focus, while others do not.

7.2   Extraction

Summary: *We present evidence that quantificational adverbs can associate with extracted elements that are realized in higher clauses, but exclusives cannot associate with such elements.*

As a first illustration of the interaction between extraction and focus sensitivity, we will consider modifications of the English sentences in (7.3) and (7.4). (7.3) and (7.4) arguably have the interpretations in (7.3a, b) and (7.4a, b), respectively.

---

[2] C-command is a standard syntactic relationship: informally, one item c-commands a second if the first is the sister of a node dominating (or possibly identical to) the second. The proper structural relationship cannot be simple c–command if we accept that there are examples where VP-*only* associates with the subject (König 1991; Ross and Cooper 1979), as in n. 1 example (ii) and the following example:

   (i) [They]$_F$ only are sending eggs to Marie. (Ross and Cooper 1979: 368)

A natural response would be to deny that this is an instance of VP-*only*, and say instead that it is a case of NP-*only* in a postposition, in which case it still c-commands the focus.

[3]   Krifka (1991: 132) also makes the assumption that focus operators c–command their focus. Büring and Hartmann (2001) propose that German focus sensitive expressions (e.g. *nur* 'only') must c–command their associated focus.

[4]   As noted below, Krifka (1992a) is an exception.

(7.3) I said that I always stock Kim's tank with clownfish.

    a. 'I said I stock Kim's and no other tank with clownfish.'

    b. 'I said I stock Kim's tank with clownfish and nothing else.'

(7.4) I said that I only stock Kim's tank with clownfish.

    a. 'I said I stock Kim's and no other tank with clownfish.'

    b. 'I said I stock Kim's tank with clownfish and nothing else.'

Consider the following scenario:

> I have two roommates, Kim and Sandy. I always stock their fishtanks. I stock Sandy's fishtank with goldfish and nothing else. I stock Kim's fishtank with goldfish and with clownfish.

The table in (7.5) illustrates the scenario. Sandy's fishtank is stocked with only goldfish. Kim's fishtank is stocked with goldfish and clownfish.

(7.5)

Sandy's fishtank	Kim's fishtank
goldfish	goldfish and clownfish

    In (7.6) and (7.7), *the tank* is a possible focus associate of the focus sensitive expressions *always* and *only*, but corresponds to a gap in the bare relative *I said I always/only stock with clownfish*.[5]

(7.6) Kim's is ⌐the tank⌐ I said I always stock with clownfish.[6]

    a. 'I said I stock Kim's and no other tank with clownfish.' [TRUE]

    b. 'I said I stock Kim's tank with clownfish
       and nothing else.' [FALSE]

Both (7.6a) and (7.6b) are among the possible readings of (7.6).

(7.7) Kim's is ⌐the tank⌐ I said I only stock with clownfish.

    a. *'I said I stock Kim's and no other tank with clownfish.' [TRUE]

    b. 'I said I stock Kim's tank with clownfish
       and nothing else.' [FALSE]

---

[5] It is crucial to this argument that in (7.6) (and all the extraction examples that follow) that the focus sensitive expression takes scope under an embedding verb like *said*. Since the *saying* event is not bound by *always* in (7.6), it cannot be claimed that the subject of the main clause, which is the apparent semantic focus of *always*, is within the syntactic scope or the binding domain of *always*.

[6] In the extraction examples which follow, the relevant occurrences of *always* and *only* have been underlined, and the focus associate has been boxed.

Surprisingly, (7.7) lacks the reading in (7.7a), where *only* associates with *the tank*. We confirmed these judgments in a small questionnaire study we conducted using written materials similar to that in (7.6–7.7).

The data in (7.6) and (7.7) suggest that there is a bifurcation between focus sensitive expressions. As illustrated in (7.8), *always* and *only* do not c–command the focus associate *the tank* in (7.6) and (7.7), yet (7.6) still has the reading in (7.6a), where *always* associates with *the tank*.[7] This is not the case for the variant with *only* in (7.7).

(7.8)

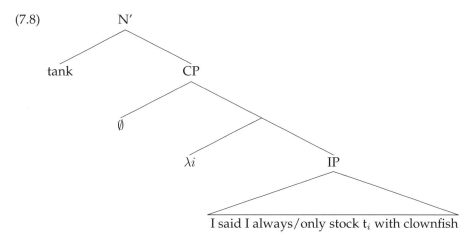

$$\text{I said I always/only stock } t_i \text{ with clownfish}$$

The contrast between (7.6) and (7.7) suggests that a structural condition like (7.2) holds for *only*, but not for *always*.

As far as we know, Krifka (1992a: 234) was the first to observe a contrast between focus sensitive expressions in extraction contexts, specifically with respect to *wh*–relatives. Krifka's examples are in (7.9).

(7.9) a. We should thank $\boxed{\text{the man}_i}$ whom Mary <u>always</u> took t_i to the movies.

   b. We should thank $\boxed{\text{the man}_i}$ whom Mary <u>only</u> took t_i to the movies.

(7.9a), with *always*, can mean 'We should thank the man such that, if Mary took someone to the movies, it was him,' where *always* apparently associates with *the man*. In contrast, (7.9b) cannot mean 'We should thank the man such that Mary took only HIM to the movies,' the reading where *only* associates with *the man*.

Compare also the *which*-relatives in (7.10) and (7.11). The naturally occurring example in (7.10)[8] has the reading where *always* associates with the extracted

---

7 In (7.8) we adopt an analysis of relative clauses in the style of Heim and Kratzer (1998).

8 *Polo*. Cooper, Jilly. London: Bantam (Corgi), 1991, pp. 162–267. (British National Corpus text CAO: some data extracted from the British National Corpus, distributed by Oxford University Computing Services on behalf of the BNC Consortium. All rights in the texts cited are reserved.)

focus *Pedro's polo helmet*: 'Whenever Angel was playing in a match, he wore Pedro's polo helmet.' In contrast, the constructed variant of (7.10) in (7.11), with *only* substituted for *always*, fails to have the reading where *only* associates with *Pedro's polo helmet*.

(7.10)   Besides these photographs were ⌐Pedro's polo helmet¬, which now had a map of the Malvinas stamped on the front (**which Angel always wore in matches**), and a jar of earth he'd dug up from the Islands on the day he'd been sent home as a prisoner of war.

(7.11)   Besides these photographs were ⌐Pedro's polo helmet¬, which now had a map of the Malvinas stamped on the front (**which Angel only wore in matches**), and a jar of earth he'd dug up from the Islands on the day he'd been sent home as a prisoner of war.
Cannot mean: '. . . Pedro's polo helmet such that Angel wore that helmet and no other in matches . . .'

We looked through fifty naturally occurring examples of *which*-relatives with *only* in their argument without finding any extracted foci associating with *only*. For example, the naturally occurring (7.12)[9] lacks an ambiguity which is found in the constructed variant in (7.13).

(7.12)   [As compared with] ⌐the more usual situation¬ in which we only know the activity of people over a short period, [such data raise some challenging statistical and econometric problems].
Cannot mean: [As compared with] the more usual situation which is such that we know the activity of people over a short period in that situation but not in other situations, [such data raise some challenging statistical and econometric problems]

(7.13)   We only know the activity of people over a short period in the more usual situation.
Can mean: 'We know (the activity of people over a short period) in the more usual situation, but not in other situations.'

Example (7.13) has a reading where *only* associates with *the more usual situation*, as in 'We know the activity of people over a short period in no other situations but the more usual situation.' This reading is not available for (7.12); i.e. *only* fails to associate with the extracted element *the more usual situation*.

If we look beyond relative clauses to other (leftward) extraction constructions, we see the same contrast between different focus sensitive expressions such as *only* and *always*. To illustrate, *wh*–interrogatives in English also suggest

---

[9] *Rapid* (archive of ESRC grant abstracts), British National Corpus.

that extraction of the focus of *only* is impossible, but extraction of the apparent focus of *always* is possible.

For example, the interrogative in (7.14) has the reading in (7.14a) where *always* associates with the extracted *wh*–phrase *what*. For the interrogative in (7.15) with *only*, the reading in (7.15a), where *only* associates with *what*, is unavailable.

(7.14) | What | do you think Kim always gives his mother?

    a. 'What is the thing such that Kim gives that thing and nothing else to his mother?'

    b. 'What do you think Kim gives his mother and noone else?'

(7.15) | What | do you think Kim only gives his mother?

    a. *'What is the thing such that Kim gives that thing and nothing else to his mother?'

    b. 'What do you think Kim gives his mother and noone else?'

Likewise, (7.16)–(7.18) illustrate other (leftward) extraction constructions in English. In all cases, *only* fails to associate with an extracted element (the (b') readings) while *always* can do so (the (a') readings).

(7.16) **Topicalization**

    a. | Fishsticks |, I believe Kim always buys.

    a'. 'I believe that Kim buys fishsticks and nothing else.'

    b. | Fishsticks |, I believe Kim only buys.

    b'. *'I believe that Kim buys fishsticks and nothing else.'

(7.17) **Adverb Preposing**

    a. | On Sunday |, I thought you always went to the store.

    a'. 'I thought that you went to the store on Sunday and no other day.'

    b. | On Sunday |, I thought you only went to the store.

    b'. *'I thought that you went to the store on Sunday and no other day.'

(7.18) **Inverted *wh*–Cleft**

    a. | Guinness | is what I think Kim always wants to drink.

    a'. 'I think Kim wants to drink Guinness and nothing else.'

    b. | Guinness | is what I think Kim only wants to drink.

    b'. *'I think Kim wants to drink Guinness and nothing else.'

These data show that the generalization that *only*, but not *always*, fails to associate with extracted elements holds for a range of leftward extraction constructions in English.

To sum up, we have shown that focus sensitive expressions do not act as a homogeneous class in leftward extraction constructions in English. This suggests that some, but not all, focus sensitive expressions must associate with a focused element in their c–command domain. We explore further evidence for this split in the next section.

7.3 Cross-linguistic Evidence on Extraction

Summary: *We show that differences between exclusives and quantificational adverbs are found in a range of extraction constructions across German, Dutch, Swedish, Spanish, and Italian.*

In addition to English, other Germanic languages reveal a similar pattern with respect to the interaction of focus sensitive expressions and extraction. For example, in Dutch, *alleen maar* 'only' fails to associate with (leftward) extracted elements, whereas the adverb of quantification *altijd* 'always' can associate in such cases.

To illustrate, in (7.19), *altijd* can associate with the extracted object *wat* 'what' of *geeft* 'give' (reading (7.19a)).

(7.19) Dutch

        | Wat | denk jij   dat Kim altijd   aan haar moeder geeft?
        What think you that Kim always to   her   mother gives

    a. 'What is the thing such that you believe that Kim gives that thing (and nothing else) to her mother?'

    b. 'What do you believe that Kim gives her mother (and nobody else)?'

In contrast, the reading in (7.20a) where *alleen maar* associates with extracted foci is unavailable as an interpretation of (7.20).

(7.20) Dutch

        | Wat | denk jij   dat Kim alleen maar aan haar moeder geeft?
        What think you that Kim only   to her   mother gives

    a. *'What is the thing such that you believe that Kim gives that thing (and nothing else) to her mother?'

    b. 'What do you believe that Kim gives to her mother (and nobody else)?'

A similar contrast is found with the *wh*-relative examples in (7.21) and (7.22): *altijd* can associate with the extracted focus associate (reading (7.21a)), whereas *alleen maar* cannot (the unavailable reading (7.22a)).

(7.21) Dutch

| De stoel | waarop | Hans zegt Jan altijd | heeft gezeten is stuk. |
| The chair | on-which | Hans says Jan always | has   sat   is broken |

    a. 'The chair such that Hans says that Jan sat on that chair and no other chair is broken.'

    b. 'The chair on which Hans says Jan sat and did nothing else to it is broken.'

(7.22) Dutch

| De stoel | waarop | Hans zegt Jan alleen maar heeft gezeten |
| The chair | on-which | Hans says Jan only   has   sat |

is stuk.
is broken

    a. *'The chair such that Hans says Jan sat on that chair and no other chair is broken.'

    b. 'The chair on which Hans says Jan sat and did nothing else to it is broken.'

(7.23) and (7.24) show Swedish examples in which focus sensitive expressions *alltid* 'always' and *bara* 'only' interact with extraction.

(7.23) Swedish

| Vem | har han alltid | givit kakor? |
| Who | has he   always | given cookies |

    a. 'Who is the person such that he gave that person and nobody else cookies?'

    b. 'Who is the person such that he gave that person cookies and nothing else?'

The question in (7.23) has at least three meanings, including (7.23a), the reading where *alltid* associates with the extracted element *vem* 'who'. The question in (7.24) can mean (7.24b) among other readings.

However, (7.24) cannot mean (7.24a), the reading where *bara* associates with the extracted element *vem*.

(7.24) Swedish

> [Vem] har han <u>bara</u> givit kakor?
> Who has he only given cookies

>> a. *'Who is the person such that he only gave that person and nobody else cookies?'

>> b. 'Who is the person such that he only gave that person cookies and nothing else?'

Romance languages such as Spanish and Italian display a similar split between focus sensitive expressions in extraction contexts. For example, the counterparts of *only* in Italian and Spanish, but not the counterparts of *always*, fail to associate with their extracted focus associate in extraction constructions like relativization.

Examples (7.25a) and (7.25b) illustrate the contrast between Spanish *sólo* 'only' and *siempre* 'always'.

(7.25) Spanish

>> a. [A su novia], Pedro <u>siempre</u> lleva al   cine.
>>   his fiancée   Pedro always takes to the cinema
>>   Can mean: 'If Pedro takes someone to the movies, it's his fiancée.'

>> b. [A su novia], Pedro <u>sólo</u> lleva al   cine.
>>   his fiancée   Pedro only takes to the cinema
>>   Cannot mean: 'Pedro takes his fiancée and nobody else to the cinema.'

(7.25a) has the reading where *siempre* associates with the fronted element *a su novia* 'his fiancée.' In contrast, the variant with *sólo* in (7.25b) does not have that reading.

Examples (7.26) and (7.27) illustrate the same contrast for Italian *sempre* 'always' and *solo* 'only.'

(7.26) Italian

> Giulia sa   [quale ragazzo] Maria ha <u>sempre</u> portato
> Giulia knows which boy   Maria has always brought
> al   cinema.
> to-the cinema

>> a. 'Giulia knows which boy is such that Maria has always brought him to the cinema but nobody else.'

>> b. 'Giulia knows which boy is such that Maria has always brought him to the cinema while not taking him anywhere else.'

(7.27) Italian

| Giulia sa | quale ragazzo | Maria ha | solo portato |
| Giulia knows | which boy | Maria has | only brought |

al cinema.
to-the cinema

a. *'Giulia knows which boy is such that Maria has only brought him to the cinema and nobody else.'

b. 'Giulia knows which boy is such that Maria has only brought him to the cinema and nowhere else.'

In sum, we have provided evidence that the split between focus sensitive expressions in English also holds for cross-linguistic counterparts of *only* and *always* in Germanic and Romance languages.[10] The data that we presented in this and the previous section suggest that focus effects on interpretation must be encoded in the meaning of *only* and its cross-linguistic counterparts. In contrast, the availability of readings where *always* and its cross-linguistic counterparts associate with extracted foci suggests that a pragmatic account may be more appropriate. In the next section we provide an analysis of the extraction facts.

7.4 Analyzing the Extraction Data

Summary: *We account for the extraction data from §7.2 and §7.3 in terms of an event-based model (c.f. §6.5) that minimizes the semantic differences between quantificational adverbs and exclusives, and highlights the fact that whereas quantificational adverbs are restricted by free association, exclusives associate with focus conventionally.*

In §7.2 and §7.3 we gave evidence that suggests that *only* (and its cross-linguistic counterparts) fails to associate with extracted elements, whereas *always* (and its counterparts) successfully associates. Before we turn to our analysis, we show that standard accounts of association with focus do not capture this observation.

Consider a semantic account of association with focus (e.g. Rooth 1985 and Krifka 1992a).[11] Most semantic accounts of association assume that the focus associate of a focus sensitive expression is in the syntactic scope of the focus

---

[10] In §7.5 we discuss some apparent exceptions in German and Dutch to the generalization that morphemic counterparts of *only* in these languages cannot associate with extracted elements.

[11] The argument we make here also applies to movement theories of focus (Chomsky 1977; Drubig 1994).

sensitive expression at some level of representation. Recall the principle in (7.2), repeated as (7.28), from Tancredi (1990):

(7.28)   *The Principle of Lexical Association*
          An operator like *only* must be associated with a lexical constituent in its c–command domain.

For extraction, semantic accounts of focus sensitivity have two options: (i) traces are F-marked[12] or (ii) traces are not F-marked. One instantiation of option (i) appears in Barbiers (1995: 65) (see also Jacobs 1983), given as (7.29). (7.29) claims that a focus-sensitive operator can associate with the trace of its extracted focus.

(7.29)   A focus particle immediately c-commands (the trace of) its semantic argument.

If semantic accounts choose option (i) they incorrectly allow the impossible reading (7.30a) of (7.30).

(7.30) Kim is the guy who Sandy says she only gives chocolate.

    a. *'Kim is the guy such that Sandy says she gives him and nobody else chocolate.'

    b. 'Kim is the guy such that Sandy says she gives him chocolate and nothing else.'

(7.31) Kim is the guy who Sandy says she always gives chocolate.

    a. 'Kim is the guy such that Sandy says she gives him and nobody else chocolate.'

    b. 'Kim is the guy such that Sandy says she gives him chocolate (and nothing else).'

The paraphrase in (7.30a) gives the reading where *only* associates with the extracted focus. However, if semantic accounts of focus sensitivity choose option (ii), where traces are not F-marked, they will be no better off. Under option (ii), such accounts would incorrectly disallow the reading in (7.31a) of (7.31), where the extracted focus *the guy* is not in the c-command domain of *always*.

---

[12] See Chapter 2 for discussion. Selkirk (1996: 561) makes use of F-marked traces in her theory of focus projection. Her theory includes the principle: "F-marking of the antecedent of a trace left by NP– or *wh*–movement licenses the F-marking of the trace." Note that what Selkirk is referring to is what in §2.4 we notated as f-marking rather than F-marking. This difference is significant, for the principle as Selkirk stated it cannot be right. It implies that f-marking on a constituent extracted out of a VP could lead to f-marking of the entire VP. Thus, e.g. *BEANS, Fred ate* could, in Selkirk's account, lead to the VP *ate __* being f-marked. Selkirk's principle should perhaps be recast to refer to *Foc*-marking rather than f-marking.

Purely pragmatic accounts of focus sensitivity (e.g. Martí 2003; Roberts 1996; Schwarzschild 1997; and Geurts and van der Sandt 2004) would make incorrect predictions about the extraction example in (7.30). Consider the predictions that Roberts (1996) makes in the account discussed in §2.7 and §5.4. Roberts bases her theory of focus sensitivity on an extension of Hamblin's (1973) theory of questions, whereby the question in (7.32a) introduces a set of alternative propositions corresponding to sentences of the form 'Sandy gives X chocolates.' For example, if only Morgan, Lee, and Kim are relevant, then (7.32a) has the question meaning in (7.32b).

(7.32) a. Who does Sandy give chocolates?

    b. {Sandy gives Morgan chocolates, Sandy gives Lee chocolates, Sandy gives Kim chocolates}

Roberts allows that the set of propositions in (7.32b) may become salient either because (7.32a) has been uttered or because it is implicit in the discourse that this question is of interest. If the set constitutes a question under discussion when (7.30) is uttered, it will be used to determine the quantificational restrictor of *only*. According to the relevance-based criterion she sets out, a discourse consisting of (7.32) followed by (7.30) (as in (7.33)) is predicted to be coherent.

(7.33) A. Who does Sandy give chocolates?

    B. #Kim is the guy who Sandy says she only gives chocolates.

Consequently, a model like that of Roberts incorrectly predicts that (7.30), with reading (7.30a), will be felicitous in this context. However, (7.30a) is not a possible reading of (7.30) in this context or any other, thus falsifying a purely pragmatic theory like that of Roberts.

More generally, anyone advancing a purely pragmatic theory of focus sensitivity (one in which what we call *quasi* and *free* association were the only mechanisms at work) will have trouble explaining the interaction between focus and focus sensitive expressions in extraction constructions. This type of data points towards there being some degree of syntactic sensitivity and thus conventionalized sensitivity to focus in the account.

We will now see how examples (7.6) and (7.7), repeated below as (7.34) and (7.35), can be analyzed along the same lines as the analysis of reduction data in Chapter 6. The other extraction examples we have considered can be treated along similar lines.

(7.34)   Kim's is the tank I said I always stock with clownfish.

(7.35)   Kim's is the tank I said I only stock with clownfish.

By definition, extraction gaps cannot be prosodically prominent. But syntactic theories often assume that when there is a gap, there is a trace at some level of syntactic representation, and Selkirk (1996: 561) even assumes that traces can be F-marked (see note 12).

The extraction facts involving *only* and *always* can be explained if overt movement generally does not leave F-marked traces behind, independently of whether the trace is coindexed with a F-marked element. Specifically, we assume that in none of the extraction examples we have presented is there a F-marked trace. Making this assumption, we predict that (7.35) can only be felicitous if one of *stock*, *with*, *clownfish*, *with clownfish*, or *stock with clownfish* is F-marked.

For example, if *clownfish* is F-marked, then the gapped clause in (7.36) will have an underlying meaning, the ordinary interpretation of (7.37), given by q in (7.38), and a VP-defocused meaning as given by p in (7.39). Plugging p and q into the template $\forall e\ p(e) \rightarrow q(e)$, and reducing, we derive the meaning given by ϕ in (7.40) for the gapped clause.

(7.36)   I only stock t_i with [clownfish]$_F$.

(7.37)   I stock t_i with [clownfish]$_F$.

(7.38) $q = \lambda e\ [stock(e) \wedge AG(e, speaker) \wedge LOC(e', x_i) \wedge TH(e, clownfish)]$

(7.39) $p = \lambda e\ [stock(e) \wedge AG(e, speaker) \wedge LOC(e', x_i)]$

(7.40) $\phi = \forall e\ (stock(e) \wedge AG(e, speaker) \wedge LOC(e', x_i)) \rightarrow TH(e, clownfish)$

To give a meaning for (7.35), we need to make some assumptions about both the semantics of attitude verbs and the binding of gaps. We make the following assumptions: (i) the verb *said* introduces a separate event; (ii) the complement of *said* has an intensional thematic role ATTITUDE (ignoring tense); and (iii) the trace variable is bound by an existential quantifier. Based on these assumptions we arrive at the following for the interpretation of (7.35):

(7.41) $\exists e' \exists x_i\ owner(x_i, kim) \wedge fishtank(x_i) \wedge say(e') \wedge AG(e', speaker) \wedge$
            $ATT(e', {}^\wedge\phi)$

Crucially, (7.41) does not describe a scenario like the one in (7.5), in which the speaker admitted to having stocked Kim's tank with two types of fish.

What if some other element than *clownfish* had been F-marked in (7.35)? If *stocked* had been F-marked, we would have derived an interpretation that could be paraphrased as *Kim's is the tank of which I said that stocking was the only thing I did that involved it and clownfish*. In fact, the speaker had made no such prior claim, so this possibility for focus either produces a false interpretation, or is simply ruled out pragmatically as an implausible interpretation. Similarly, pragmatic implausibility or clear falsity would presumably rule out focus on the entire VP *stock with clownfish*, or on *with*, although we do not attempt full analyses here.

The only remaining alternative, that there is no focus within the scope of *only*, would produce a trivial interpretation for the embedded clause: 'Kim's is the tank such that all occasions of stocking it with clownfish are occasions of stocking it with clownfish.' Once again, such a trivial reading could be ruled out on grounds of pragmatic infelicity, for example if there was a requirement on relative clauses that they should function to identify some individual. Alternatively, the example could be ruled out simply on the grounds of a grammatical stipulation like (7.28) that *only* must have a focus marked constituent in its syntactic scope.

Returning to (7.34), in which *always* seems to associate with a missing (focused) fishtank, we start by examining the embedded clause (7.42):

(7.42)   I always stock t_i with clownfish.

The interpretation of a sentence with *always* is semantically underspecified, and we need to consider how to resolve the domain restriction. Various sets of events have been mentioned explicitly in the context, and still others are available through further reasoning.

Suppose that the only focus marked constituent in (7.34) is *Kim's*. Then (7.42) is completely de-stressed.[13] Perhaps the hearer takes this as evidence that of the many salient sets of events, it is the set of events of the speaker stocking tanks with clownfish that is now under discussion. If so, the domain restriction of *always*, σ, may be set as follows:

(7.43) $\sigma = \lambda e \ [stock(e) \wedge \text{AG}(e, speaker) \wedge \text{TH}(e, clownfish)]$

If the domain relation ρ is set to identity, then what will result for the meaning of (7.42) will be as in (7.44), which may be plugged into (7.45) to get the complete interpretation of (7.34).

(7.44) $\psi = \forall e \ (stock(e) \wedge \text{AG}(e, speaker) \wedge \text{TH}(e, clownfish)) \rightarrow \text{LOC}(e', x_i)$

(7.45) $\exists e' \exists x_i \ owner(x_i, kim) \wedge fishtank(x_i) \wedge say(e') \wedge \text{AG}(e', speaker) \wedge$
$\text{ATT}(e', {}^\wedge\psi)$

---

[13]   It is possible to read (7.34) with no further pitch accent after *Kim's,* although the length of the sentence makes this seem a little forced. Alternatively, *clownfish* can have a secondary accent. More exactly, *Kim's* can be given an H*LL%, and *clownfish* can be given a rise-fall-rise accent that is sometimes said to mark contrast and/or topic, H*LH% in ToBI – c.f. §2.3 and the discussion of negation in §3.2.

If the entire H*LL% were to fall on *Kim's,* then we should also find significant lengthening in this word, and a slight hiatus (possibly difficult to detect given the slow decay of the final sibilant) before the onset of *is.* The intonation phrase boundary marker, H%, might also appear later in the sentence, for instance on *tank,* which could then be followed by a perceived hiatus before the onset of *I,* which itself might get a small pitch accent. If the secondary accent on *clownfish* does mark topicality, that would be grist to our mill.

Note that *only* can associate with H*LH% as well as with H*LL%. Tancredi (1997) suggests the situation is more complex, with a three-way interaction between the focus sensitive expression, the accent type, and the presence of syntactic islands. Further empirical work is needed here.

This, of course, is just the meaning that would be blocked for the equivalent sentence with *only*, (7.35). What we must stress is that it is not essential to our main claims that we detail a convincing route by which (7.34) gets the interpretation we have just described. On the contrary, we suggest that there are many routes, and many other interpretations. What is important is that this interpretation is not blocked.

Since *always* obtains its domain pragmatically, syntactic contingencies like extraction are of little significance to the interpretation of *always*, except insofar as they mark information structure. In the case at hand, the use of a construction which makes *Kim* the focus is plausibly connected with the availability of a reading in which the *always*-clause ends up saying of a certain set of events that they all involved Kim in some way (they were events of stocking Kim's tank). But other plausible connections could also be made.

What we predict, in fact, is that there will typically be no single dominant reading (i.e. single choice for the domain restriction) for a sentence with *always*, but that a number of readings should be available, whereas the range of readings available for utterances of comparable sentences with *only* should be much reduced.

In other words, if one is not convinced that in the context we described (7.34) gets the reading in (7.45), that is unsurprising, although many respondents give judgments in accord with them having obtained this reading. The only strong claim we make about how any one person will interpret the examples at hand is that they will definitely *not* interpret (7.35) as having the meaning in (7.45). The reason is simple: *only* associates with focus, and the gap in (7.35) is not F-marked.

7.5   An Extraction Puzzle

Summary: *We discuss potential counterexamples from Dutch and German to our generalization that the focus associate of an exclusive must appear overtly in the exclusive's syntactic domain.*

We have provided evidence that exclusives must associate with an F-marked element in their syntactic scope. In this section, we discuss some apparent counterexamples to this claim from German and Dutch.

It has been observed that in German V2 constructions focus sensitive expressions such as *nur* 'only' and *sogar* 'even' can follow their focus associate (Jacobs 1983; Büring and Hartmann 2001; Jaeger and Wagner 2003). To illustrate, in (7.46) (from Büring and Hartmann 2001) the focus sensitive expression *nur* follows its associated focus *küsste* 'kissed.' In (7.47) (from Krifka 1999) sentence-medial focus sensitive expressions like *nur*, *auch* 'also', and *sogar* 'even' can associate with the initial NP subject *Peter*.

(7.46)   German
            Peter | KÜSSTE$_i$ | Maria nur t$_i$.
            Peter kissed   Maria only
            "Peter kissed and did nothing else to Maria"

(7.47)   German
            | PETER$_i$ | hat nur/auch/sogar t$_i$ die Ausstellung besucht
            Peter   has only/also/even the exhibition   visited
            "Peter has only/also/even visited the exhibition"

Data like (7.46) and (7.47) have been taken to indicate that German focus sensitive expressions like *nur* can associate with extracted elements. However (7.46) and (7.47) alone do not counterexemplify the claim that *nur* and *sogar* cannot associate with extracted elements. In (7.46), *nur* associates with the lexical verb *küsste*, and both expressions are within the same clause. Similarly, *Peter* is within the same clause as the focus sensitive expressions in (7.47).[14]

   Extraction constructions in German, such as *wh*-interrogatives like those in (7.48) and (7.49), conform to our generalizations. None of the speakers we consulted could get the assocation with focus reading (7.49a) of (7.49). In (7.49), *nur* crucially takes scope under the *believing* event.

(7.48) German
       | Was | glaubst du daß Hans immer seiner Mutter gegeben hat
       What believe you that Hans always his   mother gave   have

   a. 'What was the thing such that you believe that Hans gave always that thing to his mother?'
   b. 'What do you believe that Hans always gave his mother but nobody else?'

(7.49) German
       | Was | glaubst du daß Hans nur seiner Mutter gegeben hat
       What believe you that Hans only his   mother gave   have

   a. *'What was the thing such that you believe that Hans gave only that thing to his mother?'
   b. 'What do you believe that Hans only gave his mother but nobody else?'

---

[14] It was crucial to our argument above that focus sensitive expressions in extraction contexts took scope under an embedding verb like *said* or *believe* (see e.g. (7.34) and (7.35)). That way it could not be claimed that the extracted element is within the syntactic scope or the same binding domain of the focus sensitive expression.

Barbiers (1995) claims that Dutch focus sensitive expressions like *pas* 'just' can associate with extracted elements. In (7.5) (Barbiers 1995: 68), the focus sensitive expression *pas* associates with the initial object *twee boeken* 'two books.'

(7.50)   Dutch
      | TWEE | boeken$_i$ denk ik dat Jan *pas* t$_i$ heeft gekocht
      Two   books   think I   that Jan just t$_i$ has   bought
      'I think that Jan has bought just two books.'

We have failed to reproduce this result with other Dutch focus sensitive expressions. (7.51) is a variant of (7.5) with the exclusive *alleen maar* 'only' replacing *pas*. In (7.51), *alleen maar* completely fails to associate with the extracted element *twee boeken*.

(7.51)   Dutch
      | TWEE | boeken$_i$ denk ik dat Jan *alleen maar* t$_i$ heeft gekocht
      Two   books   think I   that Jan only   t$_i$ has   bought
      *'I think that Jan has bought only two books.'
      (not a possible reading)

It is arguable that *pas* in (7.50) is not an exclusive at all, although it's meaning is certainly comparable with the English *just*. We suggest that, quite generally, *pas* combines with quanties.[15]

In sum, German and Dutch have been claimed to counterexemplify the claim that focus sensitive expressions fail to associate with extracted elements. However, upon closer inspection, German and Dutch extraction behavior is broadly in line with the main claims of this book, and the existence of a contrast in extraction possibilities between exclusives and adverbs of quantification in these languages is clear. In Chapter 10, we return to the German and Dutch extraction facts and suggest an analysis within the QFC theory of focus sensitivity.

7.6 Ellipsis

Summary: *We show that in the English ellipsis construction, quantificational adverbs can associate with elided material, but exclusives cannot.*

---

[15] One hypothesis worth exploring is that *pas* measures out events in the sense that *pas* adds a MEASURE thematic role to a verb's lexical semantics (e.g. *gekocht* 'bought' in (7.5)) (Tenny 1994). The *measure* role measures out and defines the temporal boundary of the event denoted by the sentence.

If this hypothesis is on the right track, a more accurate interpretation of (7.5) is *I think that Jan has just reached the stage of buying two books out of a larger intended purchasing procedure.* If *pas* does measure out events in this way, then this case might be analyzed as a *free* association rather than *conventional* association: it is the salience of a larger event that produces an interpretation comparable to that involved when a true exclusive associates conventionally via the alternative set. However, we will not pursue this analysis any further here.

English VP ellipsis constructions provide us with another way to remove an element from the syntactic scope of focus sensitive expressions. Given that an element has been removed from the syntactic scope of the focus sensitive expression, we can then examine whether the element can still be the expression's semantic focus. In this section we discuss a contrast between *always* and *only* in English VP ellipsis contexts.

Always can associate with elided elements, but *only* cannot. Consider the following context and the continuations in (7.52a) and (7.52b).

> **Context**: At the ceremony, some soldiers salute and others fire a round in the air. Some do both. What about Kim and Sandy?

(7.52) a.   Kim always SALUTES because Sandy always does.
>   (can mean: 'Kim salutes at every ceremony because Sandy salutes at every ceremony.')

   b.   *Kim only SALUTES because Sandy only does.
>   (cannot mean: 'Kim salutes (and does nothing else) because Sandy salutes (and does nothing else).')

The VP ellipsis example in (7.52b) fails to have the reading 'Kim salutes (and does nothing else) because Sandy salutes (and does nothing else)' while (7.52a) can have the association with focus reading 'At every ceremony, Kim salutes because Sandy salutes.'

Examples (7.53a) and (7.53b) are naturally occurring examples of VP ellipsis in which *always* and *usually* are followed by an elided VP. Both have readings in which the quantificational adverb associates with the elided VP.

(7.53) a.   Oh well ... it will all work out (it always does).
>   *[web example]*
>   (can mean: 'It always works out.')

   b.   A bus did come, but not surprisingly it was not going through the City as it usually did.
>   *[British National Corpus, Frances Saunders-Veness, Oh! sister
>   I saw the bells go down, Lewes, East Sussex,
>   The Book Guild Ltd, 1989, pp. 7–73.]*
>   (can mean: 'Most of the time, when the bus came, it went through the City.')

In contrast, searching for *only did* (in the British National Corpus and on the web) produced almost exclusively examples in which *only did* follows *not*. Among the fifty examples we checked, we found some occurrences of genuine anaphoric *did*, but it was not the focus, and was followed by an adjunct phrase containing the focus. For example, in (7.54) *did so* is anaphoric, but the associated focus of *only* is the *when*-clause.

(7.54)   Originally Marlowe had no intention of following what we now call
           'Tamburlaine Part I' with a sequel, and only did so when public
           acclaim demanded it.

                                                                    [*web example*]

There is a clear contrast between the behavior of exclusives and quantificational adverbs in English ellipsis constructions. We now present a simple
account of that contrast in terms of the ability of quantificational adverbs to
freely associate, but the requirement of exclusives that they associate conventionally.

7.7 Analyzing the Ellipsis Data

Summary: *We present an analysis in event semantics which explains the data in
terms of quantificational adverbs manifesting free association, but exclusives requiring conventional association.*

How can the ellipsis data we have presented be explained in terms of the
theoretical analysis presented in Chapter 6? Let us consider the examples in
(7.52a) and (7.52b), which involve Kim and Sandy saluting (as opposed to
shooting).
     The crucial clause of (7.52b) is that in (7.55a), where we have added an
anaphoric index. Let us assume that the semantics of the VP anaphor *does$_i$* can
be represented as $\lambda x \lambda e\ [X_i(e) \wedge \text{AG}(e, x)]$. For (7.55a), the underlying sentence
meaning q will be (7.55b).

(7.55) a.   Sandy only does$_i$.

       b. $q = \lambda e\ [X_i(e) \wedge \text{AG}(e, sandy)]$

Because the VP-defocused meaning p is defined as being the underlying sentence meaning minus the contribution of focal elements in the VP, and since we
assume that *does* is not a bearer of focus, p must be the same as q.
     Under these circumstances we would derive the truth-conditions in (7.56)
for (7.55a), prior to anaphoric resolution of X_i:

(7.56) $\forall e\ (X_i(e) \wedge \text{AG}(e, sandy)) \rightarrow (X_i(e) \wedge \text{AG}(e, sandy))$

However X_i is resolved, the form in (7.56) will be trivial. We assume this
triviality is related to the infelicity of the sentence, either directly, or because

of an underlying grammatical principle that prevents such trivial meanings from occurring.[16,17]

Turning to *always*, we must consider the last clause of (7.52a): *Sandy always does$_i$*. The context given was one which made salient military ceremonies at which Sandy was present, so one plausible value for the quantificational domain of *always* would be that given in (7.57).

(7.57) $\sigma = \lambda e \, [military\text{-}ceremony(e) \wedge present\text{-}at(e, sandy)]$

We assume that the domain relation ρ is given by the higher order constant *temporal-and-physical-part-of*. If the underlying sentence meaning q takes the same value as q in (7.55), and X_i is resolved to a property of events *salute*, then the truth conditions for *Sandy always does$_i$* end up as:

(7.58) $\forall e \, (military\text{-}ceremony(e) \wedge present\text{-}at(e, sandy)) \rightarrow$
                 $\exists e' \, temporal\text{-}and\text{-}physical\text{-}part\text{-}of(e, e') \wedge X_i(e') \wedge \text{AG}(e, sandy)$

This seems a reasonable meaning, so we correctly predict felicity of *Sandy always does* in this context, and hence show the desired contrast between *always* and *only*.

In general, the apparent association of *always* with ellipsis targets will be seen whenever the set of salient situations quantified over are not situations in which the content expressed by the target is known to hold. For instance, if there is a salient set of military ceremonies S where Sandy is present, and it is

---

[16] Jason Merchant (p.c.) comments correctly that triviality is not in general sufficient to cause infelicity. However, it is worth bearing in mind that in the case under discussion, there is no obvious pragmatic function that utterance of a tautology could take on. Thus the perceived infelicity might require an explanation at the level of discourse coherence, in terms of the lack of relevant connection between the meanings of (7.55a) and the prior sentence.

Another approach to explaining why the triviality of (7.56) leads to infelicity would be to follow Gajewski (2002). Gajewski distinguishes sentences which are analytic because of the extensions of the content words which they contain, and sentences which are analytic because of their logical form. He offers a general principle to the effect that the latter class, into which we suggest (7.56) might fall, are ungrammatical.

Note that in other cases discussed in this chapter, we do not rely on triviality producing infelicity, but merely on contentful interpretations being strongly preferred over trivial ones in cases of ambiguity. Also note that in Chapter 10, §10.6, we describe in terms of our more detailed account of the meaning of *only* how the infelicity of (7.56) relates to discourse incoherence.

[17] Note that although *does* was not focused in the above examples, there are cases when *does* is focused. In this case, it seems to be the polarity of the sentence which is being contrasted with that of some other sentence, as in the familiar routine: *Punch: Oh no I didn't!, Policeman: Oh yes you did!* In that case we would assume that the VP–defocused meaning p is just the disjunction $q \vee \neg q$, so that a sentence like (7.55a) would receive a meaning of the form $\forall e \, (q(e) \vee \neg q(e)) \rightarrow q(e)$. This is logically equivalent to $\forall e \, q(e)$, which in the case at hand, after anaphora resolution, would express the obviously false proposition *every event is one of Sandy saluting*. This result is in line with the data, i.e. the fact that the sentence is infelicitous.

not established that in each of these Sandy salutes, and the property of saluting is also salient, then *Sandy always does* can mean that in each member of the set S, Sandy salutes.

7.8 An Ellipsis Puzzle

Summary: *Normally an exclusive must have an overt focused element in its syntactic domain, and cannot associate with elided material. However, we present examples showing that English exclusives apparently can associate with elided material when the exclusive itself is stressed.*

In §7.6 we made the observation that exclusives cannot associate with elided elements. The example in (7.52b), repeated here as (7.59), illustrates the observation. (7.59) has two important properties. First, *only* in the ellipsis target *Sandy only does* is a repeat of *only* in the ellipsis source. Second, *only* is not accented in the ellipsis target.

(7.59)   *Kim only SALUTES because Sandy only does.
           (cannot mean: 'Kim salutes (and does nothing else) because Sandy salutes (and does nothing else)')

Note, however, that when *only* is accented and not repeated, as in (7.60) and (7.61), *only* seems to be able to associate with an elided element.[18]

(7.60) A: Which store do your friends prefer to shop at?
        B: John sometimes goes to the FANCY store, and Sue ONLY does.

(7.61) A: Mary never feeds NUTRAPUP to Fido.
        B: Whaddya mean? She ONLY does.
            (... She wouldn't dream of feeding him anything less.)

In speaker B's utterance of (7.60), *only* is accented in the ellipsis target *Sue ONLY does* and can mean 'Sue goes to the fancy store and nowhere else.' Crucially, *only* is contrastive with *sometimes* in the ellipsis source *John sometimes goes to the fancy store*. Similarly, in (10.39), the ellipsis target *she ONLY does* in speaker B's utterance can mean 'She feeds nutrapup and nothing else to Fido.' In (10.39), *only* contrasts with *never* in Speaker A's utterance.

One hypothesis worth exploring is the idea that focus structure is normally not reconstructed in ellipsis contexts, but may be reconstructed in highly echoic utterances, such as denials. We return to this puzzle in §10.6 and sketch an alternative solution.

---

[18] Thanks to Delia Graff and Michael Wagner for these observations.

7.9 Summary

In this chapter we provided evidence showing that the structural condition in (7.62) holds for some but not all focus sensitive expressions.

(7.62)   *The Principle of Lexical Association*
          An operator like *only* must be associated with a lexical constituent in its c–command domain.

Only and its cross-linguistic counterparts must normally be associated with a lexical constituent in their c–command domain. This condition does not hold for *always* and its translation equivalents.

Consequently, we have further evidence for the claim that some expressions that have been classified as focus sensitive involve obligatory dependence on focus, while other expressions do not. This result, along with the evidence in Chapter 6, provides a compelling argument for the QFC model. Specifically, the evidence speaks in favor of a conventionalized account of the focus sensitivity of exclusives, but a purely pragmatic account of the focus sensitivity of quantificational adverbs.

Though we provided evidence from extraction and ellipsis that supports our account of *only* and *always*, we also presented evidence from German and Dutch showing that the interaction between extraction and the interpretation of focus sensitive expressions may be more complicated than we have argued is the case for English. Consequently, more data is needed to give a cross-linguistic picture of how focus interacts with various types of extraction constructions. The same could be said of the interaction of ellipsis and focus cross-linguistically: English VP-ellipsis constructions are unlike those in even typologically similar languages, so much more research would be needed to generalize our results on ellipsis cross-linguistically. Despite these caveats, it should be clear that a major prediction of our account of focus sensitivity is borne out: to the extent that it happens at all, association of exclusives with an elided focus is far more restricted than is the case for quantificational adverbs.

Chapter 8

Monotonicity and Presupposition

Opposition on so tender a subject would only attach her the more to her own opinion.
Jane Austen, 1811, *Sense and Sensibility*

8.1   Introduction

In Chapter 6, we considered phonological effects on association with focus. We showed that the focus associate of a quantificational adverb can be reduced or dependent material, whereas the focus associate of an exclusive cannot. Then, in Chapter 7, we considered syntactic effects. We showed that the focus associate of a quantificational adverb is relatively independent of syntactic operations like extraction and ellipsis, whereas the focus associate of an exclusive must normally be explicitly realized in the syntactic domain of the exclusive.

In this chapter, we turn to semantic and pragmatic effects, namely effects related to *monotonicity* and *presupposition*. Once again, we will show that an exclusive, like *only*, behaves quite differently than a quantificational adverb, like *always*. Furthermore, the difference will accord with the generalization we have been arguing for throughout this book: *only* associates conventionally, but *always* associates freely.

8.2   Background on Monotonicity, NPIs, and PPIs

Summary: *We introduce the concepts of* upward *and* downward monotonicity *and then the related notions of* negative *and* positive polarity items. *The distribution of polarity items is shown to have a bearing on the interpretation of exclusives and quantificational adverbs, and hence on the types of focus sensitivity that these expressions manifest.*

The notion of MONOTONICITY relates to inferential properties of parts of sentences. Material that can be arbitrarily strengthened while maintaining truth of the sentence is said to occur in a downward monotone position. One way to strengthen something is to conjoin it with something else, so e.g. *Mary and Sam laughed* is stronger than *Mary laughed*. If α is a sub-part of a sentence ϕ, then we write the result of replacing α with the conjunction of α and β as $\phi[\alpha/\alpha \wedge \beta]$, producing the following definition:

> **Definition 1 (Test for (simple) downward monotonicity)** *The expression α occurs in a simply downward monotone position in a sentence ϕ iff for any β which is stronger than α, ϕ entails $\phi[\alpha/\beta]$. If α is a set denoting term, then a stronger term would be a narrower one, i.e. one denoting a subset. If α is a proposition, then strength means logical strength, so β ranges over expressions that entail α, e.g. a conjunction containing α as one conjunct.*

We can give a similar statement of a test for the opposite property, upward monotonicity:

> **Definition 2 (Test for upward monotonicity)** *The expression α occurs in an upward monotone position in a sentence ϕ iff for any β which is weaker than α, ϕ entails $\phi[\alpha/\beta]$.*

The notions of upward and downward monotonicity are standardly used in accounting for the distribution of *polarity items* (PIs), of which there are two basic categories, NEGATIVE POLARITY ITEMS (NPIs), and POSITIVE POLARITY ITEMS (PPIs). We start with NPIs.

At an intuitive level, NPIs are expressions which tend to occur in negative rather than positive statements, words like *any, ever, give a damn*, and *lift a finger*. It is widely accepted that downward monotonicity is a necessary condition for licensing of *Negative Polarity Items* (NPIs) (Fauconnier 1975; Ladusaw 1979).[1]

Similarly, upward monotonicity (i.e. the validity of inferences involving weakening) is widely held to be a necessary condition for licensing PPIs. These are expressions like *rather, somewhat*, and *a tad* which tend to occur in positive statements, hence the infelicity of # *She wasn't rather/somewhat/a tad drunk*, except as an echoic denial.

Because PIs are sensitive to monotonicity, we can use the distribution of PIs as a diagnostic test to see whether a given environment is upward or downward monotonic (if either). For example, consider universal quantifiers like the determiner *every*, which is downward monotonic in its restrictor argument and upward monotonic in its scope argument. As a result of these monotonicity properties, NPIs are licensed in the restrictor but not the scope of *every*. The example in (8.1) shows licensing of the NPI *ever*:

(8.1)   a.   Every bear that ever there was is going to be down in the woods because ...[2]

     b.   *Every bear is ever going to be down in the woods.

---

[1]   See Giannakidou (1998, 1999) for an alternative view.
[2]   James B. Kennedy, *The Teddy Bear's Picnic*, 1913. (Tune composed John W. Bratton, 1907, presumably inspiring use of an NPI.)

We must now relate the notion of monotonicity to the meaning of *always* and *only*. As in the previous two chapters, we will assume in this chapter that *always* and *only* semantically express event quantifiers with universal force, as illustrated by examples (6.31) and (6.32), repeated below as (8.2) and (8.3). Thus, like *every*, *always* and *only* have a restrictor and a scope.

(8.2)   a.   Sandy always feeds [Fido]$_F$ Nutrapup.

      b.   Sandy only feeds [Fido]$_F$ Nutrapup.

      c. $\forall x\ feed(sandy, x, nutrapup) \rightarrow x = fido$
        "Everything Sandy feeds Nutrapup to is Fido"

      d. $\forall e\ (feeding(e) \wedge \text{AG}(e, sandy) \wedge \text{TH}(e, nutrapup)) \rightarrow \text{GO}(e, fido)$

(8.3)   a.   Sandy always feeds Fido [Nutrapup]$_F$.

      b.   Sandy only feeds Fido [Nutrapup]$_F$.

      c. $\forall x\ feed(sandy, fido, x) \rightarrow x = nutrapup$
        "Everything Sandy feeds to Fido is Nutrapup"

      d. $\forall e\ (feeding(e) \wedge \text{AG}(e, sandy) \wedge \text{GO}(e, fido)) \rightarrow \text{TH}(e, nutrapup)$

Herburger (2000) also treats *only* and *always* as event quantifiers and offers the following generalization: "All the nonfocused material in the scope of the event quantifier Q also restricts Q" (Herburger 2000: 18). Data involving negative polarity items (NPIs) can help us test whether this generalization is accurate by showing which material in a sentence with focus sensitive expressions like *always* and *only* is interpreted in the restrictor. Therefore, if Herburger's generalization is correct, then NPIs should be licensed by both *only* and *always*.

On the basis of this prediction, we present data in §8.3–8.6 that verifies Herburger's generalization with regard to *only*, but disconfirms it with regard to *always*. The theoretical importance of this result is that it supports our claim that focus sensitivity of these expressions results from different mechanisms.

8.3   Polarity Item Licensing by *only*

Summary: *We show that in English, German, Dutch, and Spanish, VP-modifying exclusives license NPIs in non-focal material.* Contra *Horn (1996), this is not restricted to weak NPIs, but includes strong NPIs too. We also demonstrate that VP modifying exclusives do not license NPIs in focal material: NPIs appearing in focal material in the scope of an exclusive either do not have their idiomatic NPI interpretation, or else are licensed independently of the exclusive.*

We now present naturally occurring and constructed cross-linguistic data showing that *only* and its cross-linguistic counterparts license NPIs outside of their focus position. This observation (for English) is originally due to Klima (1964).

Subsequent discussions of NPI licensing in non-focal positions in the scope of *only* include Atlas (1993, 1996, 2002), Beaver and Clark (2003), von Fintel (1999), Giannakidou (1998, 1999, 2006), Herburger (2000: 100–4), Horn (1992, 1996, 2002a), Ladusaw (1979), Linebarger (1987), McCawley (1981, 1993: 83, 1998: 587), and Wagner (2006, 2007).

NPIs have been divided into two main sub-classes (Zwarts 1998; Jackson 1995; Krifka 1995), *weak* and *strong*. Weak NPIs in English include unstressed *any* and *ever*, *care to* and *bother with*. Strong NPIs include such locutions as *lift a finger* and *give a damn/fuck/shit*. The NPIs in these classes are differentiated by their distribution: weak NPIs are standardly taken to be licensed in all downward monotone contexts, and (according to Zwarts 1998) strong NPIs are licensed in a subset of these contexts having the property of ANTI-ADDITIVITY.[3] We return to the formal definition of these properties in §8.5.

Horn (1996: 8) claims that *only*, although an NPI licenser, does not produce an anti-additive context and does not license strong NPIs. The data we will now present shows that, in fact, *only* licenses both weak and strong NPIs. Our study differs from previous ones in two ways. First, we concentrate on VP modifying *only*, studying licensing in non-focal material in the VP, whereas almost all prior research concentrated on NP modifying *only*. Second, our data is primarily naturally occurring.

Examples (8.4)–(8.13) all show NPIs occurring within the scope of VP *only*. In each case, the relevant instance of *only* is underlined and the NPI has been boxed. The first four examples show weak NPIs, and the remainder strong NPIs. In all of the examples, the NPI is not the focus of *only*.

Weak NPIs:

(8.4)   We only ┃ever┃ had cream of mushroom.[4]

(8.5)   The central problem is that it is only ┃ever┃ possible to sample a child's language over a fixed period of time and within a finite number of situations.[5]

---

[3] Examples (i)–(iv) show that weak polarity items such as *any* and *ever* and minimizers such as *lift a finger* are licensed in the restrictor, but not the scope, of *every*.

(i) Every student who had ┃ever┃ read ┃anything┃ about phrenology attended the lecture.

(ii) *Every student who attended the lectures had ┃ever┃ read ┃anything┃ about phrenology. (Ross 1967: 451, 454; Ladusaw 1980)

(iii) Every group that ┃lifts a finger┃ for animals needs funds to fight the evil that is done to animals.

(iv) *Every group ┃lifts a finger┃ for animals.

[4] Muriel Gray, *The First Fifty*, Mainstream Publishing, Edinburgh, 1990.
[5] John Harris, *Early Language Development*, Routledge and Kegan Paul, London, 1990.

(8.6)   Because we found one order of this group to be much more likely than any other, we probably only | care to | see the map distances for this single order.[6]

(8.7)   According to his viewpoint, the Miatas are prone to this partly because they don't accumulate miles the way most cars do. The timing belt should be changed at 60,000 miles OR 60 months, and most people only | bother with | the mileage.[7]

Strong NPIs:

(8.8)   The only words coming out of my mouth is a lyrical thang
          So please back tha fuck up off my screen tho
          Since i was four you was known to be the enemy
          Like rintintin you only | give a shit | for me
          The community took four steps higher
          86ing motherfuckas working for the suppliers[8]

(8.9)   … if the left flipper is too weak for a bearkick, as it often is because people who run arcades are usually assholes and only | give a shit | about their street fighter shit games, use that left flipper to send the ball back into the swamp.[9]

(8.10)   Well, I certainly don't give a damn. I only | gave a damn | because I thought you did.[10]

(8.11)   If you were a kid in Cleveland (then), you only | gave a damn | about two things – the Beatles and Ghoulardi.[11]

(8.12)   Work is the curse of Stevie Thomas Jackson and Christopher Thomas Geddes. Stuart David, visionary and poet, cursed it before trying it, and would only | lift a finger | to pick his nose or write a book.[12]

---

[6]   Stephen Lincoln, Mark Daly and Eric Lander, *Constructing Genetic Linkage Maps with MAPMAKER/EXP Version 3.0: A Tutorial and Reference Manual*, Whitehead Institute for Biomedical Research Technical Report, January, 1993.

[7]   http://www.socalm.org/crank/crank199609.pt1.html – archived email.

[8]   The Coup, "Interrogation", on *Genocide and Juice*, Wild Pitch/EMI Records, 1994 (CD).

[9]   http://www.acc.umu.se/oscar/pinball/gbook/guestbook.html – A page for pinball lovers.

[10] Jamie Malankowski, "Five Finales: How to wrap up Seinfeld? We offer some suggestions", *Time Magazine* 151: 17, May 4 1998. Note: we take it that in this example the focus of *only* is the *because* clause although *gave* would also be read with contrastive stress to mark the past tense morpheme.

[11] Mike Olszewski, quoted in the *Akron Beacon Journal*, October 9, 1998.

[12] Belle and Sebastian, *If You're Feeling Sinister* (CD Sleeve Notes), Jeepster 1996.

(8.13)   You may think faeries are sweet, good and kind, but they're not.
         They're vicious, greedy buggers who'd only | lift a finger | to save their
         best friend if they thought they'd profit from it. They have sharp teeth
         too and, as many people have found out, won't hesitate to use them.[13]

We have not collected large amounts of data on NPI licensing of cognates
of *only* in languages other than English. However, our initial research on other
languages is encouraging.[14] The Dutch equivalents of *only* also license NPIs.
Van der Wal (1996) mentions *alleen maar* and *slechts* as members of a class of
"inherently negative" expressions which license NPIs. Zwarts (1998: 195) clas-
sifies phrases of the form *slechts* n N (n a number, *N* a noun) and *alleen NP*
as monotone decreasing, like their English counterparts *only* n N and *only NP*,
respectively.
   Using web searches, we located several naturally occurring examples of
Dutch equivalents of *only* licensing NPIs. Note that, with the possible exception of example (8.16), these are not VP-modifying uses of equivalents of *only*.

(8.14)   Dutch
         Spreker vindt dat het multicultureel erfgoed niet bestaat. Er vol-
         gens hem maar één spreker, die | enig benul | heeft van Vlaamse iden-
         titeit … [15]
         "Speaker finds that the multi-cultural inheritance does not exist. In
         his view, [there is] only one speaker who has | any notion | of the
         Flemish identity."

(8.15)   Dutch
         Waarschijnlijk is het altijd al zo geweest dat slechts een kleine min-
         derheid | enig benul | heeft van de methoden en resultaten van de
         wetenschap.[16]
         "Probably it has always been the case that only a small minority has
         any notion of the methods and results of science."

(8.16)   Dutch
         De motor is wonderlijk sterk en klein. Als we een bacterie opblazen
         tot de afmetingen van een auto heeft zijn motor een doorsnee

---

[13] Online text at http://www.angelfire.com/me/Spero/folks.html.
[14]   Giannakidou (1998, 1999, 2006) argues that the Greek exclusive *monon* 'only' does not license
NPIs at all. We return to this claim in §8.7 below. The languages for which we have positive data
are all Romance or Germanic.
[15] De heer Raets, quoted in the minutes of the meeting of the Provincieraad van Antwerpen,
October 1998.
[16] Maarten van Rossem, *Geloof en Wetenschap*, September 1999. Note first that *minderheid* ('minority') could also be the relevant NPI licensor. Second, there is an occurrence of *altijd* ('always') in the
first clause. However, the NPI falls clearly in the semantic scope of *altijd*, not its restrictor, so this is
presumably irrelevant.

van slechts vijf centimeter – een verhouding tussen kracht en afmetingen die onze techniek <u>alleen</u> met gasturbines en raketten ☐kan evenaren☐.[17]

"The motor is wonderfully strong and small. If we blew up a bacterium to the size of a car, it's motor would only be 5 centimeters across – a power to weight ratio with which in our technology <u>only</u> gas turbines and rockets ☐can compare☐."

A native Dutch informant reports that the following constructed example in which VP *alleen maar* licenses the NPI *ooit* 'ever' is acceptable:

(8.17)   Dutch
         Jan heeft ☐ooit☐ <u>alleen maar</u> geld aan zijn [moeder]$_F$ gegeven.
         "Jan <u>only</u> ☐ever☐ gave money to his [mother]$_F$."

We have also found some initial evidence that *nur*, the German equivalent of *only*, licenses NPIs, on the basis of native speaker judgments of the following constructed examples:

(8.18)   German
         Hans hat <u>nur</u> in dem [haus]$_F$ ☐einen Muckser von sich gegeben☐.
         "Hans <u>only</u> made ☐so much as a peep☐ in the [house]$_F$."

As a last NPI example, we found the following case of *solamente* 'only' licensing an NPI in Spanish:

(8.19)   Spanish
         <u>Solamente</u> una lámpara ☐dijo una palabra☐
         y me condujo a salva hasta la habitación[18]
         "Only a lamp said a word
         And led me in safety up to our quarters"

It is clear from the data we have presented so far in this section, that exclusives license both weak and strong NPIs, and that this effect holds across a range of languages. However, it is essential to the argument we will develop that this licensing of NPIs is specific to non-focal expressions in the domain of the exclusive. So we must now consider the issue of whether NPIs are licensed in focal positions. This turns out to be a vexed issue.

---

[17]   "Bouwen in een kleine wereld", KIJK.
[18]   Benjamín Valdivia, "Sobre un afortunado papel de fotografía", in *El Juego del Tiempo*. Secretaría de Educación Pública/CREA Mexico, 1985.

NPI licensing in the focus associate of exclusives

The scope of *every* does not license NPIs, so if *only* is akin to a universal as suggested, we would expect that NPIs would not be permitted in the focus position of *only*. However, Linebarger (1987) and Horn (1996: 27f) provide constructed examples showing that the NPIs *any* and *ever* are licensed in the focus position of *only*. The example in (8.20) is from Linebarger (1987: 373).

(8.20)   Only people who have ever had a debilitating illness themselves can appreciate what an ordeal this was.

Note that (8.20) is also acceptable without *only*, as in (8.21):

(8.21)   People who have ever had a debilitating illness themselves can appreciate what an ordeal this was.

It is easy to find naturally occurring examples of bare plural and definite *wh*-clauses licensing NPIs to which *only* can freely be added.

(8.22) a.   In fact, among the 30.4 million US adults who made any purchase via the Web in the past month, one out of 11 reads PC World.[19]

       b.   In fact, among only the 30.4 million US adults who made any purchase via the Web in the past month, one out of 11 reads PC World.

(8.23) a.   People who had ever been heavy marijuana users cost the nation $34.2 billion in diminished worker productivity in 1980.[20]

       b.   Only people who had ever been heavy marijuana users cost the nation $34.2 billion in diminished worker productivity in 1980.

Based on the above examples, it is clear that Linebarger's (1987) and Horn's (1996) data does not establish that *only* licenses weak NPIs in its focus position. Their data shows merely that independently licensed NPIs may appear there. This is unsurprising (cf. von Fintel 1997: 23–4 and Beaver 2004: 48–50). As Horn (1996: 28) says: "polarity items are possible in this context [the focus position of *only*-DIB/BZC] not *because* of the semantic properties of *only* but in *spite* of them."

Further, note that certain NPs which mark the lowest points on scales are licensed in the focus of *only*; e.g., *She only drank a [drop]*$_F$. In such cases *only* has a scalar reading rather than an exhaustive reading. We posit that whenever a phrasal NPI occurs in the focus of *only*, it has a referential interpretation, derived compositionally, that puts it on the endpoint of a scale, rather than a purely conventional non-compositional interpretation.

---

[19]   http://marketing.pcworld.com/site/pressreleases/fall2001mri.html
[20]   Ed Falk, *Lies in the War on Drugs*, post on misc.activism.progressive, 1/25/1993.

For example, *Did Mary have any whiskey?* can be followed by *She only drank [a drop]$_F$!* This reply would only be a true statement if there is some drop of whiskey that Mary drank. Further, it is possible to say (ironically) *She drank a whole drop!*, which exploits the compositional nature of the NPI. So, here we have a case of an expression that often has an idiomatic NPI interpretation in the focus associate of *only*. But when the expression occurs in the focus associate of *only*, it lacks its idiomatic NPI interpretation. Thus the occurrence of the expression in the focus associate of *only* does not provide any evidence that this position is inherently downward monotone.

We have reached the conclusion that NPIs are licensed in non-focal positions in the syntactic domain of *only*, but not in the focus associate of *only*. We now consider the distribution of NPIs by the quantificational adverb *always*.

8.4   Polarity Item Licensing by *always*

Summary: *It is shown that NPIs are not licensed in non-focal material in the scope of* always.

Neither corpus searches in the British National Corpus, nor corpus searches in ten years of the *New York Times*, nor web searches have produced any credible examples in which the six NPIs from (8.4)–(8.13) occur in positions licensed by *always* (or *usually*) in the same clause.[21] Furthermore, replacement of *only* by *always* in sentences involving NPIs produces infelicity even after appropriate adjustments have been made.

Witness the effects of replacing *only* by *always* in variants of (8.4)–(8.13):

(8.24)   People only/*always ever have [cream of mushroom soup]$_F$.[22]

(8.25)   It is only/*always ever possible to sample a child's language over [a fixed period of time]$_F$.

---

[21]   However, we do find examples of *any* and its variants (*anything*, etc.) in VPs modified by *always*. It seems that we are forced to regard *any* as exceptional. This, of course, is not an unusual move. There is a large literature attempting to explain the distribution facts of *any*, much of which simply assumes that *any* is ambiguous between NPI and so-called *free-choice* readings – see Kadmon and Landman (1993) and Krifka (1995) for attempts to do without this ambiguity.

[22]   The impossibility of *always* and *ever* in (8.24) could result from a mismatch between the temporal interpretations of *always* and *ever*, and have nothing to do with polarity *per se*. However, *never ever* is felicitous, suggesting that the issue is one of monotonicity not temporality. Note also that there are positive uses of *ever*, meaning roughly *forever*, as in (i): these are common in the scope of *always*, generally as a form of emphasis. Ideally a diagnostic should be developed to separate positive and negative uses of *ever*.

(i) Forever? Forever ever? Foreverever?
     (Outkast, "Ms. Jackson", *Stankonia*, LaFace, 2000)

(8.26)   We probably only/?always care to see the map distances for [this single order]$_F$.

(8.27)   People only/?always bother with [the mileage]$_F$.

(8.28)   People only/?always give a shit for [me]$_F$.

(8.29)   People only/?always give a shit about [street fighter games]$_F$.

(8.30)   I only/?always gave a damn because I thought [you did]$_F$.

(8.31)   If you were a kid in Cleveland, you only/*always gave a damn about [two things]$_F$.

(8.32)   Stuart would only/?always lift a finger to [pick his nose]$_F$ or [write a book]$_F$.

(8.33)   Faeries would only/?always lift a finger to [save their best friend]$_F$.

Cross-linguistic counterparts of *always* also seem not to license NPIs. Neither Van der Wal (1996) nor Zwarts (1998) list any Dutch equivalents of *always* as NPI licensors. Further, *nur*, the German equivalent of *only*, licenses NPIs (see example (8.18)), but *immer* 'always' does not, on the basis of native speaker judgments of the example in (8.34):

(8.34)   German
          ? Hans hat <u>immer</u> in dem [haus]$_F$ | einen Muckser von sich gegeben |.
          "Hans <u>always</u> made | so much as a peep | in the [house]$_F$."

We have now shown that there is a contrast as regards NPI licensing by *only* and *always*. The former licenses NPIs in non-focal material in its domain, while the latter does not. The interpretation we give to this is that non-focal material in the syntactic domain of *only* is interpreted in a downward monotone position, while non-focal material in the syntactic domain of *always* is interpreted in an upward monotone position. But if this conclusion is valid, then there should also be distributional effects for PPIs, and this is the issue we now consider.

A brief look at PPI licensing

How does the distribution of positive polarity items (PPIs; e.g., *rather*, *pretty*, *quite*) differ between *only* and *always*? The parallel with *every* would lead to the negative prediction that PPIs should not be licensed in the scope of *only* and *always* outside of the focus. However, as the following examples show, once again there is a contrast between *only* and *always*: PPIs are licensed in non-focal positions in the scope of *always*, but not *only*.

(8.35) a.   Mary's ?only/always rather tired on [Sunday]$_F$.

       b.   Mary's ?only/always pretty (damn) tired on [Sunday]$_F$.

Corpus searches for PPIs have not been revealing. However, (8.36) is an example which is ambiguous as to whether the PPI *quite* occurs in the focus of *always* or not. The fact that the phrase *always been quite useful* can be read without stress provides some further support for our claim that PPIs are licensed in non-focal positions in the scope of *always*. We have found no such examples involving *only*.

(8.36)   Traditional economics has <u>always been</u> $\boxed{\text{quite}}$ useful for understanding the market forces that shaped industries and governed competition among firms during the first and second revolutions.[23]

We interpret the polarity item data we presented in this section and the previous one in terms of monotonicity. But we can also study the issue of monotonicity directly, by considering patterns of inference involving exclusives and quantificational adverbs. This is what we turn to in the next section.

8.5   Monotonicity Inferences

Summary: *We study monotonicity inferences involving* only *and* always. *These inferences are complicated by the presence of presuppositions associated with* only. *We follow von Fintel (1999) in considering inference patterns which account for these presuppositions. Having done so, we are able to give evidence that non-focal material in the scope of* only *is interpreted in a context which is both downward monotone and anti-additive, while this is not the case for* always.

We assume in this chapter that *only* expresses a universal quantifier, following argumentation of Horn (1996), who himself cites medieval authority for his position (e.g. Peter of Spain's *Tractatus Exponibilium*). On Horn's account *Only As are Bs* is logically equivalent to *All Bs are As*. Since *All Bs are As* is downward monotone in the B position, *Only As are Bs* should be downward monotone in the B position. Assuming a uniform semantics for NP and VP *only*, non-focal material in the syntactic scope of VP *only* should also license NPIs. This is in complete agreement with the data we presented above.

Is the data from NPI licensing backed up by inference tests based on definition 1? The answer is no (Atlas 1996, 2002; Giannakidou 2006; von Fintel 1999; Horn 2002a). In the following example, the diagnostic for downward monotonicity fails, because the validity of the argument from (8.37a) to the strengthened (8.37b) is dubious.

---

[23]   David Evans and Matthew Leder, "Economics for the Third Industrial Revolution", *Viewpoint 1*, Marsh and McLennan Companies, 1999.

(8.37) a.   Only Nathan drank to make others seem more interesting.

     b.   Only Nathan drank mojitos to make others seem more interesting.

Von Fintel (1999) presents an example like (8.37) that shows failure of the monotonicity inference for NP *only*, and also notes that strengthening non-focal material in the scope of VP *only* is not clearly truth preserving. Thus, for example, it is not clear that (8.38b) can be inferred from (8.38a).

(8.38) a.   Nathan only drank [to make others seem more interesting]$_F$.
       [→?]

     b.   Nathan only drank mojitos [to make others seem more interesting]$_F$.

More generally, it has been observed by Ladusaw (1979) and others (see e.g., Linebarger 1987) that NPIs are licensed in many cases where strengthening inferences do not appear to hold. Apart from *only*, examples of constructions which license NPIs but do not cleanly support monotonicity inferences include emotive factives, superlatives and embedded questions.

Von Fintel (1999) discusses a variant of downward monotonicity which is a better predictor of NPI licensing. In partial adoption of von Fintel's terminology, we term this *Strawson downward monotonicity*. We arrive at the following diagnostic:

Definition 3 (Test for Strawson downward monotonicity) *Let presupposition* (ψ) *be the strongest sentence presupposed by* ψ. *The expression* α *occurs in a Strawson downward monotone position in a sentence* ϕ *iff for any* β *which is stronger than* α, *the combination of* ϕ *and presupposition* ($\phi[\alpha/\beta]$) *entails* $\phi[\alpha/\beta]$.

The idea is that *only Nathan drank to make others seem more interesting* entails *only Nathan drank mojitos to make others seem more interesting*, under the assumption that the presuppositions of the second are satisfied.

For an analysis we follow (for the moment) Horn (1996), according to whom the presuppositions connected with *only* are existential (i.e. in this case the presupposition is that someone drank mojitos to make others seem more interesting).[24] With the von Fintel inspired revision of the downward monotonicity diagnostic, we can show for NP and VP *only* that downward monotonicity inferences are valid. From (8.39a, b) and (8.40a, b), we can infer (8.39c) and (8.40c) respectively.

---

[24] Note that strengthening the presupposition to *Nathan drank mojitos to make others seem more interesting*, in accord with Horn (1969), would not affect our account, although as Horn (1996) argues, it is less motivated. In Chapter 10, we will motivate another presupposition for exclusive sentences. On the account presented in that chapter, *Only Nathan drank mojitos to make others seem more interesting* neither presupposes someone drank mojitos to make others seem more interesting nor does it presuppose that Nathan drank mojitos to make others seem more interesting. Rather, *Only Nathan drank mojitos to make others seem more interesting* presupposes that an answer to the Current Question at least as strong as *Nathan drank mojitos to make others seem more interesting* is true.

(8.39) a.   Someone drank mojitos to make others seem more interesting.

     b.   Only Nathan drank to make others seem more interesting.
       $[\rightarrow]$

     c.   Only Nathan drank mojitos to make others seem more interesting.

(8.40) a.   Nathan drank mojitos (for some reason).

     b.   Nathan only drank [to make others seem more interesting]$_F$.
       $[\rightarrow]$

     c.   Nathan only drank mojitos [to make others seem more interesting]$_F$.

Anti-additive positions are a subset of downward monotone positions:

> **Definition 4 (Test for (simple) anti-additivity)** *The expression α occurs in an anti-additive position in a sentence ϕ iff ϕ and $\phi[\alpha/\beta]$ are together equivalent to $\phi[\alpha/\alpha$ or $\beta]$.*[25]

For example, the restrictor of *no* is anti-additive. From the conjunction of *No woman is 300 years old* and *No man is 300 years old*, we can infer *No man or woman is 300 years old*. It is easily seen that the restrictor of *every* is also anti-additive. Not only does the inference from (8.41b) to (8.41a) hold (downward monotonicity), but also the inference from (8.41a) to (8.41b) (Here α is *girl*, β is *boy*.)

(8.41) a.   Every girl is happy and every boy is happy.
       $[\leftrightarrow]$

     b.   Every girl or boy is happy.

For an example of a non-anti-additive context, consider the restrictor of *less than three*: note that there is a valid (downward monotonicity) inference from (8.42a) to (8.42b), but not *vice versa*.

(8.42) a.   Less than three girls are happy and less than three boys are happy.
       $[\nleftrightarrow]$

     b.   Less than three boys or girls are happy.

Horn (1996: 8) claims that *only NP*, although a polarity licenser, is a non-anti-additive quantifier. If *only* is semantically equivalent to a universal, as Horn argues at length, and if universal restrictors are anti-addititive, then Horn is incorrect to say that non-focal material in the scope of *only* occurs in a non-anti-additive context. But perhaps part of the problem is that presupposition complicates the data we obtain using the standard inference test for anti-additivity.

---

[25]   Note that the leftward direction of this bi-implication is equivalent to downward monotonicity, since α is just a strengthening of α or β, and so is β.

As with the superset inference test for downward entailment, a sentence *Only Nathan drank mojitos and only Nathan drank Cajun martinis* is equivalent to *Only Nathan drank mojitos or Cajun martinis* only if all presuppositions are satisfied. Accordingly, we modify the definition of anti-additivity:

Definition 5 (Test for Strawson anti-additivity) *The expression α occurs in an anti-additive position in a sentence ϕ iff ϕ and $\phi[\alpha/\beta]$ are together equivalent to the combination of $\phi[\alpha/$ α or $\beta]$, the presuppositions of ϕ and the presuppositions of $\phi[\alpha/\beta]$.*

Note that for cases that occur to us, if the presuppositions of ϕ and those of $\phi[\alpha/\beta]$ are satisfied, then the presuppositions of $\phi[\alpha/$ α or $\beta]$ will also be satisfied. So it is not necessary to add presuppositions to the lefthand-side of the bi-implication in the above definition.

There is a bi-implication between (a, b) and (c, d, e) in each of (8.43) and (8.44), showing that both NP and VP *only* produce Strawson anti-additive contexts outside of their foci. Note that this result corroborates the analysis of *only* as a universal quantifier.[26]

(8.43) a.   Only Nathan drank to make others seem more interesting, and

b.   Only Nathan smoked to make others seem more interesting. [↔]

c.   Only Nathan drank or smoked to make others seem more interesting,

d.   Someone drank to make others seem more interesting and

e.   Someone smoked to make others seem more interesting.

(8.44) a.   Nathan only drank [to make others seem more interesting]$_F$, and

b.   Nathan only smoked [to make others seem more interesting]$_F$. [↔]

c.   Nathan only drank or smoked [to make others seem more interesting]$_F$,

d.   Nathan drank and

e.   Nathan smoked.

The combination of NPI licensing data and inference test data allows us to refute some analyses of *only* which do not account for presuppositions adequately. For example, the cross-categorial analysis of *only* presented by Bonomi and Casalegno (1993) incorporates as a principal part of the meaning of *only* (i.e. as ordinary (at-issue) content) what Horn gives as an existential presupposition.

---

[26]   Note that Atlas (1996) argues that *only Count Noun* is a downward monotonic, anti-additive quantifier expression, while *only Proper Name* is a non-monotonic, pseudo-anti-additive quantifier expression. We would claim that neither *only Count Noun* nor *only Proper Name* are simply downward monotonic, and, *a fortiori*, neither are simply anti-additive. We would also claim that both are Strawson anti-additive and, *a fortiori*, both are Strawson downward monotonic.

In Bonomi and Casalegno's (1993) event framework *Sandy only eats [nuts]*$_F$ has the following meaning:

(8.45) $(\exists e \; eating(e) \wedge \text{AG}(e, sandy) \wedge \text{TH}(e, nuts) \wedge$
$(\forall e \; eating(e) \wedge \text{AG}(e, sandy) \rightarrow \text{TH}(e, nuts))$

That analysis predicts that non-focused material in the scope of NP and VP *only* is in a non-monotone context, neither upward monotonic nor simply downward monotonic nor Strawson downward monotonic. This is incompatible with either the NPI data presented earlier, or the inference test data presented in this section.[27]

To end this section, let us consider monotonicity inferences involving *always*. Our observation here is that monotonicity inferences involving *always* are far less clear than those involving *only*. In some cases, it seems clear that *always* creates a Strawson downward monotonic context in non-focal material:

(8.46) a.   Nathan sometimes drank mojitos.

b.   Nathan always drank [to make others seem more interesting]$_F$. [→]

c.   Nathan always drank mojitos [to make others seem more interesting]$_F$.

However, consider the contrast between (8.47) and (8.48).

(8.47) a.   Kids care deeply about something these days.

b.   Kids only care about [music]$_F$ these days. [→]

c.   Kids only care deeply about [music]$_F$ these days.

(8.48) a.   Kids care deeply about something these days.

b.   Kids always care about [music]$_F$ these days. [→?]

c.   Kids always care deeply about [music]$_F$ these days.

Whereas the monotonicity inference in (8.47) is clear, there is no clear inference from (8.48a, b) to (8.48c). On the contrary, it seems possible to infer (8.48b) from (8.48c), indicating an upward monotonic context.

Perhaps the explanation of this puzzling result is that stress in (8.48b, c) is taken to mark broad focus on *care (deeply) about music*, in which case we would be observing inferences involving focal material. But it is not clear why this should not also be the case for the parallel sentences involving *only* in (8.47), and we have no basis for claiming that focus projection in the scope of *only*

---

[27] The question arises as to whether *every* creates an anti-additive context, or merely a Strawson anti-additive context. Note that many people would be queasy about the equivalence of *Every American head of state has been male* and *Every American president has been male and every American monarch has been male*, even under the assumption that all heads of state are either presidents or monarchs. So perhaps we should say that *every*, like *only*, creates a Strawson anti-additive context.

should work differently from focus projection in the scope of *always*. On the basis of the NPI licensing data we presented earlier, we take a different tack.

We suppose that while compositional semantics causes non-focal material in the scope of NP or VP *only* to be interpreted in the restrictor of a universal, the mechanism determining the restrictor of *always* (when that restrictor is not explicit) is pragmatic. Thus non-focal material in a sentence containing *always* is not interpreted in the restrictor of a universal. Rather, this material gets interpreted in the universal's scope, and NPIs are not licensed there since it is not a (Strawson) downward monotone context. Indeed, it is upward monotone. The variability of inference data involving sentences with *always* would then be explained by the fact that the formation of the restrictor of *always* does not result from an orderly grammatical process, but from pragmatic reasoning.

8.6   A Formal Account of PI Licensing

Summary: *In order to account for the data on PI distribution and monotonicity inferences, we extend the event semantics of Chapters 6 and 7 to allow for presuppositions. The resulting formal system correctly predicts that non-focal material in the syntactic domain of* only *(but not* always*) is interpreted in a downward monotone, anti-additive context.*

In this section we describe our proposal for the semantics of *only* and *always*, show formally how *only* and *always* differ in terms of downward monotonicity and anti-additivity, and hence account for the polarity item licensing behavior that we have observed.

We use a three-valued logic, first order predicate logic with the addition of one propositional operator, the presupposition operator ∂ of Beaver (2001).[28] The existential and universal quantifiers have classical satisfaction conditions and, for simplicity, $\exists\varphi$ and $\forall\varphi$ are false if not true. The connectives are Weak Kleene; i.e., defined *iff* all arguments are defined, and classical in this case. The presupposition operator produces undefinedness when its argument is not true, and is defined as follows:

Definition 6 (Presupposition operator) $[\![\partial\phi]\!]_M = 1$ *iff* $[\![\phi]\!]_M = 1$,
$= *$ *otherwise.*

We next give a logical reformulation of the downward monotonicity diagnostics.

Definition 7 (Simple downward monotonicity) *A formula α occurs in a simply downward monotone position in ϕ iff for any β such that $\beta \models \alpha$, $\phi \models \phi[\alpha/\beta]$.*

---

[28] We treat presupposition in a partial logic because of the formal simplicity of this approach, although nothing hinges on it. For a compositional account of presupposition in partial logic, see Beaver and Krahmer (2001).

Thus, for example, the subformula *bark(fido)* is in a simply downward mono-tone position in $\neg bark(fido)$, since classically $\neg bark(fido) \models \neg(bark(fido) \wedge \phi)$ for any ϕ.

The following presupposition sensitive notion of entailment differs from classical entailment in that it is restricted to models in which both premises and conclusion are defined, i.e. their presuppositions are satisfied:

Definition 8 (Strawson Entailment) $\phi_1, \ldots \phi_i \models \psi$ *iff*
$\forall M$ *if* $[\![\phi_1]\!]_M = \ldots = [\![\phi_i]\!]_M = 1$ *and* $[\![\psi]\!]_M \in \{0, 1\}$ *then* $[\![\psi]\!]_M = 1$

Relative to this presupposition sensitive notion of entailment, we can easily define what it means to be in a Strawson downward monotonic position or Strawson anti-additive position.

Definition 9 (Strawson downward monotonicity) *A formula α occurs in a Strawson downward monotone position in ϕ iff for any β such that $\beta \models \alpha$, $\phi \models \phi[\alpha/\beta]$.*

Definition 10 (Strawson anti-additivity) *A formula α occurs in a Strawson anti-additive position in ϕ iff α is in a Strawson downward monotone position in ϕ and for any β, $\phi \wedge \phi[\alpha/\beta] \models \phi[\alpha/\alpha \vee \beta]$.*

We now proceed to the semantics of *only* and *always*. As in previous chap-ters, we define the semantics of these two operators as uniformly as possible, so as to highlight relevant differences. We assume both words to be universal quantifier relations defined between sets of events, and both words to carry a presupposition that the quantificational restrictor is a non-empty set.

A presuppositional universal quantifier relation may be defined in our par-tial logic as follows:

Definition 11 (Presuppositional universal operator)
$\boxed{\forall}(\phi, \psi) \equiv_{def} \partial(\exists e\phi) \wedge \forall e(\phi \rightarrow \psi)$.

Now let **SUB** be the content of the subject NP in a sentence, **NF** be the content of the non-focal material in the VP, and **F** be the content of the focal material in the VP. Then the interpretation of a sentence containing VP *only* is given as follows:

Definition 12 (Semantics of *only*) NP only VP *translates to* $\boxed{\forall}(SUB \wedge NF)(F)$

For example, in the sentence *Mary only has a [lamb]*_F, the variables would be set as follows: **SUB** is AG(e, m); **NF** is POSSESSION(e); **F** is $\exists x\ (lamb(x) \wedge TH(e, x))$. Thus the meaning of the sentence would be (8.49).

(8.49) $\boxed{\forall}(AG(e) = m \wedge POSSESSION(e))\ (\exists x\ (lamb(x) \wedge TH(e) = x))$

This formula presupposes that there is some eventuality of possession by Mary, and asserts that every such eventuality is one in which the object possessed is a lamb.

One crucial difference between *only* and *always* explains the polarity licensing contrasts we have presented. Whereas the restrictor of *only* is constrained by non-focal material, the restrictor of *always*, in the absence of an explicit restrictive subordinate clause, is provided by context.

Let σ be a contextually given property of events. Then we interpret sentences containing *always* as follows:

Definition 13 (Semantics of *always*)
NP always VP *translates to* $\boxed{\forall}(\sigma)(SUB \wedge NF \wedge F)$

Thus the compositionally derived meaning of *Mary always has a [lamb]*$_F$ would be (8.50).

(8.50) $\boxed{\forall}(\sigma)(\text{AG}(e) = m \wedge \text{POSSESSION}(e) \wedge \exists x \, (lamb(x) \wedge \text{TH}(e) = x))$

Questions arise as to how σ should be resolved, and how its resolution should be related to focus. Here we do not answer these questions, and merely make the claim that σ is resolved pragmatically, and not compositionally.[29]

Let us assume that weak NPIs are licensed in Strawson downward monotone positions and strong NPIs are licensed in Strawson anti-additive positions. The following fact can now be easily derived from the above definitions and predicts the NPI licensing data presented earlier.

FACT: NF is in a Strawson Downward Entailing and Strawson Anti-additive position in the translation of *NP only VP*, but NF is not in a Strawson Downward Entailing or (*a fortiori*) in a Strawson Anti-additive position in the translation of *NP always VP*.

The above result establishes that our formal system correctly predicts both the NPI distribution and monotonicity inferences that we observed in previous sections of this chapter. The difference in predictions between *only* and *always* derives directly from the hypothesis that *only* is conventionally focus sensitive, but *always* is not, and hence provides further support for that hypothesis. But there are some loose ends to tie up. Several phenomena have been discussed in the literature suggesting that NPI licensing by exclusives involves more than just a contrast between focal and non-focal positions. We now consider these phenomena.

---

[29] Note that the above meanings for *only* and *always* differ not only in the restrictor position, but also in the scope, i.e. the second argument of the universal operator. However, this difference is superficial. Since $\boxed{\forall}(SUB \wedge NF)(F) \equiv \boxed{\forall}(SUB \wedge NF)(SUB \wedge NF \wedge F)$, we could equally well have written out the meanings for *only* and *always* such that the scope of the quantifier was the same in both cases, i.e. SUB $\wedge$ NF $\wedge$ F.

8.7   Restrictions on PI Licensing by *only*

Summary: *We consider two puzzling restrictions on the distribution of NPIs by exclusives. First, in English, certain NPIs are not licensed. Second, in Greek, no NPIs are licensed. We show that in both cases the licensing patterns for exclusives mirror precisely the licensing patterns for universal determiners. We conclude that the restrictions shed no further light on the interpretation of exclusives, although they remain a puzzle that must be solved in a complete account of NPI licensing.*

Certain NPIs are not licensed outside of the focus of *only* (Atlas 1993: 313, 1996: 285, 2002; Gajewski 2005; Giannakidou 2006; Nathan 1999). For example, the NPI *either* is not licensed in the scope of *only*, as illustrated in example (8.51) (Nathan 1999: 43).

(8.51)   [Context: Only John likes broccoli.]
          *Only John likes tomatoes either .

As illustrated by (8.52)–(8.54), all negative time adverbials (e.g., *until yesterday*, *yet*, *in years*) are ruled out outside the focus of *only* (Atlas 1993: 313, Gajewski 2005; Giannakidou 2006).[30]

(8.52)   *Only Bill arrived until yesterday .

(8.53)   *Only John has arrived yet .

(8.54)   *Only Sue has visited John in years / decades / months .

All that and *a red cent* also fail to be licensed outside the focus of *only* (Atlas 1993: 313; Giannakidou 2006):

(8.55)   ?Only I was all that keen to go to the party.

Regarding *a red cent* (Atlas 1993: 313), it is difficult to find reliable informants:

(8.56)   ?Only Phil will give Lucy a red cent .

Note that these NPIs are licensed in canonical negative contexts:

(8.57) a.   Nobody likes tomatoes either .

       b.   Nobody wants Sam to finish that report until Friday .

---

[30]   See Horn (1970: 318) on constraints on the occurrence of negative time adverbials: "The constraints on occurrence of *yet* and *anymore* are stronger than the constraints on … *any* and *ever*, while … the constraints on negative polarity *until* are stronger still" (quoted in Horn 1996: 31).

  In recent talks, Dmitry Levinson has suggested that such NPIs have an additional licensing condition: they must be in a context which forms part of the *asserted* content of the utterance, in a sense he defines. Restrictors of universals do not satisfy this condition.

c.   Nobody has arrived $\boxed{\text{yet}}$.

d.   Nobody has visited John $\boxed{\text{in years}}$.

e.   Nobody was $\boxed{\text{all that}}$ keen to go to the party.

f.   Nobody will give Lucy $\boxed{\text{a red cent}}$.

Atlas (1993: 313; 1996: 285; 2002) takes the data in (8.51)–(8.56) to indicate that "*only* is not, in general, a trigger for Negative Polarity Items" (1993: 313). Giannakidou (2006) concludes that the restricted licensing of *only* undermines the Strawson downward monotonicity account of *only*.

However, none of these NPIs (*either*, negative time adverbials, *all that*) sit well in the restrictor of English universals such as *every*. This is illustrated in (8.58).

(8.58) a.   *Everybody that likes tomatoes $\boxed{\text{either}}$ returned.

b.   *Everybody that wants Sam to finish that report $\boxed{\text{until Friday}}$ returned.

c.   *Everybody that visited Kim $\boxed{\text{yet}}$ returned.

d.   *Everybody that has visited John $\boxed{\text{in years}}$ returned.

e.   *Everybody that was $\boxed{\text{all that keen}}$ to go to the party returned.

f.   ?Everybody that will give Lucy $\boxed{\text{a red cent}}$ returned.

The licensing conditions for *either*, negative time adverbials, *all that*, and *a red cent* must go beyond those available in the restrictor of a universal. Thus these items form part of a distinct class of NPIs with their own licensing properties. Consequently, the distribution of NPIs such as negative time adverbials does not provide evidence for or against the (Strawson) downward monotonicity account of exclusives such as *only*.

What, then, are the licensing conditions for *either*, negative time adverbials, *all that*, and *a red cent*? These NPIs are only permitted in ANTIVERIDICAL contexts (Bernardi 2002; Giannakidou 1998, 1999, 2006; Zwarts 1995). Antiveridical contexts may be defined as follows (Zwarts 1995; Giannakidou 1999; Bernardi 2002: 132).[31]

Definition 14 (Antiveridicality)

Let O be a truth-conditional operator,

i.   O is VERIDICAL *iff* O(p) ⇒ p *is logically valid. Otherwise O is* NONVERIDICAL.

ii.   A nonveridical operator O is ANTIVERIDICAL *iff* O(p) ⇒ ¬p *is logically valid.*

---

[31]   The set of antiveridical contexts form a proper subset of nonveridical ones. See Bernardi 2002 for a general definition of (non)veridicality.

Downward monotone contexts (a proper subset of nonveridical contexts; Zwarts 1995) such as the restrictor of universals are not antiveridical, as illustrated by (8.59), and, consequently, rule out NPIs such as *either* that can only appear in antiveridical contexts.[32]

(8.59) a.   Every student who attended the lecture fell asleep. $\not\to$

b.   No student attended the lecture.

If exclusives and universals are mutually convertible, then NPIs such as *either* are correctly predicted to be ruled out in nonfocal positions in the scope of *only*.

Giannakidou (2006) observes that the Greek exclusive *monon* 'only' does not license NPIs at all: neither weak NPIs such as nonemphatics (e.g., *kanenan* 'anybody') nor strong NPIs such as emphatics (e.g., *KANENAN*) and minimizers (e.g., *dini dhelara* 'gives a damn'), as illustrated in (8.60) (from Giannakidou 1998: 154) and (8.61) (from Giannakidiou 2006).

(8.60)   *monon i   Theodora idhe | kanenan |
          only   the Theodora saw.3sg anybody
          "Only Theodora saw anybody"

(8.61)   *monon o   Janis | dini dhelara |
          only   the John give.3sg damn
          "Only John gives a damn"

However, the same NPIs that are ruled out by Greek exclusives are banned in the restrictor of universals such as *kathe* 'every' (example (8.62) is from Giannakidou 1998: 127 and examples (8.63) and (8.64) are from Giannakidou, p.c.).

(8.62)   *Kathe fititis   pu gnorize | tipota | sxetiko me   tin
          every student that knew.3sg **anything** about   with the

          ipothesis apodixtike poli xrisimos
          case   proved.3sg very helpful

          "Every student who knew anything about the case proved very helpful"

(8.63)   *Kathe fititis pu | dini dekara | na to anaferi sto diefthindi
          "Every student who | gives a damn | should report to the chair"

(8.64)   *Kathe fititis pu | ipe tipota | to petaniose.
          "Every student | who said a word | regretted it"

---

[32]   In fact, "no determiners require that their NP or NP ∩ CP be empty" (Giannakidou 1999: 399). See also Bernardi (2002: 133–4).

Universals such as *kathe* **can** license nonemphatic NPIs when the VP contains a future-oriented subjunctive, e.g., *as milisi tora* 'should speak now' in (8.65) (from Giannakidou 1998: 119).

(8.65)   <u>Kathe</u> fititis   pu gnorize   tipota   sxetika me   tin ipothesi,
          every student that know.3sg **anything** about   with the case,
          as   milisi   tora.
          subj talk.3pl now

          "Every student who knows anything about the case should speak
          now"

Similarly for the exclusive *monon* (Giannakidou, p.c.):

(8.66)   <u>Monon</u> i   theodora prepi na   milisi   me   kanenan
          only   the Theodora must subj talk.3sg with anybody
          "Only Theodora must talk with anybody"

In contrast, strong NPIs such as emphatics and minimizers are never licensed in the restrictor of universals or outside the focus of exclusives.

Generally speaking, the distribution of NPIs in English and Greek supports the interdefinability of exclusives and universals in (8.67):

(8.67)   only As are Bs ↔ all Bs are As
          (only [felines]$_F$ are immortal ↔ every immortal is feline)

Why, though, are certain NPIs (e.g., minimizers) ruled out in the B position of universals and exclusives in Greek, but licensed in English? These differences can be located in the NPIs themselves.

We have already seen that there are multiple classes of NPIs (Zwarts 1998). Languages also vary as regards which NPIs appear in which classes, but given that a NPI is in a given class in a given language, the contexts that the NPI can appear in are determined by the logic of the surrounding operators. Greek NPIs such as emphatics and minimizers and English NPIs such as *until*, *all that keen*, and *either* are licensed in antiveridical contexts (Giannakidou 1998, 1999), a proper subset of nonveridical contexts. This correctly predicts that these NPIs will never appear in the restrictor of universals and outside the focus of exclusives. Greek nonemphatics are licensed in a subset of nonveridical environments (Giannakidou 1998, 1999); e.g., in the restrictor of universals and outside the focus of exclusives when the VP contains a future-oriented subjunctive. English NPIs such as unstressed *any*, *ever*, and minimizers are licensed in Strawson downward monotone environments. This accurately predicts the availability of these NPIs in the restrictor of universals and outside the focus of *only*.

So far in this chapter, we have considered monotonicity data which supports the hypothesis that non-focal material in the scope of *only*, but not *always*, is interpreted in the restrictor of a universal. In the next two sections, we will present data which differentiates once more between *always* and *only*, and which also provides clearer evidence as to just how *always* gets its interpretation.

8.8   Association with Presupposition

Summary: *Association with presupposition effects have been argued to support purely pragmatic models of focus sensitivity. We use constructed and naturally occurring data to show that these effects are found for* always, *but not for* only.

The last section provided evidence that whereas all non-focal material in the scope of *only* is interpreted in the restrictor of a universal, this is not the case for *always*. In this section, we return to a phenomenon discussed in Chapter 5, *association with presupposition*, that shows a converse effect: whereas stressed material in the scope of *only* becomes the semantic focus of the expression, sometimes *always* does not associate with stressed material in its scope. Rather, the restrictor of *always* is determined contextually.

As we discussed in Chapter 5, a number of previous authors have concluded that *always* may associate with presupposition. We use minimal pairs to show that in this respect the interpretation of sentences involving *always* contrasts with that of those involving *only*.

Example (5.9), from Cohen (1999) and repeated below in (8.68), involves both a presupposition ('Mary took exams') and a focus (*exams*) in the argument to the adverb of quantification *always*.

(8.68) Mary always managed to complete her [exams]$_F$.

    a.   'Whenever Mary took exams, she completed them.'

    b.   ?'Whenever Mary completed something, it was invariably an exam.'

We might imagine that there are two readings associated with (8.68), given in (a) and (b). In the (a) reading, the restrictor clause contains the material associated with the implicative verb *manage* (i.e. the presupposition 'Mary took exams'), and in the (b) reading the restrictor contains all non-focal material. Cohen observed that, contrary to the predictions of semantic accounts of focus sensitivity such as Rooth (1985), the (a) reading in (8.68) is the preferred one.

Note that Cohen's observation about (8.68) holds in a context that is neutral with respect to the two readings, like *Tell me about Mary*. Now consider (8.69), in which we have substituted *only* for *always*.

(8.69) Mary only managed to complete her [exams]$_F$.

    a.   *'What Mary did when taking exams was complete them and do nothing else.'

    b.   'What Mary completed was an exam and nothing else.'

Here the (a) reading, involving association with presupposition, is impossible in the *Tell me about Mary* context, while the association with focus reading, as in (b), is unproblematically available.

This contrast can be brought out more clearly if we consider possible continuations to (8.68) and (8.69).

(8.70)   Mary always managed to complete her [exams]$_F$, and she always managed to complete her [assignments]$_F$.

In contrast, (8.71) is clearly inconsistent showing that the association with focus reading is the only one available.

(8.71)   #Mary only managed to complete her [exams]$_F$, and she only managed to complete her [assignments]$_F$.

If (8.68) had only the association with focus reading, then (8.70) would be contradictory, since it would imply both that whenever Mary completed something it was an exam and whenever she completed something it was an assignment. However, on the association with presupposition reading, (8.70) would be consistent, meaning that whenever Mary took an exam she completed it, and whenever she did an assignment she completed it. Since (8.70) is consistent, something like the association with presupposition reading is available.

Another phenomenon that can be explained in terms of the (un)availability of association-with-presupposition readings is the fact that focused *someone* can occur in the argument to *always*, but not *only*:

(8.72)   Mary always took [someone]$_F$ to the cinema.

(8.73)   ? Mary only took [someone]$_F$ to the cinema.

The infelicity of (8.73) is unsurprising if it has the association with focus reading 'The single person that Mary took to the cinema was someone', which is uninformative. In contrast, the felicity of (8.72) is unsurprising if it has the reading 'Whenever Mary went to the cinema, she took someone.'

This reading could loosely be described as association with presupposition, in that a plausible pragmatic presupposition of someone discussing *who Mary took to the cinema* is that Mary went to the cinema.[33,34] The remaining examples

---

[33]   Given that we believe that the focus on *someone* in (8.72) is not serving to restrict *always*, what licenses the focus at all? Without attempting to give a general answer to this question, we note that one context in which *someone* could receive nuclear stress in (8.72) is where it was contrastive, for example because some occasion had been mentioned on which there was reason to believe Mary had taken *no-one* to the cinema.

[34]   Note that although *Mary took someone to the cinema* implies that Mary went to the cinema, this may not be a semantic presupposition. Consider *Most weekends Mary takes someone to the cinema, but last weekend she did not take anyone to the cinema.* It does not follow from the final negated clause that Mary went to the cinema last weekend, so we see that at least in some cases the putative presupposition does not project from negation, and so perhaps is not a lexical presupposition at all.

in this section show that the apparent ability of *always*, but not *only*, to associate with presuppositions is common to a wide range of presupposition types in English.

Example (8.74) and (8.75) demonstrate the effect for a factive use of the verb *remember*.

(8.74) Mary always remembers to go to [church]$_F$.

    a. 'Whenever it's time for church, Mary remembers to go.'

    b. ?'Whenever Mary remembers to go somewhere, it's to go to church.'

(8.75) Mary only remembers to go to [church]$_F$.

    a. *'The single thing Mary does when it's time for church, is remember to go.'

    b. 'The single place Mary remembers to go is to church.'

(8.74), with the focus sensitive operator *always*, has an association with presupposition reading, as in (a), but (8.75), with the focus sensitive operator *only*, has an association with focus reading, as in (b).

The next two examples demonstrate the same effect for the lexical presupposition of *beats*:

(8.76) Kim always beats Sandy at [ping-pong]$_F$.

    a. 'When Kim plays ping-pong with Sandy, Kim invariably beats Sandy.'

    b. ?'When Kim beats Sandy at something, it is invariably ping-pong.'[35]

(8.77) Kim only beats Sandy at [ping-pong]$_F$.

    a. *'What Kim does when playing a game of ping-pong with Sandy is beat her and do nothing else.'

    b. 'Kim beats Sandy at ping-pong and nothing else.'

We now turn to naturally occurring examples. To be sure that the reading we get for a sentence corresponds to association with presupposition rather than association with focus, we have to know what the focus is. When looking at naturally occurring textual examples, the focus is not explicitly marked, so it can be difficult to say of a given textual example that it counter-exemplifies the association of *always* with focus.

However, looking at naturally occurring textual examples involving *always* is still instructive. We have found that the difference in interpretation that would be obtained if *only* were substituted for *always* is often stark, even if an

---

[35] This reading is dispreferred in a neutral context but may be available when *ping-pong* is clearly contrastive.

effort is made to make sure that the two variants are read with identical intonation. In many cases, it seems clear that the difference is best explained by saying
that *always* is being restricted in a way that is impossible for *only*.

In (8.78a), the presupposition of *answer your prayers* is presumably earlier
prayer. Thus *God didn't always answer your prayers* means that there are exceptions to the rule that every situation in which the addressee prayed is one which
received a response.

(8.78) a. More important, you could get medicine guaranteed to cure you,
           whereas God didn't always answer your prayers.[36]

       b. God didn't only answer your prayers.

Furthermore, we get this reading whether stress is placed on *always, answer,
prayers*, or all three. In (8.78b), *always* has been replaced by *only*. Here, stress
affects the interpretation considerably. With stress on *answer*, the implication is
that some of the addressee's prayers received something other than an answer.
With stress on *prayers* the implication is that not only your prayers, but perhaps
also some of your telephone calls, faxes, post-it notes, and emails received heav-
enly responses. Finally, with stress on both *answer* and *prayers*, the implication
is that higher powers had been responsible for actions that the addressee had
not actually requested.

In example (8.79a), concerning the sport of rugby, various readings are
available.

(8.79) a. It's a high-speed collision sport and a prop forward always takes the
           brunt of the punishment.[37]

       b. A prop forward only takes the brunt of the punishment.

The subject *a prop forward* can be understood as the semantic focus of *always*.
What is notable is that this reading obtains even if the example is read with
stress on *punishment*, but not on *prop forward*. What is presupposed is a set of
high-speed collisions, from which punishment will necessarily follow, and from
which some group of players will bear the brunt. Against this background, we
learn the identity of the unfortunate recipients of the punishment, namely the
prop forwards. A reading of this sort is not available in (8.79b), although this
is unsurprising given that the focus of VP *only* is restricted to the VP. Rather,
the reading that we obtain is that a prop forward does not take the brunt of
anything apart from the punishment. This is presumably true, but we are not
sure what it means.

(8.80a) involves the implicative *manage* in the scope of *always*. The final
clause can be read with main stress on *rehomed*.

---

[36] K. Carmichael, *Ceremony of Innocence*, Macmillan Publishers Ltd., Basingstoke, 1991.
[37] *The Daily Mirror*, London 1992 (British National Corpus).

(8.80) a.   Technically, if they're not claimed within seven days, then they should be put to sleep, but we always manage to get them rehomed.[38]

     b.   We only manage to get them rehomed.

Salient in the context is a set of occasions when dogs are at a pound and, against the background of this pragmatically presupposed set of occasions, it is claimed that every member of the set is also an occasion where a dog gets rehomed.

    Note that the lexical presupposition of *manage* – that the rehoming is difficult or that the subject makes considerable effort to achieve the rehoming – does not directly restrict the quantification. We claim that the sentence makes a claim about all instances of dogs requiring rehoming, not just the difficult cases. The variant with *only* once again produces an entirely different reading. Given the same sentence final stress, (8.80b) means that the only thing that the representatives of the pound manage to do to the dogs is rehome them, and not, for instance, treat them to a new hair-style at the local grooming parlor.

    The data we have presented in this section demonstrates that presuppositions can never completely override the effects of accentual focus in the interpretation of sentences containing *only*. But concerning *always* we do observe such apparent overrides. In the next section we will consider more closely the nature of the association with presupposition effect for quantificational adverbs like *always*.

8.9   What Does *always* Associate With?

Summary: *We argue that presupposition does not directly determine the restrictor of a quantificational adverb. Rather, the restrictor should be anaphoric on a salient set of events, and, for the discourse to be coherent, that set of events must satisfy the presuppositions.*

While we will continue to hold that *only* associates with focus, it will now be shown that it would be wrong to conclude that *always* associates with presupposition. Using an argument similar to that developed in Beaver (2001, 2005), we now show that if *presupposition* means the set of conventional presuppositions triggered by linguistic items (definites, factives, etc.) in the sentence, then *always* does not directly associate with presupposition.[39] Consider (8.81):

(8.81)   Every Friday Sandy goes to town. She always realizes that the Harley Davidson she's riding there is going to attract a lot of attention.

---

[38] *Dogs Today*. Burlington Publishing Company Ltd, Windsor, 1992.

[39] The original argument developed by Beaver was used to counter-evidence the process of *intermediate accommodation* of presuppositions. This mechanism is more general than presuppositional restriction of *always*, including any accommodation of presuppositions into a context other than the global context of discourse or the local context of the presupposition trigger. For instance, intermediate accommodation could theoretically take place in the antecedent of a conditional, or the restrictor of a quantificational determiner.

The first sentence makes a set of events salient, events which take place on Friday and involve Sandy going to town. The second sentence involves a definite description *the Harley Davidson she is riding* which conventionally triggers the presupposition that there is such an object, and a factive verb *realizes*, here conventionally triggering the presupposition that the bike will attract attention.

Suppose that *always* associated with conventionally triggered presuppositions, and this was the principal mechanism by which the domain restriction of *always* was set. Then we should expect the second sentence in (8.81) to mean 'Whenever Sandy is riding a Harley Davidson and it attracts a lot of attention, Sandy realizes that it is attracting attention.' But (8.81) does not mean this.

One might consider a weaker position: the domain restriction of *always* is constrained by a combination of what is salient in the context and what is presupposed in the sentence. But then the predicted meaning of (8.81) would be paraphrasable as 'Whenever Sandy rides her Harley to town on Friday and it attracts a lot of attention, Sandy realizes that it is attracting attention.' This is also incorrect, as can be seen from the fact that (8.82) is difficult to process, and seems contradictory.

(8.82) ? Every Friday Sandy goes to town. She always realizes that the Harley Davidson she's riding there is going to attract a lot of attention. So mostly she goes by bus.

(8.83) Every Friday Sandy goes to town. When she rides her Harley Davidson there, she always realizes that it's going to attract a lot of attention. So mostly she goes by bus.

If the presuppositions were providing a restriction which merely added to that given by context, the interpretation of (8.82) would be the same as that of (8.83). But (8.83) is perfectly coherent.

To summarize, *always* does not associate with the conventional presuppositions of its VP argument. So what is the relationship between the domain restrictions of *always* and conventional presuppositions? Returning to (8.81), what a hearer will commonly conclude is that every Friday Sandy rides her Harley to town, every Friday it attracts attention, and every Friday she realizes that it is attracting attention.

We must draw a fine distinction. A model in which *always* associates with presupposition would not be the same as one in which *always* associates with something else but all the while respecting presuppositions. It is the latter sort of model we advocate, echoing conclusions of Beaver (2005), von Fintel (1994), and Geurts and van der Sandt (1997).

In the example at hand, the presupposition that Sandy is riding a conspicuous Harley does not help the hearer choose which set of events is the domain restrictor of *always*, since there is only one salient set of events. But the presupposition does tell the hearer that amongst the set of events chosen, there are none where Sandy fails to ride a conspicuous Harley.

We can summarize our conclusions about how the domain restriction of *always* is established as follows: first, if *always* associates with anything, it is with contextually salient sets of events or situations; second, the presuppositions of the VP argument are not what determines which set of events or situations *always* associates with; third, whatever set of situations or events *always* associates with, it must be one which satisfies the presuppositions triggered in the scope of *always*.

If *always* associates with a contextually salient set of events or situations, then what explains the appearance of association with presupposition? The most important reason is simply that it is often hard to tell the difference between an anaphoric link to a set of events that satisfies the presuppositions, and a direct dependency on the presupposition.

But there is more at work here. What we have shown so far is that when a suitable antecedent set of events is available for *always*, anaphoric resolution takes place. But what if there is no fully explicit antecedent? For example, in the relevant clause of (8.79), *a prop forward always takes the brunt of the punishment*, there is no linguistically explicit antecedent set of events. The set of all rugby games is salient, but there is nothing in the previous text which a linguist might tag with an index to be coindexed with the implicit argument of *always*.

Where the linguistic context does not provide a suitable antecedent explicitly, hearers accommodate one. When accommodating, thinking is presumably colored not only by what was salient in the context, but also by what would be needed in order for the utterance containing *always* to make sense. Thus, in cases where the antecedent is not explicit, conventionally triggered presuppositions should be expected to constrain the process of accommodation. Nonetheless, we maintain that this is a pragmatic and inferential process, not a grammaticized linking of presuppositions to the content of the restrictor.

Regarding *always*, the conclusions we have reached are very much in tune with previous work of Beaver (2005) and von Fintel (1994). As stressed by Beaver (2005), the mistake of concluding that presuppositions directly constrain restrictors is particularly tempting when confronted with decontextualized single sentence examples, still the stock in trade of most papers on semantics. In cases where the context is not known, it is often impossible to distinguish between direct presuppositional modification of the restrictor and inferential accommodation of the domain of quantification.

Neither Beaver (2005) nor von Fintel (1994) advances a proposal that all association with focus effects might be reduced to association with presupposition or association with accommodated variables. This is what we take Rooth (1999), Cohen (1999) and van der Sandt and Geurts (1997) to be considering. The data we have presented in this section places an obstacle in the way of the complete reduction of association with focus to association with presupposition or even to association with accommodated variables. If a theory based on such a reduction works for VP *always*, it is unlikely to work for VP *only*, and *vice versa*.

8.10 Summary

In this chapter we provided evidence from monotonicity and presupposition that exclusives, but not quantificational adverbs, have a conventionalized dependency on focus, as predicted by the QFC taxonomy of focus sensitive expressions presented in Chapter 3. We showed that NPIs are licensed in non-focal positions in the scope of exclusives, but not in focal positions. This demonstrates that non-focal material is grammatically constrained to limit the restrictor of exclusives, while focal material only affects the scope. In contrast, the NPI data suggested that non-focal material does not limit the restrictor of adverbs of quantification. We provided evidence from association with presupposition that showed that the restrictor of adverbs of quantification does not always associate with focal material in its scope. The restrictor of an adverb of quantification is instead determined contextually.

In Chapters 4 and 5, we examined how semantic and pragmatic theories of focus interpretation work. In Chapters 6 and 7 and the current chapter, we discussed a mountain of evidence which demonstrates that the class of focus sensitive expressions is not uniform, thus providing motivation for a taxonomy of focus sensitive expressions like that presented in Chapter 3. Now, equipped with an understanding of how exclusives fit into the wider taxonomy of focus sensitive expressions, we turn to one of the richest and most difficult problem areas in semantics and pragmatics: the meaning of sentences containing exclusives.

Chapter 9

Exclusives: Facts and History

Where to use only _in a sentence is a moot question, one of the mootest questions in all rhetoric. The purist will say that the expression:_ He only died last week, _is incorrect, and that it should be:_ He died only last week. _The purist's contention is that the first sentence, if carried out to a natural conclusion, would give us something like this:_ He only died last week, he didn't do anything else, that's all he did. _It isn't a natural conclusion, however, because nobody would say that and if anybody did it would be likely to lead to stomping of feet and clapping of hands, because it is one of the singy-songy expressions which set a certain type of person to acting rowdy and becoming unmanageable. It is better just to let the expression go, either one way or the other, because, after all, this particular sentence is of no importance except in cases where one is breaking the news to a mother. In such cases one should begin with:_ Mrs Gormley, your son has had an accident, _or:_ Mrs Gormley, your son is not so good, _and then lead up gently to:_ He died only last week.

The best way is often to omit only _and use some other expression. Thus, instead of saying,_ He only died last week, _one could say:_ It was no longer ago than last Thursday that George L. Wodolgiffing became an angel. _Moreover, this is more explicit and eliminates the possibility of a misunderstanding as to who died. The greatest care in this regard, by the way, should be taken with the verbs_ to die, to love, to embezzle, _and the like. In this connection, it is well never to use_ only _at the beginning of a sentence –_ Only one person loves me, _for example. This of course makes it necessary to capitalize_ Only _and there is the risk of a hurried reader taking it for a proper noun and confusing it with the late Richard Olney, who was Secretary of State under Cleveland._

James Thurber, in _The Owl in the Attic and Other Perplexities_, Universal Library, 1931, (section III, Ladies' and Gentlemen's Guide to Modern English Usage.)[1]

9.1 Introduction

We have reviewed a huge amount of evidence that the focus sensitivity of exclusives like _only_ is conventionalized, unlike the apparent focus sensitivity of _always_. But we have not given any explanation of why exclusives should

---

[1] This quote was brought to our attention by Caroline Heycock (http://www.ling.ed.ac.uk/~heycock/thurber–only.html).

differ from quantificational adverbs in this way. Indeed, we went to some lengths to give *only* and *always* maximally similar semantic descriptions. Yet describing the meanings of *only* and *always* in such similar ways was a didactic trick designed to set their different behaviors in stark relief. The fact is that we believe that *only* and *always* have dramatically different functions, reflected in their meanings, and that an understanding of those functions is precisely what explains why one of them is conventionally focus sensitive, and the other is not.

Broadly speaking, all the action concerns exclusives. That is, we do not claim that the model of quantificational adverbs we have sketched is the last word, and there are several far more careful discussions of both the semantics and the pragmatics of quantificational adverbs (e.g. de Swart 1993; von Fintel 1994). For example, we would be perfectly happy to drop our analysis of quantificational adverbs as counting events, since we have not provided any direct evidence for such an events analysis. Instead, adverbs could quantify over situations à la von Fintel, over cases à la Lewis (1975), or (relatedly) over DRS universes à la Kamp and Reyle (1993).

The one important claim about quantificational adverbs we want to stick by – and this is exactly the point that von Fintel makes very forcibly – is that their restrictor, when it is not made explicit by e.g. an *if* or *when* clause, is an anaphoric element. It is not constrained directly by focus, or for that matter by presuppositions triggered in its scope. Rather, it is constrained by an anaphoric dependency on previous discourse. Both focus and presuppositional effects are best understood as secondary, relating to the fact that in order for a discourse to be coherent, presuppositions must be justified by salient individuals, and focus structure must mirror what is under discussion about those individuals. These effects constrain the antecedent discourse referent that *always* picks up, be it a set of events, a set of situations, or an abstract referent for a DRS, and it is only after the pragmatic process of anaphoric resolution that the quantificational restrictor, in effect, inherits the focus or presupposition derived constraints.

We will now study in detail the meaning and function of exclusives. In the current chapter, we take a critical look at the mass of evidence that has been collected in prior literature as regards the inferences that can be drawn from sentences containing exclusives, and the conclusions that have been derived. This will provide the background to the new theory of the meaning of exclusives that will be presented in Chapter 10.

This theory, though it uses many of the theoretical insights from the discussion in Chapters 4 and 5, puts a completely different emphasis on the study of *only* than that of prior authors, an emphasis on discourse function rather than truth conditions. The goal will be to explain both the data in the current chapter on inferences associated with *only*, and the data in Chapters 6–8 on focus sensitivity effects.

Now it is time to burrow into the tortuous and ever growing literature on the interpretation of exclusives.

9.2 Positive and Negative Parts of Exclusive Meanings

Summary: *There are two primary components of the meaning of exclusives, one positive and one negative. While the negative component is generally agreed to be an entailment, the status of the positive component is controversial. We introduce the conjunction analysis of exclusives, which says that the meaning of an exclusive sentence is the conjunction of the positive and negative components.*

Let us begin by considering the primary two components entering into prior discussions of the meaning of exclusives, one positive and one negative. The positive component of *only Jane smokes* might be taken to be the proposition that Jane smokes – this is also termed the *prejacent*. But as we will see, some authors take the prejacent to be a secondary inference rather than a core component of the meaning of an exclusive, and some authors consider a weaker existential to be either part of the at-issue meaning[2] or part of the presupposed meaning of an exclusive, in this case the proposition that someone smokes.

The negative component – also known as the *exclusive* or, as we will term it, the *universal* – is the proposition that nobody else smokes. While there is some disagreement as to exactly what the negative component is, it is generally agreed to be a vanilla entailment, something that gets, e.g., asserted by an assertion, negated by a negation, and questioned by a question. In the case of the positive component things are not so simple. There is both disagreement about the exact content of the positive component, and disagreement about its semantic/pragmatic flavor.

In what follows we will discuss the various observations that have driven scholars to a wide range of positions. But to start with, observe that both the prejacent and the universal inference follow from what we will call the *base sentence* or *exclusive sentence*, a simple sentential clause with an occurrence of NP or VP *only*, and no other operators. This is shown by (9.1) and (9.2) for NP *only*, and in (9.3) and (9.4) for VP *only*.

(9.1) Basic Positive Inference (NP *only*)
   a. Only Mary smokes. $\mapsto$
   b. Mary smokes.

(9.2) Basic Negative Inference (NP *only*)
   a. Only Mary smokes. $\mapsto$
   b. Nobody other than Mary smokes.

(9.3) Basic Positive Inference (VP *only*)
   a. Mary only smokes [Luckies]$_F$. $\mapsto$
   b. Mary smokes Luckies.

---

2 Potts (2005: 6) uses *at-issue entailments* "as a cover term for regular asserted content ('what is said', in Grice's terms)."

(9.4)   Basic Negative Inference (VP *only*)

      a.   Mary only smokes [Luckies]$_F$. $\mapsto$

      b.   Mary smokes no brands apart from Luckies.

The most obvious reaction to this data is simply to take the meaning of the base sentence to be the conjunction of the prejacent and the universal (or an equivalent proposition). This is the tack taken, as Atlas (1991) points out, by William of Sherwood in the early thirteenth century (Kretzmann 1968).[3] More recent adherents include Taglicht (1984), and also (though in a slightly different form) Rooth (1992) and Herburger (2000).

    Atlas himself advocates a variant of the conjunction analysis in which the positive conjunct for (9.1a) would be the proposition that exactly one person smokes rather than the proposition that Mary smokes (Atlas 1991, 1993, 1996). As Atlas is well aware, the conjunction of *exactly one person smokes and everybody who smokes is Mary* is classically equivalent to the conjunction *Mary smokes and everybody who smokes is Mary*, so his analysis is only a stone's throw from William of Sherwood's.

    One difference is that Atlas represents the interpretation at a level of logical form which not only has truth-conditional interpretation, but also represents aspects of information structure. On Atlas' analysis, information structural differences in turn have both distributional and inferential effects. That is, Atlas takes the meaning of *Exactly one person smokes and everybody who smokes is Mary* to be distinct from *Mary smokes and everybody who smokes is Mary* in terms of information structure, so that it makes a difference to the expected distribution of exclusive sentences whether their meaning is represented in the form of the first version (Atlas' preference) or the second.

    In the coming sections we consider why the conjunction analysis is not sufficient, and what prior scholars have suggested be done about it. After that we attempt to motivate and describe our own integrated model to account for both the meaning of exclusives and their focus sensitivity. Note that we give most of the basic data in the next two sections using NP *only*. For all cases, we have checked comparable examples for VP *only* too, in many cases we have also checked for other exclusives (*just, merely, exclusively*), and in some cases we will later have observations to make about the interpretational effects of syntactic position or the exclusive chosen.

9.3   The Prejacent Presupposition Theory

Summary: *Evidence from negation, order asymmetries, and reason clauses suggests that there is an asymmetry between the positive and negative inferences from*

---

[3]   Horn (1996) sees Peter of Spain (Mullally 1945) as the primary progenitor of the conjunction (or *symmetricalist*) account under which the positive and negative components of the meaning of *only* are simply conjoined. But Peter of Spain wrote later than William of Sherwood.

*exclusive sentences. We introduce the prejacent presupposition theory of exclusives,
which says that the positive component of the meaning of an exclusive sentence is a
presupposition, whereas the negative component is an ordinary entailment.*

So far we have established that both the prejacent and the exclusive follow from
an utterance of a sentence involving an exclusive. Horn (1969) pointed out that
there is an asymmetry between the two inferences. This asymmetry can be seen
in a wide range of phenomena, the most striking of which is behavior under
negation. While the prejacent is implied by the negation of the base sentence
(9.5), the universal is not (9.6):

(9.5) Embedding under negation: positive component

  a. Not only Mary smokes. ↦

  b. Mary smokes.

(9.6) Embedding under negation: negative component

  a. Not only Mary smokes. ↦̸

  b. Nobody other than Mary smokes.

Survival of implications under negation is the best known test for presupposition. Thus the data in (9.5) and (9.6) provides evidence that while the universal
is an ordinary entailment of the base sentence (and thus targeted by negation),
the prejacent is a presupposition (and thus ignored by ordinary negation). This
prejacent presupposition theory, as we will call it, is the position Horn (1969)
adopted. A variant of it has recently been robustly defended by Roberts (2006),
despite being very much against the tide of contemporary work on the issue.

   Neither the presuppositions nor assertions of simple affirmative sentences
can normally be directly canceled. Because of this, the fact that neither the prejacent nor the universal inference are cancelable in this way (as in 9.7) suggests
that an implicature analysis of prejacent inferences may be wrong. However,
it says nothing about whether the prejacent is a presupposition or a plain
entailment.[4]

(9.7) Failure of simple cancellation

  a. ## Only Mary smokes, but Mary doesn't smoke.

  b. ## Only Mary smokes, but somebody else does (too).

   However, there are at least two further types of evidence that the prejacent
is presupposed while the universal is not. First, the base sentence can be used
as a strengthening of a statement of the prejacent, but not as a strengthening of
a statement of the universal (9.8).

---

[4] Note that by "##" we mean pragmatically odd, and even more so than sentences marked by just
a single hash.

(9.8) Order asymmetries

   a.   Mary smokes, and indeed [only]$_F$ Mary smokes.

   b.   #Nobody but Mary smokes, and indeed only Mary smokes.

Second, when a sentence with *only* is given as the cause for something (9.9), or is the target of an emotive attitude (9.11), it is usually the universal which is understood as the cause or the target of the attitude, not the prejacent.

(9.9) Reason Clause

   a.   And aides and allies were instructed not to characterize Thursday's vote as a victory or a defeat, even though many viewed it as a partial win because only 31 Democrats voted for Hyde's resolution.

                                             (*Washington Post*, 10/10/98)

   b.   ↛They were instructed not to characterize it that way (partly) because 31 Democrats voted for Hyde's resolution.

(9.10) Reason Clause

   a.   Aides and allies were given certain instructions because only 31 Democrats voted. (Artificial variant of above)

   b.   ↛They were given those instructions (partly) because 31 Democrats voted.

(9.11) Emotive Factive Clause

   a.   I am disappointed that only $3 billion dollars will be paid against the approximately $480 billion dollar federal debt.

                                                         [*web example*]

   b.   ↛I am disappointed partly by the fact that $3 billion dollars will be paid.

Because the naturally occurring example in (9.9) is complex, a simplified variant is given in (9.10): the point being that (9.10b) is *not* an appropriate statement of the reason for instructions being given. The reason the instructions were given is that the number of Democrat voters was not higher than 31. Both the strengthening pattern and the reason-clause data are what would be expected if the prejacent is a presupposition.[5]

---

[5] Compare, e.g., to the behavior of *the woman smiled* which presupposes the existence of a (unique) woman, and asserts that she smiled:

   (i)   There is a woman and indeed the woman smiled.
   (ii) ## She$_i$ smiled and indeed the woman$_i$ smiled.
   (iii) I smiled because the woman smiled. ↛ The existence of the woman was part of the reason I smiled.
   (iv) I'm disappointed that the woman smiled. ↛ The existence of the woman is part of the reason I'm disappointed.

9.4 The Existential Presupposition Theory

Summary: *We consider arguments for the existential presupposition theory of exclusives, which says that exclusives carry an existential presupposition rather than presupposing their prejacent. We present survey data that does not provide much support for either the existential presupposition theory or the prejacent presupposition analysis. Any theory which predicts that an exclusive sentence should always be infelicitous when the prejacent or existential proposition fails must be at least a little off the mark.*

After 27 years of reflection, Horn (1996) suggested, *contra* his position in Horn (1969), that exclusives might not presuppose their prejacent but rather carry a weaker existential presupposition. This is the analysis that we followed in Chapter 8.[6] According to the existential analysis, the base sentence *only Mary smokes* would presuppose that somebody smokes, and we will term this the existential proposition.

On this analysis, the prejacent is not given any clear independent status as part of the meaning of the base sentence. Rather, it is an inference that arises when both the presupposition and the assertion hold, since e.g. *somebody smokes* and *everybody who smokes is Mary* together classically entail *Mary smokes*.

Horn cited several arguments, including the authority of medieval logicians, the analogy between exclusives and ordinary universals like *all* and *every*, and a number of empirical arguments, one of which is based around the wager in (9.12).

(9.12) Horn's Bet
        Only Seattle will win more than 60 games in the upcoming regular
        season for the National Basketball Association.
   a.   Seattle 62, all others below: WIN
   b.   Seattle and Orlando above 60: LOSE
   c.   Nobody makes 60: ALL BETS OFF?
   d.   San Antonio 62, all others below: LOSE?

The observation is that if presuppositions are definedness conditions on meaningfulness, then the wager should become void whenever the presuppositions fail.

On the conjunction analysis involving no presupposition, one would expect the bet to be lost in all situations except (a), when Seattle wins more than 60 games and everybody else wins less than 60. On the prejacent presupposition theory, the wager should be void whenever Seattle fails to win 60 games, i.e. in

---

[6] Although it must be pointed out that all the arguments concerning NPI licensing in Chapter 8 would also have gone through if we had adopted the stronger position that the prejacent was presupposed.

situations (c) and (d). On the existential presupposition analysis, the wager should only be void when no team at all wins 60 games, situation (c). Horn's claim is that this latter prediction is correct, i.e. his judgments of the situation are those in capital letters in (a–d).

Horn's bet provides an interesting type of evidence for the existential analysis. But it is far from a knockdown argument. We have found speakers whose intuitions tally better with the conjunction analysis, at least when the speakers are put in the position of the person accepting the bet rather than the position of a person offering it. We have also found speakers who wonder whether the situation is clear in case (d), suggesting there might be something right about the prejacent presupposition analysis.

To help sort through the confusion, we performed an email survey of undergraduate students in a Stanford University dorm (*Arroyo*) and an in-class survey of students at UT-Austin. The results we report are pooled, the results being similar for each of the two surveys.[7]

(9.13)   The Arroyo Purity Wager

```
At Jason's suggestion, a bunch of people in the dorm take
an online purity test. Amina makes the following wager:
"I bet only Jason has a purity score lower than 25%!" "OK,
you're on!" says Adassa.

1) Now, suppose everybody's score turns out to be over
30%. Then...
a) Amina wins her bet.
b) Amina loses.
c) In that case, the bet's off.
d) Don't know.

2) Suppose instead that Peling gets a purity score of 20%
(whoa!), while Jason has a purity score of 30%. Then...
a) Amina wins her bet.
b) Amina loses.
c) In that case, the bet's off.
d) Don't know.

3) Jason's computer melts down while he's taking the test
so he doesn't finish, and everybody's score turns out to
```

---

[7] The survey appearing here is a slightly edited version of that used in the Stanford dorm, the UT-Austin survey being similar, but appropriately localized. A *purity test* is a questionnaire about personal habits and behaviors which participants answer, and, on the basis of their answers, a *purity score* is calculated, typically as a percentage, with 100% meaning the participant is completely pure. For an off-beat discussion of the Arroyo purity test, see David Beaver, *A Sudden Loss of Innocence*, at http://itre.cis.upenn.edu/~myl/languagelog/archives/003230.html.

be over 30%. Then...
a) Amina wins her bet.
b) Amina loses.
c) In that case, the bet's off.
d) Don't know.

4) Jason doesn't finish the test, and Peling gets
a purity score of 20%. Then...
a) Amina wins her bet.
b) Amina loses.
c) In that case, the bet's off.
d) Don't know.

Questions 3 and 4 of the survey suggest a radical case of pragmatic presupposition failure, since if Jason does not finish the test, he doesn't even have a score, and the question of whether his score is lower than 30% does not even arise. For this reason the test was designed to allow us to compare this fairly clear case of presupposition failure with what happens when the existential or prejacent fails (in questions 1 and 2 respectively).

We obtained 34 responses to the survey across the two polls, shown graphically, alongside what we take to be the predictions Horn would make, in Figure 9.1.

In keeping with Horn's observations, almost all respondents ($33/34 = 97\%$) said the bet was lost in the scenario for question 2, in which someone other than Jason is the only person with a purity score below 30% (with one *don't know*).

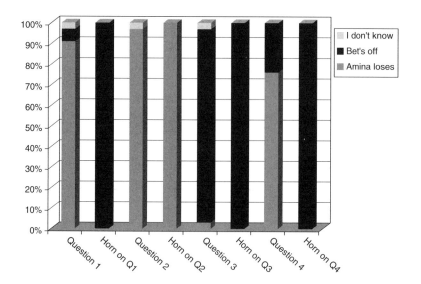

Figure 9.1 Purity wager results (n $= 34$)

In other words, failure of the prejacent is treated just like falsity of the wagered proposition.

However, with respect to question 1, in which nobody scores below 30%, so that the existential fails, the great majority of respondents ($31/34 = 91\%$) said that in this case the bet was lost, while relatively few ($2/34 = 6\%$) said the bet was off (again, one *don't know*). This evidence runs counter to Horn's claims because he says the bet should be off in an analogous situation. It appears that relying on his own intuitions here did not provide him with a very general perspective. While our sample is not large, it looks to us like Horn is in a minority.[8]

Why did respondents fail *en masse* to say the bet was off when the prejacent failed? Was it because the hard-nosed students in the sample set always take a bet to be lost when a presupposition fails? Far from it. In answer to question 3, in which computer malfunction prevented satisfaction of a *precondition* of the prejacent, almost all respondents ($32/34 = 94\%$) said the bet was off. So, in this case of presupposition failure, not a single respondent thought the bet was lost. For most respondents, failure of the existential was not in the same league as failure of a computer.

The scenario for question 4 was a variant of the computer failure situation in which it was clear that even if the computer had functioned normally the bet could not have been won. Here most respondents ($26/34 = 76\%$) thought the bet was simply lost, while a significant minority ($8/34 = 24\%$) said the bet was off.

Those who are partial to three-valued logics may be reminded of the intuition behind Strong Kleene connectives. The semantics for these connectives allows a complex expression to be given a truth value even if one of its elements suffers presupposition failure, provided the truth value of the complex expression can be calculated without reference to the part suffering presupposition failure.

For example, the expression *the Pope is catholic or the King of France is bald* is interpreted as true because although *the King of France is bald* may have an indeterminate truth value, the truth of the left disjunct guarantees the truth of the whole. Irrespective of the merits or otherwise of the Strong Kleene semantics as a model of natural language connectives (see Beaver 1997 for discussion), it does seem as if people judging a wager tend to adopt a Strong Kleene approach, providing a definite judgment as soon as there is sufficient information to guarantee what the hypothetical outcome would be if all information were present.

The results of the Arroyo Purity Wager do not provide much support for the existential presupposition or prejacent presupposition analysis, although the fact that at least a small number of respondents judged the bet to be off

---

[8]   Despite the survey results above, it turns out that Horn is not in a minority of one. We have found a subject whose intuitions match Horn's across the board, determining e.g. that the bet should be off in the scenario for question 1. Anna Beaver (age 12;4), choosing answer *c*, commented: "That isn't what the bet was about."

when the existential failed perhaps provides those supporting the existential presupposition theory with a glimmer of hope.[9]

As regards the implications of Horn's Bet for the presuppositions of exclusives, one is tempted to conclude that all bets are off. Roberts (2006) comes to a similar conclusion regarding the difficulty of using Horn's Bet to shed light on what is presupposed and what is at-issue. But we want to suggest something just slightly stronger: on the basis of our survey, it seems that any theory must be at least a little off the mark if it predicts that an exclusive sentence should always be infelicitous when the prejacent or existential proposition fails.

Despite the complexities of Horn's wager, the existential analysis is compelling in a number of ways, perhaps most obviously because the analysis of exclusives is seen as part of a more general principle with roots as far back as Aristotle. This is the principle that strong quantifiers, and universals in particular, carry existential import on their domain of quantification. As discussed in Chapter 5, Geurts and van der Sandt (2004) argue for an interesting variant of the existential presupposition analysis: they ascribe the source of the presupposition to the underlying focused sentence, not to the meaning of the exclusive. Their analysis is therefore comparable to Horn's in that the existential presupposition is motivated in general terms, but unlike Horn's in that the particular motivation they use is quite different.

Geurts and van der Sandt mention at least one further argument for preferring the existential presupposition analysis to the prejacent presupposition analysis (an argument which Horn also gives), which is the fact that an exclusive can be used as a direct answer to a *wh*-question in cases where the prejacent is clearly not pragmatically presupposed, i.e. clearly not part of the common ground between the conversational participants.

A simple artificial example is the discourse in (9.14a). Although we have found it difficult to locate naturally occurring examples with this pattern, two are given in (9.14b) and (9.14c).

(9.14) New prejacents in answers.

      a.   Q: Which of them smokes?
           A: Only Mary.

---

[9] Tangentially, in turf betting the rules for what happens in cases of presupposition failure (though not stated in such terms) may be more complex than assumed in Horn's analysis of (9.12). In a case where a horse does not run, the presuppositions of a bet that the horse would win fail.

In this situation some bookies and institutional bodies overseeing betting operate under *ante-post betting rules*, under which the bet is lost. Others operate a *non-runner, no bet* rule, meaning that the bet is void, though this may be rarer. Some bookies sportingly return a percentage of the stake. And still others have a complex code, so that the result depends on when the bet was placed, when the horse was pulled, and why. Sometimes the bet is off, sometimes the bet is on, and sometimes a race steward or some other official must adjudicate. Of course, the reason for putting in a complex set of governing principles is presumably to avoid punters or bookies gaming the system, rather than to analyze the semantics of bets.

b. What did Lenin have in mind? Only that the victory of socialism in the sense of the establishment of a dictatorship of the proletariat is possible at first in one country, which because of this very fact, will be counterposed to the capitalist world.

(Leon Trotsky, *The Third International after Lenin, Part 2*, 1996, Pathfinder Press, NY.)

c. What did they have? Only the rights to gather and to move from one place to another. That's not land ownership.

[web example; they = aboriginals]

To deal with such data would require a well-tuned theory of accommodation that enabled the presuppositions of *only* to be added when needed, yet that still made sufficient distinction between presupposition and assertion to account for the differences.[10]

9.5 The Implicational Presupposition Theory

Summary: *Evidence from negation and plural foci shows that the existential presupposition analysis of exclusives faces a number of empirical problems. We consider Ippolito's implicational presupposition theory of exclusives, which says that exclusive sentences presuppose the implication existential→prejacent. This theory fails to make the right predictions for Horn's bet and does not explain simple inferences to the prejacent in unembedded contexts.*

While the existential analysis has strong motivation and at least some empirical support, it faces a number of problems. Most obviously, it fails to account for the fact that the prejacent typically remains an inference from the negated

---

[10] Geurts and van der Sandt's argument hinges on whether in general answers to questions can be presupposed: they maintain not, and this seems to be supported by the oddity of (ii) and (iii) below as answers to (i). However, we note that all of (iv–vi) seem to us to be quite reasonable responses to (i), at least when *Mary* is focused, and all of them semantically presuppose that Mary smokes, which is a partial answer to the question:

(i)   Which of them smokes?
(ii) # Jane regrets that Mary does.
(iii) # The fact that Mary does is surprising.
(iv) Well, John has found out that Mary does.
(v)   I'm afraid that Mary does.
(vi) Well, Mary still hasn't stopped.

Roberts (2006) argues that the important issue is not whether the information answering a question is presupposed, but whether the at-issue content of the answer is relevant to the question. We are sympathetic to this view but we still feel there is an issue to be addressed as to why it is so natural to use an exclusive sentence to inform the hearer of the truth of the prejacent. We address the issue in detail in Chapter 10.

base sentence, as in (9.15). Simple logic dictates that combining the existential *Somebody smokes* with the proposition that it is not the case that nobody who is not identical to Mary smokes, generates the inference that at least one person who is not identical to Mary smokes. But such an analysis fails to address the issue of whether Mary smokes.

(9.15) Embedding under negation: positive component [= (9.5)]

    a. Not only Mary smokes. $\mapsto$

    b. Mary smokes.

Another problem, pointed out by van Rooij and Schulz (2003, 2007) and Ippolito (2006), is seen when the focus of the exclusive is a plural, as in (9.16a). To even evaluate examples in which an exclusive combines with a plural, we need a more subtle variant of the universal component than we have been using in this section so far, as discussed back in Chapter 4.

Suppose we state the universal component for (9.16a) informally as follows: everything that smokes is a subset of Mary and Jeff. If we combine that with the existential proposition that somebody smokes, what we derive is the inference that at least one of Mary and Jeff smokes. But the desired inference is that both of them smoke, i.e. the prejacent (9.16b). For the negative case in (9.17) the situation is, of course, even worse: the desired inference is that both smoke, but the existential and (modified) universal together do not entail that either of them smoke.

(9.16) Plural foci

    a. Only Mary and Jeff smoke. $\mapsto$

    b. Mary and Jeff smoke.

(9.17) Negated plural foci

    a. Not only Mary and Jeff smoke. $\mapsto$

    b. Mary and Jeff smoke.

Based on this data, Ippolito (2006) suggests an interesting variant presupposition. According to Ippolito the base sentence presupposes neither the prejacent nor the existential, but rather an implication: existential→prejacent. Thus *Only Mary smokes* would presuppose that if anyone smokes then Mary does. This presupposition immediately gets the desired inferences for the negative cases. If *Not only Mary smokes* is true, then *Someone smokes* is true, and combining with the presupposition using *modus ponens* takes us to the conclusion that *Mary smokes* holds. The same argumentation works for the negative plural cases in (9.17).

Unfortunately, and as Ippolito realizes (indeed, advertises) such a presupposition is not sufficient. For it does not account for the inferences we need in the simple positive cases, i.e. the inference from the unembedded base sentence to the prejacent. For example, in the case of *Only Mary smokes*, it does not follow from the presupposition that if anyone smokes then Mary does, and the assertion that nobody who is not Mary smokes, that anybody smokes at all. So for simple unembedded exclusive sentences, the implicational presupposition not only fails to predict that the prejacent holds, it fails even to lead to the inference that the relevant existential is true.

Let us return to a case that we considered at length already in §9.4, namely Horn's bet. What would Ippolito's theory predict in this case? Horn wagered that *Only Seattle will win more than 60 games in the upcoming regular season for the National Basketball Association*. Ippolito's implicational presupposition is the proposition that if any team wins more than 60 games, then Seattle will.

Now consider the scenario where Seattle fails to make 60 games, but another team, San Antonio does. In that case and its *purity test* counterpart, intuitions are clear: both Horn and 97% of our survey respondents said that the bet is lost. But this is not what Ippolito predicts. For according to her this is precisely the case when the presupposition fails, so she would apparently predict that the bet should be off. This does not seem encouraging for the implicational presupposition theory. But let us allow Ippolito that at least part of the problem may be that, *contra* Horn's tacit assumption, such wagers are not necessarily judged to be void when a presupposition fails.

Let us sum up what we have observed about various theories of the inferences associated with exclusives that we have considered so far. Both the simple conjunctive theory and all the presupposition theories we have considered face problems. The simple conjunctive theory fails to account for any of the asymmetries between positive and negative implications, including, for example, the NPI licensing data discussed in Chapter 8.

The prejacent presupposition theory has fared well so far, but it fails to account for Horn's bet, and also faces some *prima facie* counter-evidence from examples of new prejacents in answers (9.14). The existential theory solves some problems but fails to account for inferences from the negated base sentence, fails to account for cases involving plural foci, and also makes incorrect predictions as regards the results of the surveys we conducted to study Horn's bet.

Lastly, Ippolito's implicational presupposition also fails to make the right predictions for Horn's bet, and also does not by itself explain simple inferences to the prejacent in unembedded contexts. In the next section we will see why Ippolito thinks this latter property is a strength of her theory, and, more generally, how theories like those we have considered may be supplemented by an account of implicatures.

9.6 Implicatures for Unembedded Exclusives

Summary: *The prejacent inference associated with exclusive sentences can be suspended, whereas the universal inference cannot be. We consider the conversational*

implicature account of (unembedded, non-negated) exclusives, which says that infer-
ences to the prejacent associated with exclusive sentences are examples of conversa-
tional implicatures. Evidence from direct non-modalized cancellation shows that the
conversational implicature account is empirically flawed. We discuss the limitations
of the conversational implicature accounts presented in van Rooij and Schulz (2003,
2007) and Ippolito (2006).

We begin this section with a phenomenon which, while it does provide further evidence for an asymmetry between prejacent and universal inferences, is
potentially problematic for the conjunctive theory, the prejacent presupposition
theory, and the existential presupposition theory: suspension of the prejacent
implication. Although we saw above that neither the prejacent nor the universal can ordinarily be canceled by a direct denial (9.7), the prejacent can be
suspended in some cases (9.18a, 9.18c, 9.18d, 9.19a, 9.20a). In these cases, the
universal inference cannot be suspended (9.18b, 9.19b, 9.20b).[11]

(9.18) Suspendability/Cancelability of modalized *only* statements

    a.   # Only Superman can save us now, and even he can't.

    b.   ## Only Superman can save us now, but some other people can too.

    c.   Only one person could absolve her, and maybe not even him.

                                              [web example]

    d.   Only Arnold Schwarzenegger can save us now, but he's busy work-
        ing for – you guessed it – The Government. We are therefore doomed.

                                              [web example]

(9.19) Suspendability with modalized denials.

    a.   . . . it was written on MASS-11 on a VAX, and now exists only on
        paper. And maybe not even in that form.

                                              [web example]

    b.   # It was written on MASS-11 on a VAX, and now exists only on paper.
        And maybe also in other forms. (Artificial variant of above)

---

[11] We could have described the examples in (9.18a, 9.18c, 9.18d, 9.19a and 9.20a) as involving *can-*
cellation, but they are better described using Horn's (1972/1976) notion of *suspension*. The standard
frame for the suspension diagnostic involves a right-adjoined *if not* phrase, as in *They were smoking,*
if not actually burning. But such cases involve suspension of an inherently negative inference, i.e. that
they were not burning. In the cases under consideration, the inference is itself positive, so a positive
suspension clause is required. Thus we have (i), in which the positive component is suspended,
which contrasts with the vapid sounding (ii), an attempt to suspend the negative component:

   (i) It now exists only on paper, if, indeed, it even exists in that form.
   (ii) # It now exists only on paper, if not in other forms.

(9.20) Suspendability with modalized denials.

    a. Google Calendar, Spreadsheet and the rest only serve to tie home users to Google and maybe not even that.

[web example]

    b. # Google Calendar, Spreadsheet and the rest only serve to tie home users to Google and maybe even have other functions too. (Artificial variant of above)

It should be born in mind that presuppositions of sentences cannot normally be canceled (9.21a, 9.22a) unless the sentence is embedded, e.g. under negation (9.21b, 9.22b). Presuppositions can be suspended using an *if* clause, as in (9.23, 9.24), but cannot be suspended using a modalized denial, as in (9.25, 9.26).

(9.21) Cancelability of factive presuppositions.

    a. ## Mary discovered that Bill was happy, though he wasn't.

    b. Mary didn't discover that Bill was happy, because he wasn't.

(9.22) Cancelability of aspectual presuppositions.

    a. ## Mary stopped smoking, although she never had smoked.

    b. Mary didn't stop smoking, since she never did.

(9.23) *If*-clause suspendability of factive presuppositions.

    a. Mary discovered that Bill was happy, if indeed he even is happy.

    b. Mary didn't discover that Bill was happy, if indeed he even is happy.

(9.24) *If*-clause suspendability of aspectual presuppositions.

    a. Mary stopped smoking, if indeed she ever did smoke.

    b. Mary didn't stop smoking, if indeed she ever did smoke.

(9.25) Modal suspendability of factive presuppositions.

    a. # Mary discovered that Bill was happy, though maybe he wasn't.

    b. # Mary didn't discover that Bill was happy, though maybe he wasn't.

(9.26) Modal suspendability of aspectual presuppositions.

    a. # Mary stopped smoking, although maybe she didn't ever smoke.

    b. # Mary didn't stop smoking, although maybe she didn't ever smoke.

Returning to the examples involving *only* in (9.18) and (9.19), the occurrence of modals is clearly significant.[12] But the fact that there is some suspension effect cannot be attributed to an interaction between modality and presupposition *per se*, since comparable constructed examples in which the denial of a presupposition is caveated with a modal (9.25, 9.26) are not generally felicitous.[13]

---

[12] See Roberts (2006) for recent discussion of exactly this point.

[13] For classic discussions of suspension and cancelability effects, see Horn (1972/1976, 1996, 2002b) and Atlas (1993b, 1996).

The question then arises: what sort of inference could be suspended in this way? One possible answer is: whatever it is, it cannot be part of the conventional meaning of *only*. Thus many authors, from Geach (1972) onwards, have denied that exclusives even have a positive component to their conventionalized meaning. Geach himself was motivated by the fact that he thought it logically simpler if *only* was a pure universal, and was not interested in justifying inferences to the prejacent. But a more standard line is to use the apparatus of Grice (1975), agree with Geach that the positive component is not part of the conventional meaning, and instead explain inferences to the prejacent as examples of conversational implicatures. This is the line taken by McCawley (1993) and Horn (1992), and most thoroughly explored by van Rooij and Schulz (2003, 2007).

Atlas (1993b, 1996), as we saw above, analyzes the inference to the prejacent from simple unembedded occurrences of the base sentence as full-blooded entailment. But he turns to Gricean reasoning to justify inferences to the prejacent when the base sentence is negated. Beaver (2004), who assumes that an existential presupposition is responsible for the prejacent inference in unembedded cases, also resorts to conversational implicature to explain the inference when the base sentence is negated.

On the other hand, Ippolito (2006) justifies the inference to the prejacent when the base sentence is negated using her unusual implicational presupposition. So for her it is only the unembedded cases that require additional pragmatic work, and for which she takes the prejacent to be a conversational implicature.

Can we find any empirical basis on which to decide whether the inference to the prejacent in unembedded cases is a conversational implicature, whether the inference under negation is a conversational implicature, or whether both inferences are conversational implicatures?

The first observation to make is that the facts as we have seen them so far are not supportive of a conversational implicature analysis of the inference to the prejacent in unembedded cases. Conversational implicatures in comparable cases are easily cancelable, whereas, as we have seen, direct non-modalized cancellation of the prejacent inference is impossible. What is possible in at least some cases, as we have seen, is modalized denial of the prejacent, though this might be better seen as suspension rather than cancellation.[14] Both Ippolito (2006) and van Rooij and Schulz (2003, 2007) explain this in terms of a distinction between weak implicatures and strong implicatures.

Van Rooij and Schulz claim that an utterance of *Only Mary smokes* produces a weak implicature that the speaker knows that Mary smokes, and a strong implicature that the speaker takes it to be possible that Mary smokes. Simple denial

---

[14]   What class of exclusive sentence permits suspension through modalized denial? Ippolito's (2006) conclusion, translated into our terminology, is that modalized denial of the prejacent is generally possible when the main predicate in the sentence is gradable, and is also possible when circumstances independently make her implicational presupposition intuitively plausible.

of the prejacent would amount to cancellation of both implicatures, and thus is ruled out, while the modalized denials cancel only the weaker implicature, and thus are felicitous.[15]

The approach seems coherent, but it is unmotivated. First, why should the 'strong' implicatures, which depend on standard Gricean apparatus, be stronger than the 'weak' implicatures, which depend on an additional non-standard assumption regarding the competence of the speaker to make judgments in the given conversational domain? Second, why should the strong implicatures in this case not be cancelable, when implicatures apparently created by similar mechanisms clearly are cancelable?[16] By analogy, one would expect (9.27a) to generate the strong implicature in (b), and the weak implicature in (c). If it were generally the case that only weak implicatures could be canceled, one would expect that the denial of the strong implicature in (d) would be infelicitous, and the denial of the weak implicature in (e) would be felicitous.[17] But in fact both (d) and (e) are felicitous: so what we have called 'strong' implicatures are not necessarily very strong after all.[18]

(9.27) Strong and weak scalar implicatures.
   a.   Mary ate some of the cake.
   b.   The speaker takes it to be possible that Mary did not eat all of the cake.
   c.   The speaker knows that Mary did not eat all of the cake.
   d.   Mary ate some of the cake. In fact, she ate all of it.
   e.   Mary ate some of the cake, and maybe even all of it.

Ippolito says of the inference from a simple unembedded occurrence of *only* to the prejacent: "trying to deny the implicature [...] is a pragmatically

---

[15] We can distinguish between cases where the denial is modalized, and cases where the proposition being denied is modal, as in (9.19a, c). Roberts (2006) provides an enlightening discussion of the latter cases.

[16] Roberts (2006) also discusses this point.

[17] Van Rooij and Schulz (2007: 223) argue that cancellations such as (9.27d) are not counterxamples to their assumption that implicatures with weak epistemic force are not easily cancellable. They claim that expressions such as *in fact* change the topic of the conversation. However, one can not explain away the equal felicity of (9.27d) and (9.27e) by saying that *in fact* changes the topic. (9.27d) is all about how much cake Mary ate.

[18] Van Rooij and Schulz use slightly different terminology. *Only Mary smokes* gives rise to what they call an inference of *weak epistemic force* that says that the speaker takes it to be possible that Mary smokes, and an inference of *strong epistemic force* that says that the speaker knows that Mary smokes. The inference with strong epistemic force (the speaker knows that Mary smokes) is easy to cancel, whereas the inference with weak epistemic force is not. There is potential for terminological confusion since what we have termed the *weak* implicature is the one with strong epistemic force, and what we have termed the *strong* implicature is the one with weak epistemic force. Despite these terminological issues, it remains the case that as yet van Rooij and Schulz have not offered a complete explanation of why an implicature with weak epistemic force is not cancelable, though they do discuss the issue at length.

illegitimate move." She considers the case of *only* modifying a singular proper noun as in (9.28):

(9.28)   Only [Hillary]$_F$ trusts Bill.

Ippolito now argues: "the speaker's utterance presupposes that Hillary is salient. Second, by uttering *Only [Hillary]$_F$ trusts Bill*, the speaker set Hillary aside from every other salient person. Now, if the speaker knew that Hillary does not trust Bill, then since Hillary is salient too, the speaker would (and should) have said nobody trusts Bill. She did not; therefore, it must be the case that the speaker does not believe that Hillary does not trust Bill." We see two major (related) problems with this analysis. Consider the following:

(9.29) a.   Q. How many famous people does only Hillary trust?

       b.   A. ## Four: Bill, Al, George, and John. Of course, nobody trusts George or John.

(9.30)   ## Al thinks that only [Hillary]$_F$ trusts Bill, though I don't know whether Al thinks that anybody trusts Bill.

The answer (9.29b) to the question in (9.29a) is infelicitous because it involves direct cancellation of a prejacent inference. But on Ippolito's analysis, the question is asking how many people are such that either Hillary trusts them, or nobody trusts them. Nothing in Ippolito's argument suggests that such a question should have been asked in a different way, and no implicatures are generated by Ippolito's analysis, which, as stated, applies only to assertions containing exclusives. So Ippolito's argument, because it applies specifically to simple assertions of unembedded exclusive sentences, does not predict the infelicity of the answer in (9.29b).

Similarly, Ippolito's argument does not predict appropriate inferences for the first conjunct in (9.30). What is needed is the inference that Al believes the prejacent, i.e. that he thinks that Hillary trusts Bill. Now the speaker, as is admitted in the following sentence, is not in a position to say that Al thinks that nobody trusts Bill. Therefore, Ippolito does not rule out the speaker uttering the first conjunct in (9.30), and does not predict the clear infelicity of the example.

So, we have now seen a problem with Ippolito's argument, namely that it is too specific: it works for completely unembedded exclusives, but not for more complex cases. But as we will now see, there is also a sense in which her argument is too general. Conversational implicatures of the type Ippolito describes are expected to be NON-DETACHABLE, in the sense that an utterance using an alternate expression with the same meaning should convey the same implicatures.[19] But what we in fact find is that expressions with apparently very similar

---

[19]   Thus saying that an inference is *non-detachable* means that the inference cannot be detached from an utterance simply by replacing words or expressions with truth-conditionally equivalent synonyms. For classic discussion, see Grice (1975) and Levinson (1983).

truth conditions to *only*, or at least to those Ippolito takes *only* to have, do not necessarily produce the analogous inferences with the same robustness. We will consider two classes of expression, *at most*, which might be considered a *maximizing downtoner* (see Chapter 3), and exceptives like the *apart from* phrase in *everyone apart from Mary*.[20]

We begin with *at most*, which, like *only*, (i) can appear as both an NP modifier and a VP modifier, (ii) leads to both negative and positive inferences (from (9.31a) to (b) and (c) respectively), and (iii) manifests focus sensitivity in its VP modifying use. Significantly, and also like *only*, simple denial of the positive inference associated with *at most* is at least mildly infelicitous, both for NP-*at most* (d) and VP-*at most* (e).

(9.31) Comparison with *at most*.

    a.   At most Hillary trusts Bill.

    b.   Nobody other than Hillary trusts Bill.

    c.   Hillary trusts Bill.

    d.   (#) At most Hillary trusts Bill, and she doesn't trust him either.[21]

    e.   (#) Hillary at most trusts [Bill]$_F$, and she doesn't trust him either.

Judgments of differences between *only* and *at most* are occasionally quite subtle. However, three native speakers (two being the authors) found that for each of the following three minimal pairs, disappearance of the prejacent inference was problematic for *only*, but unproblematic for *at most*. This suggests that in the case of *at most*, the inference might be a conversational implicature, but for *only*, something stronger is needed. Yet as far as we can see, Ippolito's reasoning applies equally to both cases, and predicts no differences.

(9.32) Contrast between *at most* and *only*.

    a.   I can confirm that everybody at most took [one]$_F$ of the suspect pills: in fact, most people took none at all.

    b.   # I can confirm that everybody only took [one]$_F$ of the suspect pills: in fact, most people took none at all.

(9.33) Contrast between *at most* and *only*.

    a.   Q: Do you owe money at most on [a student loan]$_F$?
        A: Yes – In fact, I owe no money at all.

    b.   Q: Do you owe money only on [a student loan]$_F$?
        A: # Yes – In fact, I owe no money at all.

---

[20] Horn (1972/1976: 14–15) performs a similar comparison of the behavior of exclusives to that of exceptives.

[21] By a bracketed hash mark "(#)", we mean that at least some people find the sentence slightly odd, or at least marked, though this might just be a matter of finding the right context of utterance.

(9.34) Contrast between *at most* and *only*.

    a. There are 15 people who at most recognized [the Mona Lisa]$_F$, and, of them, 10 didn't recognize any paintings at all.

    b. # There are 15 people who only recognized [the Mona Lisa]$_F$, and, of them, 10 didn't recognize any paintings at all.

Now we turn to exceptives, a class including *but, other than, apart from, except, with the exception of*, and more besides. Here things are considerably more complicated, since exceptives themselves do not form a completely uniform class. However, all the exceptives tend to give rise to an inference parallel to the prejacent inference triggered by *only*, e.g. from (9.35a) to (9.35b) for *other than*. There may or may not be infelicity when this inference is canceled, but this depends on the choice of exceptive (9.35c, d), and there may be variation among speakers.

(9.35) Comparison with *other than*: basics.

    a. Nobody other than Hillary trusts Bill.

    b. Hillary trusts Bill.

    c. Nobody other than Hillary trusts Bill, and she doesn't trust him either.

    d. # Nobody but Hillary trusts Bill, and she doesn't trust him either.

In the following three triples, (9.36a, b, c)–(9.38a, b, c), the behavior of *other than* in the (a) example is contrasted with that of the exceptive *but* in (b) and with *only* in (c). Again, what is being tested is whether the prejacent proposition is required to hold, and what the examples show is that it is much easier to cancel the prejacent inference for *other than* than it is for *only*. On our judgments, *but* patterns more like *only* than like *other than*, although nothing rides on this for us.

The important point is that Ippolito's account appears to make the same predictions for *other than* as it does for *only*. The fact that we derive different results, and that the prejacent inference is more robust for *only* than it is for some exceptives, strongly suggests that the prejacent inference is not purely a matter of conversational implicature, but is in some way part of the conventional meaning of *only*.[22]

(9.36) a. I can confirm that every single patient took none of the pills other than the blue ones, and most patients took no pills at all.

    b. (#) I can confirm that every single patient took no pills but the blue ones, and most patients took no pills at all.

    c. # I can confirm that every single patient only took the blue pills, and most patients took no pills at all.

---

[22] As a side note, whatever that conventionalized part of the meaning of *only* is, our data suggests that the exceptive *but* (a word which historically functioned as an exclusive) shares that meaning in some way.

(9.37) a. Q: Did you give no students other than Fred a passing grade?
A: Yes, and I failed Fred too

b. Q: Did you give no students but Fred a passing grade?
A: (#) Yes, and I failed Fred too

c. Q: Did you only give [Fred]$_F$ a passing grade?
A: # Yes, and I failed Fred too

(9.38) a. Each of the 15 students recognized no paintings other than the Mona Lisa, and 10 of them didn't recognize the Mona Lisa either.

b. # Each of the 15 students recognized no paintings but the Mona Lisa, and 10 of them didn't recognize the Mona Lisa either.

c. # Each of the 15 students recognized only the Mona Lisa, and 10 of them didn't recognize the Mona Lisa either.

We have now seen two reasons to be cautious about explaining prejacent inferences from non-negated exclusives as conversational implicatures. First, the explanation is overly specific, working for completely unembedded exclusives, but failing for various more complicated cases, such as Horn's bet. Second, the explanation is too general, since it would apply to various expression types with similar descriptive meanings to exclusives, and yet not all such expression types produce those inferences.

9.7 Denial Isn't Just a River in Egypt

Summary: *We present evidence that the prejacent inference from negated (scalar and non-scalar) exclusives are not as robust as previous literature has suggested.*

As we saw, the negation of a sentence involving an exclusive tends to yield an inference to the truth of the prejacent. But what sort of inference is this? And what inferences are produced under embeddings other than negation?

Ippolito (2006) comments on inferences to the prejacent in embedded and unembedded cases as follows:

[the existential presupposition analysis] predicts that (i) in the positive *only* sentence *Only John is at the party*, the positive implicatum follows from the presupposition together with the assertion and, therefore, it should not be cancelable; (ii) in the negative *only* sentence *Not only John is at the party*, the positive implicatum is a scalar implicature, and therefore, should be cancelable, like other scalar implicatures. The problem is that the judgments point exactly in the opposite direction.

She goes on to say in the conclusion of the paper:

Differently from any other implicature analysis that I know of, the current proposal accounts for the mixed behavior of the positive implicatum (its survival under negation and its cancelability) by suggesting that it is the scalar implicature of a positive *only* sentence but an entailment of its negative counterpart.

We are not sure in what sense Ippolito intends her claim that the prejacent inference is "an entailment" of a negated sentence with an exclusive, since her theory appears to make the prejacent follow from a combination of the presupposition and the ordinary meaning. But let us put that aside, for we want to concentrate here on empirical issues. Do the judgments really point in the direction Ippolito claims?

In the last section we observed that, *contra* Ippolito, prejacent inferences from unembedded exclusives are too robust to be mere conversational implicatures, at least as generated by strategic conversational reasoning that we are familiar with. We will now see the converse: though the picture is complex, inferences from negated exclusives are *not* as robust as Ippolito imagines.

Before going on, we must point out a rather obvious fact that for some reason tends not to enter the discussion of this issue: *not only* is highly idiomatic and behaves differently than *only* and *not* when either of them appear alone. The most extreme case is when *not only* fronts a subject-verb inversion, as in (9.39a), where there is no equivalent inverted structure headed by *not* (9.39b) or *only* (9.39c) alone.

Furthermore, the *not only* inversions themselves are subordinate clauses, invariably followed by an non-inverted main clause, which itself often (about a third of the time in naive web counts) begins with *but also*, as in (9.39a). This collocation was immortalized by the Dudley Moore/Peter Cook TV show *Not Only, but Also*. For this rather special type of *not only* sentence, in agreement with Ippolito's claim, inference to the prejacent is mandatory.

(9.39) *Not only*+inversion

    a.   Not only have linguists seen language evolution as a decaying process (cf. Schleicher 1852: 14–30), but also pundits and plain speakers have themselves tried to block evolution by pouring scorn on the replacement of canonical items by more efficient, but in their eyes, more 'lax' alternatives. (Bernard H. Bichakjian (1999), *Language Evolution and the Complexity Criterion* Psycoloquy: 10(033), lead article on language complexity.)

    b.   * Not have linguists seen it as a decaying process.

    c.   * Only have linguists seen it as a decaying process.

Another special case occurs when *not only* modifies an NP, as in *not only the book but also the T-shirt*. Again, inference to the prejacent seems mandatory. We suggest that what the *not only* inversions and the NP internal *not only* cases have in common is that the negation narrowly focuses on the exclusive. We return to the possible significance of this below, but what we want to consider now are cases where the inference to the prejacent is not so reliable.

As observed in Beaver (2004), from which the following examples are drawn, inference to the prejacent becomes much less robust when the negation is not string adjacent to the exclusive. Thus while (9.40a+b) is inconsistent, once *not* is moved into a pre-verbal position, as in (9.40a+c), consistency is restored.

Note that while (9.40a+b) is bad whether stress is on *only* or *Hubert* or both, (9.40c) requires stress on *only*, and has optional stress on *Hubert*. The optionality of stress on *Hubert* presumably relates to the fact that it is old information, having been mentioned in the previous sentence. So it could be argued that in (9.40c) the whole constituent *only Hubert* is in focus.

(9.40) Negation of NP *only*

    a. I don't know whether Muriel likes Hubert, but …

    b. ## Muriel likes not only Hubert.

    c. Muriel does not like only Hubert.

We see similar effects when *only* is pre-verbal. (9.41) again provides evidence that the prejacent implication (here that Muriel likes Hubert) is inviolable only when *not* and *only* are adjacent, and perhaps form a constituent. In (9.41a+c) they clearly do not form a constituent, since the negation is cliticized onto a verbal auxiliary, and here the truth of the prejacent is not required.

(9.41) Negation of VP *only*

    a. I don't know whether Muriel likes Hubert, but …

    b. ## Muriel not only likes Hubert.

    c. Muriel doesn't only like Hubert.

In the cases we will now consider, the prejacent does not follow from a negated scalar use of an exclusive. The possibility of disappearing prejacent implications with scalar uses of exclusives is memorably illustrated by the occurrence of the exclusive *just* in the old saw *Denial isn't just a river in Egypt*, though the metalinguistic aspects of this particular example make it a rather special case.

However, consider the naturally occurring examples in (9.42–9.44), all of which involve a negation outscoping an exclusive (and we have highlighted the exclusive using **bold** type). The phenomenon is very widespread, and we illustrate it for all three of the most common English exclusives, *only*, *just*, and *merely*. In none of these cases does the prejacent follow. (9.42a) does not imply that the cinematic production in question is a "shoot 'em up" pointless movie, (9.43a) was not intended to imply that in 1947 Russia was a degenerated workers' state, (9.44a) does not imply that Lost Lake is an imaginary spot on an old government map, and so on.

(9.42) Negated Scalar Exclusives: *only*

    a. And contrary to what many say I found the level of violence high but not excessive. This isn't **only** a "shoot 'em up" pointless movie; there's more than just stage blood.

                                         [web example]

b. I think people wouldn't marry any other person at the drop of a hat because marriage isn't **only** a one way street, it gives other people rights as well.

[web example]

c. She's one of the first that really represents the country and isn't **only** some blond bimbo with no brains.

[web example]

(9.43) Negated Scalar Exclusives: *merely*

a. I was in Paris in 1947, trying to convince Trotskyists they should believe that Russia isn't **merely** a "degenerated workers' state," it's a state-capitalist society.

(Raya Dunayevskaya. 1978, *Dialectics: The Algebra of Revolution*,
Marxist-Humanist Archives)

b. How can I be certain that the universe isn't **merely** a figment of my imagination?

[web example]

c. The registered office address must be a street address, and not **merely** a post office box.

[web example]

(9.44) Negated Scalar Exclusives: *just*

a. Lost Lake isn't **just** an imaginary spot on an old government map. David Cripe, 92, is a lifelong area resident and clearly remembers a lake in the area ...

(Chase Squires, "Lost lake found", *St. Petersburg Times*, 7–12–1998)

b. Is it not all one whether Amazon physically distributes a modified program, or keeps the program to itself and distribute[s] the fruits via the Internet? I said, no, it isn't all one. The former activity may be banned by copyright or contract; the latter is not **just** a special case of it, is clearly not banned by copyright, and should not be banned by contract.

[web example]

c. Do-it-yourself medical testing isn't **just** some crazy scheme for hypochondriacs and penny-pinchers. It can help your doctor to better help you.

(Mary Desmond Pinkowish, "Patient, Heal Thyself [. . .]", CNN
Money.com, 3–1–2003.

A theory like that of Horn (1969) or Roberts (2006) in which the prejacent is presupposed, would predict incorrect inferences in these cases. The same applies, for that matter, to the presupposed implication theory of Ippolito (2006). In all cases above, the relevant existential proposition holds, so Ippolito predicts that the prejacent should also hold. What (9.42a) instead suggests is that the relevant movie is *better* than "shoot 'em up" pointless movies. And what (9.43a) implies is that, in 1947, Russia was something in some way superior to a degenerated workers' state.

We must point out here that the issue of scalarity of exclusives is a complex one, and that the prejacent presupposition theories make correct predictions even in many cases that might naturally be thought of as scalar. The trouble is that up to now there has been no clear criterion for when an exclusive is scalar, and that most scales that have been discussed in the literature are special cases of entailment.

For example, numbers form an obvious scale, but on the (much discussed) assumption that *seven* means 'at least seven', an example in which an exclusive focuses on a number could rely on an entailment scale, since, e.g., 'At least seven cats purred' entails 'At least six cats purred.' Indeed, we suggest that negated exclusives might be used as a diagnostic for scalarity: an exclusive is scalar when its negation can be used without implying the prejacent, even in the absence of explicit presupposition denial.

Based on our informal observations, the exclusive *exclusively* is, in this sense, not scalar. For this reason, the naturally occurring examples in (9.42–9.44) become infelicitous when the existing exclusive is replaced by *exclusively*, or at least substantially change their meaning. For example, (9.42c) implies that the woman under consideration is *not* a blond bimbo with no brains, but if *only* were replaced by *exclusively*, the sentence would imply she was exactly that.[23]

Given that a distinction can be made between scalar exclusives and non-scalar exclusives, a defender of the previous analyses of exclusives discussed in this chapter might say that the data in (9.42–9.44) is simply not relevant, for those theories were not intended to apply to scalar cases. That is a line that could be taken, at least if those theories made correct predictions as regards all the other phenomena we have discussed, which they don't. But it troubles us. For we believe that scalar uses of *only*, *just* and *merely* do not involve a lexically different meaning from non-scalar uses, they involve a different pragmatic context where an ordering over alternatives is salient. If so, then the theories of

---

[23]   Note that judgments vary about the examples in (i) and (ii). For some speakers, (i) does not necessarily imply that Sandy met a lieutenant, whereas (ii) does imply this.

   (i) Sandy didn't meet only a lieutenant, but a general.
   (ii) Sandy met not only a lieutenant, but a general.

   In contrast, both (iii) and (iv), with the negated exclusives *not just* and *not merely*, do not necessarily imply that Sandy met a lieutenant.

   (iii) Sandy met not just a lieutenant, but a general.
   (iv) Sandy met not merely a lieutenant, but a general.

See Beaver (2004) for further discussion.

exclusives we reviewed in this chapter would be almost exclusively theories of the exclusive *exclusively*, a legitimate quarry, to be sure, but is it enough?

9.8   The Arroyo Tequila Test

Summary: *We present survey data that shows that the prejacent inference from negated exclusives does not behave like a presupposition. The prejacent presupposition theory, the implicational presupposition theory, and the existential presupposition theory are disconfirmed by our survey data.*

To understand better the nature of the inference from a negated exclusive sentence to the prejacent, we conducted a light-hearted survey comparable to the Arroyo Purity Wager we reported on earlier.

Again, there were two versions, one an email survey in a Stanford dorm, and the second an in-class survey at UT-Austin. Below we present the Stanford version of the survey.[24]

(9.45)   The Arroyo Tequila Test

```
Scenario:
One year there were 90 students in Arroyo.
  30 drank Tequila and nothing else.
  30 drank EANABs and nothing else.
  30 drank everything, no matter what.

1) How many Arroyans didn't only drink Tequila?
  a. 30
  b. 60
  c. Don't know. (If possible please explain.)
  d. Maybe a Tequila would help me figure this out.

2) How many Arroyans didn't drink only Tequila?
  a. 30
  b. 60
  c. Don't know. (If possible please explain.)
  d. Can I get another of those?
```

The scenario described in the survey is designed to test whether people counted individuals lacking the prejacent property amongst those in the negation of an expression involving an exclusive. If subjects insist on counting individuals who satisfy the prejacent (i.e. who drink Tequila), the answer should be the

---

[24]   It may help to understand that in Stanford-speak, EANABs are Equally Attractive Non-Alcoholic Beverages, provision of which the university administration strongly encourages whenever Attractive Alcoholic Beverages are present. Unfortunately for the University's policy, what many students find most attractive about typical EANABs is that they make good mixers.

Table 9.1 Results for the Arroyo Tequila Test Survey in (9.45)

	Question 1 VP-only	Question 2 NP-only
Answer a: 30	$17/41 = 41\%$	$9/41 = 22\%$
Answer b: 60	$23/41 = 56\%$	$31/41 = 76\%$
Answer c: Don't know	$1/41 = 2.4\%$	$1/41 = 2.4\%$

number who both drink Tequila and something else, thus 30, which is answer (a). If they allow also individuals who lack the prejacent property, i.e. the 30 who just drink EANABs, they should get the answer 60.[25]

We received 41 responses to the survey, and the results are summarized in Table 9.1.

The standout result from the survey is that for both questions, a clear majority of respondents counted both those in the extension of the prejacent and those not in the extension of the prejacent. A second result is that there is considerable individual variation for both questions, but the effect was stronger for NP-*only* than for VP-*only*.

Now we ask the crucial question: is the pattern of results in Table 9.1 what we would expect if the prejacent inference involved a presupposition? To test this, we ran yet another survey, this time in a UT class only.

The survey, in (9.46) consists of four questions. These involve negated presupposition triggers, the triggers being the aspectual verb *stop*, the factive *realize*, a possessive definite description, and the emotive factive *regret*, respectively.

(9.46)   Presuppositional Tequila Tests

```
1) Scenario: There are 90 students: 30 never drank
Tequila, 30 currently drink Tequila, and 30 used to drink
but gave up.

How many students didn't stop drinking Tequila?
  a. 30
  b. 60
  c. Don't know. (If possible please explain.)
```

---

[25] In a more carefully controlled study, we might have separated the subjects into two groups and asked one of them the first question, and the other the second, or at least we might have distributed surveys with random ordering of the two questions. So at best the Arroyo Tequila Test can be regarded as a pilot experiment. Also note that although the table appears to show a difference between the behavior of NP-*only* and VP-*only*, a χ^2 test reveals that this is not significant: there is insufficient evidence (at $p = 0.05$) to conclude that responses differ according to whether *only* is an NP modifier or a VP modifier.

2) Scenario: There are 90 students who all drank at a party. 30 drank Tequila, and 60 drank what they thought were Margaritas, but which in fact were virgin Margaritas containing no Tequila at all. 30 of these latter students have since found out what they were drinking.

How many students don't realize they've been drinking virgin Magaritas?
  a. 30
  b. 60
  c. Don't know. (If possible please explain.)

3) Scenario: A recent party was attended by 90 students. 30 students were drinking soda, and the remainder were drinking Margaritas. When the party was busted, 30 students hid their Margaritas in the dorm piano.

How many students didn't hide their Margaritas in the dorm piano?
  a. 30
  b. 60
  c. Don't know. (If possible please explain.)

4) Scenario: After the party in (3), 30 students who were found in possession of alcohol were threatened with Minor In Possession charges. Although all charges were dropped, and although everyone else left the party happy, these 30 students came to regret having been drinking Margaritas.

How many students didn't regret drinking Margaritas?
  a. 30
  b. 60
  c. Don't know. (If possible please explain.)

This single survey was the smallest that we conducted, with 13 respondents. The numerical results for this survey are shown in Table 9.2 and are presented graphically, alongside those for NP-*only* and VP-*only*, in Figure 9.2.

The results are quite unlike those for the comparable test involving *only* in (9.45). For both NP-*only* and VP-*only*, Table (9.1) shows that respondents were more likely to answer *60* than *30*, but for all four cases of standard presupposition triggers, Table (9.2) shows that respondents were more likely to answer *30* than *60*. Indeed, and despite the relatively small sample size, the results are statistically highly significant.

To check for statistical significance, we pooled the data from both NP-*only* and VP-*only* across both the Stanford and UT-Austin versions of the survey

Table 9.2 Results for the Presuppositional Tequila Test Survey in (9.46)

	Question 1 stop	Question 2 realize	Question 3 their	Question 4 regret
Answer a: 30	9/13 = 69%	12/13 = 92%	10/13 = 77%	5/13 = 38%
Answer b: 60	3/13 = 23%	0/13 = 0%	3/13 = 23%	4/13 = 31%
Answer c: Don't know	1/13 = 7.7%	1/13 = 7.7%	0/13 = 0%	4/13 = 31%

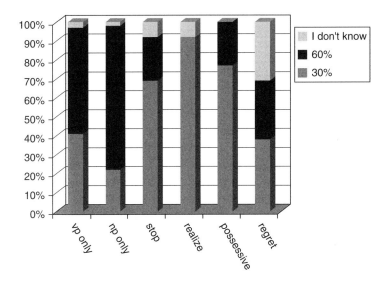

Figure 9.2 *Only* vs. presupposition triggers

in (9.45), and we pooled the data across all presupposition types in (9.46). We then examined the null hypothesis that the underlying distribution of responses across the three answers (a, b, and c) was the same for the *only* cases as for the standard presupposition triggers. A χ^2 test then disconfirms the null hypothesis, indicating that the distribution of responses for *only* is different from that for standard presupposition triggers, with probability of error $p \leq 0.001$ (2 degrees of freedom, $\chi^2 = 28.6$).

Let us now consider why the standard presupposition triggers behave as they do under negation, why *only* behaves differently, and what the consequences are for the various accounts of presupposition we have looked at. Consider (9.47), repeated from question 2 of the survey in (9.41), and involving the *factive* verb *realize*:

(9.47)   How many students$_i$ don't realize they$_i$'ve been drinking virgin
          Margaritas?

The factive verb triggers the presupposition that the student in question has
been drinking virgin Magaritas.[26] As discussed in the discussion of presupposition in §5.2.4, there are various ways this presupposition might be dealt with.
It cannot be globally accommodated because that would cause a free variable
to become unbound, what we referred to in §5.2.4 as *trapping*. That leaves the
three interpretational possibilities given in (9.48), below.

(9.48) a. Of those students who have been drinking virgin Margaritas, how
           many students don't realize it?
           (*Answer: 30*)

       b. How many students are such that they've been drinking virgin
           Margaritas and don't realize it?
           (*Answer: 30*)

       c. How many students are such that it's not the case that they've been
           drinking virgin Margaritas and realize it?
           (*Answer: 60*)

In (9.48a), the question is understood as implicitly restricted to a domain of
individuals who satisfy the presupposition.[27] In (9.48b), the presupposition is
accommodated in an intermediate position as if it was part of the at-issue content of the question, though outside the negation. This reading is not easily
distinguishable from that in (9.48a), since it yields the same answer, 30. Third,
in (9.48c), the material that is normally thought to be presupposed for this trigger could be treated just as if it was a standard at-issue entailment. In this case,
the presupposition (if it even is one) stays under the scope of the negation. As
described in §8.3.2, presupposition theorists generally treat such cases as *local
accommodation* of the presupposition.

So, we have suggested three logically possible readings for (9.47): which do
people prefer? Even though our survey was small, the result was solid: most
get a reading for (9.47) like that in (9.48a) or (9.48b). Indeed, for all classes of

---

[26]   Here we assume that *they* is bound by *How many students*, i.e. that its value covaries with the
student in question. Another reading is available where *they've been drinking virgin Margaritas* is
understood as meaning that the whole group is collectively engaged in an activity characterized
as drinking virgin Margaritas. This reading is not immediately available, perhaps because in this
scenario a use of *they* with that interpretation is blocked by the alternative *some of them*.

[27]   In van der Sandt and Geurt's theory, as described in §5.2.4, this would be a case of *intermediate
accommodation*. This is related to the issue of how *always* is restricted (§8.2.2). See Beaver (2001, 2005)
and Beaver and Zeevat (2007) for further critical discussion of intermediate accommodation.

standard presupposition trigger, more people get one of these two readings than get the reading in (9.48c).

Our null hypothesis was based on the assumption that when *only* is negated, the prejacent behaves just like the presuppositions of standard presupposition triggers. To make this clearer, let us suppose that the prejacent inference under negation was just a simple presupposition. Under that assumption, we can state the comparable readings for one of the survey questions involving *only*. Example (9.49) would be expected to have the three possible readings in (9.50). As for (9.48), the three readings in (9.50) correspond to restriction of the domain of the question, intermediate accommodation, and treatment of the prejacent as if it were an ordinary at-issue entailment, respectively.

(9.49)   How many Arroyans didn't only drink Tequila?

(9.50) a.   Of those Arroyans who drank Tequila, how many didn't only drink Tequila?
            (*Answer: 30*)

       b.   How many Arroyans are such that they drank Tequila and didn't only drink Tequila?
            (*Answer: 30*)

       c.   How many Arroyans did not both (i) drink Tequila and (ii) only drink Tequila?
            (*Answer: 60*)

Now we can ask which of these readings best represents the interpretations of subjects in our survey. The answer is clear: they generally preferred the reading in (9.50c) to either of the readings (9.50a) and (9.50b). That is, whereas standard presuppositions generally escape the negation in cases like these, for most speakers the prejacent of *only* does not. Barring any factors we may have overlooked, the statistical significance of the result means that we can safely conclude that the prejacent inference from *only* under negation does not behave like a standard presupposition.

Our survey data is also inconsistent with the hypothesis, based on Ippolito's work, that inferences associated with *only* under negation result from an implicational presupposition. Example (9.51) lists the three possible readings we might expect, in the same order as we used for (9.48) and (9.50).

(9.51) a.   Of those Arroyans who are such that if they drank anything, they drank Tequila, how many didn't only drink Tequila?
            (*Answer: 30*)

       b.   How many Arroyans are such that (i) if they drank anything they drank Tequila and (ii) they didn't only drink Tequila?
            (*Answer: 30*)

c. How many Arroyans are not such that (i) if they drank anything they drank Tequila and (ii) they only drank Tequila?
(*Answer: 60*)

The readings that might be predicted under Ippolito's model are complex, so it takes a little more effort to calculate what answers might result from each reading. But note that the Arroyans who are *such that if they drank anything, they drank Tequila* are just the same as the Arroyans who drank Tequila. Having realized this, the calculation is no harder than for the earlier cases, and what we quickly come to see is that assuming an implicational presupposition leads to just the same predictions for our survey as assuming the simple prejacent presupposition does.

It now follows that the implicational presupposition theory, like the prejacent presupposition theory, is falsified by our survey data. To the extent that the prejacent has a special status in negated examples, it does not behave like a presupposition. And to the extent that the implication considered by Ippolito has any special status, that too is not the status of a standard presupposition. At best, the variation in the survey results could be used to argue that these inferences *sometimes* have the character of standard presuppositions. That is, we could argue that e.g. Ippolito's implication is a genuine presupposition, but that for some reason it is usually accommodated differently than standard presuppositions.

And what of the idea that exclusives have an existential presupposition? That is a non-starter for negated exclusives, for it makes incorrect predictions for much simpler cases than in our survey. To consider how it would fare for the survey data, note that all 90 students in our invented survey scenario for (9.49) drank something, and drinking something is exactly the relevant existential presupposition for the examples at hand.

Because the existential presupposition is satisfied for all individuals, the existential presupposition theory makes the same predictions as a theory in which there is no presupposition at all. Thus all the readings predicted under this theory are equivalent in the given scenario, and lead to the answer 60. Though it is indeed the case that a majority of respondents chose this answer, the fact that the existential presupposition theory does not have any logically distinct readings means that no variation at all is predicted. Thus the existential presupposition theory is also disconfirmed by our survey data.

9.9 Is the Prejacent Entailed?

Summary: *We consider the hypothesis that the prejacent inference of exclusive sentences is an entailed presupposition. We conclude that this position is defensible.*

As we have established, the prejacent is not a standard presupposition. But is it entailed? Horn (2002b), having previously argued first for a strong presupposition and then for a weaker one, gave up on the presupposition altogether.

The position he ended up supporting is that both the positive and negative components form part of the entailed meaning of *only*.

However, the positive component suffers from a peculiar impediment Horn calls *inertia*, an impediment which apparently prevents the positive component from getting caught up in all the hustle and bustle that normal entailments face in their everyday life. For example, inert entailments do not like to be the main target of an assertion, a negation, or an emotive attitude. In fact, they behave suspiciously like presuppositions, and Horn does suggest that many inferences which have previously been regarded as presuppositions might in fact be inert entailments. He offers no diagnostics which differentiate assertorically inert elements from presuppositions. So we are inclined to classify Horn's assertorically inert elements as a subset of presuppositions.

What, then, did Horn (2002b) achieve beyond a shift in terminology? The main change seems to be that whereas in Horn's previous work the prejacent was not treated as presupposed and not part of the entailed meaning, now it is treated as presupposed (by another name) and part of the entailed meaning. But how can that be? How can something be presupposed and entailed?

Well, actually, far from being a new concept, this is the standard position taken on most types of presupposition trigger, including cognitive factives (*realize, know*), definite descriptions (*the, her*), aspectual verbs (*start, stop*), aspectual adverbs (*still, already*), and implicatives (*manage, succeed*). The arguments were made explicit by Gazdar (1979), and the data is discussed at length by Beaver (1997, 2001).

Broadly speaking, for most presupposition triggers it is natural to say that the presupposition is entailed, while for a number of cases there is controversy about data that might be interpreted to mean that the presupposition is not entailed. This latter, controversial class includes the temporal operator *before*, and, in addition, several of our possibly focus sensitive friends, the emotive factives (*regret, be happy that*) and the additives (*too, also*).[28]

So if Horn now thinks that the positive component of exclusive meaning is something very much like an entailed presupposition, what then of the phenomenon of cancelation of the positive component for simple exclusive sentences?

Herburger (2000), defending a variant of a conjunction analysis, made an important observation on this phenomenon: sometimes even clear cases of entailment may be weakened, and these cases have something important in common with the cases in which the positive component of an exclusive sentence is, as Horn (1972/1976) himself put it, suspended. A web search using

---

[28] It should be noted, however, that in all the cases listed above, the reason for saying that the presupposition is not entailed is *not* that it is easily cancelable. Indeed, if anything the presuppositions of emotive factives and additives are harder to cancel than other presuppositions. Rather, the point is that for these triggers the presupposition need not hold in the local context of the trigger. For recent discussion, see Beaver and Zeevat (2007).

variants of the phrase *and maybe not even* picks up a number of cases of the relevant sort:

(9.52) Suspension of entailed material.

    a. They learn a little Braille – thirty words a minute – and maybe not even that.

                                                                                             [web example]

    b. Factually correct, if a bit devious, and maybe not even that.

                                                                                            [web example]

    c. Hal, It seems that the issues you bring up here are clarification (and maybe not even that) issues and not issues to remove the Expiration feature.

                                                                                             [web example]

    d. Besides, Soros is just a single vote, and maybe not even that (does he live and vote in CT?)

                                                                                             [web example]

    e. This one's for hardcore fans . . . and maybe not even them.

                                                                                             [web example]

It seems that sometimes freshly asserted, entailed material can be suspended without giving the impression that the speaker is in any way confused. But, as is clear from Herburger's discussion, this is a highly restricted operation. The generalization seems to be that material can be suspended provided the speaker is using a particular rhetorical strategy which we term *letting the hearer down gently*. To use this strategy, there must be a salient scale of propositions such that there is reason to think another conversational participant might believe a relatively strong proposition to be the case. The speaker argues against the truth of stronger propositions on the scale by first offering as true a relatively weak, but still palatable proposition, and then questioning whether even that holds.

    Given the existence of such a strategy, Horn's position that the prejacent is entailed (albeit in a special way) is defensible. And, in the next chapter, we will adopt a similar position. However, we will not follow Horn in taking the prejacent to be inert, for the simple reason that we have no clear understanding of what that means.

9.10 Summary

To summarize the point we have reached: (i) we suggest that a uniform mechanism should explain the positive inference from both simple exclusive sentences and negated exclusive sentences, (ii) implicature analyses fail to account for the relative robustness of both the positive and negative inferences, (iii) the fact that the positive inference cannot be directly denied is more consistent with a presupposition analysis than with an implicature analysis, but it is not clear that the behavior of exclusives precisely mirrors the behavior of standard presupposition trigger types, (iv) the fact that the positive inference is subject to modalized denial (*suspension*) in unembedded cases is compatible with both a presuppositional and a conjunction account, given that even entailments can be denied in this way in similar circumstances, (v) to the extent that prejacent inferences are more robust for negated exclusive sentences than for simple unembedded exclusive sentences, this may be understood in terms of the discourse functions that exclusives have, the fact that they are negatively oriented.

More generally, we think that discourse function should be at the heart of any theory of what exclusives mean. In the next chapter, we will develop a theory of the meaning and function of exclusives which is consistent with all these desiderata, and also explains the place of exclusives in the QFC model.

Chapter 10

Exclusives: a Discourse Account

I therefore propose for only *(and similarly for a range of other particles) that its semantic properties are exhaustively characterised by the fact that it marks contexts in which the reported fact falls short of what was expected to be the case: the answer to the topic question is less than the conversational partners expected.*
Henk Zeevat, Position Paper, *One Day Only*, Amsterdam, May 10 2002

10.1   Introduction

Summary: *A proposed model of the meaning of exclusives is situated relative to other models surveyed in Chapter 9.*

Only, *just*, and *merely* are not like *cheese*, *pickles*, and *beer*. The latter triplet are words that pick out stuff in the world, and this helps us put together propositions about that stuff. Exclusives, too, can help a speaker express propositions about stuff in the world, since they have clear effects on compositionally derived truth conditions of the sentences that contain them. But to concentrate on the truth conditions of exclusives is to miss most of the action.

The primary function of exclusives is not to refer to stuff, or even to refer (as determiners and many adverbs do) to quantificational relations that might hold between different lumps of stuff. The primary function of exclusives is to mediate the flow of discourse.[1]

There has been much work on the focus sensitivity of exclusives, and much work on the entailments, implicatures, and presuppositions of exclusives, and there has also been some work on how scalar exclusives relate to non-scalar exclusives (van Rooij 2002).

---

[1]   The only extended piece of work we have been able to locate which puts the discourse function of exclusives at center stage is that of Aijmer (2002: ch. 4). Aijmer discusses the discourse functions of the exclusive *just* on the basis of an extensive corpus study. Unfortunately, we came across this too late in the publication process to attempt a detailed comparison.

However, by and large, previous authors have attempted a divide and conquer strategy, e.g. looking at the presupposition/implicature question and ignoring focus, or *vice versa*. Indeed, sometimes the same author has worked carefully through both issues, for example Roberts (1996) on the focus sensitivity of *only* and Roberts (2006) on the meaning of *only*, even in the same book (Herburger 2000). We are indebted to both of these authors, but nonetheless feel that neither of them has succeeded in providing the link between the question of why exclusives are focus sensitive and the question of what exclusives mean. What we lay out in this chapter is a uniform theory that accounts for both the meaning and the focus sensitivity of exclusives, and accounts for them in terms of the function of exclusives in discourse.

We suggest that *only*, unlike *always*, is not anaphoric on a mere set of events or situations: it is anaphoric on a question. But didn't Rooth, von Fintel and Roberts already claim just that? Yes, they did, but we go a step further. In principle, a quantificational adverb can pick up any highly salient set of events (or situations, or DRSs if you prefer). And, in principle, Rooth, von Fintel and Roberts allow an exclusive to pick up any salient set of alternatives, provided the result is rhetorically coherent. In contrast, we claim that exclusives are grammatically constrained to pick up the Current Question, in the sense we introduced in Chapter 2.

The reader may recall that on our Roberts inspired model (as in the models of Büring 2003 or Carlson 1985), discourse is structured as a hierarchy of questions, such that at any point in the discourse there is a stack of questions waiting to be answered, with more general questions being lower down the stack, and more specific questions higher up. The Current Question associated with an utterance is the question which that utterance addresses, the most specific of the questions on the stack. If the utterance answers the question fully, and the answer is accepted, that question will then be popped off the stack.

So in the model we propose, it is part of the lexical meaning of an exclusive that it comments not just on a salient question, but specifically on the Current Question. But we go further still, and claim that exclusives place heavy constraints on the Current Question and its expected answer. It is these constraints that explain a slew of problems that have prompted one of the most controversial debates in the history of semantics, the debate over the meaning of *only* that we presented in Chapter 9. And it is because of their grammaticized interaction with the Current Question that exclusives manifest the phenomenon of focus sensitivity that we studied in detail in Chapters 1–8. Now is the time when we attempt to bring everything we presented together in the form of a single, integrated theory of the meaning and function of exclusives.

10.2 The Discourse Function of Exclusives

Summary: *We motivate a model of the meaning of exclusives that makes discourse function primary: exclusives challenge an overly strong expectation. We show that inappropriate expectations lead to sentences with exclusives becoming infelicitous.*

Exclusives have a peculiar duality that seems almost paradoxical. Positive and negative. At one and the same time, they can add emphasis, by saying that some alternative is the strongest that is true, and they can downtone, by underlining the fact that the alternative is not the strongest that in principle might have been the case. We suggest that while exclusives have truth conditional effects, their function is partly MIRATIVE,[2] to say that the true answer to the Current Question is surprisingly weak, and control the flow of discourse by resetting expectations about that answer.

Typically, the expectation on which an exclusive comments is from the perspective of a hearer, though this will not always be the case.[3] The dual nature of exclusives is central to how they are used to reset expectations, allowing the speaker to strike a balance between what is interesting (i.e. relevant and strongly informative) and what is true. The presuppositions, entailments, and maybe also implicatures of exclusives should all be understood in terms of this discourse function.

We now state our proposal for the interpretation of exclusives. We use a number of ideas and terms we introduced earlier in our descriptions and developments of prior work, and in particular Rooth's (1992) Alternative Semantics and Roberts' (1996) question based model of discourse. There is also obvious inspiration from various analyses of Horn's.[4]

But the theory of exclusives we present is distinct from this prior work: if anything, it is the theory of exclusives that Roberts (1996) and Roberts (2006) would have written if they had ever coauthored a paper.[5] The core idea is simple:

---

[2] The term *mirative*, not, as yet, recognized by the Oxford English Dictionary, is from DeLancey (1997), and refers to "grammatical marking of unexpected information." This is generally understood as implying that information marked by a *mirative* is a *hearer-new* proposition, in the sense that Prince (1981) uses *hearer-new*. We do not know of any previous account of a *mirative* marker which indicates that a *hearer-old* proposition departs from expectation. Yet, on our view, that is precisely what exclusives do. This makes for a natural extension of DeLancey's work, since exclusives, like the *miratives* and *evidentials* that are his primary concern, are often grammaticized as functional morphemes. And as we already observed in §2.2, there is at least one language (Quechua) where evidential morphemes, like exclusive morphemes in e.g. Japanese and Hindi, can indicate what is in focus.

[3] To simplify, we assume by default for the examples we discuss that it is the hearer who is doing the expecting.

[4] We are reminded of Horn's Zen-like tendency to present theories with mirrored positive and negative components. This tendency runs through his very relevant discussion of *only*, *almost* and *barely* (Horn 1996; Horn 2002b), his analysis of conditional perfection (Horn 2000), and most obviously of all, his reformulation of Grice's maxims as mirror Q and R principles (Horn 1984). Horn's lower bounding R-principle ("say no more than you must") corresponds to what, for us, is the presupposition of an exclusive in our analysis, while his upper bounding Q-principle ("say as much as you can") corresponds to what, for us, is the entailment of an exclusive. In our brief discussion of *even* in this chapter, below, the relationship is reversed.

[5] In adopting a mirative analysis of exclusives, we are also influenced by the approach of Iván García Álvarez in as yet unpublished dissertation work on the analysis of exceptives, exceptives being closely related in their semantics to exclusives. Further, and as the quote that heads this

(10.1)   **Meaning of exclusives**
         The lexical meaning of exclusives is exhaustively described by:
         Discourse function: *To make a comment on the Current Question (CQ, as defined in Chapter 2), a comment which weakens a salient or natural expectation. To achieve this function, the prejacent must be weaker than the expected answer to the CQ on a salient scale.*
         Presupposition: *The strongest true alternatives in the CQ are* **at least** *as strong as the prejacent.*
         Descriptive Content: *The strongest true alternatives in the CQ are* **at most** *as strong as the prejacent.*

So, potential answers to the CQ are ordered from weak to strong, either because some answers entail other answers, or through a pragmatically relevant ordering such as newsworthiness. In general, this structure will be a PRE-ORDER, i.e. a reflexive and transitive relation. It is more standard in the literature to assume a stronger requirement on scales, i.e. that they are PARTIAL ORDERS, but we will see at least one case below where this does not hold.[6] The prejacent is one potential answer. To be general, what is expected will correspond to a probability distribution over stronger alternatives. For our purposes, it is simpler to conceive of a categorical distinction between one set of alternatives which the hearer expects to contain the strongest true answers, and another set which the hearer does not expect to contain the strongest true answers. Put differently, the alternatives in the CQ which remain open from the perspective of the hearer is a subset of the set of alternatives which are left open in the common ground. This may be either because some of the hearer's beliefs as regards

---

chapter indicates, much of what we say here is prefigured by Henk Zeevat's proposal (see Zeevat 2007: 182) that *only* marks that an answer falls short of the interlocutor's expectations. Our account of exclusives is also anticipated by van Rooij's (2002) insight that *only* ϕ means that ϕ is the unique best answer to the Current Question.

[6]   *Pre-orders* are also sometimes known as QUASI-ORDERS. A *partial order* is a *pre-order* which is antisymmetric, meaning that two distinct propositions cannot each be as strong as the other. Discussion of the use of partially ordered sets for pragmatic problems is found in e.g. Hirschberg (1991), Ward and Hirschberg (1985), Ward (1988), Ward and Prince (1991). For a very recent application of partially ordered sets to the meaning of exclusives, see Riester (2006). His conclusions, especially the idea that *only* is always scalar, are very similar to ours. Note that the particular partial ordering we use could also be based on e.g. relative probability given the common ground, or relative utility for a salient goal. Appropriate notions of relative utility for communicative acts have been developed furthest in the work of Robert van Rooij. As well as his joint work with Katrin Schulz, already cited, see the developments in van Rooij (2004).

   Particular delicacy may be required in developing a fuller theory of relative strength of alternatives, because we have not distinguished between cases in which one answer is more exhaustive than another, and cases where one answer is more fine-grained than another. For example, *She lives in London* is more fine-grained than *She lives in England*, and the former entails the latter, but it is not clear that the former will always be pragmatically stronger than the second. One way to approach this issue would be to limit alternative sets to answers at a pragmatically appropriate level of precision. But we will not pursue this avenue here.

the answer to the CQ have not been officially introduced into the conversation, or else because some of those beliefs have been announced but not accepted.

For example, if *How much does Sandy earn?* is the CQ, Speaker 1 may comment *Well, he works in an investment bank*, implicating that Sandy earns a lot. However, the implicated proposition is only accepted if it is not challenged. Speaker 2 could reply *He only earns $25,000: he cleans the floors there!* Suppose that the open alternatives to the CQ in the common ground before Speaker 1's comment included alternatives *He earns X* for a wide range of values for X. Speaker 1 is suggesting that some of the alternatives with low values of X can be eliminated because he does not consider these alternatives plausible. Speaker 2 could accept this suggestion, e.g. by saying *Oh, I see*, and proceeding with a new topic. But instead, Speaker 2 challenges Speaker 1's expectations regarding the CQ, and uses the exclusive *only* to say that the strongest true alternative is weaker than the strongest true alternative Speaker 1 expected would hold.

The presence of an expectation that something stronger than the prejacent is true is an essential part of the meaning of *only*. This is reflected in the pairs in (10.2–10.4). For each of these pairs, the (a) version is a naturally occurring example in which an expectation is set, and then an *only* sentence is used to say that the truth is less than expected. Reversing the expectation and the prejacent, as in the constructed (b) examples produces a text which, while logically consistent, is extremely infelicitous.

(10.2) a. I really expected a suite but only got a single room with 2 beds.

[web example]

   b. # I really expected a single room with 2 beds but only got a suite. [Constructed variant]

(10.3) a. London police expected a turnout of 100,000 but only 15,000 showed up. What happened?

[web example]

   b. # London police expected a turnout of 15,000 but only 100,000 showed up. What happened? [Constructed variant]

(10.4) a. On the other hand, seven people expected a negative result but only two received one.

[web example]

   b. # On the other hand, two people expected a negative result but only seven received one. [Constructed variant]

Previous authors have said that a focus sensitive expression *may* be anaphoric on the CQ (Roberts 1996) or discourse topic (von Fintel 1994). In contrast, we say that by nature of their discourse function, exclusives *must* comment on the CQ, and this is a grammatical constraint, part of the lexical meaning of the exclusive. Thus, the process of *resolving* the restrictor of the exclusive is very different from that in Roberts' or von Fintel's models, as we understand them, where in principle the hearer could choose any salient set of alternatives.

Here are two other things that previous authors have said: (i) exclusives carry a presupposition which explains various of the complex inference patterns we studied in Chapter 9, and (ii) exclusives involve a set of alternatives, or even a presupposed set of alternatives. We say that the presupposition which explains the complex inference patterns is the same as the presupposition of alternatives. That is, what an exclusive presupposes is not anything like the prejacent or existential proposition *per se*. What an exclusive presupposes is an open question of a certain type, namely one that the speaker takes to have been partially answered, and for which there is a salient expectation of a much stronger answer.

We may put it this way: when the speaker utters a sentence containing an exclusive, the speaker takes the hearer to believe that some answer stronger than the prejacent is true, and the speaker himself thinks that something as strong as the prejacent is true (typically the prejacent itself). The speaker, therefore, takes it as uncontroversial that something at least as strong as the prejacent is true, and presupposes that these alternatives are the only ones left open.

At this point, there are two possibilities. Either the speaker's utterance was congruent to the existing CQ, or it was not. If the utterance was congruent, the hearer does not need to accommodate a new CQ, but may be forced to accommodate a change as regards which alternatives are considered still open for the existing CQ.

Even if such a change is needed, however, it should not involve closing any alternatives that the hearer expected to be complete answers to the question. If the speaker is right about the hearer's expectations, each of these alternatives will be weaker than the answer that the hearer expects to be true. Thus, in this first case, even if accommodation is necessary, it should be unproblematic. And, of course, even this limited form of accommodation, removal of some alternatives that are weaker than the expected complete answer, may not be necessary. For it may be that the presuppositions of the exclusive sentence are already in the common ground.

If the utterance was not congruent, a CQ must be accommodated from scratch. According to the generalizations given in Chapter 2 (2.56), this is possible provided that CQ is part of a strategy to answer other open questions, or to meet common discourse goals. And in this case, the CQ that is accommodated will be some (not necessarily strict) subset of those focal alternatives of the utterance that are at least as strong as the prejacent.

Once the hearer has performed whatever accommodation is necessary, the CQ will contain only alternatives in which something at least as strong as the prejacent is true. It is in this sense that the question that the prejacent would have naturally answered, is taken to have already been partially answered. And against this background, what the speaker asserts is that, *contra* the hearer's expectations, all the alternatives stronger than the prejacent can also be closed. So we can see that ordinary declarative utterances with exclusives form a natural part of conversational strategy: they allow the speaker to presuppose something he considers uncontroversial, and assert something he considers controversial.

In many cases that have been discussed in the literature, the relevant scale of strength is just entailment. Often, there is a total ordering among the alternatives. For example, if the question was *How many fish did you catch?*, the answer *only three* can be understood in terms of a scale *(at least) one fish, (at least) two fish . . .*, and on this scale answers to the right strictly entail all answers to the left. In these cases, the simplest of all, there is little difference between presupposing the prejacent and presupposing a CQ containing only alternatives at least as strong as the prejacent. Thus, for these cases we make similar predictions to a prejacent presupposition theory.

However, unlike a prejacent presupposition theory, even in these simple cases we also make predictions about focus sensitivity. Further, because we take the discourse function of exclusives as basic, we also make a prediction about the discourse phenomena of suspendability even in these cases. Specifically, it is because exclusive sentences are used to weaken expectations that they can be part of a strategy of *letting the hearer down gently*, in the sense of §9.9. But we won't dwell on the simple cases. Instead, we will turn to cases where the scale of strength is more interesting.

10.3 Examples of Scales

Summary: *A central feature of the discourse based model of exclusives is its use of scales, which in general are* pre-orders. *We show how three different types of scale lead to different inferences for simple constructed examples.*

First case: objective invite scale

Consider (10.5a), an answer to the CQ in (10.5b):

(10.5) a.   Jim only invited [Mary and Sam]$_F$.
      b.   Who did Jim invite?

The prejacent for (10.5a) is the proposition that Jim invited Mary and Sam (10.6a). We now consider alternative possible answers to the question in (10.5b). Let us suppose that the question is asked by someone who needs the information in order to make an alphabetical guest list, rather than, e.g., to judge how good a job Jim did at inviting people. We might say that the question is asked objectively, or, as the standard phrase goes, *purely for information*. The scale of strength is then ordinary entailment. Based on this scale, we can subdivide possible answers according to whether they are stronger than the prejacent, weaker, or neither.

(10.6) a. **Prejacent proposition:** Jim invited X, with X = {Sam, Mary}

b. Breakdown of alternative values of X:

Stronger: Any strict superset of {Sam, Mary}.
Weaker: {Sam} and {Mary}.
Neither: Any set including people other than Sam and Mary, and at
most one of Sam and Mary.

In this context, the answer in (10.5a) indicates that the speaker believes there is
an expectation that Jim invited others besides Mary and Sam. The speaker then
presupposes that the only open alternatives in the CQ are those which entail
that Jim invited at least Mary and Sam. The utterance entails that Jim invited
nobody other than Mary and Sam. It then follows from the utterance that Jim
invited Mary and Sam and nobody else. The combination of presupposition,
entailment and overall implications is summarized in (10.7):

(10.7) Inferences associated with (10.5a) *Jim only invited [Mary and Sam]*$_F$ in the
context in (10.6).

a. **Presupposition:** Jim invited Mary, Sam, and possibly others.

b. **Entailment:** Jim invited nobody other than Mary and Sam.

c. **Implication:** Jim invited Mary and Sam and nobody else.

This can be compared with the inferences associated with the negation of
(10.5a), *Jim didn't only invite [Mary and Sam]*$_F$. The presuppositions remain as
before. But whereas for (10.5a) the entailment was that none of the strictly
stronger alternatives were true, now the entailment is reversed: the truth must
lie among the strictly stronger alternatives. this is summed up in (10.8):

(10.8) Inferences associated with *Jim didn't only invite [Mary and Sam]*$_F$ in the
context in (10.6).

a. **Presupposition:** Jim invited Mary, Sam, and possibly others.

b. **Entailment:** Jim invited Mary and Sam and at least one other.

c. **Implication:** (as for entailment)

In this particular case, we see that the predictions of our model are comparable
to those of the prejacent presupposition theory of §9.3, proposed by Horn (1969),
and recently defended in heavily nuanced form by Roberts (2006). But for us,
this is a very special case. The fun starts when we switch to other scales.

Second case: subjective invite scale

Suppose that Jim was expected to invite a lot of people to a party, and the discourse in (10.5) is between people who's primary concern is to evaluate whether
the party will rock.

Our hypothetical interlocutors care about the actual identity of the invitees only to the extent that establishing their identity will help determine whether sufficient warm bodies will later be on the dance floor. In this context, to say that Jim invited a whole bunch of people would be to make a stronger statement than to say that Jim invited John and Mary, regardless of whether that bunch of people includes John and Mary. Accordingly, the strength ordering is not ordinary entailment, but a relation which supplements entailment, e.g. as in (10.9):

(10.9) a. **Prejacent proposition:**   Jim invited X, with $X = \{$Sam, Mary$\}$

b. Breakdown of alternative values of X:

Stronger: Any set of people with cardinality significantly larger than 2, and any set strictly containing $\{$Sam, Mary$\}$.
Weaker: Any singleton set of people.
Neither: Any set with cardinality of 2 or not significantly more, containing at most one of Sam and Mary.

The hearer has the expectation that Jim invited many people, although, depending on what else is known about Jim, this expectation may have been overly charitable. Nonetheless, the expectation is there, so the speaker feels justified in presupposing that various possible answers are out of contention. The speaker knows, e.g. that Jim did not invite Pete and Pippa, and knows that the hearer does not expect Jim to have invited Pippa and Pete and nobody else. So the speaker feels justified in removing the alternative *Jim invited Pippa and Pete* from contention.

There is a subtle point here: although the alternative *Jim invited Pippa and Pete* is removed from contention, the CQ that the speaker presupposes still includes alternatives which entail that Jim invited Pippa and Pete. The effect of removing an alternative must be understood in the light of the Current Question Rule, which requires that at least one alternative in the CQ is true. The effect of removing the alternative *Jim invited Pippa and Pete* is to restrict the possible answers to those which imply that if Jim invited Pippa and Pete, then he invited others besides them.

By taking the alternative *Jim invited Pippa and Pete* to be ruled out, the speaker is in effect presupposing that a certain exhaustive answer is ruled out. The speaker is presupposing that a complete statement of those who Jim invited does not consist of the pair Pippa and Pete alone.[7]

---

[7]   At a more general level, even though our question alternatives are not exhaustive propositions as in the question semantics of Groenendijk and Stokhof (1984), they still reflect exhaustive alternatives. When a question has been completely answered, and there is only one alternative left, it follows that all the answers which strictly entailed that alternative have been removed. Therefore the interlocutors will have exchanged the information not merely that this final alternative is true, but that it is exhaustively true.

The speaker feels justified in assuming that most alternatives that involve Jim inviting around two individuals are ruled out. Of course, there is one alternative of this sort that the speaker does not take to be ruled out, namely the alternative *Jim invited Mary and John*. Unlike the other alternatives that involve Jim inviting around two individuals, the speaker knows that this one happens to be true.

We end up with presuppositions, entailments, and overall implications as follows:

(10.10) Inferences associated with (10.5a) *Jim only invited [Mary and Sam]*$_F$ in the context in (10.9).

　　a. **Presupposition:** Jim invited a large group, or a small group (possibly as small as cardinality 2) including Mary and Sam.

　　b. **Entailment:** Jim invited nobody other than Mary and Sam.

　　c. **Implication:** Jim invited Mary and Sam and nobody else.

What we have ended up with is a presupposition that is not quite like that seen in any previous model of the meaning of exclusives. For an entailment scale, like that in the objective invite scenario above, we predict something very close to a prejacent presupposition, with the caveat that this is presupposed *via* a restriction on open alternatives in the CQ. However, in the case at hand, the prejacent is not presupposed at all. The set of open alternatives that the speaker assumes includes some which do not entail that John and Mary were invited. The presupposition is similar to that in an existential presupposition theory, but it is not exactly existential either: a special status is given to the prejacent, and yet without necessarily requiring that it is true.

This, in turn, may remind the reader of the implicational presupposition of Ippolito (2006). But our presupposition is not that either. For according to her model it would follow in this case that if Jim invited anyone then he invited Mary and Sam. In the type of scenario we have described it could be the case that Jim invited a thousand people and completely overlooked Mary and Sam, without the presupposition being falsified. This possibility falsifies the implicational presupposition theory, but is no problem at all for the model we have described.

The inferences in (10.10) can be compared with the inferences in (10.11) associated with the negated exclusive sentence *John didn't only invite [Mary and Sam]*$_F$. The presupposition associated with the negated exclusive is the same

---

Similarly, when an alternative is removed, it follows that it is impossible to narrow down the alternative set further so as to end up with just this alternative. Therefore removing an alternative corresponds to accepting the claim that the alternative would not exhaust what can truly be said in answer to the question.

as the presupposition associated with *Jim only invited [Mary and Sam]*$_F$. In contrast, the entailment is now that Jim invited a large group, or a group (larger than cardinality 2) including Mary and Sam.

(10.11) Inferences associated with *Jim didn't only invite [Mary and Sam]*$_F$ in the context in (10.9).

     a.   **Presupposition:**   Jim invited a large group, or a group (possibly as small as cardinality 2) including Mary and Sam.

     b.   **Entailment:**   Jim invited a large group, or a group (larger than cardinality 2) including Mary and Sam.

     c.   **Implication:**   (as for entailment.)

Third case: subjective autograph scale

The first case we considered in this section involved an entailment scale. The second case involved a more sophisticated scale. But the scale used in the second case still respected entailment in the sense that any proposition which entailed the prejacent was classed as stronger, and only propositions entailed by the prejacent were considered weaker. The minor departure from ordinary entailment in the scale used in the second case was that certain logically unrelated propositions were considered stronger than the prejacent. With apologies in advance to the philosophers Soames, Bealer, and Perry, we now consider a more radical departure, a case where the scale of strength is not a *partial ordering* in the mathematical sense.

     Consider (10.12a) as an answer to the CQ in (10.12b):

(10.12) a.   Brady only got a [Soames]$_F$.

        b.   CQ: What celebrity signatures did Brady get at the Philosophy of Language party?

     The interlocutors value philosophers' autographs based on what they consider the philosophers' sociological importance, such that it is better to get the autograph of someone whose work has firmly entered the western philosophical canon than the work of someone who is merely currently trendy. Likewise, it is better to get a trendy philosopher's signature than that of some nobody whose work may never make a broad impact. Furthermore, one Putnam beats any number of second or third tier philosophers' autographs. In fact, it not only beats them, it renders them totally irrelevant: it is no better to get both Putnam's and Schmuckski's autographs than to get Putnam's alone, because, after all, who's ever heard of Schmuckski?

     It is the irrelevance of Schmuckski that means that what we are dealing with here is not a *partial order* but only a *pre-order*. Under a *partial order*, distinct propositions could never both be as strong as the other, whereas in this case the distinct propositions *Brady got a Putnam* and *Brady got a Putnam and a Schmuckski* are as strong as each other.[8]

The scale, then, is as in (10.13):

(10.13) a. **Prejacent proposition:** Brady got a X, with X = Soames.

  b. Breakdown of alternative values of X:

  Stronger: Any set containing Putnam, Kripke, Kaplan, Searle, or similarly influential philsopher, and any set containing multiple philosophers of similar significance to Soames.

  Weaker: Any set not containing a philosopher as significant as Soames.

  Neither: Any set containing exactly one philosopher other than Soames but of comparable significance (Bealer, Perry ...), and any number of less significant philosophers.

  Equal: Any set containing Soames and some number of less significant philosophers.

The expectation is that Brady got a really worthwhile autograph. The speaker feels it is uncontroversial that Brady didn't get the autographs of no-names alone, so alternatives that mention no-names and no names are excluded. Similarly, the speaker feels it is uncontroversial that Brady didn't get the autograph of Bealer and nobody else of even similar influence, so this alternative is excluded. And so on.

What we end up with is the presupposition that Brady got a Soames or better. The entailment, meanwhile, is that Brady didn't get anything the interlocutors consider really good, like a Putnam, and didn't even get multiple autographs from philosophers of comparable stature to Soames. The inferences are summarized in (10.14):

(10.14) Inferences associated with (10.12a) *Brady only got a [Soames]$_F$* in the context in (10.13).

  a. **Presupposition:** Brady got a Soames, or else something better.

  b. **Entailment:** Brady got no better autograph than Soames'.

  c. **Implication:** Brady got Soames' autograph, and possibly others of lower significance.

---

[8] As noted earlier, the possibility of equally strong propositions means that we have dropped the anti-symmetry requirement of a *partial order*, leaving us with an ordering that satisfies reflexivity and transitivity. These seem to be the absolute minimal conditions that the scale of propositions must satisfy: it is hard to conceive of something which fails either of them being a scale at all.

It is the fact that in general we take our scales to be *pre-orders* rather than always being *partial orders* which explains what might have been a puzzling feature of the definition of the meaning of exclusives in (10.1). There we talked of "the strongest true alternatives" (plural) rather than "the strongest true alternative" (singular). Whenever the scale of strength is a partial ordering, and provided the CQ Rule is not broken, there will be a unique strongest true alternative.

An interesting side of our autograph example is that it involves an exclusive being used, in a sense, non-exclusively. That is: saying *Brady only got a Soames* does not imply that Brady didn't get a Schmuckski autograph. Who cares whether he did or not? Similarly, if we say of someone *she only became a chief petty officer*, we don't mean she never became a petty officer third class (a lower US naval rank), but rather that she never proceeded any further, e.g. never becoming the Master Chief Petty Officer of the Navy.

For completeness, we consider one further example in the autograph scenario, namely the negation of (10.12a). By now the style of reasoning should be clear, and, in (10.15), we merely state the results. Note that this is a case which combines all the features we have seen in the previous examples: (i) the prejacent is not presupposed, (ii) the prejacent does not follow, and (iii) there is no entailment at all as regards whether there is a unique individual in the extension of the property in question, i.e. in this case the property of being amongst those whose autograph Brady managed to acquire at the Philosophy of Language party.

(10.15) Inferences associated with *Brady didn't only get a [Soames]*$_F$ in the context in (10.13).

    a. **Presupposition:** Brady got a Soames, or else something better.

    b. **Entailment:** Brady got something better than a single Soames.

    c. **Implication:** (as for entailment.)

10.4 Formal Analysis

Summary: *We show how the meaning of a simple constructed example with an exclusive can be derived formally in a compositional grammar. The basic techniques are taken from Chapter 2 (§2.7) and Chapter 4.*

We now sketch a formal account of how the meaning of a sentence with an exclusive is built up. We note along the way a host of simplifications we have made. Despite this, the model is still sufficient to account for many of the properties of exclusives described in Chapter 9, more so, we believe, than any formal model that has been proposed elsewhere.

As our first simplification, we treat exclusives as if they were sentential operators. This makes the compositional derivation, and the application of the Focus Principle, much more manageable. The interpretation of exclusives modifying NPs, VPs, and PPs will all be given via the equivalence $[[_S X [O\ Y] Z]] = [[_S O [_S X Y Z]]]$, where O is an exclusive and X, Y, Z are parts of syntactic trees, and neither X nor Z contain any focused elements. The effect of using the equivalence is the same as if exclusives were moved syntactically to a sentence modifying position prior to interpretation, which is the approach taken by, for example, Herburger (2000). We assume that the Focus Principle treats the discontinuous X Y Z as if it were a constituent, and allows its alternative set to be congruent to the CQ.

We now give formal definitions of the lower and upper bounding operators MIN and MAX that are at the heart of our analysis of the meaning of exclusives. These are stated in terms of an information state σ, which is assumed to provide a value for CQ_σ, the open alternatives in the CQ in σ, as well as for the *Context Set*, the set of worlds compatible with all propositions taken to be in the common ground between the interlocutors. In a fully formalized model, the state σ would be updated dynamically as the conversation unfolded, but we make no attempt here to formalize how σ changes over time.

(10.16)   Definitions of lower and upper bounding operators.

$$\text{MIN}_\sigma(\pi) = \lambda w \forall p \in CQ_\sigma \ p(w) \rightarrow p \geq_\sigma \pi$$
$$\text{MAX}_\sigma(\pi) = \lambda w \forall p \in CQ_\sigma \ p(w) \rightarrow \pi \geq_\sigma p$$

Using MIN and MAX, we can now restate more formally the presupposition and content of an exclusive from (10.1). In a full analysis, the state σ would keep track not only of the common ground of the participants and the questions under discussion, but also their expectations. However, to keep the compositional analysis manageable, we omit what we described in (10.1) as the discourse function of exclusives, except insofar as it is reflected in the presupposition and content.

(10.17)   Presupposition and content of X *[only Y]* Z.

$$\text{presupposition}(X \text{ [only Y] } Z) = \text{MIN}_\sigma(\llbracket X \ Y \ Z \rrbracket^I)$$
$$\llbracket X \text{ [only Y] } Z \rrbracket^I = \text{MAX}_\sigma(\llbracket X \ Y \ Z \rrbracket^I)$$

Let us now consider a specific example, (10.18), for which we will assume that the context makes no special strength ordering over propositions available beyond ordinary entailment:

(10.18)   Alex only likes [Bill and Callie]$_\text{F}$.

This sentence involves focus on a group denoting NP, *[Bill and Callie]*$_\text{F}$. Let us immediately make another simplification: rather than dealing with all the complexities of introducing individual concepts into the system, we will just treat NPs extensionally, so that, e.g. *Bill* is represented by a constant b of type e, rather than being an individual of type $\langle s, e \rangle$.[9] We assume an algebra over sums of individuals, so that *Bill and Callie* denotes a sum entity, also of type e, written $b \oplus c$. We also assume basic subpart operations over these sum entities. Specifically, $x \sqsupseteq y$ means that x contains y, or, equivalently, that y is a subpart of x. Thus e.g. $b \sqsupseteq b$, and $(b \oplus c) \sqsupseteq b$, but $b \not\sqsupseteq (b \oplus c)$.

---

[9]   The reader is referred back to Chapter 4 for derivations which do not make the simplifying assumption that NPs are type e.

The compositional build-up of the underlying sentence lacking the exclusive would proceed, modulo some of the extra simplifications we have made, along the same lines as any of the Alternative Semantics derivations in Chapter 4. Rather than working through such a derivation again, we jump straight to the level at which the content and alternative set for *Alex likes [Bill and Callie]*$_F$ has been derived:

(10.19)   Content and alternative set for *Alex likes [Bill and Callie]*$_F$

$$[\![\text{Alex likes [Bill and Callie]}_F]\!]^I = \lambda w \, [\text{likes}(w, a, b \oplus c)]$$
$$[\![\text{Alex likes [Bill and Callie]}_F]\!]^A = \lambda p \, \exists x \, p = \lambda w \, [\text{likes}(w, a, x)]$$

The meaning of a sentence with an exclusive depends essentially on the CQ. But not just any CQ will do, for two reasons. First, the CQ must satisfy the congruence condition from the Focus Principle (2.54), which ensures that the focus marking in an utterance is appropriate for the question that the utterance helps answer. In the case at hand, this will mean that all the alternatives in the CQ must be propositions corresponding to sentences of the form *Alex likes X*. Second, the CQ must obey the additional constraint imposed by the presupposition of the exclusive, placing a lower bound on the strength of the alternatives that are still open. In this case, every alternative must be at least as strong as the proposition *Alex likes Bill and Callie*.[10] The constraining effect of the Focus Principle and the presuppositions of the exclusive are stated in (10.20):

(10.20)   Constraints on CQ from *Alex only likes [Bill and Callie]*$_F$

$$\text{CQ}_\sigma \subseteq \lambda p \exists x \, p = \lambda w \, [\text{likes}(w, a, x)]$$
         (Focus Principle *applied to* Alex likes [Bill and Callie]$_F$)
$$\text{CQ}_\sigma \subseteq \lambda p \, p \geq_\sigma \lambda w [\text{likes}(w, a, b \oplus c)]$$
         (*presupposition of* Alex only likes [Bill and Callie]$_F$)

We are taking the strength ordering to be ordinary entailment, as was the case for the first example discussed in §10.3. This allows the two constraints in (10.20)

---

[10]   In accord with the Roberts' derived model presented in §2.7, the state, here σ, provides a Context Set, a set of worlds corresponding to what is in the common ground of the discourse participants. It is this Context Set that must be updated with the content of an assertion: the Context Set is intersected with the set of worlds compatible with the asserted proposition. A side effect of updating the Context Set in this way is to reduce the set of open alternatives of the CQ, for we take the open alternatives in the CQ to be just those which are compatible with at least some worlds in the Context Set.

But now consider the case of the presupposition of *only*, which imposes a constraint on the set of open alternatives of the CQ. If this constraint is not met, it appears that there are potentially two different ways that an interlocutor can react. First, the interlocutor can accommodate by throwing out worlds from the Context Set until the presuppositional constraint is satisfied. Second, the interlocutor can just remove improper alternatives directly from the CQ. The net effect, however, will be the same, provided the Current Question Rule holds, for this will ultimately force the interlocutor to remove worlds from the Context Set which are not compatible with at least one alternative in the CQ.

to be simplified considerably. If strength is just entailment, and assuming *likes* is distributive, then $likes(w, a, x) \models likes(w, a, y)$ if and only if $x \sqsupseteq y$. Let us also assume that there is no further information constraining the open alternatives in the CQ, so that the set of open alternatives can just be the maximal set obeying both constraints in (10.20). In that case, the set of open alternatives is just any proposition corresponding to a sentence of the form *Alex likes X*, where X contains both Bill and Callie, and possibly others besides:

(10.21)   Value of CQ if $\geq_\sigma$ is entailment, and CQ is the largest set compatible with all constraints.

$$\text{CQ}_\sigma = \lambda p\,[\exists x\; x \sqsupseteq (b \oplus c) \wedge p = \lambda w\,[\text{likes}(w, a, x)]]$$

Now that we have CQ_σ, we can calculate the content of (10.18). This is the proposition that no open alternatives should be stronger than the proposition that *Alex likes Bill and Callie*. Using the same approach as we employed for (10.21), we can replace the notion of strength for entailment, and then cash out entailment in terms of the containment relation between sums of individuals. Thus the content of (10.18) is the proposition that every true open alternative is a proposition of the form *Alex likes X* where X is the sum of Bill and Callie or some subpart of that sum, i.e. X is Bill, or X is Callie:

(10.22)   Content of (10.18) *Alex only likes [Bill and Callie]*F assuming $\geq_\sigma$ is entailment.

[Alex only likes [Bill and Callie]F]^I
   $= \lambda w \forall p \in \text{CQ}_\sigma\; p(w) \rightarrow \exists x\, (b \oplus c) \sqsupseteq x \wedge p = \lambda w\,[\text{likes}(w, a, x)]$

The content of (10.18) expressed in (10.22) can be simplified in obvious ways. First, plug in CQ_σ from (10.21). This yields the proposition that the only true alternatives among those which involve Alex liking at least Bill and Callie are those which involve Alex liking at most Bill and Callie. In other words, there aren't any true alternatives which involve Alex liking more than Bill and Callie. Second, if we assume two likings are distinct iff they are between different individuals,[11] then we can replace quantification over propositions with quantification over individuals. We are left with the proposition that for every sum containing Bill and Callie such that Alex likes the sum, that sum is just Bill and Callie:

(10.23)   Content of (10.18) *Alex only likes [Bill and Callie]*F using (10.21), and assuming appropriate constraints on *likes*.

[Alex only likes [Bill and Callie]F]^I
   $= \lambda w \forall x(((b \oplus c) \sqsupseteq x \wedge \text{likes}(w, a, x)) \rightarrow x = (b \oplus c))$

---

[11]   Formally, what we need is a meaning postulate on the extension of the predicate *like*. This postulate would be parallel to that in (4.9).

Finally, we can combine the presupposed and asserted content to derive the implications we expect from (10.18), i.e. the proposition that Alex likes Bill and Callie, and he doesn't like anyone else:

(10.24)　Combined implication of presupposition and content of (10.18) *Alex only likes [Bill and Callie]*$_F$, using assumptions in (10.23) and Current Question Rule.

$$\lambda w \; \text{likes}(w, a, b \oplus c) \wedge \neg \exists x \sqsupseteq (b \oplus c) \wedge \text{likes}(w, a, x)$$

We have now seen how the account of the meaning of exclusives in the second and third sections of this chapter can be used in a compositional derivation, albeit one in which we made many simplifications. We certainly do not want to claim that it would be trivial to give a more complete account in which none of those simplifying assumptions were made. But we do want to claim that we cannot see any principle reason why a more comprehensive formal account, complete with a statement of a substantial fragment of English that included (10.18), could not be given.

Rather than pursuing this line of technical development, we would like to return to the various phenomena involving exclusives that we have discussed over the last few chapters. In the remaining sections of this chapter we review these phenomena, and show how the model we have developed accounts for them.

10.5 Unembedded Exclusives

Summary: *It is shown that the discourse theory of exclusives explains (i) why the prejacent follows from simple positive uses of exclusives, including cases where the focus is a plural, (ii) why the inference is not directly cancelable, but is suspendable, and (iii) why the exclusive sentence can be used to inform a hearer of the identity of the focus in answer to a wh-question.*

The first and most basic item of data to consider is the fact that the prejacent follows from an unembedded exclusive sentence. According to our discourse based model of exclusives, the reason is that the prejacent is entailed by all remaining alternatives once the (lower bounding) presupposition and (upper bounding) content of an exclusive sentence have been applied.[12] This holds

---

[12]　Technically, we can generate a situation where this would not be so. Suppose that with the ordering described in the third case in §10.3, the speaker were to say (i) *Brady only got [a Soames and a Schmuckski]*$_F$. The reader may verify that in that case the update will leave open the alternative corresponding to (ii) *Brady got a Soames*. But this sentence (though it is equally strong) does not entail the prejacent (iii) *Brady got a Soames and a Schmuckski*. We suggest that in this case the very fact that the speaker mentioned the Schmuckski implies, by the Gricean maxims of Relevance and Quantity, that it is valuable information that Brady got a Schmuckski. Therefore, the speaker cannot be using a scale in which (ii) *Brady got a Soames* is equally strong as the prejacent (iii) *Brady got a Soames and a Schmuckski*.

even when the focus is a plural NP, a class of examples that, as we discussed in Chapter 9, is problematic for some accounts (those which derive the prejacent from a combination of an existential presupposition and the assertion). Further, when the salient ordering is just entailment, the prejacent is not merely entailed, but presupposed, since the exclusive sentence presupposes a question that corresponds to a set of alternatives at least as strong as the prejacent. The Current Question Rule then requires that at least one alternative is satisfied, so it immediately follows that the truth of the prejacent is not at issue, on pain of infelicity.

The prejacent is not cancelable by the same speaker that uttered the exclusive sentence, because it is part of the core meaning. Although the prejacent is presupposed, entailed presuppositions are not generally cancelable (i.e. cancelable by direct denial of the presupposition) in unembedded contexts, and even in embedded contexts (to which we turn shortly) such cancellation typically has a marked metalinguistic quality to it.

The fact that the prejacent can be suspended is expected because it is the function of exclusives to lower expectations, so that, like other assertions which suggest that the truth is weaker than an interlocutor believed, they may be part of a strategy of letting the hearer down gently.[13]

Suspension is a special case of hedging, or introducing a caveat. It is typical for suspension to target something other than the main claim of the utterance, and to have the effect of conditionalizing the assertion. Thus compare (10.25a) to (10.25b). Example (10.25a), complete with suspension, is not a strong claim, but at least the hearer might walk away with a conditional: if Mary is a student, then she is the tallest in the class. But in the second case, the main assertion is suspended. While this is not clearly infelicitous, it might well leave the hearer wondering why the speaker spoke in the first place, since all that is conveyed is that if none of the students is taller, then Mary is the tallest.

(10.25) a. Mary is the tallest student in the class, although, then again, maybe she isn't a student.

b. Mary is the tallest student in the class, although, then again, maybe some other student is taller.

The prejacent of an exclusive sentence is comparable to the presupposition of a superlative. But the prejacent is even more naturally suspendable than a presupposition of a superlative. As we have discussed, the function of

---

[13] On our analysis, the fact that exclusive sentences are suspendable may also be related to the fact that presuppositions of questions tend to be more easily suspendable, as in the embedded questions *who ate my donut* in (ia), than cancelable, as in (ib).

(i) a. I want to know who ate my donut, although perhaps nobody did.
b. # I want to know who ate my donut, although in fact nobody ate it.

an exclusive sentence is to weaken the hearer's expectations, and weakening yet again using suspension merely extends the rhetorical game plan one step further.

We now turn to the issue of why exclusive sentences can be used to inform a hearer of the truth of the prejacent, and specifically why sentences of the form *Only X has property P* can be used to answer a *wh*-question aimed at identifying who has property *P*. A naturally occurring example is given in (10.26). Though the example is not one of literal, informative dialogue, it's nonetheless clear that (10.26c) felicitously follows (10.26b), and could do so in a non-risible context.

(10.26) a. Knock, knock!

   b. Who's there?

   c. Only Spock.

   d. Only Spock who?

   e. Only Spock when spoken to.

(Matt Rissinger and Philip Yates, *Greatest Jokes on Earth*,
Sterling Publishing Company, 1999.)

Put simply, an exclusive sentence like (10.26c) can answer a *wh*-question like (10.26b) because the questioner does not know the answer. In fact, the utterer of the exclusive sentence would typically take the questioner to have incorrect assumptions about the answer, so the answer is not only informative, but also potentially corrective. Furthermore, the exclusive is information structurally appropriate: it presupposes a question which, in the sense of Groenendijk and Stokhof (1984), contains a subset of the partitions in the original *wh*-question. And to top it all off, the exclusive sentence provides an exhaustive answer to the question: an exclusive sentence makes a great answer. However, the issue we must address is not simply why the exclusive sentence can answer the question, but why the exclusive sentence can be used to inform the questioner of the prejacent. Here, the situation will vary according to whether a pure entailment ordering is used, or whether there is additional pragmatic ordering.

If only a pure entailment ordering is salient, an exclusive sentence like (10.26c) has plusses and minuses pragmatically as an answer to a *wh*-question like (10.26b). The plusses, we listed in the previous paragraph. The big minus, obviously, is that it is taken for granted that the hearer knows the prejacent to be true. Because of this, it is in fact quite hard to conceive of (10.26c) being used without some other salient ordering making *Spock* a weaker answer than some others. When you hear that uncomfortable line in (10.26c), doesn't your heart sink with the knowledge that the joke is bound to be dire. (This sinking feeling is, of course, essential to the genre, a part of the setup for a punch line which is invariably even worse.) For example, out of the joke context, we might imagine Spock to be a peculiarly named errand boy or gang member, as opposed to an important guest who was expected. Similarly we might calm someone who heard the noise of our arrival and took it to be the sound of an unwelcome visitor by saying *'Don't worry – it's only me.'* Two naturally occurring examples of this follow:

(10.27)   And Harry, if you're reading this, and if on your 21st birthday party you see in the corner some guy dressed up as Adolf Hitler, don't worry. It's only me.

[Aaron Barschak, Harry's Game *The Guardian*, 14–1–2005]

(10.28)   "Oh it's only you." "Who were you expecting, your knight in shining amour? Because I think he's down the hall"

[web example, Harry Potter Fan site]

The point here is that the addressee expects something stronger on a pragmatically appropriate scale. And when there is such a scale, rather than pure entailment, the exclusive sentence need not presuppose the prejacent at all.

10.6   Negated Exclusives and Other Embeddings

Summary: *Negated exclusives sentences usually, but not always, lead to inferences that the prejacent holds. We show that the discourse based model explains the inferences, and compares favorably in this regard to the prejacent presupposition model, the implicational presupposition model, and the existential presupposition model. We then turn to embeddings other than negation, considering (i) Horn's Bet (embedding in a wager) and (ii) the Tequila Test (embedding under a question and a negation). We argue that the special status of the presupposition in our model may be helpful for these cases.*

For negated exclusives we must explain not only the 'fact' that the prejacent follows, but also the 'fact' that the prejacent is a stronger inference than for unembedded exclusives.

Why the scare quotes? Well, for the first, although in this section we will just take it to be a fact that the prejacent follows, we devoted a separate section in Chapter 9 (§9.7) to an interesting class of counterexamples which had not been previously brought to light. For the second, the basis of the claim that the inference is stronger for negated exclusives than for positive exclusives (made most explicitly by Ippolito, as noted in Chapter 9) is that whereas for a simple positive exclusive sentence the prejacent can be suspended, this is not the case for a negated exclusive. We explain this observation below. But the reason for the second set of scare quotes is that there is at least one sense in which the prejacent inference is weaker for negated exclusive sentences than for simple exclusive sentences, namely that the former can be canceled.

Why does the prejacent normally follow from the negation of an exclusive sentence? There are two cases to consider: either the salient ordering is pure entailment, or not. The second case is the interesting one, but let us consider first the former.

If the ordering is entailment, then the prejacent follows from the negated exclusive because, and this will come as no surprise, it is presupposed. More precisely, the negated exclusive sentence is taken to presuppose exactly the same question as the corresponding positive sentence, and this question contains only alternatives at least as strong as the prejacent. Given an entailment ordering, this means the prejacent is true in every open alternative. And given the Current Question Rule, at least one alternative has to hold, so therefore the prejacent must hold.

Now, what of Ippolito's claim that inferences from negated exclusive sentences are more robust than inferences from positive exclusive sentences? In Chapter 9, §7, we showed that the differences between the two types of inference are not as sharp as Ippolito suggests.

Yet there is something intuitively right about Ippolito's claim that suspension is harder for negative than positive exclusive sentences. In the light of the theory we have proposed, it should be apparent what it is. Suspension using *and maybe not even* is appropriate when a speaker is letting a hearer down gently, moving the hearer from a strong proposition to a relatively weak one, and then giving a final push down to ground level. An unembedded exclusive sentence is *downward oriented*, in that it is used to say that the strongest proposition that holds is weaker than the hearer expected. So it makes an ideal middle step on the way down.

But a negated exclusive sentence is the worst possible type of sentence to use in this way. It is oriented upwards, in the sense that a speaker uses it to say that stronger propositions hold than have been already established. It would be a very cruel speaker indeed who would take a hearer up to the dizzy heights offered by a *not only* sentence entirely for the purpose of then dropping that hearer back down to zero again with a bump. One can almost hear the sadistic satisfaction in the voice that utters:

(10.29)   (#) She didn't only drink Tequila: maybe she didn't drink at all.

Indeed, it is difficult to understand (10.29) as mere hedging. In spite of the modal, it seems more like a case of cancellation than of suspension, specifically an example of presupposition denial. Yet, while denying a presupposition is a skill mastered over several millenia by philosophers and defense lawyers, it remains highly marked in everyday language. That is why (10.29) seems so forced. However, we should keep in mind that explicit denials of the presupposition of exclusives do occur, sometimes even without modals to lessen the impact. Three naturally occurring examples follow:

(10.30)   CRATYLUS: That is true, Socrates; but you see that the case of language is different; when by the help of grammar we assign the letters α or β, or any other letters to a certain name, then, if we add, or subtract, or misplace a letter, the name which is written is **not only**

written wrongly, but not written at all; and in case of any of these accidents happening, becomes other than a name.

[Plato, *Cratylus, pt. V*, tr. B. Jowett, Clarendon Press, Oxford, 1871.]

(10.31)   Franklin was a spiky personality who not only did not suffer fools gladly but did not suffer them at all.

[web example]

(10.32)   Chemical damp proofing isn't "the only option" – it isn't an option at all because it doesn't achieve anything with undamaged bricks.

[web example]

The first of these quotes, for independent reasons, has an important place in the history of semantics as one of the earliest discussions of the meaning of names. For current purposes, the crucial phrase is *not only written wrongly, but not written at all*, a clear case of the prejacent proposition (that the name is written wrongly) being canceled. Similarly, in (10.31) we see cancelation of the prejacent proposition that (Rosalind) Franklin did not suffer fools gladly. The last of the three cases is strictly not of the type we have been analyzing so far, since it involves the locution *the only*, the semantics and pragmatics of which differs slightly from other occurrences of *only*. Nonetheless, the example is notable because the author explicitly presented this example with quotation marks around the phrase containing the exclusive. This illustrates the fact that denial of an exclusive's prejacent has a character which is typical of presupposition denial, a clear, though hard to formalize, metalinguistic flavor.

Let us now turn to cases of negated exclusives where the salient ordering is not pure entailment. None of the major types of account of the meaning of exclusives that we have considered extend from the basic entailment cases to the more complex non-entailment cases. We showed with naturally occurring data in §9.7 that (even absent any metalinguistic flavor) a negated exclusive sentence can be true without the prejacent being true. A standard prejacent presupposition theory simply does not apply in this case. And we see no reason why switching from saying that the prejacent is presupposed to saying that it is assertorically inert (as Horn and Roberts have recently done) will help. Ippolito's presupposed implication theory also fails to extend to cases discussed in §9.7. It makes completely the wrong prediction, for it says that in cases of negated exclusives, the inference to the prejacent is robust.

Last, what of the existential presupposition theory? Well, in a sense it makes good predictions for the cases discussed in §9.7, since it correctly predicts that the prejacent does not have to hold. But at what cost is this prediction made? Unfortunately, existential presupposition theories do not account for why the prejacent *does* follow in cases of negated exclusives when there is no salient scale of comparison other than entailment.

What we want of a theory of negated exclusives, obviously, is that it predicts the inference to the prejacent in just the right cases. Not only do we not want the theory to predict prejacent inferences all of the time (as for the prejacent and implicational presupposition theories) but we also do not want it to predict prejacent inferences none of the time. Thus the existential presupposition theory must be rejected.

As far as we can see, this leaves only one option, which we have described at length in this chapter. As we demonstrated in §10.3, our proposed model of exclusives predicts both cases where a negated exclusive sentence implies the prejacent, for example the "objective invite scale," but also cases where a negated exclusive sentence fails to imply the prejacent, for example the "subjective invite scale" and the "subjective autograph scale."

We can summarize our discussion of negated exclusives as the following four observations:

First, the prejacent follows from a negated exclusive sentence when the salient scale is just entailment because the prejacent is true in all open alternatives in the CQ, and the Current Question Rule requires that at least one of those alternatives holds. Thus the prejacent is presupposed, though indirectly, since a felicity condition on discourse must come into play for the inference to go forward.

Second, the fact that the prejacent inference is not suspendable from a negated exclusive sentence does not imply, as Ippolito suggested, that the prejacent inference is inherently *stronger* for negated exclusives than for simple positive uses. Rather, the difficulty of suspending the prejacent in these cases results from the fact that a negated exclusive is a way of shoring up expectations rather than lowering them, and so a use of a negated exclusive sentence cannot serve as part of an attempt to let the hearer down gently.

Third, there is a sense in which inferences to the prejacent are stronger for unembedded exclusives than for negated exclusives: for unembedded exclusives, direct cancellation of the prejacent produces infelicity, whereas for negated exclusives denial of the prejacent, while marked, is possible. This latter behavior is typical for presuppositional inferences.

Fourth, no standard theory of exclusives both accounts for inferences to the prejacent in basic cases and extends to examples in §9.7 where the prejacent inference does not go through. We have explained this phenomenon in terms of the availability of salient scales other than entailment which can order alternative answers to the CQ.

A note on purity wagers and tequila tests

Let us turn to two last cases that we can view as involving embedding or negation, Horn's Bet and the Arroyo Tequila Test.

With regard to Horn's Bet, we saw earlier that the results of a small survey indicated that native speakers do not generally take failure of the existential or prejacent propositions to be a reason to call off a bet that an exclusive sentence will hold. How can it be that when the presuppositions of the bet fail, the bet is still interpretable, and the relevant exclusive sentence simply judged false by the majority of respondents?

On our model, the truth of the prejacent is not a condition on interpretability, but a condition on discourse coherence. The prejacent is a pragmatic presupposition of speakers that utter the exclusive sentence, and if it is not true then a condition on discourse felicity, the Current Question Rule, will fail. It seems that for the subjects in our surveys, discourse incoherence is not a sufficient reason to declare a bet void. However, in the situation involved in Horn's bet (and likewise for the Arroyo Purity Wager), there is no salient scale apart from entailment. For example, it is stronger to say that Seattle and Orlando will win more than 60 games than to say that Seattle will win more than 60. As a result, there is a robust inference to the prejacent. And this may be why the students we surveyed, contra Horn, did not want to pay out any money in a situation where the prejacent failed.

Similar considerations apply to the Arroyo Tequila Test. Here the issue was whether for a sentence *How many X's didn't only Y?* subjects would count X's that didn't Y at all, i.e. whether they would count X's for whom the prejacent failed. We showed that for classic presuppositional constructions, the expectation would be that subjects would usually restrict their count to individuals for whom the presupposition held. However, when we ran a survey to see what happened in the case of *only*, a slight majority of subjects counted both individuals for whom the prejacent held, and those for whom it did not. Thus the subject's behavior was not in line with what we might expect on any of the standard presuppositional accounts.

We suggest that one reason for this is that the prejacent is not, like many standard cases of presupposition, a condition on interpretability. Rather, it is a condition on discourse felicity. Thus when evaluating the *how many* question, it is not necessary for hearers to restrict attention to individuals for whom the prejacent holds in order to evaluate whether each individual counts as a plus or a minus in the final tally. If the hearer does not restrict attention to those for whom the prejacent holds, the question *How many Arroyans didn't only drink Tequila?* becomes equivalent to: *How many Arroyans drank something other than Tequila?* In the situation described, the answer to this latter question is 60. In other words, if the presupposition for exclusives is weaker than that for standard presupposition triggers, we should expect more respondents in the survey to give the answer 60 for the questions involving exclusives than for those involving standard presupposition triggers. And this is exactly what we find. It seems plausible then that the pragmatic presupposition of the prejacent affects how the exclusive sentence is to be slotted coherently into a wider discourse, but need not have a strong effect on deciding who to count.[14]

---

[14]   An alternative explanation for the Tequila Test results could be developed in terms of local accommodation of the question presupposed by an exclusive. The exclusive in the Tequila Test examples is associated on our account with a presupposed question that can be paraphrased as: *what did X drink?*, where X is bound by the earlier question phrase *how many*. Suppose that the hearer has a choice between accommodation sites for this presupposed question resulting in meanings that can be paraphrased as in (i) and (ii):

Overall, we do not want to claim that either the wagers or the Tequila test provide solid support for our proposal in and of themselves. As regards the wagers, we are happy for the reader to take away only the conclusion that they just don't provide such a good source of evidence as Horn suggested. It appears that the social institution of betting is more complicated than at least some linguists had assumed.

As regards the Tequila Test, we do want to claim that the results falsify various of the models of exclusives that we discussed, for the results were statistically quite clear in this regard. But the strongest claim we want to make about our own model is that it suggests a way to deal with the Tequila Test data: we do not yet claim to have a complete model of how focus and exclusives interact in simultaneous embedding under questions and negation.

10.7 Association with Focus

Summary: *We show that the discourse model of exclusives explains how the placement of focus can change the truth conditions of an exclusive sentence, and why, unlike for quantificational adverbs, this phenomenon is affected by manipulations of surface form like extraction and ellipsis.*

We saw in §10.4 a derivation involving association with focus for (10.18), repeated below. As focus sensitivity is the central theme of the book, it is worth repeating the main conclusions of that derivation, and contrasting them with the results that would be obtained for a sentence with a minimally different focus structure, that in (10.34):

(10.33)   Alex only likes [Bill and Callie]$_F$. [= 10.18]

(10.34)   Sandy only [likes]$_F$ Bill and Callie.

The results of our earlier compositional derivation for (10.18) can be divided into three components. First, the focal meaning for the sentence is the set of propositions which say of some individual or group that Alex likes that individual or group. Second, there is a presupposition that all open answers to the

---

(i) How many students are such that the question of what they drank is answered by "not only Tequila"? *(Intermediate accommodation, answer 30)*

(ii) How many students are such that it isn't the case that the question of what they drank is answered by "only Tequila"? *(Local accommodation, answer 60)*

Now note that (i) is at least mildly infelicitous, since it is odd to answer the question of what someone drank by "not only Tequila". On the other hand, (ii) makes more sense: for some students the question of what they drank is answered by "only Tequila", and for others it is not. If we assume that accommodation takes place preferably at a site which produces a more coherent discourse, then we correctly predict that a majority should prefer accommodation as in (ii), and the answer 60, which is what we in fact observed.

CQ are at least as strong as the proposition that Alex likes Bill and Callie. And third, the main claim of the sentence is that open answers to the CQ should be at most as strong as the proposition that Alex likes Bill and Callie.

So the compositional derivation leaves a disconnect that must be filled in pragmatically, i.e. a disconnect between the set of alternatives given by the focal meaning, and the set of alternatives in the CQ. On the proposal we have presented, that disconnect is filled in by the Focus Principle. This imposes a requirement of *congruence*, which we adapted from the work of Craige Roberts. Congruence forces the CQ (whether implicit or explicit in prior discourse) to denote a subset of alternatives given by the focal meaning of the sentence. When the CQ fits in this way, and assuming that the context only makes salient an entailment ordering, (10.18) comes to entail that Alex likes nobody other than Bill and Callie.

What of (10.34)? The focal meaning for the sentence is the set of propositions which say of some relation that Alex stands in that relation to Bill and Callie. The presupposition and main claim are the same as for (10.34), except that we must now calculate the CQ and ordering between alternatives afresh. Congruence of the focal meaning combined with the presupposition tells us that the CQ must be a set of propositions which say of some relation that Alex stands in that relation to Bill and Callie. We also know that each proposition must be at least as strong as the proposition that Alex likes Bill and Callie.

Now, in principle, there are an infinite number of such relations. So it might well be felt that some constraint should have been put into the generation of the focal set to make sure that the relations considered in some sense resemble the relation of liking, so as to rule out, e.g. the relation R which is true of any pair a and b provided a is not identical to b and it is a Wednesday afternoon. We will not attempt to introduce any such constraint into the compositional build-up, and instead assume without discussion that some questions are intrinsically more plausible than others, and some orderings over the alternatives are more plausible than others.

In this case, one possibility would be to include just the relations *likes* and *likes a lot*, and use an entailment ordering, in which case the sentence would come out meaning that Alex does not like Bill and Callie very much. Another possibility, one which is perhaps slightly more natural, is to include the relations *likes* and *loves*. As many have discovered to their cost, there is no entailment in either direction between simple sentences involving these two relations. So the ordering used has to be stronger than entailment, and the most plausible ordering is one in which *love* is considered stronger than *like*. In this case, the sentence entails that Alex likes Bill and Callie but does not love them, and it presupposes that Alex either likes or loves them.

Regarding the role of congruence in these derivations, it is as well to point out that we have presented no direct evidence in this book that the connection between the CQ and the focal meaning is filled in by such a pragmatic requirement. There is no technical reason why we could not have stipulated in the meaning of the exclusive that the CQ must be a subset of the alternatives in the focal meaning, and doing so would have made the derivations somewhat more direct.

However, even making such a move would not have obviated the need for pragmatics in the derivations: it is not a fact about compositional semantics that a natural alternative to the relation *like* is *love* and that the second is stronger than the first. Though it could be knowledge that is common to anyone who knows English, it is, nonetheless, essentially pragmatic, and perhaps not linguistic at all. So even if we added further stipulations to our model, we could not escape the essentially pragmatic nature of the comparison that an exclusive is used to perform.

We now turn to the issue of why exclusives do not associate with reduced, extracted, or elided material. On the account we have proposed, an exclusive must have a focused constituent inside its syntactic scope in order to generate a pragmatically acceptable meaning. If there is no such focus, then the focal meaning of the clause containing the exclusive is a singleton set, and, by the Focus Principle, the CQ which that clause answers either contains no alternatives, or just the prejacent. This should be ruled out by an independent condition on discourse, that the CQ contains multiple open alternatives, but in any case it conflicts with the secondary part of the presupposition of the exclusive sentence, which requires that there is a salient expectation that some stronger alternative to the prejacent holds. If there is no alternative other than the prejacent, clearly this presupposition will fail.

We can apply this explanation to data from Chapters 6 and 7:

(10.35)   I only discussed'im$_i$ with Sandy. [= (6.39)]

(10.36)   Kim's is the tank I said I only stock with clownfish. [= (7.7)]

(10.37)   *Kim only [salutes]$_F$ because Sandy only does. [= (7.52b)]

In (10.35), the leaner *im* cannot bear focus. If some constituent in the scope of *only* other than *im* bears focus, we predict that *only* associates with that constituent. If no other constituent in the scope of *only* bears focus, we predict infelicity, by the above argument. Therefore we correctly predict that there is no reading of the sentence involving association with *im*.

By contrast, if *only* were replaced with a quantificational adverb like *always*, a reading corresponding to association with *im* would be possible. Quantificational adverbs like *always* are not discourse functional, and their semantics makes no direct reference to the CQ or to expectations of the hearer. Rather, the restrictor of *always* is anaphoric on a salient set of events. If a set of events of the speaker discussing individuals with Sandy is salient, then we could get a reading with *always* with the following truth conditions: whenever the speaker discussed someone with Sandy, the speaker discussed the individual i with Sandy.

Example (10.36) involves extraction from a relative clause, and example (10.37) involves VP-ellipsis. We take it that in the relative clause construction the trace cannot bear focus, and that in the VP ellipsis construction there is no way of *reconstructing* a focus in the missing VP. Under these assumptions, precisely the same arguments will apply as for (10.35). The one minor twist is that in (10.37) there is no felicitous interpretation at all. This is because there is nothing suitable to bear focus. The one possibility which we have not yet discussed in this regard is focus on *does*, but that would not yield a suitably ordered set of alternatives. If focus on *does* were understood as polarity focus, then the alternatives would be *Sandy does not salute* versus *Sandy does salute*, but neither entails the other, and, there is no other natural ordering between them. We can hypothesize that polar opposites never stand in a strength relation, although this is not essential to our argument.

What of the special cases we identified in §7.5 in which exclusives apparently do associate with moved or elided material? The relevant cases are German V2 constructions, and utterances in which *only* is highly contrastive:

(10.38)   German
          Peter | KüSSTE$_i$ | Maria nur t$_i$.
          Peter kissed   Maria only
          "Peter kissed and did nothing else to Maria" [= (7.46)]

(10.39)   A: Which store do your friends prefer to shop at?
          B: John sometimes goes to the fANcy store, and Sue ONLY does.
          [= (7.60)]

We have said nothing which precludes us from hypothesizing that both types of example involve constructions where an unrealized element (a trace, or reconstructed material in an ellipsis site) does bear focus. Perhaps German V2 movement occurs at a level above that at which association with focus is calculated, so that the movement of *küsste* ["kissed"] still leaves it within the semantic scope of the exclusive *nur* ["only"]. It could also logically be the case that the exclusive is not in the VP, but rather in a right adjoined sentence modifying position. In that case, we would expect the exclusive to associate to its left. We have made no study of the syntactic plausibility of such an analysis. Suffice it to say that examples like (10.38) could be handled in the theory, but to do so would require some extra stipulations for which, as yet, we have no motivation.

Example (10.39) is perhaps more problematic, since syntactically it is clearly not significantly different from the VP ellipsis cases we have already considered, so one would expect the same considerations to apply. There are a number of ways forward, but we suggest that what might be called for is a weakening of the principle we assumed: that reconstructed material (or its semantic equivalent) never includes focus marking (or its semantic equivalent, i.e. multiple alternatives in the focal meaning). An appropriate weakened version of the principle would be this hypothesis: the primary focus of an utterance cannot be elided, but a focus can be elided when it is in a post-nuclear position. Such a principle would not affect examples like (10.37), because the phrase *because Sandy only does*, which we would expect to form an intonational phrase, does not contain any highly prominent material. Therefore the ellipsis site would not be in post-nuclear position.

However, in Bs utterance in (10.39), the word *only* is itself made very prominent, and carries a nuclear accent. There is then nothing preventing ellipsis of the material that would otherwise follow *only*, i.e. the phrase "goes to the [fancy store]$_F$." Such ellipsis would then be regarded as a surface phenomenon, and there would be no general principle prohibiting focus in elided/reconstructed material. Again, we conclude that ellipsis cases like (10.39) could be handled in the theory, but we do not claim to have given a fully justified analysis here.

10.8 NPI Licensing

Summary: *As shown in Chapter 8, both NP and VP modifying exclusives license a wide range of Negative Polarity Items in non-focal material. We now see how the account of NPI licensing presented in Chapter 8 transfers to the more complete theory of exclusives developed in the current chapter.*

The account we gave of NPI licensing in Chapter 8 was an application of the NPI licensing theory of von Fintel (1999). This is a variant of Ladusaw's (1979) account, and says that NPIs are licensed when strengthening inferences are valid modulo the assumption that all presuppositions are satisfied. We demonstrated in Chapter 8 that strengthening inferences are valid for exclusives, there explicated in terms of a universal quantifier, provided there is at least an existential presupposition. But according to the theory developed in the current chapter, the core meaning of an exclusive is not (just) a universal quantifier: it is a superlative. So we must examine the inference patterns predicted by the new version of the account in order to see whether NPI licensing is still predicted.

First, let us consider the issue of what a speaker who utters an exclusive sentence presupposes under the current theory. As we have noted, the characteristics of this presupposition will vary according to the ordering used. In a felicitous discourse, there are strong presuppositions. In the special case where the ordering is just entailment, the prejacent proposition is presupposed. If we allow for arbitrary orderings pragmatically stronger than entailment, then the prejacent proposition will not necessarily be presupposed. But even in this case, the combination of congruence and non-triviality of the CQ (itself a presupposition of the exclusive sentence), means that we have at least an existential presupposition.

Given that we know there is at least an existential presupposition, we can now examine the relevant monotonicity inferences. We will consider the inference from (10.40b) to (10.40c). Since we have established that (10.40c) presupposes at least the existential proposition in (10.40a), it suffices to consider the argument with this premise added. It is indeed the case that (10.40c) intuitively follows from the premises in (10.40a) and (10.40b).

(10.40) a. Mary ate something at lunchtime yesterday.

b. Mary ate only cheese yesterday.

c. (So) Mary only ate cheese at lunchtime yesterday.

Rather than going through a proof that this inference pattern is valid in the formal theory we have presented, we will restrict ourselves to showing that the paraphrase in terms of superlatives does not suggest any reason to worry about this issue. The relevant variant of the argument is given in (10.41).

(10.41) a. Mary ate something at lunchtime yesterday.

b. 'Mary ate cheese' is the strongest true answer to the question of what Mary ate yesterday.

c. (So) 'Mary ate cheese' is the strongest true answer to the question of what Mary ate at lunchtime yesterday.

Again, the argument is intuitively valid, so the new version of the theory of exclusives in this chapter correctly predicts that non-focal material in an exclusive sentence occurs in a (Strawson) downward monotone position, and therefore that NPIs should be licensed in non-focal positions in an exclusive sentence.

10.9 Non-association with Presupposition

Summary: *We recap data from Chapter 8 showing apparent association with presupposition effects for quantificational adverbs but not exclusives. We show that the explanation we gave there is compatible with the discourse model of exclusives developed in §10.1–10.4.*

We already argued, in §8.8, that neither adverbs of quantification nor exclusives associate directly with presupposition. But we did argue that quantificational adverbs show a similar effect, which we termed *contextual association*. The question, then, is why exclusives do not manifest the same effect. The contrast is exhibited by the data in (10.42) and (10.43) from Chapter 8:

(10.42) Mary always managed to complete her [exams]$_F$. [= (8.68)]

a. 'Whenever Mary took exams, she completed them.'

b. ?'Whenever Mary completed something, it was invariably an exam.'

(10.43) Mary only managed to complete her [exams]$_F$. [= (8.69)]

a. *"What Mary did when taking exams was complete them and do nothing else."

b. "What Mary completed was an exam and nothing else."

The explanation we now give follows the same lines as the explanation in Chapter 8, but we tailor it to our updated account of the meaning of exclusives. Given decontextualized examples like these, the hearer must somehow make up an appropriate context.

In the case of the sentence with *always* in (10.42), the hearer assumes that some set of events must be salient in which Mary takes exams. The quantificational adverb is then restricted to range over this set of events, an effect very much like direct association with presupposition, though distinguishable when the prior context is made explicit.

In the case of the sentence with *only* in (10.43), the hearer's options are more limited. For (10.43) carries not only a presupposition of a set of events of Mary taking exams, but also a presupposition that the CQ is a set of alternatives corresponding to sentences of the form *Mary managed to complete her* α, for different choices of α. One value for α in the alternative set must be the proposition that Mary completed her exams, all the other alternatives must be at least this strong, and there must be at least one other alternative. Furthermore, the restrictor of *only* is constrained to be identical to this alternative set. The presuppositions of the exclusive and the focus structure of (10.43) combine to place such narrow limits on the range of variation of the restrictor that the presupposition has no discernable effect.

More generally, we would expect contextual association to affect the restrictor of an exclusive, but the restrictor is typically so constrained that there is only a limited amount that further constraints can do. We predict that for an exclusive, contextual association will never override the effects of focus, and thus that for exclusives we should never even get the appearance of association with presupposition.

10.10 Summary

Rooth (1992) presented a classic theory of focus sensitivity. He assumed a certain, not unreasonable meaning for *only*. But we are struck by the fact that, while he placed constraints on the extent to which that meaning could access focus, nothing in his theory of focus motivates the particular combination of at-issue meaning and presupposition that *only* is given. The same could be said for every single theory of focus sensitivity that we have cited in this book.

On the other hand, to take one classic example, Horn (1996) motivates an interesting account of the inferences associated with *only*. But this theory of the inferential properties of *only* gives the reader no clue as to why *only* is focus sensitive. The same goes for the entire vast literature on the inferential properties of exclusives that we surveyed in Chapter 9: certainly these theories are compatible with exclusives being sensitive to focus, but then they are equally compatible with exclusives being sensitive to phases of the moon.

What is missing from all these prior theories is an account of discourse function. It is because of the discourse function of exclusives that they manifest focus sensitivity, and it is in terms of the discourse function of exclusives that we can understand the inference patterns which exclusives yield. The discourse function of an exclusive sentence is to reduce expectations as regards the strongest true answer to the CQ. Typically, the speaker thinks the prejacent is the strongest true answer but takes the hearer to expect something stronger. So the speaker presupposes that an answer at least as strong as the prejacent is true, and asserts that, *contra* expectation, nothing stronger holds.

In terms of this account, we can understand:

1   why the prejacent follows from simple exclusive sentences;
2   why the prejacent is suspendable but not cancelable in such cases;
3   why the prejacent typically follows from negated exclusive sentences;
4   why the prejacent in this case is cancelable but not suspendable;
5   why an exclusive sentence can be used to inform a hearer that the prejacent is an answer to an explicit *wh*-question;
6   why when a non-entailment ordering is salient the prejacent does not necessarily follow from a negated exclusive;
7   why exclusives are focus sensitive;
8   why the focus sensitivity of exclusives is more sensitive to syntactic manipulation than is the case for the superficially similar focus sensitivity of quantificational adverbs;
9   why exclusives license NPIs in non-focal material;
10 why exclusives, unlike quantificational adverbs, do not manifest contextual association effects where it appears that focus is trumped by presupposition.

So that makes ten *whys* for which we have given *becauses*. But where does it leave us in terms of a general theory of focus sensitivity?

Chapter 11

Conclusion

Particle is thus something of an 'escape (or cop-out) category' for grammarians. 'If it's small and you don't know what to call it, call it a particle.' seems to be the practice; and a very useful practice it is, too . . .

Hurford (1994: 153)

11.1 The Story so Far

Way back when, in the first chapter of this book, we introduced the phenomenon of focus sensitivity, and wondered whether absolutely anything could be focus sensitive, or whether there were limits. And we wondered just what mechanism or mechanisms make any expression sensitive to focus. It was in Chapter 2 that we introduced the following version of the debate on focus sensitivity:

(11.1) Is focus sensitivity

    a. lexically encoded as part of the meaning of expressions which have been identified as focus sensitive?, *or*

    b. an epiphenomenon resulting from independent pragmatic forces which make sure presuppositions are satisfied and texts are coherent?

And then we gave our answer: yes. Focus sensitivity is either lexically encoded or a pragmatically driven epiphenomenon, depending on which focus sensitive expression you consider.

Based on this conclusion, we developed a model, the QFC model, that divides focus sensitive expressions into three classes, laid out in Chapter 3. In Chapter 4, we checked that the formal underpinnings of the model (Alternative Semantics) were in good shape, i.e. that the account could be slotted into a compositional theory of interpretation, and that purported counter-examples to this theory would not cause problems. Then, in Chapter 5, we took a look at data motivating purely pragmatic models, and considered how such models might work. We found that the models we considered were not yet able to explain focus sensitivity adequately without any stipulation of conventional dependency on focus. This means that the QFC theory could be motivated on practical grounds, if no other. But as it happens, there are other grounds.

Plunging into the data, in Chapter 6, we first debunked the best known argument that exclusives are not conventionally focus sensitive (from second occurrence focus effects). The argument was based on experimental evidence from English reported by Beaver et al. (2007), supporting earlier observations of Rooth (1996b), and recently extended to German by Ishihara and Féry (2006).

We then presented, in Chapters 6–8, plenty of positive evidence that exclusives are conventionally focus sensitive. Data drawn from a range of Germanic and Romance languages showed (i) that exclusives do not associate with leaners and other phonologically dependent material, (ii) that the focus sensitivity of exclusives is sensitive to syntactic manipulations like extraction and ellipsis, and (iii) that semantic and pragmatic effects involving monotonicity and presupposition show that there is a conventionalized link between non-focal material and the restrictor argument of exclusives.

We also found that for all these phenomena, the results as regards quantificational adverbs went in precisely the opposite direction to those for exclusives. Thus, despite there being some superficial semantic similarity between exclusives and quantificational adverbs, only the former are conventionally focus sensitive.

If quantificational adverbs do not have any conventionalized lexical dependency on focus, what do they have? What explains their interactions with focus? What quantificational adverbs have is an argument position that can be filled in by a salient set of occurrences such that quantification is over the given set. This argument is filled in by anaphoric resolution to some previously mentioned set of occurrences, or to some set that is salient, even if not yet made explicit. This resolution process identifies sets of occurrences such that coherence of the discourse is maximized, and in order to maximize coherence both information structure and presupposition must be respected.

There is a good reason why we put such a great effort into the analysis of exclusives in Chapters 9 and 10, and comparatively little effort into the analysis of quantificational adverbs. We feel that prior analyses of quantificational adverbs (e.g. von Fintel 1994) are on the right track, but that prior analyses of exclusives have been barking up the wrong tree. In particular, prior analyses have barked up a semantic tree, concentrating on analysis of truth conditions, when they should have barked up a pragmatic tree, concentrating on analysis of discourse function.

Quantificational adverbs are used to describe certain rather abstract properties that may hold of the world: they quantify how many of one type of occurrence may also be classified as being of another type. But the primary function of exclusives is not to say that a certain property holds of the world external to the discourse, it is to say that a certain property holds of the discourse itself.

Specifically, an exclusive comments on the Current Question, stating that some partial answer is all there is to say. The focus dependency of exclusives results from the fact that their meaning directly concerns the Current Question, and focus structure, as argued by Roberts (1996), must be congruent to the Current Question. We argued that this perspective leads to an integrated understanding of both the focus sensitivity of exclusives and the exceedingly complex inference patterns which have shrouded exclusives in semantic mystery for literally centuries.

And here let us point out a moral of our story: the division between semantics and pragmatics (if it can be made at all) is orthogonal to the division between conventionalized and non-conventionalized meaning. The conventionalized lexical meaning of exclusives includes both a descriptive component, which helps speakers say what the world outside the conversation is like, and a discourse component, which comments on the role of a certain proposition in the conversation. Thus focus sensitivity crucially involves conventionalized pragmatics.

But haven't we known about conventionalized pragmatics since the first days of pragmatics, from Grice's (1975) notion of conventional implicature, and Austin's (1976) account of speech act verbs? Well, yes. And yet semanticists and philosophers have worked on the meaning of exclusives for many years without managing to say anything substantive about its discourse function. Maybe that's because pragmatics is hard.

11.2   What Isn't (Conventionally) Focus Sensitive?

We wanted to know if absolutely any expression could be focus sensitive, and what mechanisms cause expressions to manifest focus sensitivity. But we devoted almost all our efforts to just two classes of expression, and our plate was quite full just with these two classes. Let us move back to the bigger picture we painted in Chapter 3.

Recall Rooth's (1996a) *tolf*, introduced in Chapter 2. Sentences of the form X *tolfed* ϕ mean 'X told the focus (or foci) of ϕ that ϕ'. Rooth gave the paradigm in (2.46), repeated below:

(2.46) a.   I tolfed [that [he]$_F$ resembles her] $\equiv$ I told him that he resembles her.

b.   I tolfed [that he resembles [her]$_F$] $\equiv$ I told her that he resembles her.

c.   I tolfed [that [he]$_F$ resembles [her]$_F$] $\equiv$ I told him and her that he resembles her.

Where would *tolf* fit into the QFC taxonomy of focus sensitivity? Well, its hypothetical focus sensitivity could not result merely from quasi-association, because that would not explain how an argument (the addressee of the telling) comes to be bound. It seems more plausible that such an expression might involve free association with focus. But no, as described, *tolf* doesn't fit the bill for a freely associating expression either.

Based on the examples we have seen so far, missing arguments in the interpretation of free association expressions tend to be filled in with topical material. In the case of *tolf*, the apparently missing argument is an individual, and the hypothetical data in (2.46) suggests that this individual is actually realized as a focused NP in the utterance. The focus is the very last thing you would expect to fill in an argument position in an expression which manifests free association with focus. That leaves only the class of conventionally sensitive items. But there is no way *tolf* fits there, for, by hypothesis, this is a class reserved for expressions which primarily have a discourse function. *Tolf* is just a verb of saying: no evidence of a discourse function has as yet been reported by Rooth, the one native speaker of the *tolf* language.

We have to conclude that *tolf* fits nowhere in our taxonomy. And this, in turn, suggests that maybe we are headed in the right direction. For while our proposal might seem quite profligate in allowing not merely one, but three different mechanisms to produce focus sensitivity, it is nevertheless the case that our account is restrictive. Not just any word can join the focus sensitive club, and *tolf*, in particular, is barred for life.

11.3   Generalizations from the QFC Model

In Chapter 3, we classified dozens of expression types according to a taxonomy suggested by the QFC model. But at the time we justified our classifications on the basis of what we took to be the meaning and function of those expression types, not on the basis of diagnostic tests. We developed a battery of potential tests in Chapters 6–8, though only for the distinction between free focus and conventional focus, and in many cases specific to the pair of expression types (quantificational adverbs and exclusives) being studied.

If a researcher plans to apply these diagnostics more widely, what can he or she expect? Without going into detail, we observe that the picture is mixed: some of our diagnostics apply more widely, and others do not. Thus, on the positive side, we find that phonological reduction fairly reliably differentiates between conventional association with focus and quasi/free association (§6.6), although setting up appropriate examples is, in our experience, a delicate business.

More negatively, extraction effects do not appear to be a reliable diagnostic outside of the exclusives/quantificational adverbs contrast, perhaps for the reasons discussed in §10.6. The monotonicity effects discussed in Chapter 8 are specific to the contrast between quantificational expressions and exclusives, and should not be expected to justify other aspects of the taxonomy. But the presupposition effects discussed in the same chapter are very general: presuppositions never appear to restrict conventionally sensitive expressions, but any expression which manifests quasi-association or free association with focus will also behave as if exhibiting quasi-association or free association with presupposition, respectively.

Overall, we are optimistic that a battery of diagnostic tests can be developed which facilitate classification of focus sensitivity effects across the full range of relevant expression types, and which could be used to justify a taxonomy like the one we presented. But in the absence of such a battery of tests, the classification must stand or fall according to how plausible our analysis is of the meaning and function of individual expressions. Let us suppose that our taxonomy is completely correct. What generalizations would follow?

First, we observe that conventionally sensitive expressions are typically cross-categorial. In contrast, quasi-associating and free associating expressions usually have a more restricted distribution than conventionally associating expressions. If a free associating expression occurs as a VP or S modifier, then usually it cannot occur as an NP modifier or NP internally, and *vice versa*. But conventionally associating expressions can often occur as both VP and NP modifiers, and in many cases can occur in other positions too.

Second, expressions that associate with focus conventionally are typically superfluous and optional. That is, the meaning or discourse function of a sentence with such an expression is always a possible interpretation of the same sentence without the expression, although without the expression the interpretation is not forced. Thus exhaustivity can be achieved (as an implicature) without using an exclusive, the *so what?* effect that *even* often conveys can be achieved without a scalar additive, and intensity can be achieved without using an intensive.[1]

Third, and related to the second point, the meaning added by a conventionally sensitive expression can often be conveyed in English by a particular intonational contour. For example, exhaustification typically corresponds to a sharp pitch rise and fall (H*LL%), the meaning of a scalar additive may be conveyed by lengthening a syllable and putting a steady rise on it followed by falling and rising boundary tones (L+H*LH% approximates this), and the effect of intensives may be achieved by using a short sharp rising attack to the stressed syllable (again, perhaps notated as L+H*, but this doesn't capture the sharpness of the pitch rise and the increased pitch range). When using a conventionally sensitive expression, the same intonational contours are natural, but not required – a simple pitch rise on the focused item will suffice.

Fourth, conventionalized association with focus emerges in a late stage of grammaticalization. We do not spontaneously innovate conventionally focus sensitive expressions, which is yet another reason that Rooth's *tolf* is implausible. As Traugott (2006) observes, focus sensitive expressions such as exclusives, scalar additives, and intensives are SUBJECTIVE "in the sense that they involve the speaker's assessment and evaluation of intensity, position on a scale, ordering of alternatives, etc."

---

[1]   But note a possible exception: as discussed by Beaver and Zeevat (2007), non-scalar additives are often close to being compulsory, perhaps because they disambiguate discourse function, marking that an utterance is intended as an elaboration rather than a correction.

In general, expressions that have a conventionally encoded dependency on focus derive from expressions that have a more concrete or objectively definable meaning. As we discussed in Chapter 3, *only* is derived from an expression referring to the number one. Traugott (2006) provides evidence that the history of the scalar additive *even* follows the pathway MANNER ADVERB (meaning 'evenly', 'smoothly') > *particularizer* > *scalar additive*. The history of both *only* and *even* exemplify the process of SUBJECTIFICATION, where meanings become increasingly based on the speaker's belief state or attitude over time (Traugott 1989).[2]

The line of inquiry on which we have embarked may justify a generalization that is implicit in the above discussion as well as in standard terminology. When we began researching focus sensitivity, we were struck by the difficulty of finding a suitable label for the linguistic objects of our study. The term *focus sensitive particle* did not seem to be apt in the light of observations of Partee, Rooth, and others that effects of focus were apparently not restricted to a single grammatical category of expression, even a category as peculiar and heterogeneous as 'particles.' Quantificational adverbs, generics, counterfactual conditionals, emotive factives, and who knows how many other constructions were subject to interpretational effects comparable to those observed with respect to the canonical examples of focus sensitive particles, *only* and *even*.

In much of our previous work, and in this book too, we have attempted to finesse this issue, for example by referring to *focus sensitive expressions*, *focus sensitive constructions*, or *focus sensitive operators*. But what is now becoming clear is that the expression *focus sensitive particle* is highly apt, since expressions which conventionally associate with focus are all just that.

11.4 Closing Remarks

You have followed us on a long trek. We started by setting up the questions of what expression types can be focus sensitive and what mechanisms allow the sense of a sentence to be changed by focus. Have we given you answers? Well, at least partial answers. Take one look at the work it took us (in Chapters 9 and 10) to give something approaching a complete answer for just one class of focus sensitive expressions, and it will be obvious that there is much left to do. At this point we think we can see, in the form of the taxonomy in Section 3.5, Table 3.1,

---

[2] Another cross-linguistically common path in semantic change is the development of adverbs into sentence connectives, e.g. English *but*. Our theory of exclusives suggests an explanation for the development of *but* as an adversative coordinator from its older exclusive use in the history of English. As an exclusive (e.g. *He is but a child*), *but* says that the sentence it modifies departs from expectations relative to the Current Question. As a connective (*Kim liked the dessert but I didn't*), *but* says that the sentence it modifies departs from expectations relative to issues raised by the previous sentence. The story of this development is fractured, but the distance between the earlier meaning of *but* and its current meaning is bridgeable in the context of our theory of exclusives.

something like the promised land. But we don't know for sure if this is Mount Nebo, and you're probably skeptical about all that milk and honey.

One thing is for sure, we won't end the journey without a lot of help. We hope that our work will provide a leg-up for those who wish to study a wider range of focus sensitive expressions, but we must end on a salutory note: as the discussion of exclusives should have made clear, understanding the focus sensitivity of an expression requires as a prerequisite an understanding of the meaning and function of that expression.

Yet, as we pointed out in Chapter 3, many of the phenomena and expression types that we suggest are conventionally dependent on focus are not well understood (*downtoners, intensifiers*), or, like exclusives, are already the source of controversy (e.g. scalar additives like *even*). So justifying our taxonomy, or (surely more likely!) improving on it, will be the work of many years. And when one looks beyond the cluster of Germanic and Romance languages that we have concentrated on, it becomes apparent that the study of focus sensitivity must be a work not just of many years, but of many linguists. Please let us know how you get on!

Bibliography

Aijmer, Karin. 2002. *English Discourse Particles: Evidence from a Corpus*. Studies in Corpus Linguistics. Amsterdam/Philadelphia: John Benjamins.

Aloni, Maria. 2000. Quantification under Conceptual Covers. Amsterdam: University of Amsterdam dissertation.

Altham, James E. J., and Neil W. Tennant. 1975. Sortal Quantification. In *Formal Semantics of Natural Language*, ed. Edward L. Keenan, 46–58. Cambridge: Cambridge University Press.

Anderson, Stephen R. 1972. How to Get *Even*. *Language* 48, 893–906.

Aoun, Joseph, and Yen-Hui Audrey Li. 1993. *Wh*-elements in Situ: Syntax or LF? *Linguistic Inquiry* 24, 199–238.

Aristotle. 350 BC. *On Sense and the Sensible*. Translated by J. I. Beare. (Available on The Internet Classics Archive.)

Arnold, Jennifer. 1998. Reference Form and Discourse Patterns. Stanford University dissertation.

Asher, Nicholas. 2000. Truth Conditional Discourse Semantics for Parentheticals. *Journal of Semantics* 17, 31–50.

—— and Alex Lascarides. 1998. The Semantics and Pragmatics of Presupposition. *Journal of Semantics* 15, 239–300.

—— and —— 2003. *Logics of Conversation*. Cambridge University Press.

Atlas, Jay David. 1991. Topic/Comment, Presupposition, Logical Form and Focus Stress Implicatures: The Case of Focal Particles *only* and *also*. *Journal of Semantics* 8, 127–47.

—— 1993. The Importance of Being "Only": Testing the Neo-Gricean Versus Neo-entailment Paradigms. *Journal of Semantics* 10, 301–18.

—— 1996. "Only" Noun Phrases, Pseudo-Negative Generalized Quantifiers, Negative Polarity Items, and Monotonicity. *Journal of Semantics* 13, 265–328.

—— 2002. Negative Polarity Items and Overcoming Assertoric Inertia. A lecture given in the University of Groningen, The Netherlands, May 8 2002, ms.

Austen, Jane. 1811. *Sense and Sensibility: A Novel.* London: T. Egerton.

Austin, John L. 1962. *Sense and Sensibilia.* (G. J. Warnock, ed.). Oxford: Oxford University Press.

—— 1976. *How to do Things with Words.* Oxford: Oxford University Press.

Bach, Emmon. 1981. On Time, Tense, and Aspect: An Essay in English Metaphysics. In *Radical Pragmatics*, ed. Peter Cole, 62–81. New York: Academic Press.

—— 1986. The Algebra of Events. *Linguistics and Philosophy* 9, 5–16.

Barbiers, Sjef. 1995. *The Syntax of Interpretation*. The Hague: Holland Academic Graphics.

Barker, Stephen. 1991. Even, Still and Counterfactuals. *Linguistics and Philosophy* 14, 1–38.

Bartels, Christine. 1997. Acoustic Correlates of 'Second Occurrence' Focus: Towards an Experimental Investigation. In *Context-Dependence in the Analysis of Linguistic Meaning* (Proceedings of the workshops in Prague and Bad Teinach), ed. Hans Kamp and Barbara Partee, 11–30, University of Stuttgart. Institut fuer maschinelle Sprachverarbeitung.

Barwise, Jon, and Robin Cooper. 1981. Generalized Quantifiers and Natural Language. *Linguistics and Philosophy* 4, 159–219.

Bayer, Josef. 1999. Bound Focus or How can Association with Focus be Achieved without Going Semantically Astray. In *The Grammar of Focus*, ed. Georges Rebuschi and Laurice Tuller, 55–82. Amsterdam: John Benjamins.

Beaver, David. 1997. Presupposition. In *Handbook of Logic and Language*, ed. Johan van Benthem and Alice ter Meulen. Cambridge, MA: MIT Press.

—— 2001. *Presupposition and Assertion in Dynamic Semantics*. Stanford, CA: CSLI Publications.

—— 2004. Five 'only' Pieces. *Theoretical Linguistics* 30, 45–64.

—— 2005. Accommodating Topics. In *Context Dependence in the Analysis of Linguistic Meaning*, ed. Hans Kamp and Barbara Partee, 79–90. Amsterdam: Elsevier.

—— and Brady Clark. 2002a. Monotonicity and Focus Sensitivity. In *SALT XII: Proceedings from Semantics and Linguistic Theory XII*, ed. Brendan Jackson. Ithaca, NY: CLC Publications.

—— and Brady Clark. 2002b. The Proper Treatments of Focus Sensitivity. In *Proceedings of WCCFL XXI*, ed. Christopher Potts and Line Mikkelsen, 15–28, Somerville, MA: Cascadilla Press.

—— and Brady Clark. 2003. *Always* and *Only*: Why not all Focus Sensitive Operators are Alike. *Natural Language Semantics* 11, 323–62.

—— Brady Clark, Edward Flemming, T. Florian Jaeger, and Maria Wolters. 2007. When Semantics meets Phonetics: Acoustical Studies of Second Occurrence Focus. *Language* 83.

—— and Emiel Krahmer. 2001. A Partial Account of Presupposition Projection. *Journal of Logic, Language, and Information* 10, 147–82.

—— and Henk Zeevat. 2007. Accommodation. In *The Oxford Handbook of Linguistic Interfaces*, ed. G. Ramchand and C. Reiss. Oxford University Press, 502–38.

Beckman, Mary, and Janet B. Pierrehumbert. 1986. Intonational Structure in Japanese and English. *Phonology Yearbook* 3, 15–70.

Bennett, Michael. 1980. Review article. *Journal of Philosophical Logic* 9, 103–32.

Berman, Stephen. 1991. On the Semantics and Logical Form of wh-clauses. University of Massachusetts at Amherst dissertation.

Bernardi, Raffaella. 2002. Reasoning with Polarity in Categorial Type Logic. University of Utrecht dissertation.

Bolinger, Dwight. 1972a. Accent is Predictable (if you're a Mind-reader). *Language* 48, 633–44.

—— 1972b. *Degree Words*. The Hague and Paris: Mouton.

Bonomi, Andrea, and Paolo Casalegno. 1993. Only: Association with Focus in Event Semantics. *Natural Language Semantics* 2, 1–45.

Bowers, John. 1969. Surface Structure Interpretation in English Superlatives. MIT, ms.

Brenier, Jason, Ani Nenkova, Anubha Kothari, Laura Whitton, David Beaver, and Dan Jurafsky. 2006. The (Non)utility of Linguistic Features for Predicting Prominence in Spontaneous Speech. In Proceedings of the IEEE/ACL 2006 Workshop on Spoken Language Technology.

Bresnan, Joan. 1971. Sentence Stress and Syntactic Transformations. *Language* 47, 257–80.

Brody, Michael. 1990. Some remarks on the Focus Field in Hungarian. *UCL Working Papers in Linguistics* 2, 201–25.

Büring, Daniel. 1996. A Weak Theory of Strong Readings. In *Proceedings of Semantics and Linguistic Theory (SALT) 6*, ed. Teresa Galloway and Justin Spence, 17–34, Ithaca, NY: CLC Publications.

—— 1997. *The Meaning of Topic and Focus: The 59th Street Bridge Accent*. London: Routledge.

—— 1999. Topic. In *Focus – Linguistic, Cognitive, and Computational Perspectives*, ed. Peter Bosch and Rob van der Sandt, 142–65. Cambridge University Press.

—— 2003. On D-Trees, Beans, and B-Accents. *Linguistics and Philosophy* 26, 511–45.

—— 2005. *Binding Theory*. Cambridge: Cambridge University Press.

—— 2006a. Focus Projection and Default Prominence. In *The Architecture of Focus*, ed. Valéria Molnár and Susanne Winkler, 321–46. Berlin: Mouton De Gruyter.

—— 2006b. Towards a Typology of Focus Realization UCLA, ms.

—— and Katharina Hartmann. 2001. The Syntax and Semantics of Focus-Sensitive Particles in German. *Natural Language and Linguistic Theory* 19, 229–81.

Calcagno, Mike. 1996. Presupposition, Congruence, and Adverbs of Quantification. In *OSU Working Papers in Linguistics* vol. 49, papers in semantics, ed. Jae-Hak Toon and Andreas Kathol, 1–23. The Ohio State University.

Carlson, Gregory, and Francis Pelletier (eds.) 1995. *The Generic Book*. University of Chicago Press.

Carlson, Lauri W. 1985. *Dialogue Games: An Approach to Discourse Analysis*. Dordrecht: Kluwer Academic Publishers.

Chafe, Wallace L. 1994. *Discourse, Consciousness and Time*. University of Chicago Press.

Chierchia, Gennaro A. 1998. Reference to Kinds Across Languages. *Natural Language Semantics* 6, 339–405.

—— and Ray A. Turner. 1988. Semantics and Property Theory. *Linguistics and Philosophy* 11, 261–302.

Chomsky, Noam. 1972. *Studies on Semantics in Generative Grammar*, chapter Deep Structure, Surface Structure, and Semantic Interpretation, 62–119. The Hague: Mouton.

—— 1977. Conditions on Rules of Grammar. In *Essays on Form and Interpretation*, 163–210. Amsterdam: North-Holland.

—— 2000. *Step by Step: Essays on Minimalist Syntax in Honor of Howard Lasnik*, chapter Minimalist Inquiries: The Framework, 89–155. MIT Press.

—— and Morris Halle. 1968. *The Sound Pattern of English*. New York: Harper and Row.

Clark, Herbert H. 1996. *Using Language*. Cambridge University Press.

Cohan, Jocelyn. 2000. The Realization and Function of Focus in Spoken English. University of Texas at Austin dissertation.

Cohen, Ariel. 1999. How are Alternatives Computed? *Journal of Semantics* 16, 43–65.

—— 2001. Relative Readings of Many, Often, and Generics. *Natural Language Semantics* 9, 41–67.

Cooper, Robin, Elisabet Engdahl, Staffan Larsson, and Stina Ericsson. 2000. Accommodating Questions and the Nature of QUD. In Proceedings of Gotalog, 57–62.

Davidson, Donald. 1967. The Logical Form of Action Sentences. In *The Logic of Decision and Action*, ed. N. Rescher, 81–95. Pittsburgh University Press.

DeLancey, Scott. 1997. Mirativity: The Grammatical Marking of Unexpected Information. *Linguistic Typology* 1, 33–52.

Diesing, Molly. 1992. *Indefinites*. Cambridge, MA: MIT Press.

Dretske, Fred I. 1972. Contrastive Statements. *Philosophical Review* 81, 411–37.

Drubig, Hans B. 1994. Island Constraints and the Syntactic Nature of Focus and Association with Focus. Arbeitspapiere des Sonderforschungsbereichs 340: Sprachtheoretische Grundlagen der Computerlinguistik 51.

—— 2000. Toward a Typology of Focus and Focus Constructions. University of Tübingen, ms. Version later appeared in *Linguistics*, 41:1, 1–50, 2003.

Dryer, Matthew S. 1994. The Pragmatics of Association with *only*. Paper presented at the 1994 Winter Meeting of the L.S.A. Boston, Massachusetts, ms.

Eckardt, Regine. 1999. Focus with Nominal Quantifiers. In *Focus: Linguistic, Cognitive, and Computational Perspectives*, ed. Peter Bosch and Rob van der Sandt, 166–86. Cambridge University Press.

Faller, Martina. 2002. Semantics and Pragmatics of Evidentials in Cuzco Quechua. Stanford University dissertation.

Fauconnier, Gilles. 1975. Polarity and the Scale Principle. In *Chicago Linguistics Society* 11, 188–99.

Fernando, Tim, and Hans Kamp. 1996. Expecting Many. Proceedings of the Sixth Conference on Semantics and Linguistic Theory 53–68.

Féry, Caroline, and Vieri Samek-Lodovici. 2006. Focus Projection and Prosodic Prominence in Nested Foci. *Language* 82, 131–50.

von Fintel, Kai. 1994. Restrictions on Quantifier Domains. University of Massachusetts at Amherst dissertation.

—— 1995. A Minimal Theory of Adverbial Quantification. In *Context Dependence in the Analysis of Linguistic Meaning*: Proceeding of the Workshops in Prague, February 1995, Bad Teinach, ed. Barbara Partee and Hans Kamp, 153–93.

—— 1997. Bare Plurals, Bare Conditionals, and *Only. Journal of Semantics* 14, 1–56.

—— 1999. NPI Licensing, Strawson Entailment. *Journal of Semantics* 16, 97–148.

Fischer, Susan, 1968. On Cleft Sentences and Contrastive Stress. Cambridge, MA: MIT Press.

Foolen, Ad. 1993. De Betekenis van Partikels. Een Dokumentatie van de Stand van het Onderzoek met Bijzondere Aandacht voor 'Maar'. [The Meaning of Particles: A Compendium of the State of the Art with Special Attention to the Meaning of 'maar' ("but").] Katholieke Universiteit van Nijmegen dissertation.

Frege, Gottlob. 1884. *Die Grundlagen der Arithmetik: Eine logisch mathematische Untersuchung über den Begriff der Zahl*. [*The Foundations of Arithmetic: A Logico-mathematical Enquiry into the Concept of Number*.] W. Koebner.

Fry, John, and Stefan Kaufmann. 1998. Information Packaging in Japanese. In *Proceedings of the Joint Conference on Formal Grammar, Head-Driven Phrase Structure Grammar, and Categorial Grammar*, ed. Gosse Bouma, Geert-Jan Kruijff, and Richard Oehrle, 55–65, Saarbrücken, Germany.

Gajewski, Jon. 2002. *L-analyticity in Natural Language*. Cambridge, MA: MIT, ms.

—— 2005. *Only John* vs. *Nobody but John*: A Solution. Poster presented at *Polarity From Different Perspectives* workshop, March 11–13, 2005, NYU, ms.

Gardent, Claire. 1991. Gapping and VP Ellipsis in a Unification-based Grammar. University of Edinburgh dissertation.

Gawron, Mark. 1992. Focus and Ellipsis in Comparatives and Superlatives: A Case Study. In *Proceedings of SALT 2*, ed. Chris Barker and David Dowty, 79–98, Columbus. Ohio State University Department of Linguistics.

—— 1995. Comparatives, Superlatives, and Resolution. *Linguistics and Philosophy* 18, 333–80.

Gazdar, Gerald. 1979. *Pragmatics: Implicature, Presupposition and Logical Form*. New York: Academic Press.

Geach, Peter T. 1972. *Logic Matters*. University of California Press.

German, James, Janet B. Pierrehumbert, and Stefan Kaufmann. 2006. Evidence for Phonological Constraints on Nuclear Accent Placement. *Language* 82, 151–68.

Geurts, Bart, and David Beaver. 2007. Discourse Representation Theory. In *The Stanford Encyclopedia of Philosophy*, ed. Edward N. Zalta. CSLI, Stanford University.

—— and Rob van der Sandt. 1997. Presuppositions and Backgrounds. In *Proceedings of the Eleventh Amsterdam Colloquium*, ed. Paul Dekker and Martin Stokhof, 37–42. ILLC/University of Amsterdam.

—— and —— 1999. Domain Restriction. In *Focus: Linguistic, Cognitive, and Computational Perspectives*, ed. Peter Bosch and Rob van der Sandt, 268–92. Cambridge University Press.

—— and —— 2004. Interpreting Focus. *Theoretical Linguistics* 30, 1–44.

Giannakidou, Anastasia. 1998. Polarity Sensitivity as (Non)veridical Dependency. Amsterdam/Philadelphia: Linguistik Aktuell (*Linguistics Today*), John Benjamins.

—— 1999. Affective Dependencies. *Linguistics and Philosophy* 22, 367–421.

—— 2003. Polarity and the Presuppositions of EVEN. University of Chicago, ms.

—— 2005. The Landscape of EVEN Items. Workshop on Polarity from Different Perspectives, NYU.

—— 2006. *Only*, Emotive Factives, and the Dual Nature of Polarity Dependency. *Language* 82.

Ginzburg, Jonathan. 1995a. Resolving Questions, I. *Linguistics and Philosophy* 18, 459–527.

—— 1995b. Resolving Questions, II. *Linguistics and Philosophy* 18, 567–609.

—— and Ivan A. Sag. 2000. Interrogative Investigations. Stanford, CA: CSLI Publications.

Grice, Herbert Paul. 1975. Logic and Conversation. In *Syntax and Semantics*: Vol. 3: *Speech Acts*, ed. P. Cole and J. L. Morgan, 41–58. San Diego, CA: Academic Press.

—— 1989. Further Notes on Logic and Conversation. In *Studies in the Way of Words*, 41–57. Cambridge, MA: Harvard University Press.

Groenendijk, Jeroen. 1999. The Logic of Interrogation. Proceedings of SALT IX 109–26.

—— and Martin Stokhof. 1984. Studies on the Semantics of Questions and the Pragmatics of Answers. University of Amsterdam dissertation.

—— and —— 1991. Dynamic Predicate Logic. *Linguistics and Philosophy* 14, 39–100.

Gussenhoven, Carlos. 1983. Focus, Mode and Nucleus. *Journal of Linguistics* 19, 377–417.

Gussenhoven, Carlos. 1992. Sentence Accents and Argument Structure. In *Thematic Structure: Its Role in Grammar*, ed. Iggy M. Roca, 79–105. Berlin: Foris.

—— 1999. On the Limits of Focus Projection in English. In *Focus: Linguistic, Cognitive, and Computational Perspectives*, ed. Peter Bosch and Rob van der Sandt, 43–55. Cambridge: Cambridge University Press.

Hajičová, Eva, Barbara H. Partee, and Petr Sgall. 1998. *Topic-focus Articulation, Tripartite Structures, and Semantic Content*. Dordrecht: Kluwer Academic Publishers.

Halliday, Michael Alexander K. 1967. Notes on Transitivity and Theme in English (part 2). *Journal of Linguistics* 3, 199–244.

—— 1970. A Course in Spoken English: Intonation. Oxford University Press.

Hamblin, Charles L. 1971. Mathematical Models of Dialogue. *Theoria* 37, 130–55.

—— 1973. Questions in Montague English. *Foundations of Language* 10, 41–53.

't Hart, Johan, and Rene Collier. 1975. Integrating Different Levels of Intonation Analysis. *Journal of Phonetics* 235–55.

Hausser, Roland. 1983. The Syntax and Semantics of English Mood. Questions and Answers, Dordrecht: Reidel.

Hedberg, Nancy. 2003. The Prosody of Contrastive Topic and Focus in Spoken English. In Pre-proceedings of the Workshop on Information Structure in Context, Stuttgart University, November 15–16, 141–52.

—— and Juan M. Sosa. 2001. The Prosodic Structure of Topic and Focus in Spontaneous English Dialogue. In Topic and Focus: A Workship on Intonation and Meaning. University of California, Santa Barbara, Linguistic Society of America, Institute of Linguistics.

—— and —— 2002. The Prosody of Questions in Natural Discourse. In Proceedings of Speech Prosody 2002 (the First International Conference on Speech Prosody), 375–78, Aix-en-Provence, France.

—— and —— 2003. Pitch Contours in Negative Sentences. Poster presented at the 15th International Congress of Phonetic Sciences, Barcelona, ms.

Heim, Irene. 1982. The Semantics of Definite and Indefinite Noun Phrases. University of Massachusetts at Amherst dissertation.

—— 1985. Notes on Comparatives and Related Matters. University of Texas, Austin, ms.

—— 1992. Presupposition Projection and the Semantics of Attitude Verbs. *Journal of Semantics* 9, 183–221.

—— 1999. Notes on Superlatives. MIT, ms.

—— and Angelika Kratzer. 1998. Semantics in Generative Grammar. Malden, MA: Blackwell Publishers.

Hendriks, Herman. 2002. Links without Locations. Information Packaging: from Cards to Boxes. *Linguistische Berichte Sonderheft* 10.

Hendriks, Petra, and Helen de Hoop. 2001. Optimality Theoretic Semantics. *Linguistics and Philosophy* 24, 1–32.

Herburger, Elena. 1997. Focus and Weak Noun Phrases. *Natural Language Semantics* 5, 53–78.

—— 2000. *What Counts: Focus and Quantification*. Cambridge, MA: MIT Press.

—— 2003. A Note on Spanish ni siquiera, even, and the Analysis of NPIs. *Probus* 15, 237–56.

Higginbotham, James. 1993. Interrogatives. In *The view from Building 20: Essays in Honor of Sylvain Bromberger*, ed. K. Hale and S. J. Keyser, 195–227. Cambridge, MA: MIT Press.

—— 1996. The Semantics of Questions. In S. Lappin (ed.), *The Handbook of Contemporary Semantic Theory*. Oxford: Blackwell, 361–83.

Hirschberg, Julia. 1991. *A Theory of Scalar Implicature*. New York: Garland.

—— 1993. Pitch Accent in Context: Predicting Intonational Prominence from Text. *Artificial Intelligence* 63, 305–40.

Hoeksema, Jack, and Frans Zwarts. 1991. Some Remarks on Focus Adverbs. *Journal of Semantics* 8, 51–70.

Horn, Laurence R. 1969. A Presuppositional Analysis of *only* and *even*. In Papers from the Fifth Regional Meeting of the Chicago Linguistics Society, 98–107.

—— 1970. Ain't It Hard (Anymore). In CLS 6, 318–27.

—— 1972/1976. On the Semantic Properties of Logical Operators in English. Indiana University Linguistics Club.

—— 1984. Toward a New Taxonomy for Pragmatic Inference: Q-based and R-based Implicature. In *Meaning, Form, and Use in Context*, ed. Deborah Schiffrin. Washington, DC: Georgetown University Press.

—— 1992. The Said and the Unsaid. In *Proceedings of the Second Conference on Semantics and Linguistic Theory*, ed. Chris Barker and David Dowty, 163–92, Columbus, OH: Ohio State University.

—— 1996. Exclusive Company: *Only* and the Dynamics of Vertical Inference. *Journal of Semantics* 13, 1–40.

—— 2000. From if to iff: Conditional Perfection as Pragmatic Strengthening. *Journal of Pragmatics* 32, 289–326.

—— 2002a. Assertoric Inertia and NPI Licensing. In CLS 38-2, *The Panels*, ed. Mary Andronis, Erin Debenport, Anne Pycha, and Keiko Yoshimura, 55–82.

—— 2002b. Assertoric Inertia and NPI Licensing. In Chicago Linguistic Society 38, 55–82. University of Chicago.

Hornstein, Norbert. 1999. Movement and Control. *Linguistic Inquiry* 30, 69–96.

—— 2000. *Move! A Minimalist Theory of Construal*. Oxford: Blackwell.

Hurford, James R. 1994. *Grammar: A Student's Guide*. Cambridge University Press.

Ippolito, Michela. 2003. Presuppositions and Implicatures in Counterfactuals. *Natural Language Semantics* 11, 145–86.

—— 2006. The *only* Implicature. Boston University, ms.

Ishihara, Shinichiro, and Caroline Féry. 2006. Phonetic Correlates of Second Occurrence Focus. In Proceedings of NELS 36, Amherst, MA. GLSA.

Iten, Corinne. 2002. Even if and Even: The Case for an Inferential Scalar Account. UCL Working Papers in Linguistics 14, 119–56.

Ito, Rika, and Sali Tagliamonte. 2003. *Well* weird, *right* dodgy, *very* strange, *really* cool: Layering and Recycling in English Intensifiers. *Language in Society* 32, 257–79.

Jackendoff, Ray. 1972. Semantic Interpretation in Generative Grammar. Cambridge, MA: MIT Press.

Jackson, Eric. 1995. Weak and Strong Polarity Items: Licensing and Intervention. *Linguistic Analysis* 25, 181–208.

Jacobs, Joachim. 1983. *Fokus und Skalen*. [*Focus and Scales*.] Tübingen: Niemeyer.

—— 1991a. Focus Ambiguities. *Journal of Semantics* 8, 1–36.

—— 1991b. Negation. In *Semantik: Ein internationales Handbuch der zeitgenössischen Forschung* [*Semantics: An International Handbook of Contemporary Research*.] ed. Arnim von Stechow and Dieter Wunderlich, 560–96. Berlin: de Gruyter.

Jaeger, Florian. 2004. Only Always Associates Audibly. Even if Only is Repeated: The Prosodic Properties of Second Occurrence Focus. Stanford University.

—— and Michael Wagner. 2003. Association with Focus and Linear Order in German. Stanford University.

Jäger, Gerhard. 1999. Focus without Variables: A Multi-modal Analysis. In *Proceedings of WCCFL 17*, ed. K. N. Shahin, S. Blake, and E. Kim, Stanford: CSLI Publications.

Kadmon, Nirit. 2001. *Formal Pragmatics: Semantics, Pragmatics, Presupposition and Focus*. Oxford: Blackwell Publishers.

—— and Fred Landman. 1993. Any. *Linguistics and Philosophy* 16, 353–422.

Kamp, Hans. 1981. A Theory of Truth and Semantic Representation. In *Formal Methods in the Study of Language, part 1*, ed. Jeroen Groenendijk, Theo Janssen, and Martin Stokhof, volume 135, 277–322. Amsterdam: Mathematical Centre Tracts.

Reprinted in Jeroen Groenendijk, Theo Janssen and Martin Stokhof (eds.), 1984, *Truth, Interpretation, and Information; Selected Papers from the Third Amsterdam Colloquium*, Dordrecht: Foris, pp. 1–41.

Kamp, Hans and Uwe Reyle. 1993. *From Discourse to Logic: Introduction to Modeltheoretic Semantics of Natural Language, Formal Logic and Discourse Representation Theory*. Dordrecht: Kluwer Academic Publishers.

Karttunen, Lauri. 1974. Presuppositions and Linguistic Context. *Theoretical Linguistics* 1, 181–94.

—— 1977. Syntax and Semantics of Questions. *Linguistics and Philosophy* 1, 3–44.

—— and Stanley Peters. 1979. Conventional Implicatures in Montague Grammar. In *Syntax and semantics 11: Presupposition*, ed. Choon-Kyu Oh and David Dineen, 1–56. New York: Academic Press.

Kay, Paul. 1990. Even. *Linguistics and Philosophy* 13, 59–111.

Kayne, Richard. 1998. Overt vs. Covert Movement. *Syntax* 1, 128–91.

Keenan, Edward L., and Jonathan Stavi. 1986. A Semantic Characterization of Natural Language Determiners. *Linguistics and Philosophy* 9, 253–326.

Klima, Edward. 1964. Negation in English. In *The Structure of Language. Readings in the Philosophy of Language*, First edition, ed. Jerry A. Fodor and J. J. Katz. Englewood Cliffs: Prentice-Hall, 246–323.

Klinedinst, Nathan, 2004. Only Scalar *only*. Handout at Presupposition and Implicature Workshop, Paris.

König, Ekkehard. 1991. *The Meaning of Focus Particles: A Comparative Perspective*. London, New York: Routledge.

Kratzer, Angelika. 1977. What 'Must' and 'Can' Must and Can Mean. *Linguistics and Philosophy* 1, 337–55.

—— 1991. The Representation of Focus. In *Semantik*, ed. Arnim von Stechow and Dieter Wunderlich, 825–34. Berlin: Walter de Gruyter.

Kretzmann, Norman. 1968. *William of Sherwood's Treatise on Syncategorematic Words*. Minneapolis: University of Minnesota Press.

Krifka, Manfred. 1989. Nominal Reference, Temporal Constitution and Quantification in Event Semantics. In *Semantics and Contextual Expression*, ed. Renata Bartsch, Johan van Benthem, and Peter von Emde Boas, volume 75, p. 115. Dordrecht: Foris.

—— 1990. 4000 Ships Passed through the Lock: Object-Induced Measure Functions on Events. *Linguistics and Philosophy* 13.

—— 1991. A Compositional Semantics for Multiple Focus Constructions. In *Proceedings from Semantics and Linguistic Theory I*, ed. Steven Moore and Adam Zachary Wyner, 127–58, Cornell, NY. Cornell University Working Papers in Linguistics.

—— 1992a. A Framework for Focus–Sensitive Quantification. In *Proceedings from Semantics and Linguistic Theory II*, ed. Chris Barker and David Dowty, 215–36, Columbus, OH: Ohio State University.

—— 1992b. A Compositional Semantics for Multiple Focus Constructions. *Informationsstruktur und Grammatik* 4.

—— 1993a. Focus and Presupposition in Dynamic Interpretation. *Journal of Semantics* 10, 269–300.

—— 1993b. Review of E. König, The Meaning of Focus Particles: A Comparative Perspective. *Language* 69, 593–97.

—— 1995. The Semantics and Pragmatics of Polarity Items. *Linguistic Analysis* 25, 1–49.

—— 1997. Focus and/or Context: A Second Look at Second Occurrence Expressions. In *Context-dependence in the Analysis of Linguistic Meaning* (Proceedings of the workshops in Prague and Bad Teinach), ed. Hans Kamp and Barbara Partee, 253–76, University of Stuttgart. Institut fuer maschinelle Sprachverarbeitung.

—— 1999. Additive Particles under Stress. In *Proceedings of SALT 8*, 111–28, Cornell: CLC Publications.

—— 2001. For a Structured Meaning Account of Questions and Answers. *Audiatur Vox Sapientia. A Festschrift for Arnim von Stechow* 52, 287–319.

—— 2004. *The Semantics of Questions and the Focusation of Answers. Topic and Focus: A Cross-Linguistic Perspective*. Dordrecht: Kluwer Academic Publishers 139–51.

—— 2006. Association with Focus Phrases. In *The architecture of Focus*, ed. Valéria Molnár and Susanne Winkler, 105–36. Berlin: Mouton de Gruyter.

Kripke, Saul. 1980. *Naming and Necessity*. Cambridge, MA: Harvard University Press.

—— 1991. Presupposition and Anaphora: Remarks on the Formulation of the Projection Problem. Princeton University.

van Kuppevelt, Jan. 1994. Topic and Comment. R. E. Asher & J. M. Y. Simpson. *The Encyclopedia of Language and Linguistics* 9, 4629–33.

—— 1995. Discourse Structure, Topicality and Questioning. *Journal of Linguistics* 31, 109–47.

—— 1996. Inferring from Topics. Scalar Implicatures as Topic-Dependent Inferences, *L&P* 19, 393–443.

Kuroda, Shige-Yuki. 1965. Generative Grammatical Studies in the Japanese Language. MIT dissertation.

Labov, William. 1985. Intensity. In *Meaning, Form and Use in Context: Linguistic Applications*, ed. Deborah Schiffrin, 43–70. Washington, DC: Georgetown University Press.

Ladd, D. Robert. 1980. *The Structure of Intonational Meaning*. Bloomington: Indiana University Press.

—— 1996. *Intonational Phonology*. Cambridge University Press.

Ladusaw, William A. 1979. Polarity Sensitivity as Inherent Scope Relations. University of Texas at Austin dissertation.

—— 1980. On the Notion 'Affective' in the Analysis of Negative-polarity Items. *Journal of Linguistic Research* 12, 1–16.

Lambrecht, Knud. 1994. *Information Structure and Sentence Form: Topic, Focus, and the Mental Representations of Discourse Referents*. Cambridge University Press.

Levinson, Stephen C. 1983. *Pragmatics*. Cambridge University Press.

—— 2000. *Presumptive Meanings: The Theory of Generalized Conversational Implicature*. Cambridge, MA: MIT Press.

Lewis, David. 1973. *Counterfactuals*. Cambridge, MA: Harvard University Press.

—— 1975. Adverbs of Quantification. In *Formal Semantics of Natural Languages*, ed. E. Keenan, 3–15. Cambridge: Cambridge University Press.

—— 1979. Scorekeeping in a Language Game. *Journal of Philosophical Logic* 8, 339–59. Also in Rainer Bäuerle, Urs Egli and Arnim von Stechow (eds.) 1979, *Semantics from Different Points of View*, Berlin: Springer.

Liberman, Mark, and Ivan A. Sag. 1974. Prosodic Form and Discourse Function. In Tenth Regional Meeting of the Chicago Linguistic Society, 416–27, Chicago: CLS.

Linebarger, Marcia C. 1987. Negative Polarity and Grammatical Representation. *Linguistics and Philosophy* 10, 325–87.

Lycan, William G. 1991. Even and even if. *Linguistics and Philosophy* 14, 115–50.

Mann, William C., and Sandra A. Thompson. 1987. Rhetorical Structure Theory: A Theory of Text Organization. University of Southern California, Information Sciences Institute.

Martí, Luisa. 2003. Contextual Variables. Storrs, CT: University of Connecticut dissertation.

McCawley, James D. 1981. *Everything that Linguists Have Always Wanted to Know about Logic but Were Ashamed to Ask.* Chicago: University of Chicago Press.

—— 1993. *Everything that Linguists Have Always Wanted to Know about Logic but Were Ashamed to Ask* (Second Edition). Chicago: University of Chicago Press.

—— 1998. *The Syntactic Phenomena of English* (Second Edition). Chicago: University of Chicago Press.

Montague, Richard. 1973. The Proper Treatment of Quantification. In *Approaches to Natural Language*, ed. Jaakko Hintikka, Julius M. Moravcsik, and Patrick Suppes, 221–42. Dordrecht: Reidel.

Mullally, Joseph P. 1945. *The Summulae Logicales of Peter of Spain.* Notre Dame, IN: University of Notre Dame.

Nathan, Lance. 1999. Either: Negative Polarity Meets Focus Sensitivity. Honors thesis, Brown University.

Nenkova, Ani, Jason Brenier, Anubha Kothari, Daniel Jurafsky, Sasha Calhoun, David Beaver, and Laura Whitton. 2007. To Memorize or to Predict: Prominence Labeling in Conversational Speech. In Proceedings of NAACL-HLT 2007.

Nevalainen, Terttu. 1991. *But, Only, Just: Focusing Adverbial Change in Modern English 1500–1900.* Helsinki: Société Néophilologique.

Oshima, David Y. 2002. Contrastive Topic as a Paradigmatic Operator. Workshop on Information Structure in Context, Stuttgart University .

Pan, Shimei, and Kathleen McKeown. 1999. Word Informativeness and Automatic Pitch Accent Modeling. In Proceedings of the Joint SIGDAT Conference on Empirical Methods in Natural Language Processing and Very Large Corpora.

Parsons, Terence. 1990. *Events in the Semantics of English.* Cambridge, MA: MIT Press.

Partee, Barbara H. 1991. Topic, Focus, and Quantification. In *Proceedings of SALT 1*, ed. Steve Moore and Adam Z. Wyner, 159–87. Cornell Working Papers in Linguistics.

—— 1999. Focus, Quantification, and Semantics-Pragmatics Issues. In *Focus: Linguistic, Cognitive, and Computational Perspectives*, ed. Peter Bosch and Rob van der Sandt, 213–31. Cambridge University Press.

Paul, Hermann. 1888. *Principles of the History of Language.* London: Swan Sonnenschein, Lowrey, & Company.

Pierrehumbert, Janet B. 1980. The Phonology and Phonetics of English Intonation. Cambridge, MA: MIT dissertation.

—— and Julia Hirschberg. 1990. The Meaning of Intonational Contours in the Interpretation of Discourse. In *Intentions in Communication*, ed. Philip R. Cohen, Jerry Morgan, and Martha E. Pollack, 271–311. Cambridge, MA: MIT Press.

—— and Susan Steele. 1987. How Many rise-fall-rise Contours? In Proceedings of the XIth International Congress of Phonetic Sciences.

Postal, Paul M. 1998. *Three Investigations of Extraction.* Cambridge, MA: MIT Press.

Potts, Christopher. 2005. *The Logic of Conventional Implicatures.* Oxford University Press.

—— 2007. The Expressive Dimension. *Theoretical Linguistics* 33(2): 165–97.

Prince, Ellen. 1981. Toward a Taxonomy of Given-new Information. In *Radical Pragmatics*, ed. Peter Cole, 223–56. New York: Academic Press.

Quirk, Randolph, Sidney Greenbaum, Geoffrey Leech, and Jan Svartvik. 1985. *A Comprehensive Grammar of the English Language*. New York: Longman.

Reinhart, Tanya. 2006. *Interface Strategies: Optimal and Costly Computations*. Cambridge, MA: MIT Press.

Riester, Arndt. 2006. Only Scalar. In *Proceedings of the 11th ESSLLI Student Session*, ed. J. Huitink and S. Katrenko, Spain. University of Malaga.

Roberts, Craige. 1996. Information Structure in Discourse: Towards an Integrated Formal Theory of Pragmatics. *OSU Working Papers in Linguistics* 49. Papers in Semantics.

—— 1998. Focus, the Flow of Information, and Universal Grammar. In *The Limits of Syntax*, ed. Peter Culicover and Louise McNally, 109–60. New York: Academic Press.

—— 2004. Context in Dynamic Interpretation. In *The Handbook of Pragmatics*, ed. Laurence R. Horn and Gregory Ward. Malden, MA: Blackwell Publishing.

—— 2006. Only and Conventional Presupposition. The Ohio State University, ms.

Rochemont, Michael S. 1986. *Focus in Generative Grammar*. Amsterdam: Benjamins.

Rooij, Robert Van. 2001. Exhaustivity In Dynamic Semantics; Referential and Descriptive Pronouns. *Linguistics and Philosophy* 24, 621–57.

—— 2002. Relevance Only. In Proceedings of Edilog 2002.

—— 2003. Questioning to Resolve Decision Problems. *Linguistics and Philosophy* 26, 727–63.

—— 2004. Utility, Informativity and Protocols. *Journal of Philosophical Logic* 33, 389–419.

—— and Katrin Schulz. 2003. Exhaustification. In *Proceedings of the Fifth International Workshop on Computational Semantics*, ed. Harry Bunt, Ielka van der Sluis, and Roser Morante, 354–98, Tilburg: University of Tilburg.

—— and —— 2007. *Only*: Meaning and Implicatures. In *Questions and Answers*, ed. Maria Aloni, Alastair Butler, and Paul Dekker, 193–224. Amsterdam: Elsevier.

Rooth, Mats. 1985. Association with Focus. University of Massachusetts at Amherst: Graduate Linguistics Student Association.

—— 1992. A Theory of Focus Interpretation. *Natural Language Semantics* 1, 75–116.

—— 1995. Indefinites, Adverbs of Quantification, and Focus Semantics. In *The Generic Book*, ed. Gregory Carlson and Francis Pelletier, 265–99. University of Chicago Press.

—— 1996a. Focus. In *The Handbook of Contemporary Semantic Theory*, ed. Shalom Lappin, 271–97. London: Basil Blackwell.

—— 1996b. On the Interface Principles for Intonational Focus. In *SALT VI*, ed. Teresa Galloway and Justin Spence, 202–26, Ithaca, NY: Cornell University.

—— 1999. Association with Focus or Association with Presupposition? In *Focus: Linguistic, Cognitive and Computational Perspectives*, ed. Peter Bosch and Rob van der Sandt, 232–44. Cambridge University Press.

Ross, John Robert. 1964. A Partial Grammar of English Superlatives. University of Pennsylvania: MA Thesis.

—— 1967. Constraints on Variables in Syntax. Massachusetts Institute of Technology dissertation.

Ross, John Robert and William E. Cooper. 1979. *Like* Syntax. In *Sentence Processing: Psycholinguistic Studies Presented to Merrill Garrett*, ed. William E. Cooper and Edward C. T. Walker, 343–418. Hillsdale, NJ: Lawrence Erlbaum Associates.

Sandt, Rob A. van der. 1992. Presupposition Projection as Anaphora Resolution. *Journal of Semantics* 9, 333–77.

Scha, Remko J. H. 1983. Logical Foundations for Question Answering. Rijksuniversiteit te Groningen dissertation.

Schubert, Lenhart K., and Francis Jeffry Pelletier. 1987. Problems in the Representation of the Logical Form of Generics, Plurals, and Mass Nouns. In *New Directions in Semantics*, ed. E. LePore, 385–451. London: Academic Press.

—— and —— 1989. Generically Speaking, Or Using Discourse Representation Theory to Interpret Generics. In *Properties, Types and Meaning*, ed. Gennaro A. Chierchia, Barbara H. Partee, and Raymond Turner, volume II, 193–268. Dordrecht: Kluwer Academic Publishers.

Schwarz, Bernhard. 2005. Scalar Additive Particles in Negative Contexts. *Natural Language Semantics* 13, 125–68.

Schwarzschild, Roger, 1993. The Constrastiveness of Associated Foci. Hebrew University of Jerusalem.

—— 1997. Why Some Foci Must Associate. unpublished.

—— 1999. Givenness, Avoidf and Other Constraints on the Placement of Accent. *Natural Language Semantics* 7, 141–77.

Schwenter, Scott A. 2002. Additive Particles and Scalar Endpoint Marking. *Belgian Journal of Linguistics* 16, 119–34.

—— and S. Vasishth. 2001. Absolute and Relative Scalar Particles in Spanish and Hindi. Berkeley Linguistics Society 26.

Selkirk, Elisabeth O. 1984. *Phonology and Syntax: The Relation between Sound and Structure*. Cambridge: MIT Press.

—— 1996. Sentence Prosody: Intonation, Stress, and Phrasing. In *The Handbook of Phonological Theory*, ed. John A. Goldsmith, 550–69. London: Basil Blackwell.

Sharma, Devyani. 2003. Nominal Clitics and Constructive Morphology in Hindi. In *Nominals: Inside and Out*, ed. Miriam Butt and Tracy Halloway King. Stanford, CA: CSLI Publications.

Sharvit, Yael, and Penka Stateva. 2002. Superlative Expressions, Context, and Focus. *Linguistics and Philosophy* 25, 453–505.

Shattuck-Hufnagel, Stefanie, and Alice E. Turk. 1996. A Prosody Tutorial for Investigators of Auditory Sentence Processing. *Journal of Psycholinguistic Research* 25, 193–247.

Sidner, Candace L. 1979. Toward a Computational Theory of Definite Anaphora Comprehension in English. Technical Report No. AI-TR-537, Cambridge, MA: MIT Press.

Silverman, Kim, Mary Beckman, John Pitrelli, Mari Ostendorf, Colin Wightman, Patti Price, Janet B. Pierrehumbert, and Julia Hirschberg. 1992. ToBI: A Standard for Labelling English Prosody. In Proceedings of the International Conference on Spoken Language Processing (ICSLP), Vol. 2, 867–70, Banff.

Spector, Benjamin. 2007. Scalar Implicatures: Exhaustivity and Gricean reasoning? In *Questions in Dynamic Semantics*, ed. Maria Aloni, Alastair Butler, and Paul Dekker. Amsterdam: Elsevier.

Stalnaker, Robert. 1972. Pragmatics. In *Semantics of Natural Language*, ed. Donald Davidson and Gilbert Harman, 389–408. Reidel: Dordrecht. Reprinted in János Petöfi and Dorothea Franck (eds.) 1973, *Präsuppositionen in Philosophie und Linguistik*. [*Presuppositions in Philosophy and Linguistics*], Athanäum Verlag, Frankfurt. Page numbers in text refer to the 1973 version.

—— 1974. Pragmatic Presuppositions. In *Semantics and Philosophy*, ed. Milton Munitz and Peter Unger, 197–214. New York University Press.

—— 1978. Assertion. In *Pragmatics*, ed. Peter Cole, volume 9 of *Syntax and Semantics*, 315–22. New York: Academic Press.

Stateva, Penka. 2002. How Different are Different Degree Constructions? University of Connecticut dissertation.

von Stechow, Arnim. 1985/1989. Focusing and Backgrounding Operators. Technical report, Universität Konstanz.

—— 1991. Current Issues in the Theory of Focus. In *Semantik*, ed. Arnim von Stechow and Dieter Wunderlich, 804–25. Berlin: Walter de Gruyter.

Steedman, Mark. 2000. Information Structure and the Syntax-phonology Interface. *Linguistic Inquiry* 31, 649–89.

Stoffel, Cornelis. 1901. *Intensives and Down-toners*. Heidelberg: Carl Winter.

de Swart, Henriëtte. 1993. *Adverbs of Quantification: A Generalized Quantifier Approach*. New York: Garland Publishing.

Swerts, Marc, and Emiel Krahmer. 2007. Meaning, Intonation and Negation. In *Computing Meaning* (vol. 3), ed. H. Bunt and R. Muskens. Dordrecht: Kluwer.

Szabolcsi, Anna. 1986. Comparative Superlatives. In *Papers in Theoretical Linguistics. MIT Working Papers in Linguistics*, vol. 8, ed. Naoki Fukui, Tova R. Rapoport, and Elisabeth Sagey, 245–66. MIT.

Szendrői, Kriszta. 2001. *Focus and the Syntax-Phonology Interface*. University College London dissertation.

—— 2003. A Stress-based Approach to the Syntax of Hungarian Focus. *Linguistic Review* 20, 37–78.

Taglicht, Josef. 1984. *Message and Emphasis*. London and New York: Longman.

Tancredi, Christopher D. 1990. *Not only even, but even only*. Cambridge, MA: MIT Press.

—— 1997. Focus and Associative Operators. Yokohama National University.

Taylor, Paul. 2000. Analysis and Synthesis of Intonation Using the Tilt Model. *Journal of the Acoustical Society of America* 107, 1697–714.

Tenny, Carol L. 1994. Aspectual Roles and the Syntax-Semantics Interface. Dordrecht: Kluwer Academic Publishers.

Tovena, Lucia M. 2005. Discourse and Addition. Workshop on Discourse Domains and Information Structure .

Traugott, Elizabeth Closs. 1989. On the Rise of Epistemic Meanings in English: An Example of Subjectification in Semantic Change. *Language* 65, 31–55.

—— 2006. The Semantic Development of Scalar Focus Modifiers. In *The Handbook of the History of English*, ed. Ans van Kemenade and Bettelou Los. Malden, MA: Basil Blackwell.

Truckenbrodt, Hubert. 2006. Phrasal Stress. In *The Encyclopedia of Language and Linguistics*, 2nd edn, ed. Keith Brown. Oxford: Elsevier.

Vallduví, Enric. 1990. *Only* and Focus. *The Penn Review of Linguistics* 14, 143–56.

—— 1992. *The Informational Component*. New York: Garland Publishing.

Wagner, Michael. 2006a. NPI-Licensing and Focus Movement. In *Proceedings of SALT XV*, ed. Effi Georgala and Jonathan Howell, Ithaca, NY: CLC Publications.

—— 2006b. Association by Movement: Evidence from NPI-Licensing. *Natural Language Semantics* 14(4): 297–324.

van der Wal, Sjoukje. 1996. Negative Polarity Items and Negation: Tandem Acquisition. University of Groningen dissertation.

Ward, Gregory L. 1988. *The Semantics and Pragmatics of Preposing*. New York: Garland.

—— and Julia Hirschberg. 1985. Implicating Uncertainty: The Pragmatics of Fall-Rise Intonation. *Language* 61, 747–76.

—— and —— 1988. Intonation and Propositional Attitude: The Pragmatics of L*+HLH%. In Proceedings of the Fifth Eastern States Conference on Linguistics, 512–22.

—— and Ellen F. Prince. 1991. On the Topicalization of Indefinite NPs. *Journal of Pragmatics* 16, 167–77.

——Betty Birner, and Rodney Huddleston. 2002. *The Cambridge Grammar of the English Language*, chapter Information packaging, 1363–447. Cambridge: Cambridge University Press.

Westerståhl, Dag. 1985. Logical Constants in Quantifier Languages. *Linguistics and Philosophy* 8, 387–413.

—— 2005. Generalized Quantifiers. In *The Stanford Encyclopedia of Philosophy*, ed. Edward N. Zalta. Stanford University.

Wilkinson, Karina. 1996. The Scope of Even. *Natural Language Semantics* 4, 193–215.

Williams, Edwin. 1997. Blocking and Anaphora. *Linguistic Inquiry* 28, 577–628.

Winkler, Susanne. 1997. Focus and Secondary Predication. Berlin: Mouton de Gruyter.

Wold, Dag. 1996. Long Distance Selective Binding: The Case of Focus. In *Proceedings of Semantics and Linguistic Theory (SALT) VI*, ed. Teresa Galloway and Justin Spence, Cornell CLC Publications.

Yuan, Jiahong, Jason Brenier, and Dan Jurafsky. 2005. Pitch Accent Prediction: Effects of Genre and Speaker. In Proceedings of Eurospeech-05.

Zaenen, Annie, Staan Larsson, Agnes Sandor, and David Traum. 2001. Information State Revision and Implicit Dialogue Moves in Instructional Texts. In *The Trindi Book*, ed. TheTrindi Consortium, 261–96. University of Gothenburg.

Zeevat, Henk. 1994. Questions and Exhaustivity in Update Semantics. In *Proceedings of the International Workshop on Computational Semantics*, ed. R. M. Harry Bunt and G. Rentier, 211–21, Tilburg: Institute for Language Technology and Artificial Intelligence.

—— 2007. Exhaustivity, Questions and Plurals in Update Semantics. In *Questions in Dynamic Semantics*, ed. Maria Aloni, Alastair Butler, and Paul Dekker, 161–92. Amsterdam: Elsevier.

Zwarts, Frans. 1995. Nonveridical Contexts. *Linguistic Analysis* 25, 286–312.

—— 1998. Three Types of Polarity. In *Plurality and Quantification*, ed. Fritz Hamm and Erhard Hinrichs, 177–238. Dordrecht: Kluwer.

Zwicky, Arnold M. 1982. Stranded *to* and Phonological Phrasing in English. *Linguistics* 20, 3–57.

Index

accentless focus, 117–121, 142
accommodation, 39, 126, 131, 132, 136,
    138, 141, 210, 223, 253
  global, 100, 132, 133, 135, 136, 138
  intermediate, 132, 133, 134, 137, 208, 242
  local, 54, 56, 61, 100, 133, 242
activation, 22–23
additionally, see additives
additives, 42, 68, 71–73, 76, 78, 128, 138,
    140, 159, 245, 285
  non-scalar, 72, 127
  scalar, 4, 68, 70–72, 78, 127, 128, 140,
    159, 284
alleen maar ('only', Dutch exclusive), 78,
    150, 166, 176, 187, 188
Aloni, Maria, xiv, 101, 102
also, 72, 127, 174, 245
  see also additives, non-scalar
Alternative Semantics, *see* semantic
    approaches to focus interpretation
altijd ('always', Dutch quantificational
    adverb), 78, 150, 166, 187
always, 133, 134, 154, 177, 184, 190, 192,
    197–199, 207, 208, 212, 274
  see also quantificational adverb
analogously, 72
  see also particularizers
Anderson, Stephen, 160
anti-additivity, 194, 197
  Strawson anti-additivity, 195, 196,
    198, 199

Aristotle, 80, 222
Arnold, Jennifer, 22
Arroyo PurityWager, 219, 221, 238, 271
Arroyo Tequila Test, 238–244, 270, 271
Asher, Nicholas, 39, 73, 138
association with focus, 41–43
  conventional, 68–77
  free, 52–68
  quasi, 44–51
  taxonomy, 78
association with presupposition, 53, 79,
    118, 121–123, 140, 204–208, 211,
    278, 283
as well, 72
  see also additives
at a maximum, 76
  see also downtoners
at best, 76
  see also downtoners
at least, 254
  see also downtoners
at most, 76, 77, 231
  see also downtoners
at the very least, 75
  see also downtoners
at the very minimum, 75
  see also downtoners
at the very most, 76
  see also downtoners
Atlas, Jay David, 185, 192, 195, 200, 201,
    215, 227, 228

Austen, Jane, 142, 160, 182
Austin, John L., v, 282
AvoidF, 18, 23

Bach, Emmon, 87–88
background, 25, 30, 84, 87, 89, 93, 110
Background Presupposition Rule (BPR),
    36, 130–140
Barbiers, Sjef, 170, 176
barely, 75, 250
    see also downtoners
Barker, Stephen, 70
Bartels, Christine, 119, 145
Basic Focus Rule, 16
Bayer, Josef, 151
Beaver, Anna, 221
Beaver, David, iii, xii–xiv, 8, 61, 69, 73, 131,
    133, 135, 138, 143–149, 185, 189, 197,
    208–210, 219, 221, 228, 234, 237, 242,
    245, 281, 284
    Brenier et al. (2006), 14
    Nenkova et al. (2007), 14
because, 53, 64–67
    see also sentential connectives
Beckman, Mary, 11
    Silverman et al. (1992), 11
Bennett, Michael, 57
Berman, Stephen, 134
Bernardi, Raffaella, 201, 202
binding, 112, 115, 132, 135
Birner, Betty (Ward et al. 2002), 8
Bolinger, Dwight, 13, 14, 19, 74, 75
Bonomi, Andrea, 80, 87, 88, 90, 93, 95, 102,
    103, 106, 135, 155, 156, 195, 196
boundary tones, 11, 12
Bowers, John, 62
boy scout problem, 102–106
BPR, *see* Background Presupposition Rule
Brenier, Jason, 14
    Nenkova et al. (2007), 14
    Yuan et al. (2005), 14
Bresnan, Joan, 13
Brody, Michael, 9
Büring, Daniel, 10, 14, 19, 24, 39, 48, 55,
    58, 111, 161, 174, 249

Calcagno, Mike, 128
Calhoun, Sasha (Nenkova et al. 2007), 14

Carlson, Lauri W., 39, 249
Casalegno, Paolo, 80, 87, 88, 90, 95, 102,
    103, 106, 135, 155, 156, 195, 196
Catalan, 9
Chafe, Wallace L., 22
Chierchia, Gennaro A., 85, 94
Chomsky, Noam, 2, 3, 13–15, 169
Clark, Brady, xiv, 135, 143, 185
    Beaver et al. (2007), xiv, 143–149, 281
Clark, Herbert H., xii, 33
Cohan, Jocelyn, 8, 12
Cohen, Ariel, 55, 58, 121–123, 204, 210
Collier, Rene, 11
common ground, 33, 34, 36, 37, 73, 222,
    251–253, 261, 262
congruence, 23, 37, 49, 128, 129, 262,
    273, 276
context set, 33, 34, 38, 261, 262
contradiction contour, 47, 49
Cooper, Robin, 40, 58, 60
Cooper, William E., 160, 161
counterfactuals, 4, 52, 62, 63, 65, 66, 78
Current Question, 5, 32, 35, 36, 40, 45, 46,
    49–51, 67, 69–71, 73, 74, 77, 129, 154,
    159, 193, 249, 250, 251, 282, 285
Current Question Rule, 36, 49, 50, 66, 67,
    141, 256, 262, 264, 265, 268, 270, 271
Czech, 9

damn, 74
    see also intensives
Davidson, Donald, 87
De Swart, Henreitte, 53, 213
DeLancey, Scott, 250
denial, 47, 180, 183, 226–229, 233–238,
    268–270
determiners, *see* quantificational
    determiners
Diesing, Molly, 56
Discourse Principle, 36–40, 46, 59, 124
Discourse Representation Structure
    (DRS), 131, 132, 135, 137, 138, 213
Discourse Representation Theory (DRT),
    130, 131, 135, 137, 138
domain relation, 155, 158, 173, 179
downtoners (minimizing and
    maximizing), 68, 75–78, 159
Dretske, Fred I., 63, 64, 119

Drubig, Hans B., 169
Dryer, Matthew S., 3, 120, 147
Dutch, 78, 150, 166, 174, 176, 181, 187,
    188, 191
Dynamic Semantics, 33, 108, 111,
    112, 115

Eckardt, Regine, 55
elaboration, 73, 284
ellipsis, 106–109, 112, 115, 160, 169,
    176–182, 274–276
emotive factives, 62, 66–68, 78, 193, 245
Engdahl, Elisabet (Cooper et al. 2000), 40
entailment, 17, 18, 35, 69, 124, 198, 214,
    216, 234, 237, 243, 245, 254–263, 276
Ericsson, Stina (Cooper et al. 2000), 40
especially, 74
    see also particularizers
even, 1, 2, 4, 14, 40, 42, 70–72, 77, 86, 127,
    146, 147, 160, 161, 174, 284, 285
    see also additives, scalar
events, 87
eventualities, 87, 155
every, 55, 56, 60, 183, 185, 189, 191,
    194–196, 201, 202, 218
    see also quantificational determiner
exclusively, 68, 69, 215, 237, 238
    see also exclusives
exclusives, 2, 6, 33, 42, 68–71, 76, 77, 79,
    127, 128, 130, 154, 158, 159, 166, 169,
    174, 176, 178, 181, 184, 189, 199, 202,
    203, 211, 213, 215, 218, 222, 225, 226,
    231, 233–235, 237, 238, 247, 249–251,
    253, 260, 261, 264, 265, 267, 269, 272,
    274, 277, 278, 281, 283, 285
    detailed proposal, 248–279
    empirical/historical review, 212–247
    outline of proposal, 68–70
existential presupposition theory,
    218–223, 226, 238, 244, 257, 269
extraction, 160, 161, 163–176, 181,
    272, 274

F-marking, 8, 14–18, 31, 37, 170
factives, 208, 245, 285
    see also emotive factives
Faller, Martina, 9
Fauconnier, Gilles, 183

Féry, Caroline, 143–149, 281
Fintel, Kai von, xiv, 5, 31, 42, 52, 53, 65, 67,
    99, 104, 110, 118, 130, 152, 153, 155,
    185, 189, 192, 193, 209, 210, 213, 249,
    252, 276, 281
Fischer, Susan, 2, 45
Flemming, Edward (Beaver et al. 2007),
    xiv, 8, 143–149, 281
focus, 2, 5, 7–10, 12, 14, 43, 70, 286
    Focus Principle, 36–39, 45, 118, 124, 129,
        154, 260, 262, 273
    focus projection, 13–15, 17–19, 22–24,
        37, 170
    negated, 45, 224, 225, 228
    plural, 225
    position (Hungarian), 9
    Strong theories, 31
    Weak theories, 117
focus sensitive expressions, 2, 4–7, 31–33,
    40, 42, 78, 118, 121–123, 140, 142–144,
    149–153, 158, 160–169, 174–177, 181,
    211, 280, 284, 285
Foolen, Ad, 78
foreground, 84, 86, 87, 92, 110
fucking, 74, 75
    see also intensives

Gajewski, Jon, 179, 200
Gardent, Claire, 109
Gawron, Mark, 62
Gazdar, Gerald, 33, 245
Geach, Peter T., 228
generics, 5, 52, 55, 60, 67, 78
German, 147, 151, 174–176, 181, 188,
    191, 275
Geurts, Bart, xiii, 121, 130, 131, 139, 140,
    141, 171, 209, 210, 222, 223
Giannakidou, Anastasia, 70, 183, 185, 187,
    192, 200–203
Ginzburg, Jonathan, 27
give a damn, 183
    see also intensives
Givenness, 18, 19
Graff, Delia, 180
Greek, 187, 202, 203
Greenbaum, Sidney (Quirk et al. 1985),
    74, 75
Grice, Herbert Paul, v, 4, 40, 228, 230

Groenendijk, Jeroen, 17, 25, 26, 35, 36, 45,
    46, 48, 94, 108, 112, 117, 256, 266
Gussenhoven, Carlos, 14, 15

Hajičová, Eva, 4
Halle, Morris, 13, 15
Halliday, Michael Alexander K., 3, 61
Hamblin, Charles L., 25–27, 33, 35, 37–39,
    45, 46, 171
hardly, 75
    see also downtoners
Hartmann, Katharina, 161, 174
Hausser, Roland, 27
Hedberg, Nancy, 12, 47
Heim, Irene, xii, 18, 33, 53, 56, 62, 65, 67,
    88, 97, 108, 111, 163
Hendriks, Herman, 48
Hendriks, Petra, 55
Herburger, Elena, 45, 55, 57, 58, 70, 80, 87,
    135, 184, 185, 215, 245, 249, 260
Higginbotham, James, 25
Hirschberg, Julia, 14, 47, 48, 251
    Silverman et al. (1992), 11
Hoop, Helen de, 55
Horn, Laurence R., 70, 71, 136, 184, 185,
    189, 192–195, 200, 215, 216, 218–222,
    225–228, 231, 236, 244–246, 250, 255,
    269, 271, 272, 278
    Horn's bet, 219, 223, 233, 267, 270, 271
Hornstein, Norbert, 111
Huddleston, Rodney (Ward et al. 2002), 8
Hungarian, 9
Hurford, James R., 280

implicational presupposition theory,
    223–225
implicature, 40, 41, 48–51, 225, 226,
    228–233, 246, 249
in addition, 72
    see also additives
in particular, 73, 127
    see also particularizers
information structure, 6–8, 24, 45,
    53, 215
instead, 72
intensifiers, *see* intensives
intensives, 74–75, 159, 284
intermediate phrase, 12

intonation, 3, 7, 10, 11, 42, 47, 74, 150, 173
    intonational focus, 8
    intonational phonology, 10–12
    intonational phrase, 12
Ippolito, Michela, 65, 223–226, 228–234,
    236, 243, 244, 257, 267–270
Italian, 168
Iten, Corinne, 70

Jackendoff, Ray, 2, 14, 41, 45, 62, 107, 160
Jackson, Eric, 185, 186
Jacobs, Joachim, 14, 15, 27, 45, 69, 80, 170,
    174
Jaeger, Florian, xiv, 143, 148, 149, 174
Jäger, Gerhard, 27, 106
Japanese, 10
Jurafsky, Dan
    Brenier et al. (2006), 14
    Yuan et al. (2005), 14
just, 5, 70, 176, 215, 235, 236, 238, 248
    see also exclusives

Kadmon, Nirit, 3, 4, 10, 14, 28, 107, 117,
    119, 120, 125, 213
Kamp, Hans, xii, 33, 53, 59, 130
Karttunen, Lauri, 25, 33, 45, 70
Kaufmann, Stefan, 10
    German et al. (2006), 14
Kay, Paul, 70
Kayne, Richard, 3, 160
Klima, Edward, 184
Klinedinst, Nathan, 69
König, Ekkehard, 70, 161
Kothari, Anubha
    Brenier et al. (2006), 14
    Nenkova et al. (2007), 14
Krahmer, Emiel, 47, 197
Kratzer, Angelika, 18, 56, 61, 88, 97,
    106–108, 110–112, 115, 163
Kretzmann, Norman, 215
Krifka, Manfred, 3, 5, 27, 44, 55, 56, 70, 80,
    85, 86, 91, 106, 107, 151, 152, 155, 156,
    160, 161, 163, 169, 174, 185, 190
Kripke, Saul, 72, 81
Kuppevelt, Jan van, 39
Kuroda, Shige-Yuki, 2

Labov, William, 74
Ladd, Robert D., 8, 10–12, 14, 61
Ladusaw, William A., 183, 185, 193, 276
Lambrecht, Knud, 9, 14, 19, 22
Landman, Fred, 190
Larsson, Staffan
  Cooper et al. (2006), 40
  Zaenen et al. (2001), 40
Lascarides, Alex, 39, 73, 138
leaners, 149–154
Leech, Geoffrey (Quirk et al. 1985), 74, 75
Levinson, Stephen C., 4, 7, 200, 230
Lewis, David, 33, 53, 65, 213
Li, Yen-Hui Audrey, 160, 161
likewise, 72
  see also additives
Linebarger, Marcia C., 185, 189, 193
Lycan, William G., 70

Mann, William C., 39
many, 57–60
  see also determiners
Martí, Luisa, 3, 119, 171
Mayan, 9
McCawley, James D., 45, 185, 228
McKeown, Kathleen, 14
Merchant, Jason, 179
merely, 4, 68, 215, 235–237, 248
  see also exclusives
modal base, 61, 65–67, 78
modals, 53, 60, 78, 227
  bouletic modals, 64–66
  deontic modals, 67
  possibility modals, 50, 51
monotonicity, 182, 183, 190, 192, 203, 211
  downward monotonicity, 182, 183, 193,
    194, 197
  inferences, 183, 192, 193, 196, 276
  Strawson downward monotonicity, 193,
    198, 201
  upward monotonicity, 72, 183
most, 60
  see also determiners
mostly, 53, 57
  see also quantificational adverbs
Mullally, Joseph P., 215

Nathan, Lance, 200
negation, 41, 44–47, 49–51, 159, 214–216,
  233–235, 242, 243, 267

Negative Polarity Items (NPIs), 79,
  182–185, 187–193, 195–197, 199–203,
  211, 276, 277, 279
  strong NPIs, 184–186, 203
  weak NPIs, 184, 185, 189
Nenkova, Ani, 14
  Brenier et al. (2006), 14
net ('just', Dutch exclusive), 78
Nevalainen, Terttu, 68
new, 8, 14, 17, 20, 21, 23, 250
nog ('also/yet', Dutch additive), 78
non-association with presupposition, 277
Nuclear Stress Rule, 13, 14

only, 25, 68, 71, 72, 125, 129, 134, 135, 154,
  177, 180, 187, 189–192, 195, 197–199,
  207, 212, 238, 248, 271, 274
  see also exclusives
ook ('also', Dutch additive), 78, 151
Open Question, 35, 36, 253
Oshima, David Y., 70
Ostendorf, Marie (Silverman 1992), 11

Parsons, Terence, 88
Partee, Barbara H., 5, 55, 61, 119, 143, 285
  Hajičová et al. (1998), 4
particularizers, 4, 68, 73–74, 78, 127, 159
Paul, Hermann, 1
Pelletier, Francis Jeffry, 60, 121
Peters, Stanley, 45, 70
phonological phrasing, 10
Phrasal Focus Rules, 16
phrase accent, 11
Pierrehumbert, Janet B., 11, 47
  German et al. (2006), 14
  Silverman et al. (1992), 11
Pirelli, John (Silverman et al. 1992), 11
pitch accent, 8, 10–15, 24, 43, 47, 119, 144,
  147, 148, 173
Positive Polarity Items (PPIs), 182, 183,
  191, 192
Potts, Christopher, 74, 214
pragmatic approaches to focus
  interpretation, 6, 31, 117–141,
  142–144, 152–154, 172, 181
    presuppositional account, 130–138
    topical questions model, 123–130, 140
prejacent, 214–247, 251–260, 264–271,
  274, 276

prejacent presupposition theory, 215–217,
    218, 225, 226, 238, 244, 254, 255, 269
presupposition, 61, 65, 73, 77, 198, 208,
    211, 227, 245
    entailed, 265
    existential, 49, 73, 130, 136, 138,
        195, 276
    see also Background Presupposition
    Rule (BPR), factives
Price, Patti (Silverman et al. 1992), 11
primarily, 73
    see also particularizers
Prince, Ellen F., 17, 250, 251
prosodic prominence, see intonation:
    intonational phonology
prosody, see intonation: intonational
    phonology
purely, 68
    see also exclusives

quantificational adverbs, 4, 6, 41, 44,
    52–55, 60, 67, 78, 79, 94, 122, 127, 128,
    140, 154, 158, 159, 169, 178, 182, 208,
    211, 213, 272, 274, 279, 281, 283, 285
quantificational determiners, 52, 55, 56,
    60, 67
quantifier raising, 56
Quasi/Free/Conventional (QFC) theory,
    5, 32, 40–42, 44–79, 80, 118, 123, 141,
    158, 159, 281, 283
Quechua, 9
Question-based model, 33
questions, 7, 8, 20, 25–27, 33, 35, 39, 46, 47,
    94, 124, 126, 130, 199
    question semantics, 27, 35, 256
    sub-questions, 107
    super-questions, 107
    wh-questions, 8, 9, 20, 26, 27, 266

really, 4, 74
    see also intensifiers
Reinhart, Tanya, 14, 24
relevance, 36, 129, 171, 265
restrictor, 183, 194, 199, 211
Reyle, Uwe, 130, 213
Riester, Arndt, 251
Roberts, Craige, xiv, 3, 5, 7, 9, 33–39, 40,
    42, 94, 107, 117, 119, 123–130, 140,
    171, 216, 222, 223, 227, 229, 236, 249,
    250, 252, 255, 262, 269, 273, 282

Rochemont, Michael S., 14, 15
Rooij, Robert van, xiv, 26, 36, 46, 48, 69, 94,
    224, 226, 228, 229, 248, 251
Rooth, Mats, 3–5, 7, 14, 26, 27, 28–32, 37,
    45, 46, 51, 52, 53, 63, 65, 80, 81, 84, 91,
    93, 96, 103, 107, 117, 118, 119,
    120–123, 144, 145, 147, 152, 169, 204,
    210, 215, 249, 250, 278, 281, 282, 285
Rooth–Hamblin semantics, 27, 37, 45, 46
Ross, John Robert, 62, 160, 161, 185

Sag, Ivan A., 27, 47
Samek-Lodovici, Vieri, 14, 24
Sander, Agnes (Zaenen et al. 2001), 40
Sandt, Rob van der, 36, 100, 119, 121, 130,
    131, 132, 139, 140, 141, 171, 209, 210,
    222, 223, 242
scarcely, 75
    see also downtoners
Scha, Remko J. H., 27
Schulz, Katrin, 26, 48, 69, 224, 226, 228,
    229, 251
Schwarz, Bernhard, 70, 72
Schwarzschild, Roger, 3, 12, 14, 17–24, 37,
    69, 117, 171
Schwenter, Scott A., 70
scope, 183, 199
second occurrence focus, 119, 142–145,
    147–149, 159
Selkirk, Elisabeth O., 10, 12, 14–17, 19, 23,
    24, 170, 172
semantic approaches to focus
    interpretation, 80–116
    Alternative Semantics, 26, 28, 81–84,
        91–96
    events-based approach, 80, 87–94,
        154–158
    Structured Meanings, 27, 28, 30, 31,
        84–87, 91–94
semantic focus, 8, 119–121
Sentence Focus Rule, 16
sentential connectives, 4, 50
Sgall, Petr (Hajičová et al. 1998), 4
Sharma, Devyani, 10
Sidner, Candace L., 33
similarly, 72
    see also additives
slechts ('just', Dutch exclusive), 78, 187

solely, 68
  see also exclusives
Sosa, Juan M., 12, 47
Spanish, 168
specifically, 73, 159
  see also particularizers
Spector, Benjamin, 48
Stalnaker, Robert C., 33, 34, 39
statements of reason, 62–64
Stateva, Penka, 62
Stavi, Jonathan, 57
Stechow, Arnim von, 3, 27, 80, 123
Steedman, Mark, 3
Steele, Susan, 47
Stoffel, Cornelis, 74, 75
Stokhof, Martin, 17, 25, 26, 33, 35, 36, 45,
    46, 48, 94, 108, 112, 117, 256, 266
stress, 10, 13–15, 150, 207, 235
Structured Meanings, *see* semantic
    approaches to focus interpretation
subjectification, 285
superlatives, 5, 41, 52, 62, 63, 67, 159,
    193, 277
Svartvik, Jan (Quirk et al. 1985), 74, 75
Swart, Henreitte de, 53, 213
Swedish, 166–168
Szabolcsi, Anna, 62
Szendrői, Kriszta, 9, 10

Tagliamonte, Sali, 74
Taglicht, Josef, 119, 215
Tancredi, Christopher D., 70, 161, 170, 173
Tanglewood, 95–115
Taylor, Paul, 11
Tennant, Neil W., 57
Tenny, Carol L., 176
Thompson, Sandra A., 39
ToBI, 10–12, 15
tolf, 31, 282–284
too, 42, 72, 122, 135, 137, 140, 245
  see also additives, non-scalar
topic position, 9
totally, 74, 127, 159
  see also intensives
Tovena, Lucia M., 70
trapping, 54, 131, 133–137
Traugott, Elizabeth Closs, 284, 285

Traum, David (Zaenen et al. 2001), 40
Truckenbrodt, Hubert, 13
truly, 74
  see also intensives
Turk, Alice E., 10
Turner, Ray A., 94

uniquely, 68
  see also exclusives
universal inference from exclusives, 214
universal operator (presuppositional
    semantics), 198
usually, 53, 127, 128, 177, 190
  see also quantificational adverbs

Vallduví, Enric, 3, 117, 120
Vasishth, Shravan, 70
vooral ('especially', Dutch
    intensive/particularizer), 78

Wagner, Michael, 45, 174, 180, 185
Wal, Sjoukje van der, 187, 191
Ward, Gregory L., 8, 48, 251
Westerståhl, Dag, 57, 58
Whitton, Laura
    Brenier et al. (2006), 14
    Nenkova et al. (2007), 14
Wightman, Colin (Silverman et al.
    1992), 11
Wilkinson, Karina, 70
Williams, Edwin, 3
Winkler, Susanne, 14, 15
Wold, Dag, 107
Wolters, Maria (Beaver et al. 2007), xiv, 8,
    143–149, 281
word order determining focus, 8–10, 43

Zaenen, Annie, 40
Zeevat, Henk, xiv, 48, 73, 133, 138, 242,
    245, 248, 251, 284
zeker ('even', Dutch, intensive/scalar
    additive), 78
zelfs ('even', Dutch intensive/scalar
    additive), 78
Zwarts, Frans, 151, 185, 187, 191, 201–203
Zwicky, Arnold M., 149